尾田栄一郎

Goats are known for eating paper. They're like, "I'll eat anything!" and they'll chew on paper or whatever else comes their way. There are signs posted at zoos saying, "Don't feed the goats paper." If the paper contains chemicals, it upsets the goat's stomach. Goats... you silly... Are you trying to get on a comedy show or something?

—Eiichiro Oda, 2005

E iichiro Oda began his manga career at the age of 17, when his one-shot cowboy manga **Wanted!** won second place in the coveted Tezuka manga awards. Oda went on to work as an assistant to some of the biggest manga artists in the industry, including Nobuhiro Watsuki, before winning the Hop Step Award for new artists. His pirate adventure **One Piece**, which debuted in **Weekly Shonen Jump** in 1997, quickly became one of the most popular manga in Japan.

ONE PIECE VOL. 40
WATER SEVEN PART 9

SHONEN JUMP Manga Edition

STORY AND ART BY EIICHIRO ODA

English Adaptation/Jake Forbes
Translation/Taylor Eagle, HC Language Solutions
Touch-up Art & Lettering/HudsonYards
Design/Sean Lee
Supervising Editor/Yuki Murashige
Editor/Megan Bates

VP, Production/Alvin Lu
VP, Sales & Product Marketing/Gonzalo Ferreyra
VP, Creative/Linda Espinosa
Publisher/Hyoe Narita

Printed in the U.S.A.

Published by VIZ Media, LLC
P.O. Box 77010
San Francisco, CA 94107

10 9 8 7 6 5 4 3 2 1
First printing, April 2010

www.viz.com

THE WORLD'S
MOST POPULAR MANGA

www.shonenjump.com

THE STORY OF ONE PIECE

Volume 40

Monkey D. Luffy started out as just a kid with a dream—to become the greatest pirate in history! Stirred by the tales of pirate "Red-Haired" Shanks, Luffy vowed to become a pirate himself. That was before the enchanted Devil Fruit gave Luffy the power to stretch like rubber, at the cost of being unable to swim—a serious handicap for an aspiring sea dog. Undeterred, Luffy set out to sea and recruited some crewmates—master swordsman Zolo; treasure-hunting thief Nami; lying sharpshooter Usopp; the high-kicking chef Sanji; Chopper, the walkin' talkin reindeer doctor; and the mysterious archaeologist Robin.

After many adventures, the Straw Hats' ship, the *Merry Go*, is less than seaworthy. In order to get her repaired, they head to Water Seven, home of the best shipwrights. Furious at Luffy's decision to get a new ship instead, Usopp leaves the crew, and then Robin is linked to an assassination attempt on Mayor Iceberg and hauled off to Enies Lobby, the judicial island. To rescue Robin, Luffy joins with the Galley-La Company and the Franky Family and takes up pursuit in a defective Sea Train!
In the lead train, Sanji succeeds in finding Usopp and Franky and eventually reaches Robin. However, she and Franky end up back in the enemy's hands and are taken to Enies Lobby. Sanji joins Luffy and the others, and they make plans to storm the island together. But Luffy once again ends up going it alone!

The Franky Family

Professional ship dismantlers, they moonlight as bounty hunters.

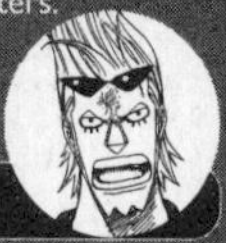

The master builder and an apprentice of Tom, the legendary shipwright.

Franky (Cutty Flam)

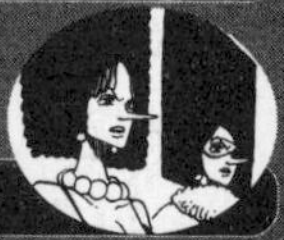

The Square Sisters

Kiwi & Mozu

Galley-La Company

A top shipbuilding company. They are purveyors to the World Government.

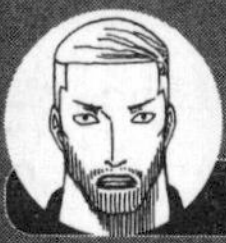

Mayor of Water Seven and president of Galley-La Company. Also one of Tom's apprentices.

Iceberg

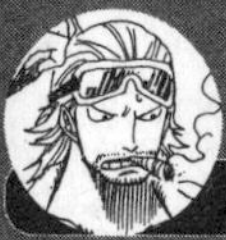

Rigging and Mast Foreman

Paulie

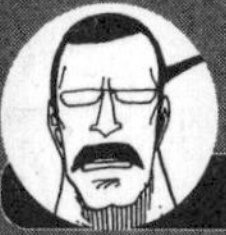

Pitch, Blacksmithing and Block-and-Tackle Foreman

Peepley Lulu

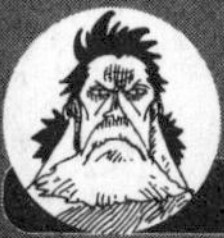

Cabinetry, Caulking and Flag-Making Foreman

Tilestone

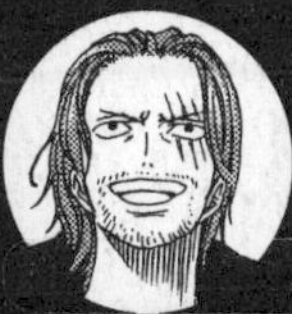

A pirate that Luffy idolizes. Shanks gave Luffy his trademark straw hat.

"Red-Haired" Shanks

WATER SEVEN

ONE PIECE

Vol. 40
Gear

CONTENTS

Chapter 378:
CASUALTIES

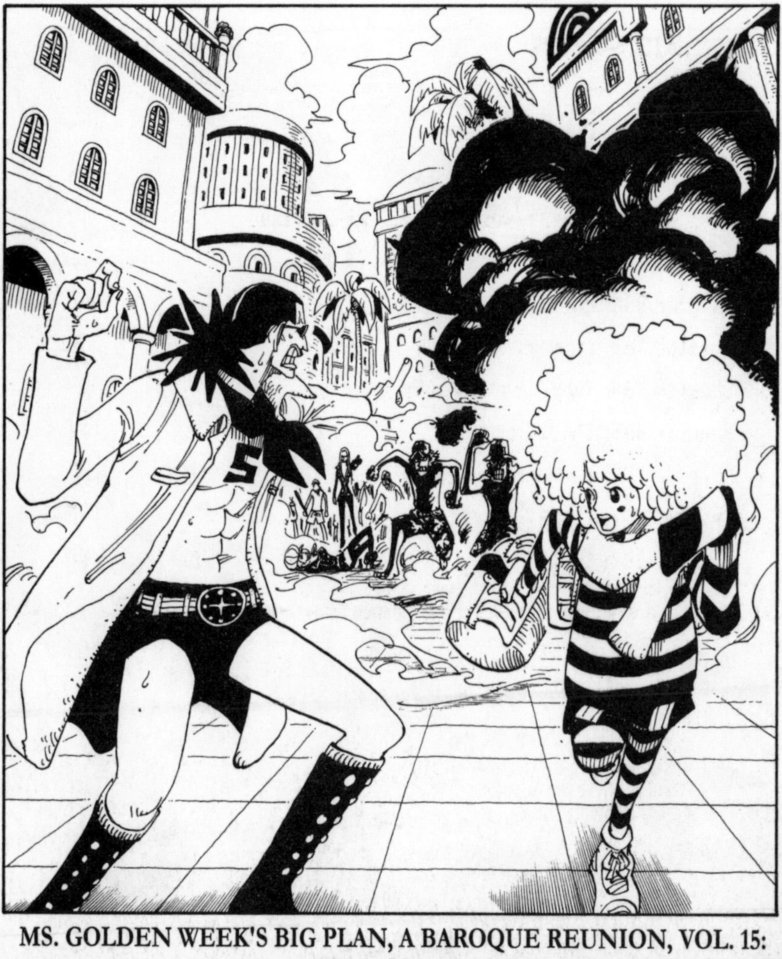

MS. GOLDEN WEEK'S BIG PLAN, A BAROQUE REUNION, VOL. 15:
"ESCAPE"

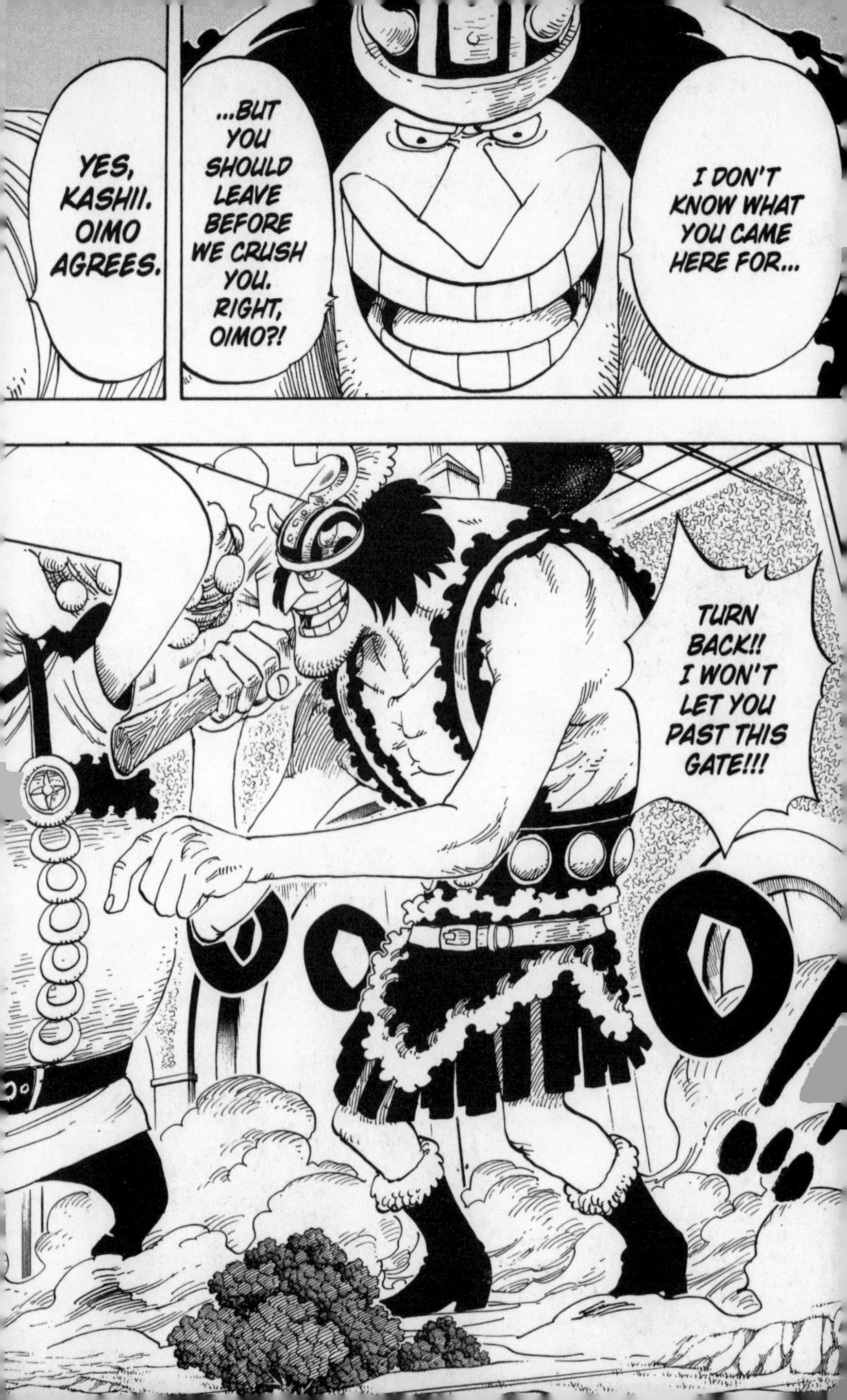
I DON'T KNOW WHAT YOU CAME HERE FOR...
...BUT YOU SHOULD LEAVE BEFORE WE CRUSH YOU. RIGHT, OIMO?!
YES, KASHII. OIMO AGREES.
TURN BACK!! I WON'T LET YOU PAST THIS GATE!!!

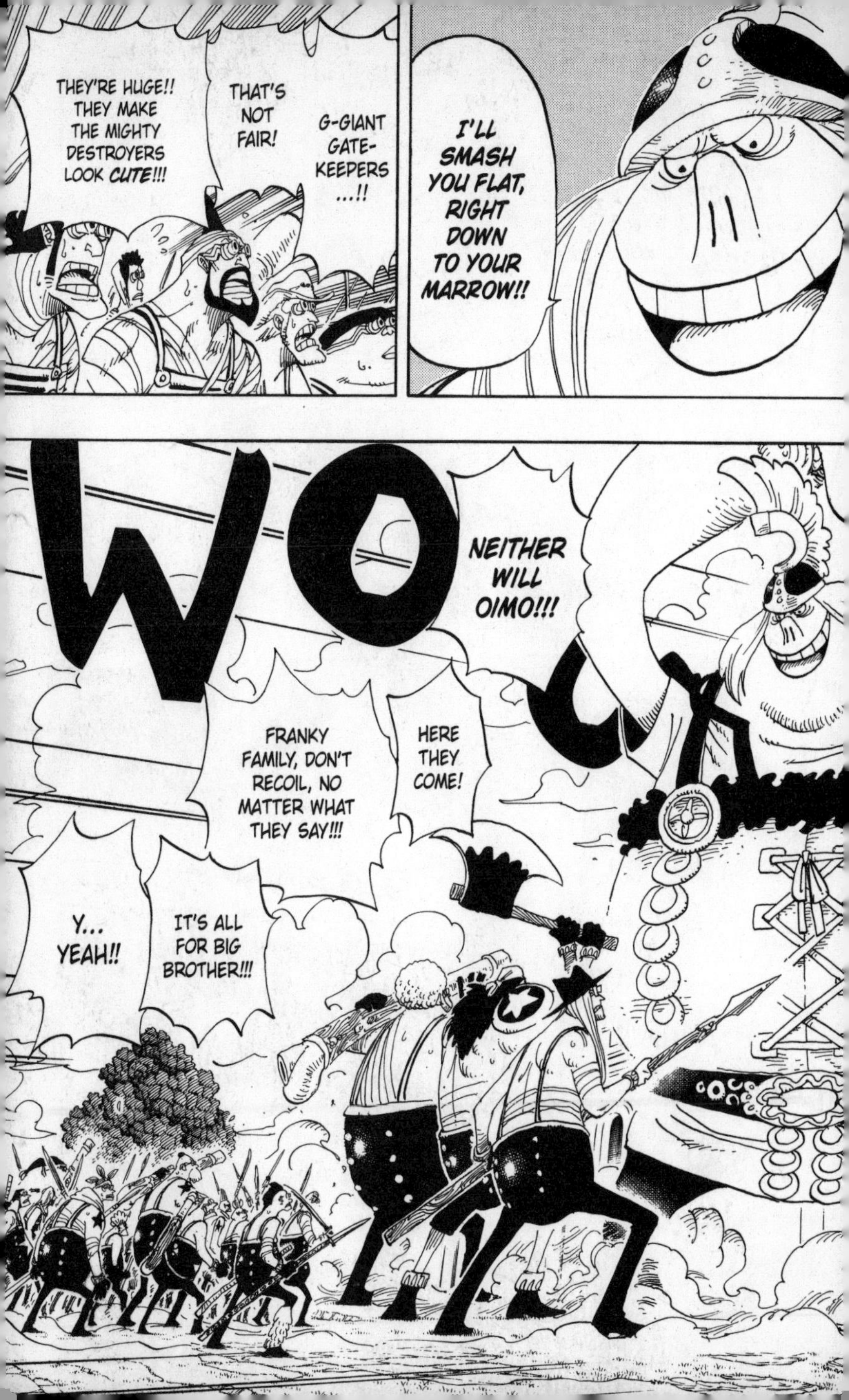
I'LL SMASH YOU FLAT, RIGHT DOWN TO YOUR MARROW!!
G-GIANT GATE-KEEPERS ...!!
THAT'S NOT FAIR!
THEY'RE HUGE!! THEY MAKE THE MIGHTY DESTROYERS LOOK CUTE!!!
NEITHER WILL OIMO!!!
WO
HERE THEY COME!
FRANKY FAMILY, DON'T RECOIL, NO MATTER WHAT THEY SAY!!!
IT'S ALL FOR BIG BROTHER!!!
Y... YEAH!!

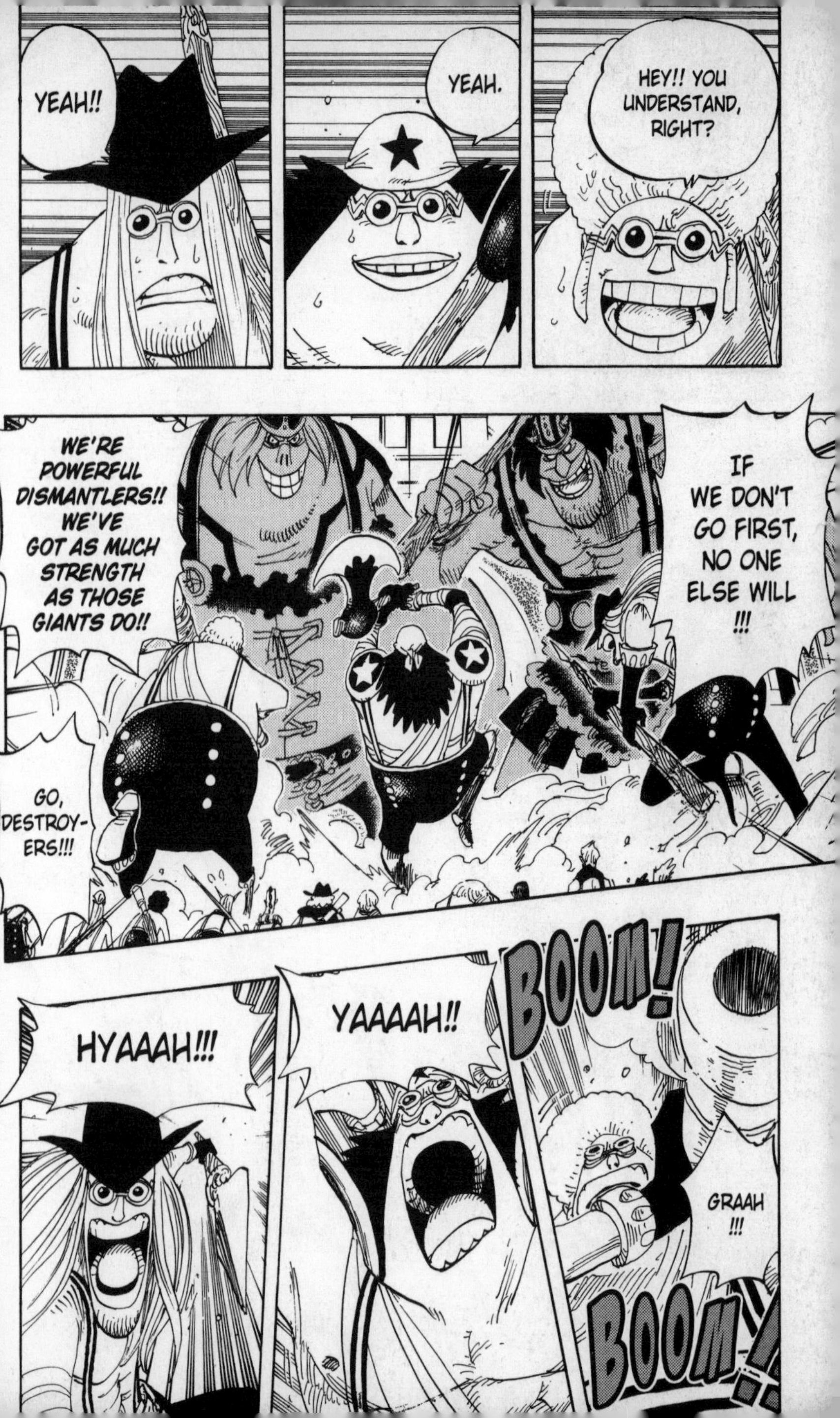
HEY!! YOU UNDERSTAND, RIGHT?
YEAH.
YEAH!!
IF WE DON'T GO FIRST, NO ONE ELSE WILL!!!
WE'RE POWERFUL DISMANTLERS!! WE'VE GOT AS MUCH STRENGTH AS THOSE GIANTS DO!!
GO, DESTROYERS!!!
BOOM!
GRAAH!!!
BOOM!!
YAAAAH!!
HYAAAH!!!

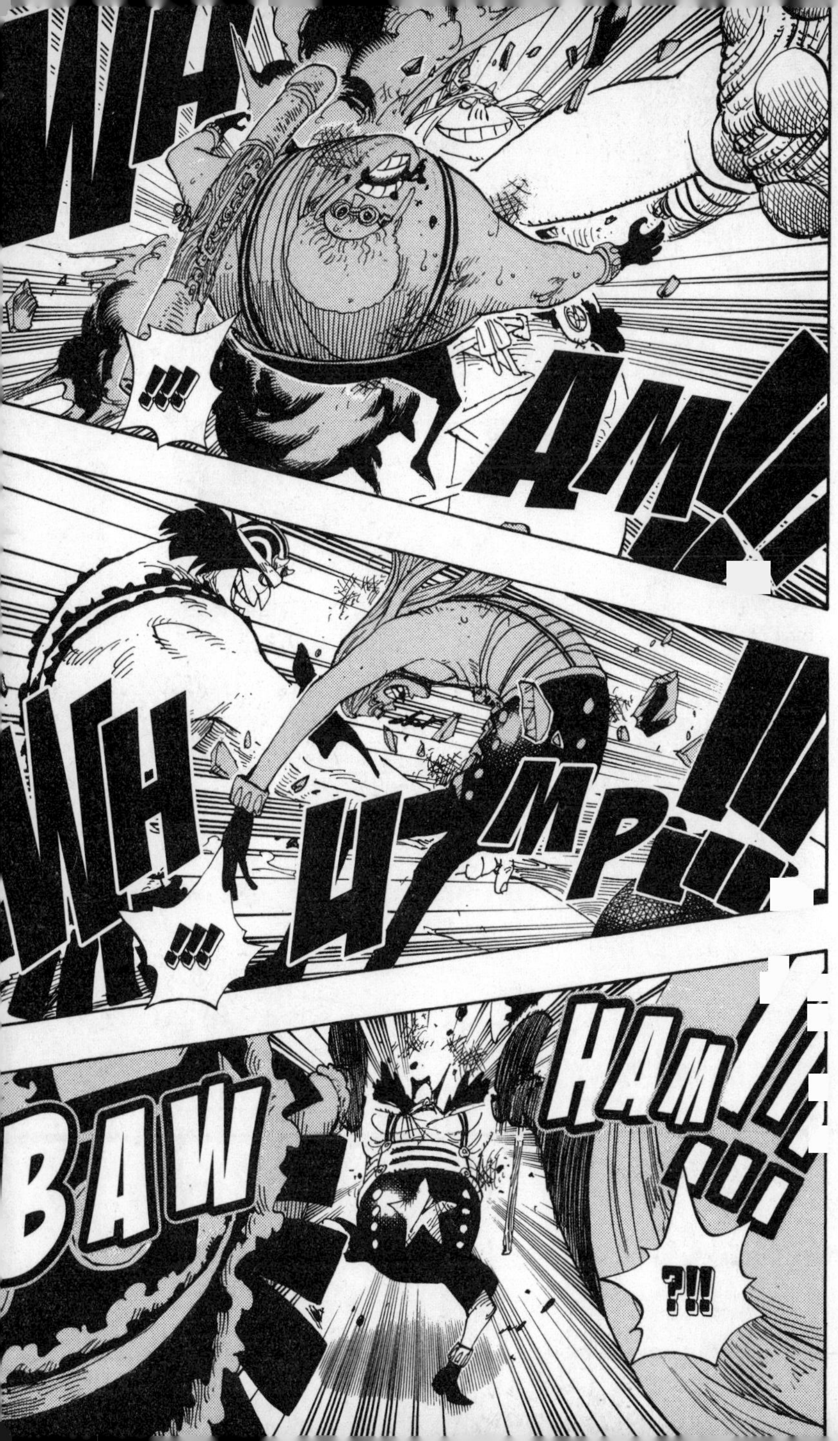
WHAM!!
!!!
WHUMP!!!
!!!
BAWHAM!!
?!!

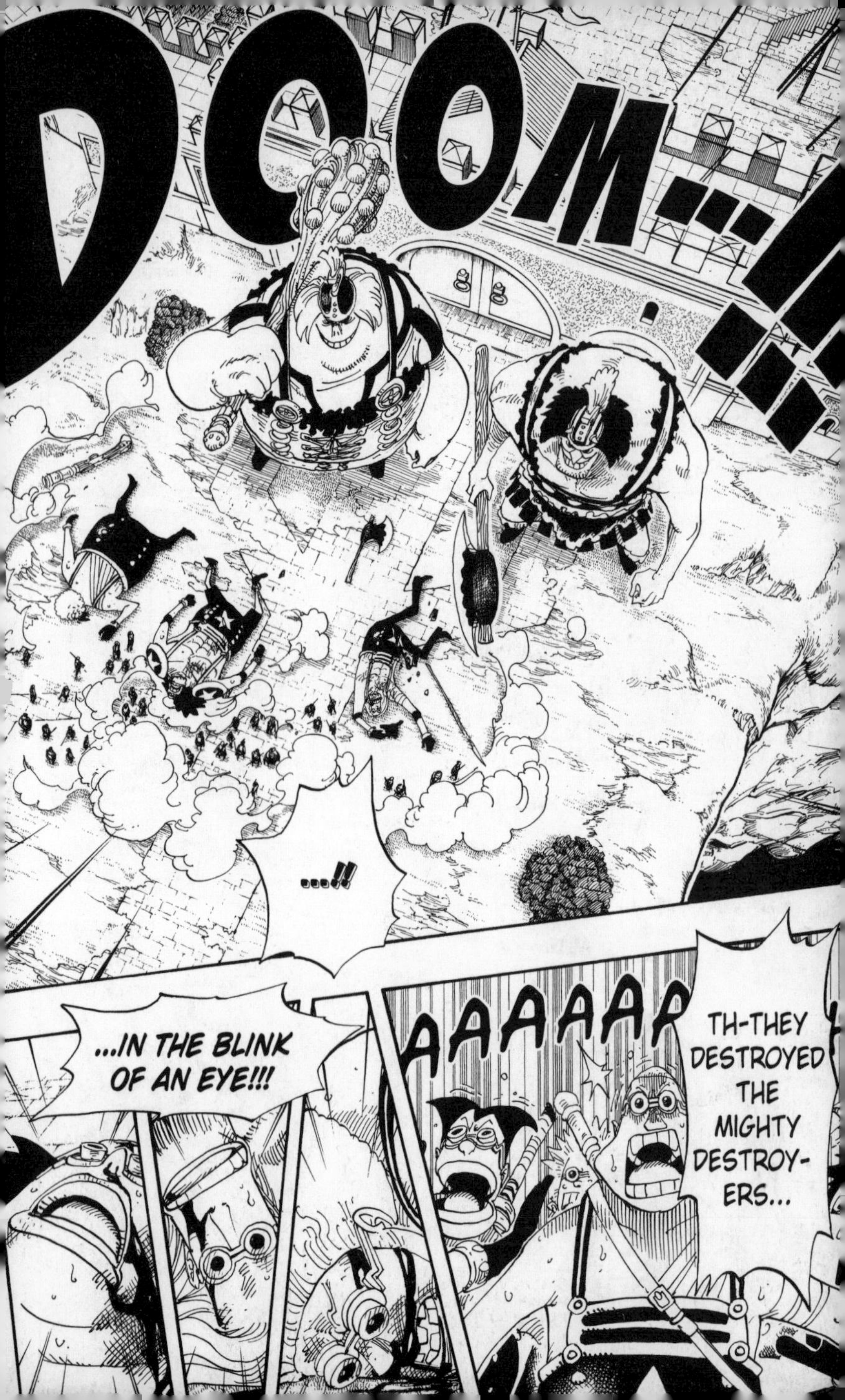
DOOM...!!!
...!!
AAAAA
TH-THEY DESTROYED THE MIGHTY DESTROY-ERS...
...IN THE BLINK OF AN EYE!!!

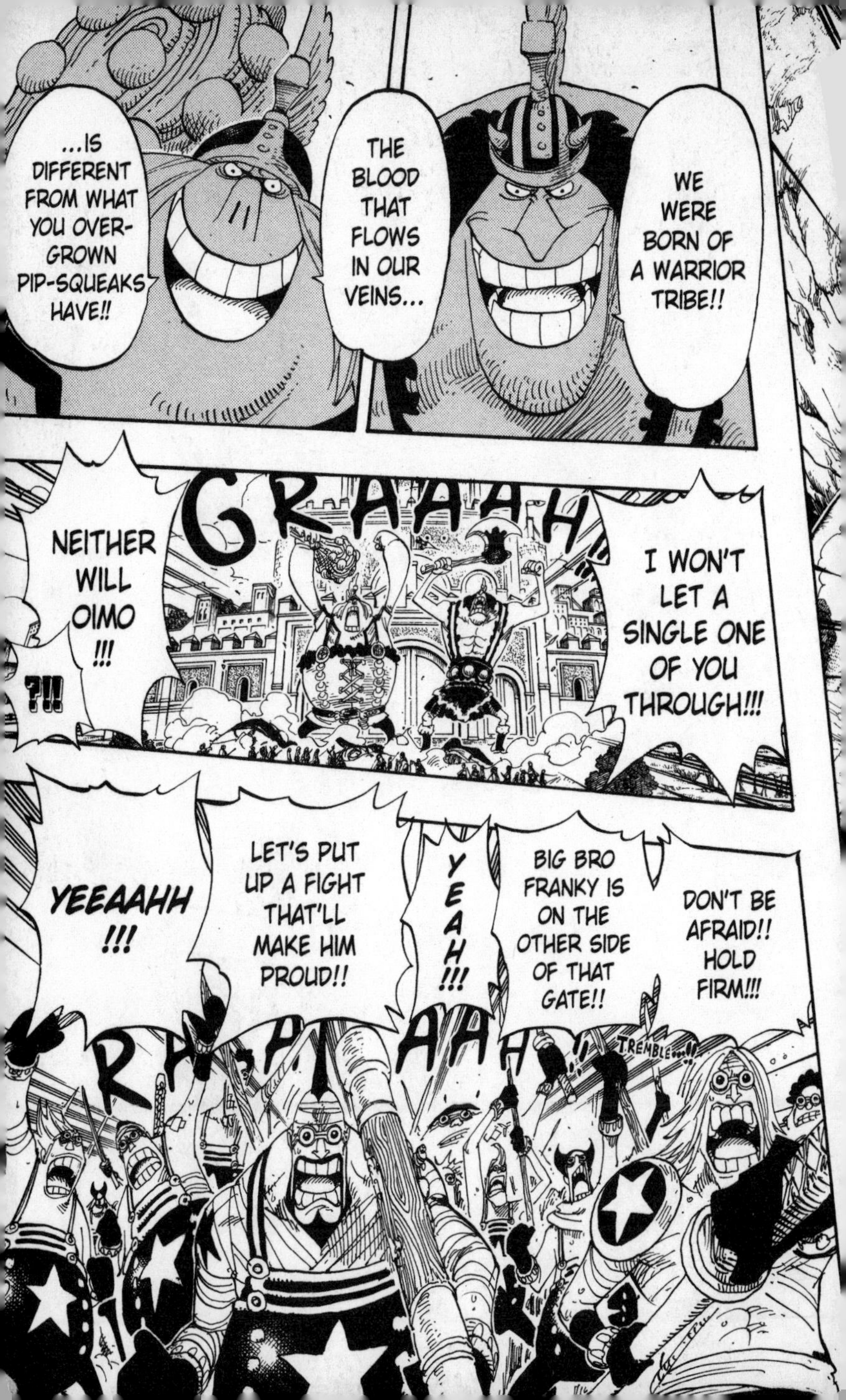
WE WERE BORN OF A WARRIOR TRIBE!!
THE BLOOD THAT FLOWS IN OUR VEINS...
...IS DIFFERENT FROM WHAT YOU OVER-GROWN PIP-SQUEAKS HAVE!!
I WON'T LET A SINGLE ONE OF YOU THROUGH!!!
GRAAAH!!
NEITHER WILL OIMO!!!
?!!
DON'T BE AFRAID!! HOLD FIRM!!!
BIG BRO FRANKY IS ON THE OTHER SIDE OF THAT GATE!!
TREMBLE...!!
YEAH!!!
LET'S PUT UP A FIGHT THAT'LL MAKE HIM PROUD!!
YEEAAHH!!!
RAAAH!!

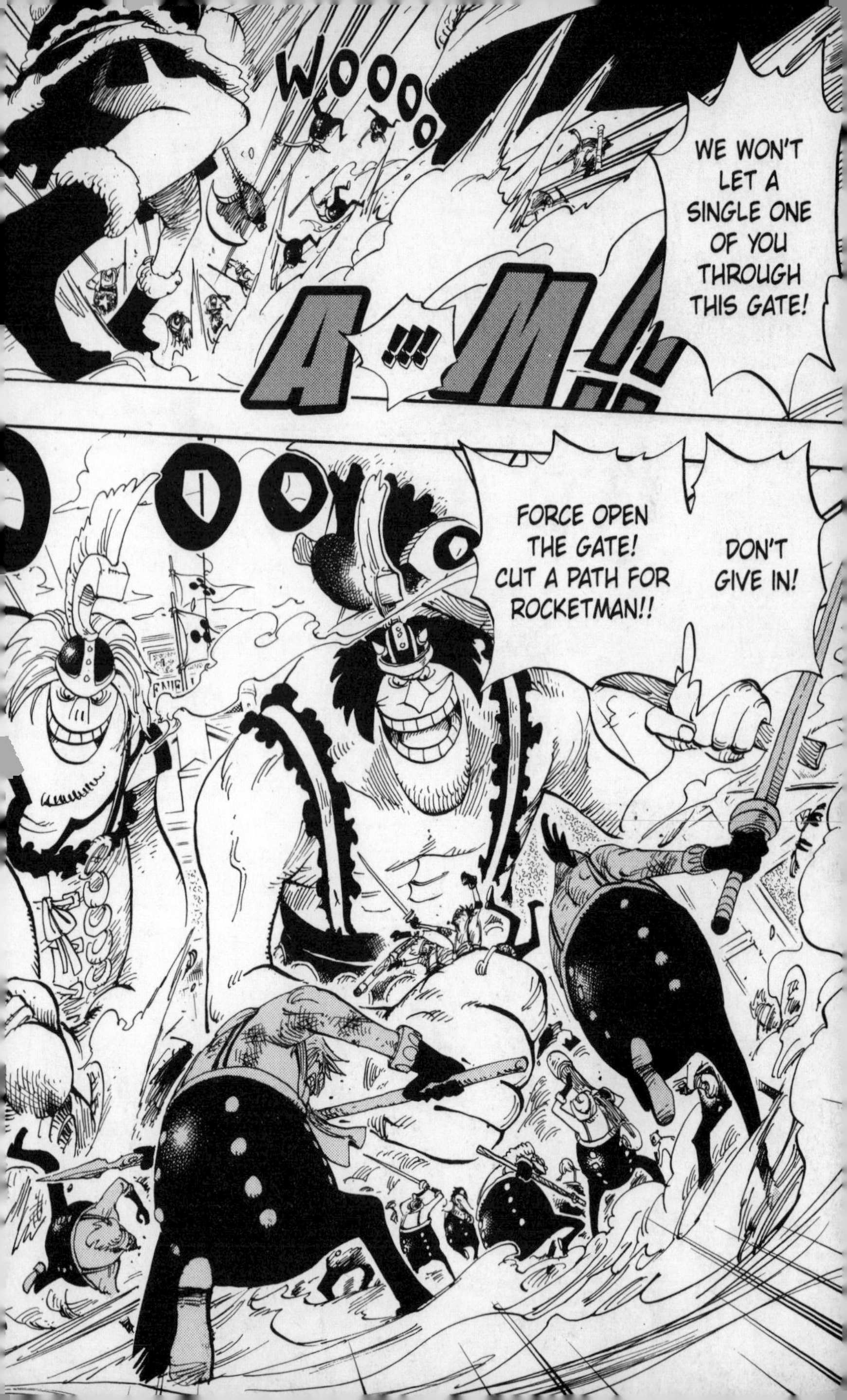
WE WON'T LET A SINGLE ONE OF YOU THROUGH THIS GATE!
WOOOO
DON'T GIVE IN!
FORCE OPEN THE GATE! CUT A PATH FOR ROCKETMAN!!

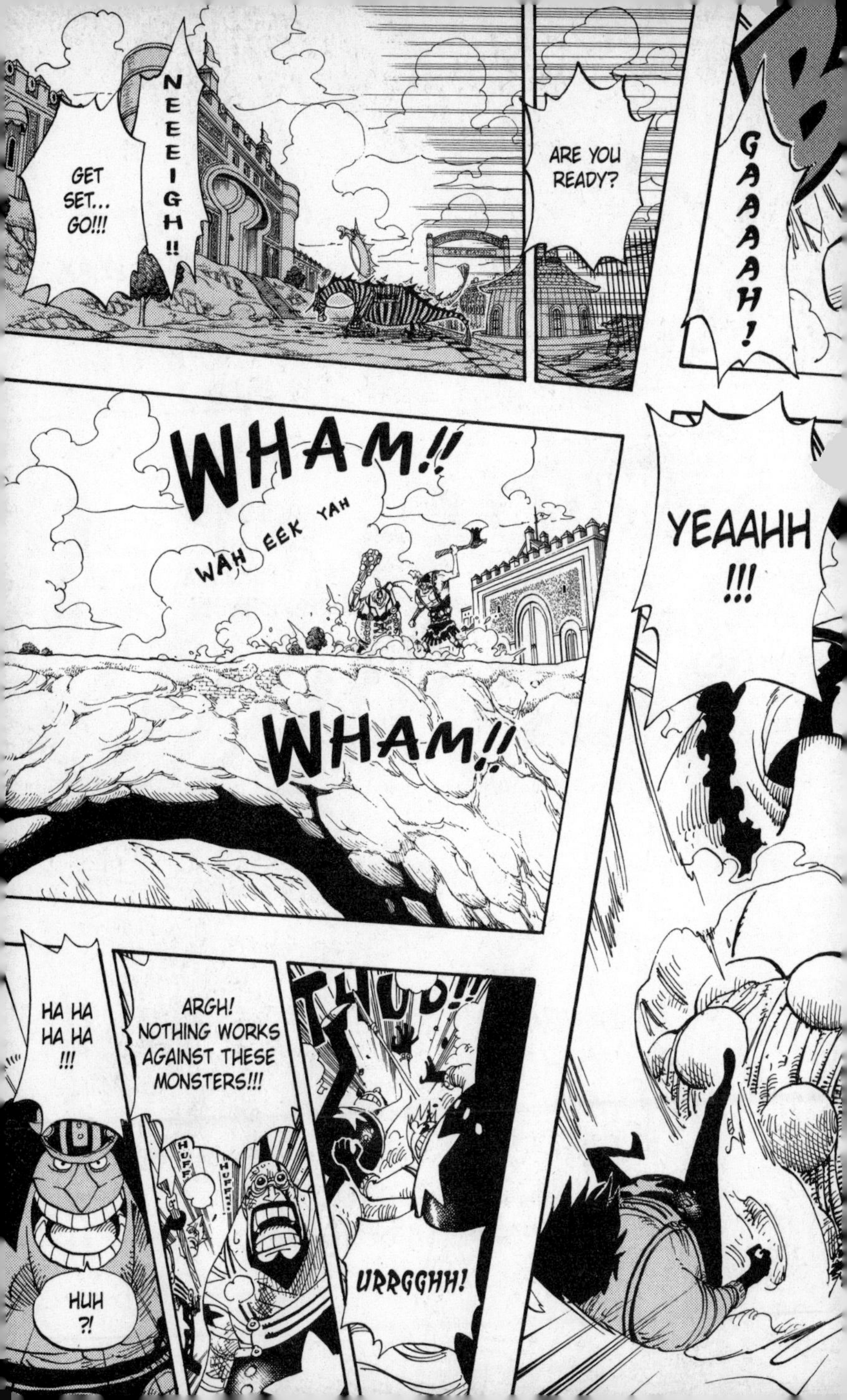

GAAAAH!
ARE YOU READY?
NEEEIGH!!
GET SET... GO!!!
YEAAHH!!!
WHAM!!
WAH EEK YAH
WHAM!!
THUD!!
URRGGHH!
ARGH! NOTHING WORKS AGAINST THESE MONSTERS!!!
HUFF
HUFF...
HA HA HA HA!!!
HUH?!

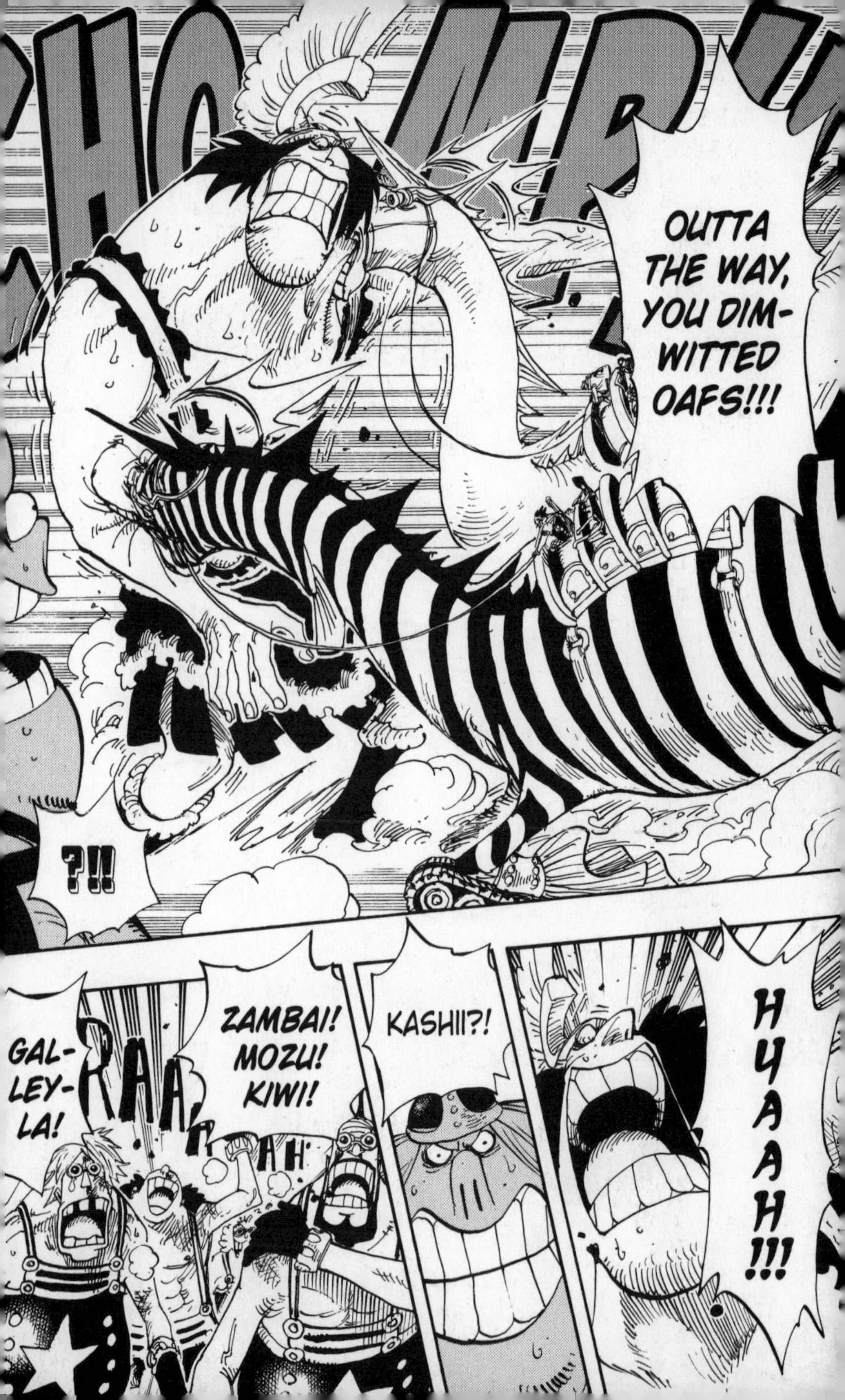

OUTTA THE WAY, YOU DIM-WITTED OAFS!!!
?!!
HYAAAH!!!
KASHII?!
ZAMBAI! MOZU! KIWI!
GAL-LEY-LA!

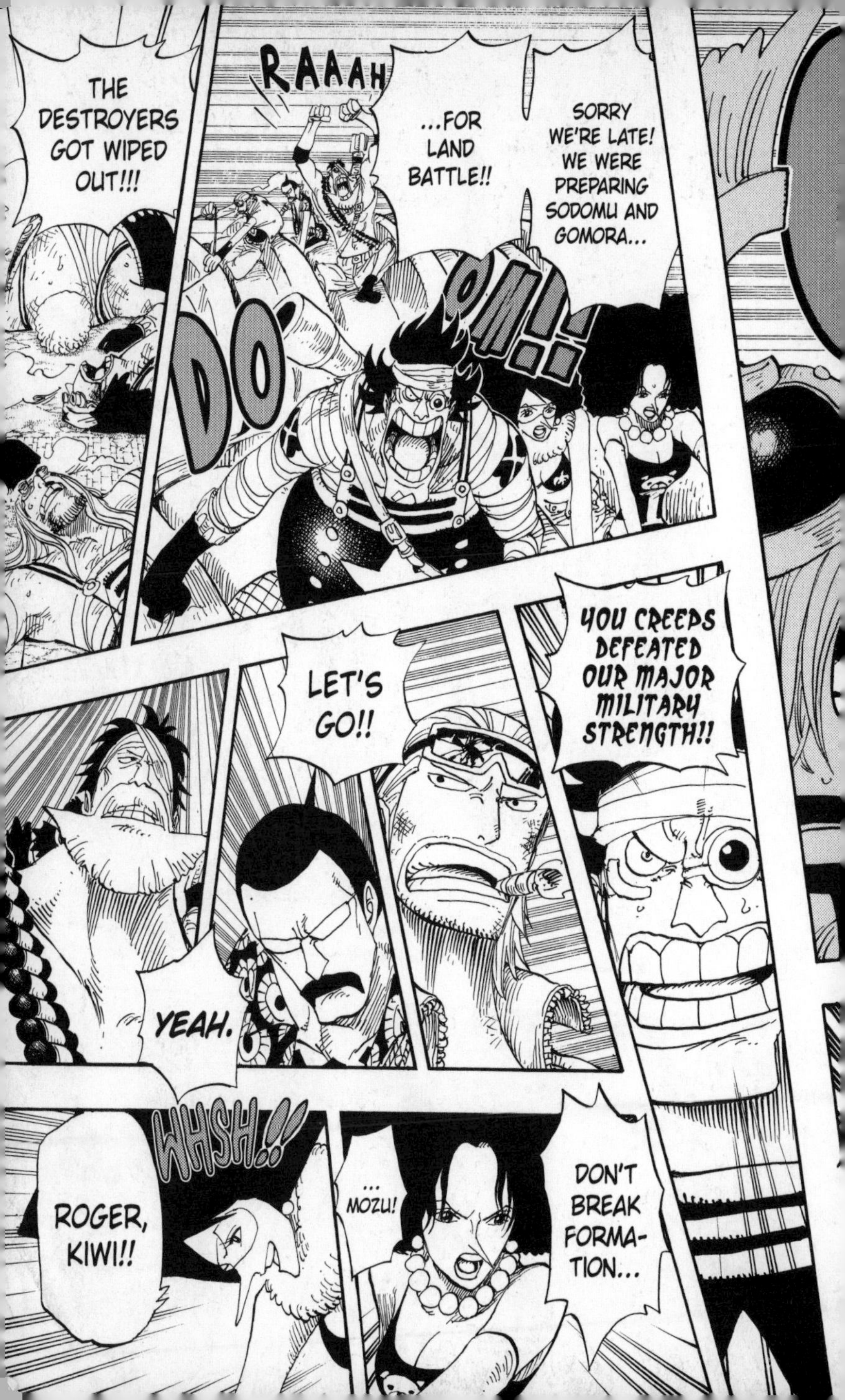
SORRY WE'RE LATE! WE WERE PREPARING SODOMU AND GOMORA...
...FOR LAND BATTLE!!
RAAAH
DOOM!!
THE DESTROYERS GOT WIPED OUT!!!
YOU CREEPS DEFEATED OUR MAJOR MILITARY STRENGTH!!
LET'S GO!!
YEAH.
DON'T BREAK FORMATION...
...MOZU!
WHSH!!
ROGER, KIWI!!

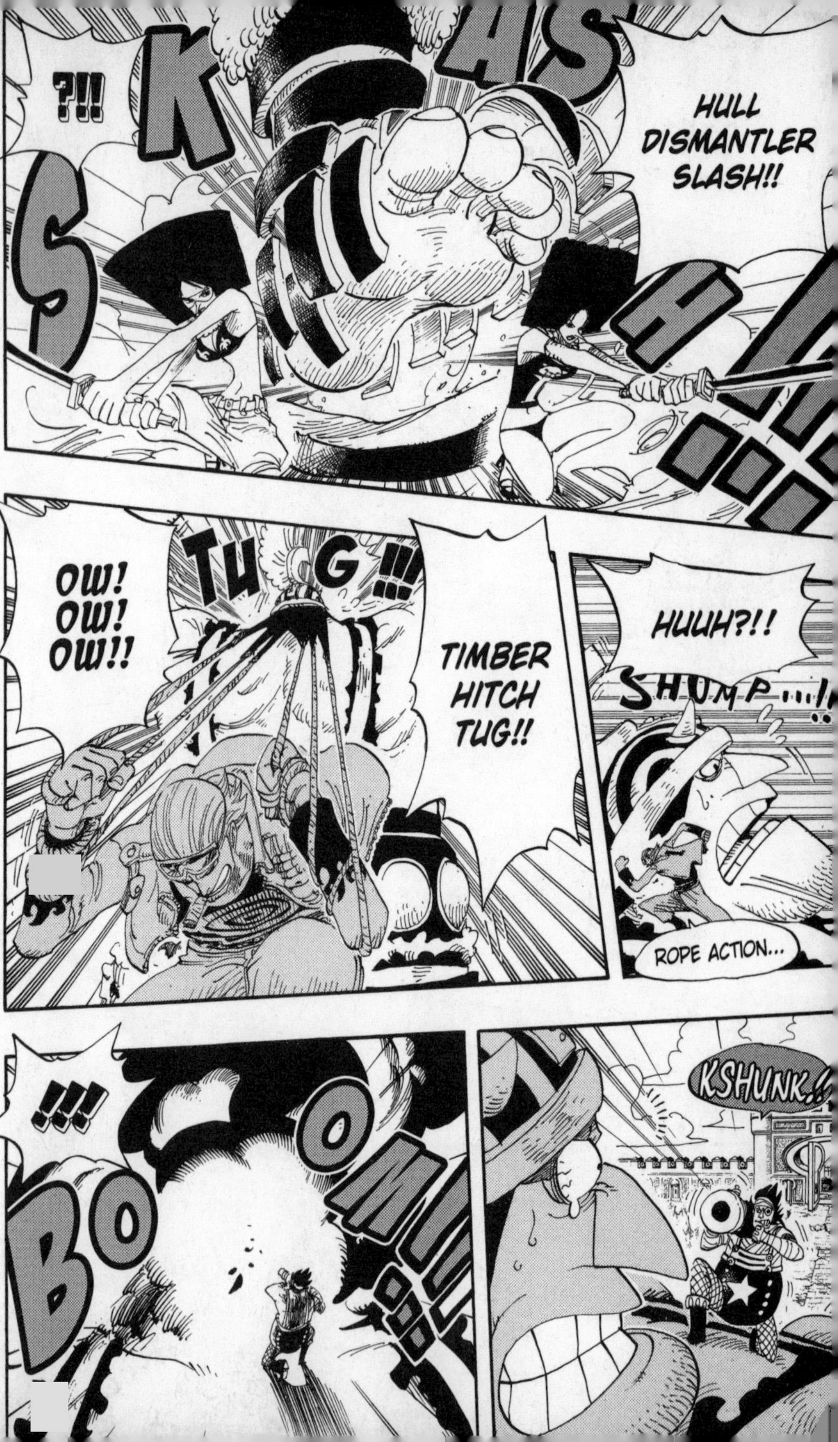
HULL DISMANTLER SLASH!!
SHASH
?!!
HUUH?!!
SHUMP...!!
ROPE ACTION...
TIMBER HITCH TUG!!
TUG!!!
OW! OW! OW!!
KSHUNK!!
!!!

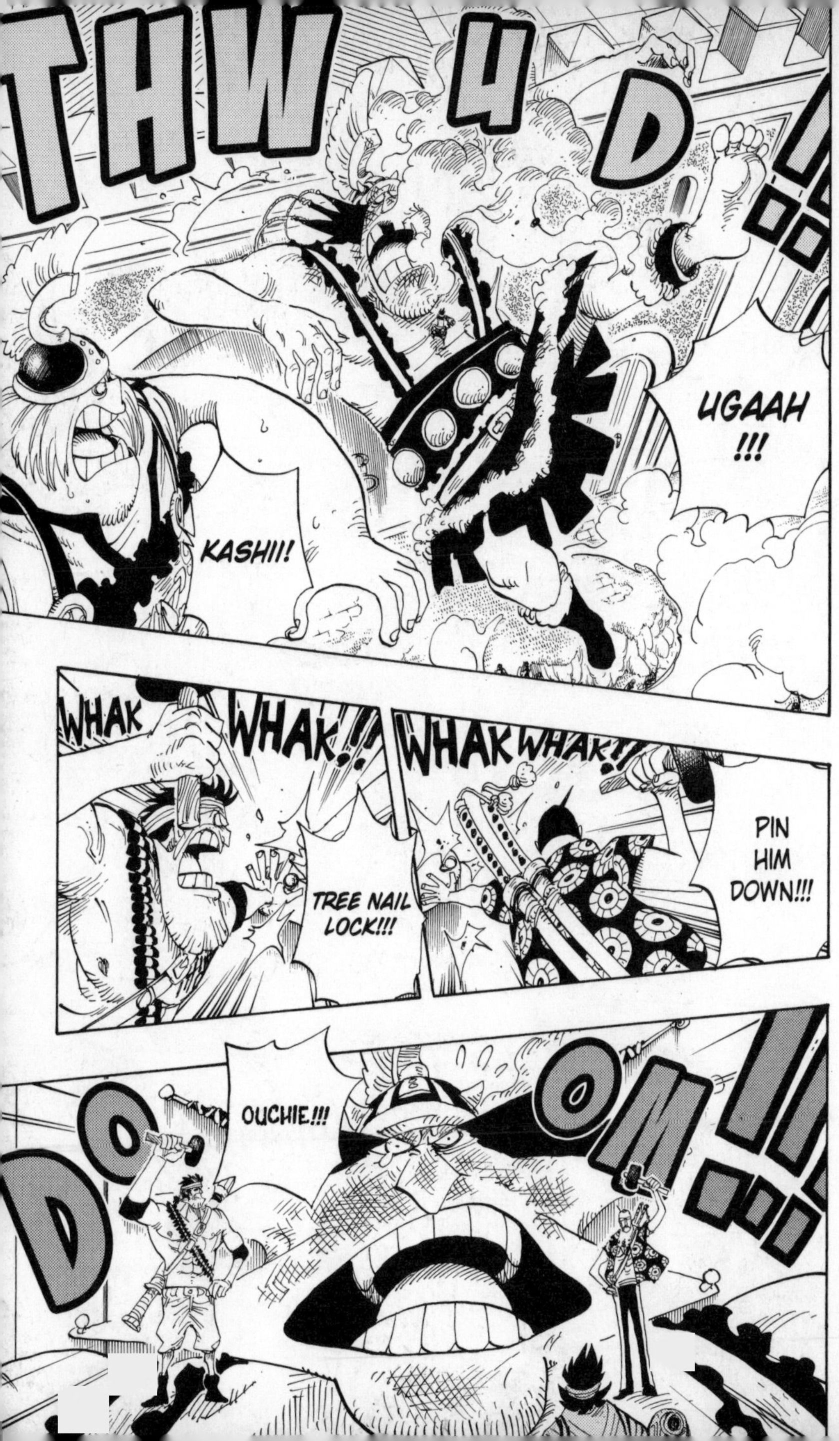
THWUD!!
UGAAH!!!
KASHII!
WHAKWHAK!!
PIN HIM DOWN!!!
WHAK WHAK!!
TREE NAIL LOCK!!!
DOON!!
OUCHIE!!!

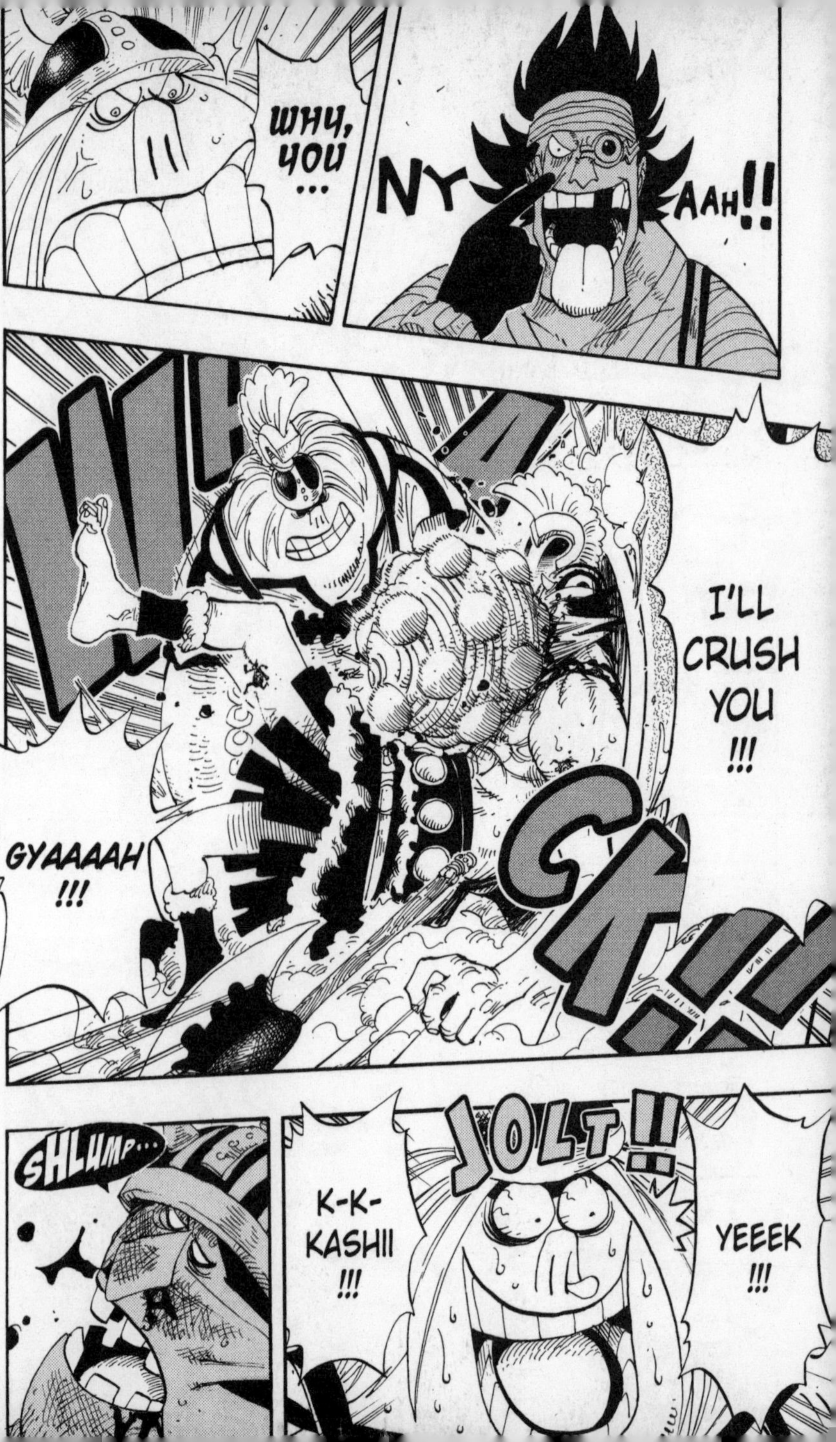
NYAAH!!
WHY, YOU...
I'LL CRUSH YOU!!!
GYAAAAH!!!
JOLT!!
YEEEK!!!
K-K-KASHII!!!
SHLUMP...

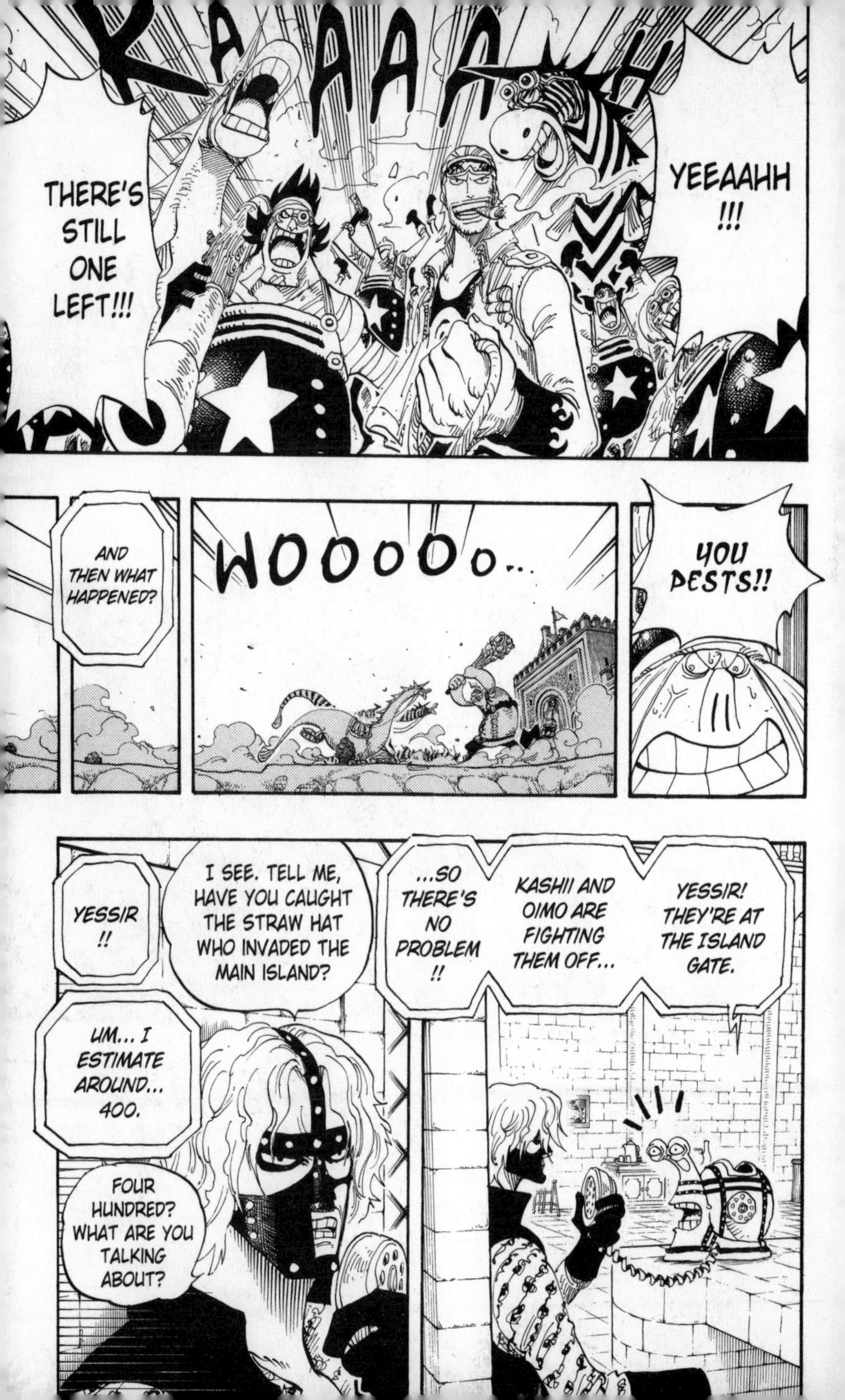
KAAAAH
YEEAAHH!!!
THERE'S STILL ONE LEFT!!!
YOU PESTS!!
WOOOOo...
AND THEN WHAT HAPPENED?
YESSIR! THEY'RE AT THE ISLAND GATE.
KASHII AND OIMO ARE FIGHTING THEM OFF...
...SO THERE'S NO PROBLEM!!
I SEE. TELL ME, HAVE YOU CAUGHT THE STRAW HAT WHO INVADED THE MAIN ISLAND?
YESSIR!!
UM... I ESTIMATE AROUND... 400.
FOUR HUNDRED? WHAT ARE YOU TALKING ABOUT?

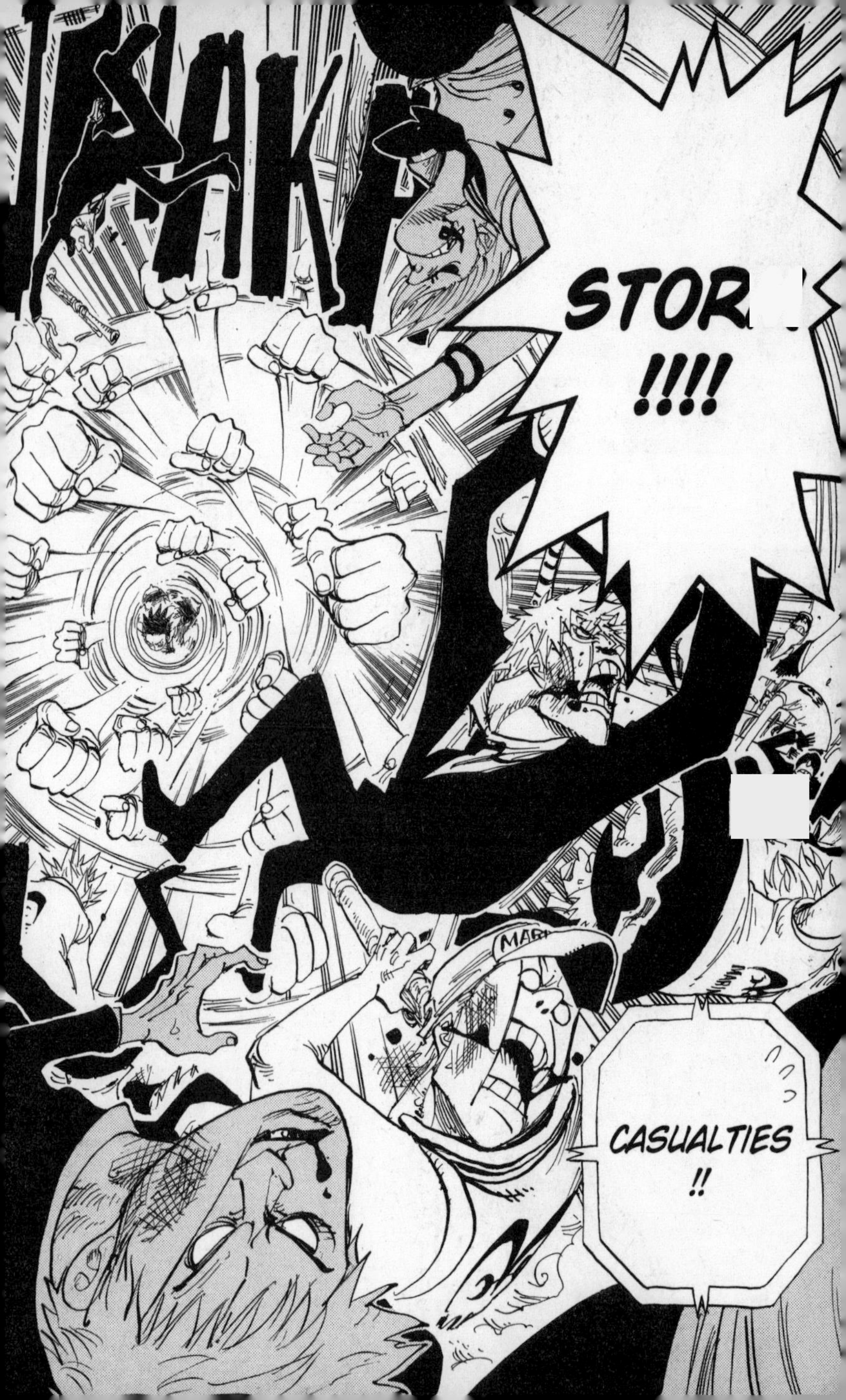
STOR
!!!!
CASUALTIES
!!

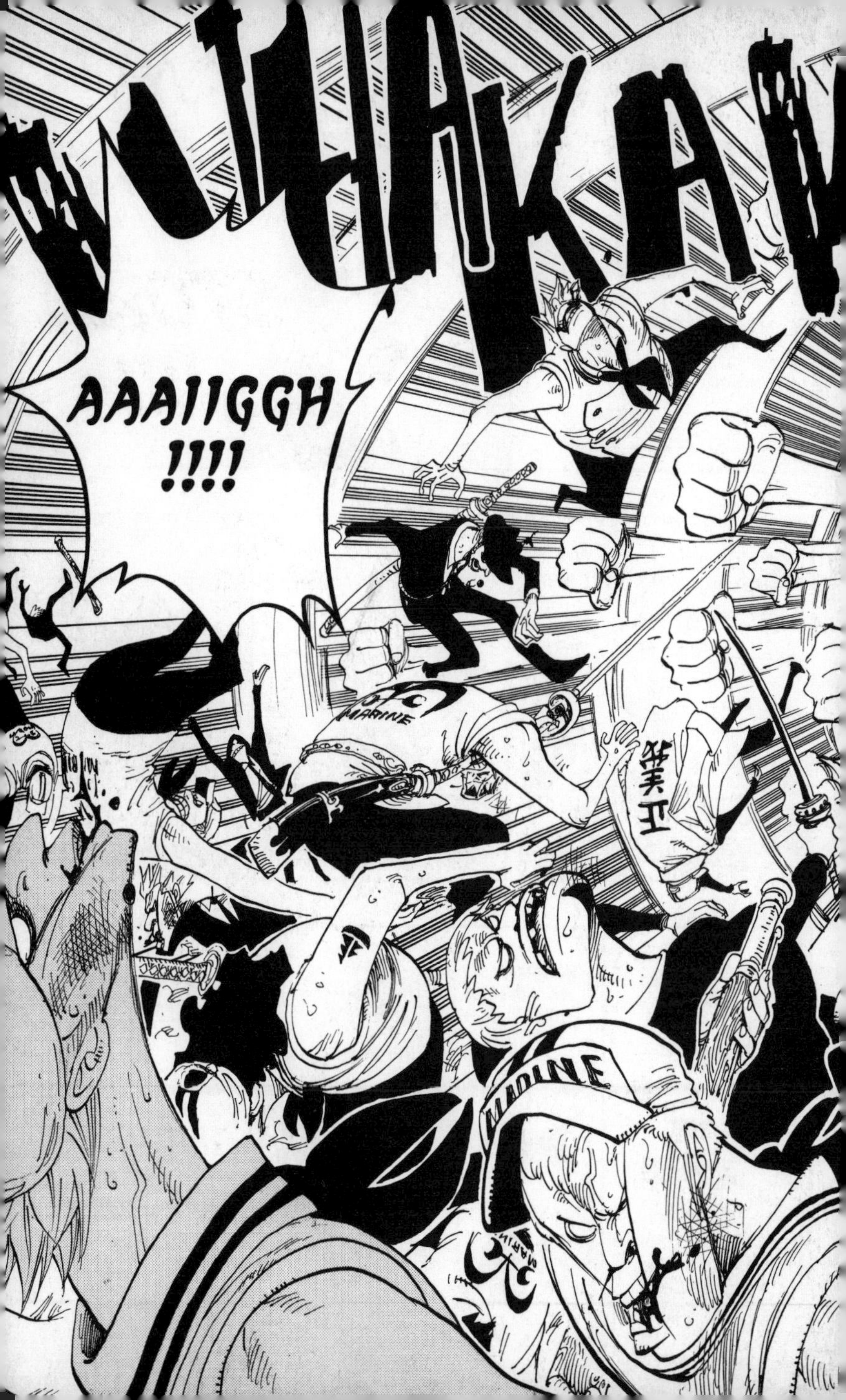
AAAIIGGH !!!!

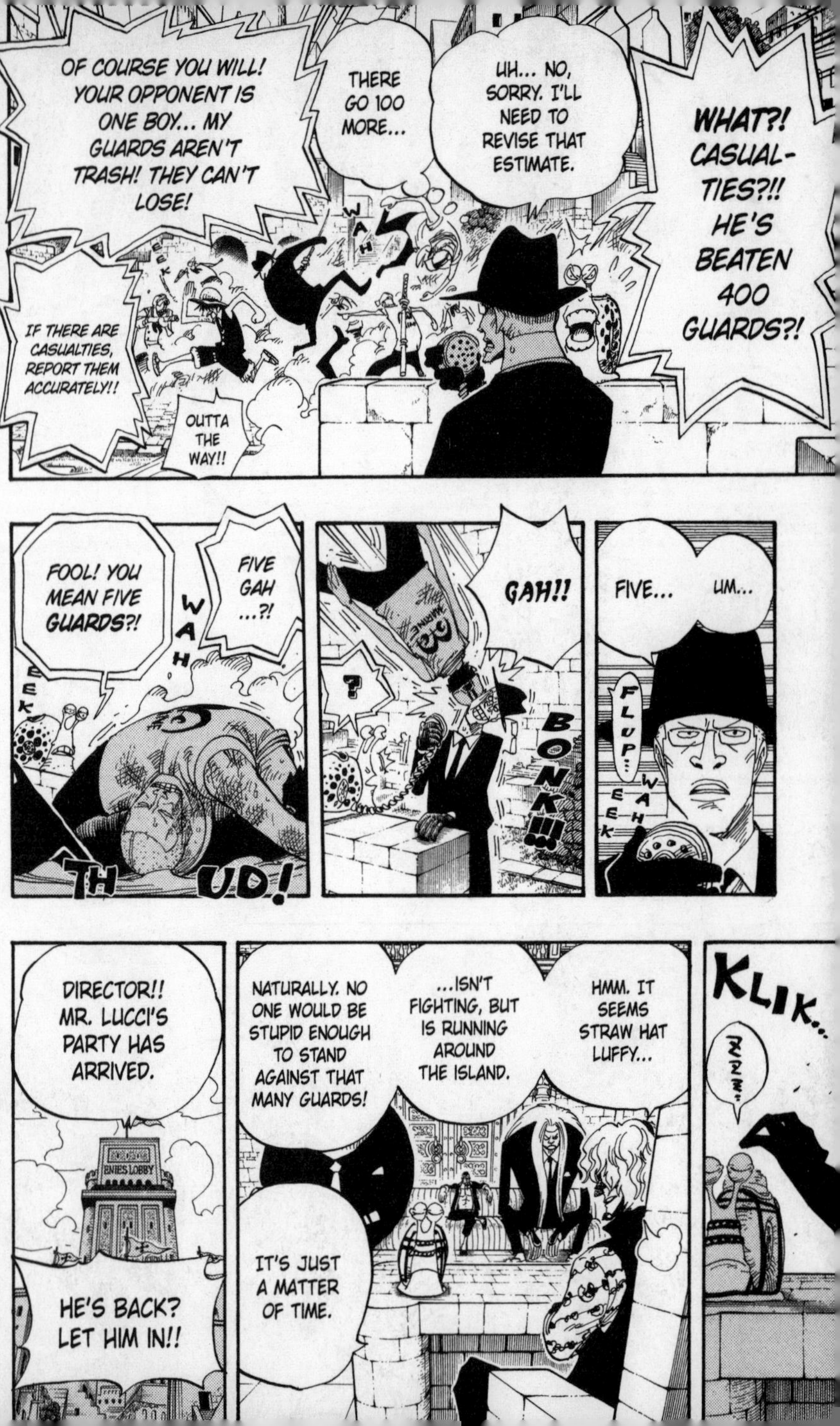

WHAT?! CASUALTIES?!! HE'S BEATEN 400 GUARDS?!
UH... NO, SORRY. I'LL NEED TO REVISE THAT ESTIMATE.
THERE GO 100 MORE...
OF COURSE YOU WILL! YOUR OPPONENT IS ONE BOY... MY GUARDS AREN'T TRASH! THEY CAN'T LOSE!
WAH
EEK
IF THERE ARE CASUALTIES, REPORT THEM ACCURATELY!!
OUTTA THE WAY!!
FIVE... UM...
FLUP...
WAH
EEK
GAH!!
?
BONK!!!
FIVE GAH ...?!
FOOL! YOU MEAN FIVE GUARDS?!
WAH
EEK
THUD!
KLIK...
ZZZ...
HMM. IT SEEMS STRAW HAT LUFFY...
...ISN'T FIGHTING, BUT IS RUNNING AROUND THE ISLAND.
NATURALLY. NO ONE WOULD BE STUPID ENOUGH TO STAND AGAINST THAT MANY GUARDS!
IT'S JUST A MATTER OF TIME.
DIRECTOR!! MR. LUCCI'S PARTY HAS ARRIVED.
ENIES LOBBY
HE'S BACK? LET HIM IN!!

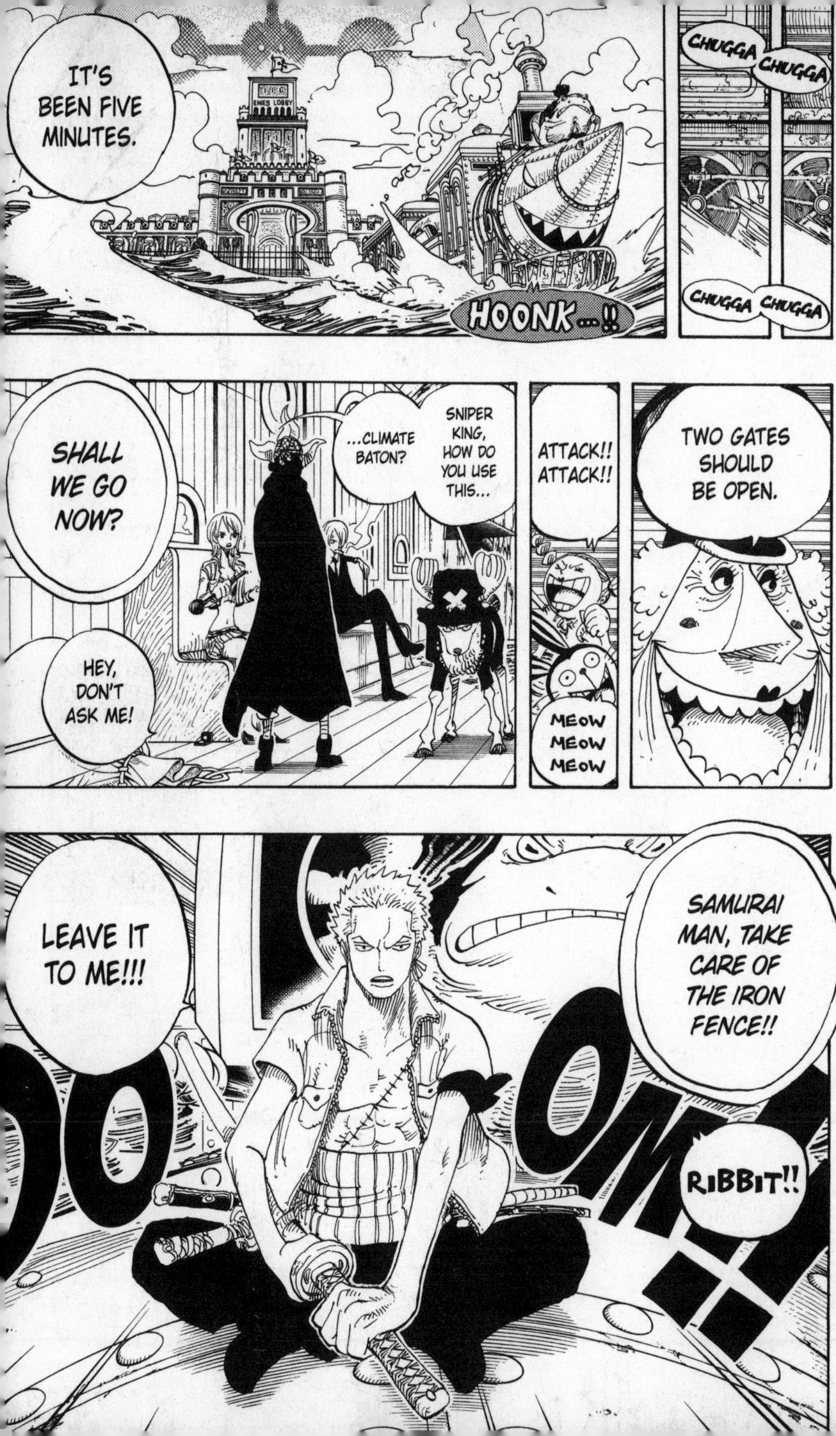
CHUGGA CHUGGA
CHUGGA CHUGGA
IT'S BEEN FIVE MINUTES.
HOONK...!!
TWO GATES SHOULD BE OPEN.
ATTACK!! ATTACK!!
MEOW MEOW MEOW
SNIPER KING, HOW DO YOU USE THIS...
...CLIMATE BATON?
SHALL WE GO NOW?
HEY, DON'T ASK ME!
SAMURAI MAN, TAKE CARE OF THE IRON FENCE!!
RIBBIT!!
LEAVE IT TO ME!!!

Chapter 379: POWER LEVEL

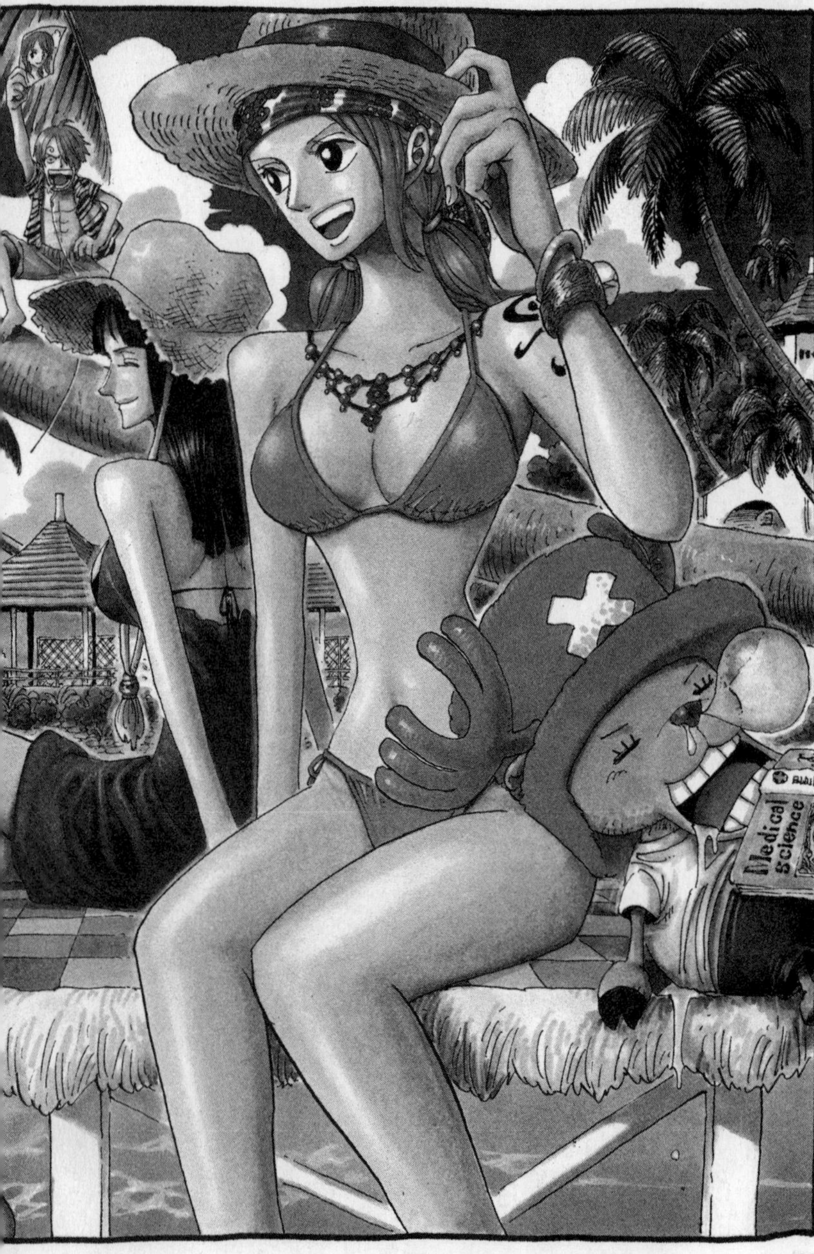
Medical science

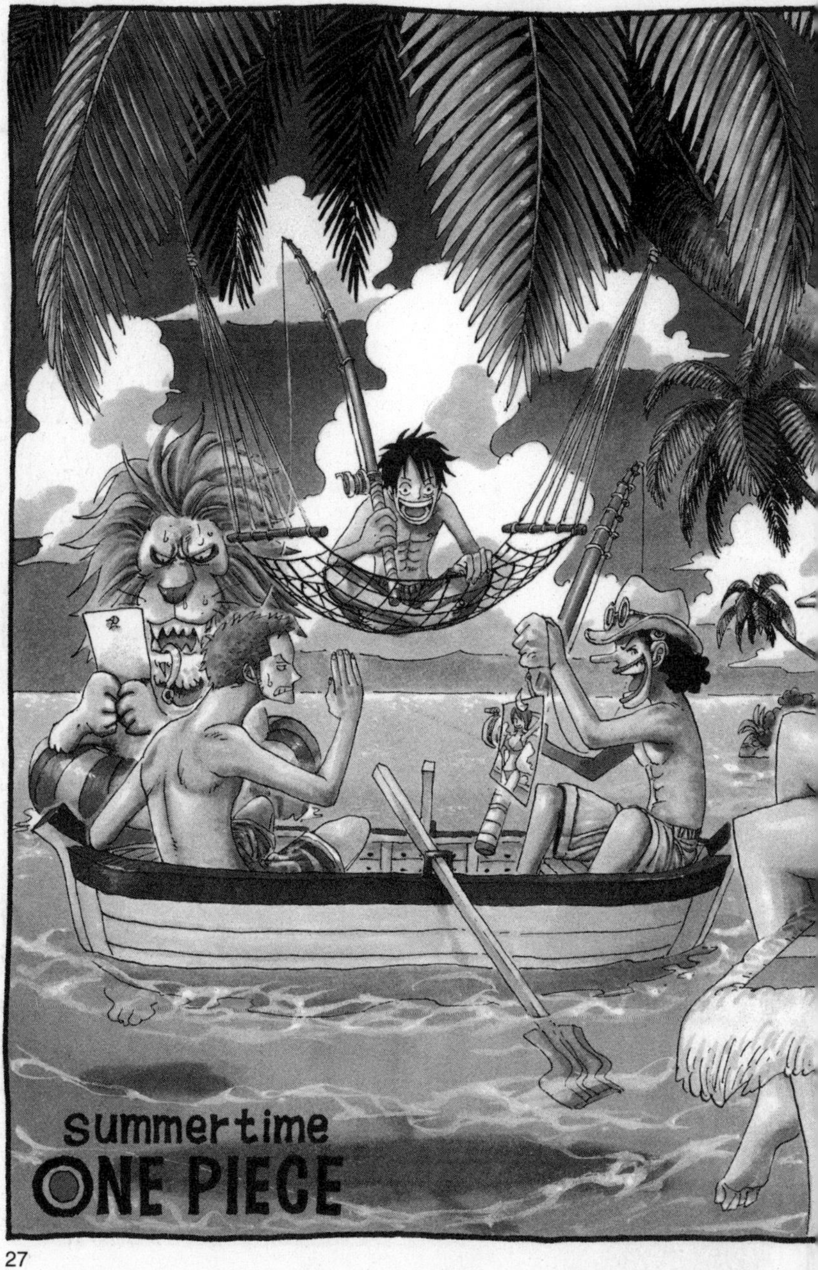
summertime
ONE PIECE

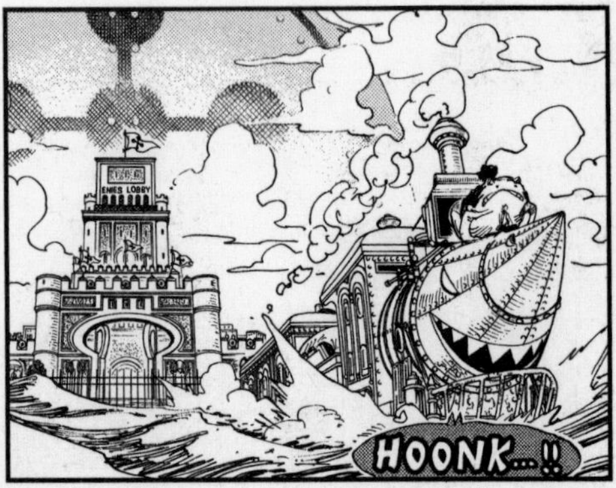
ENIES LOBBY
HOONK...!!

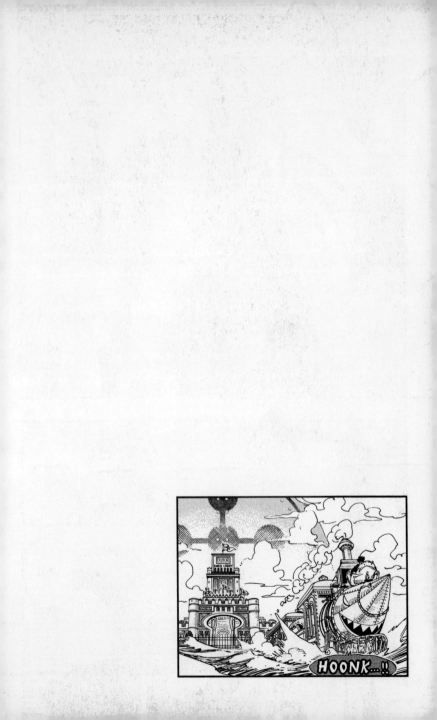

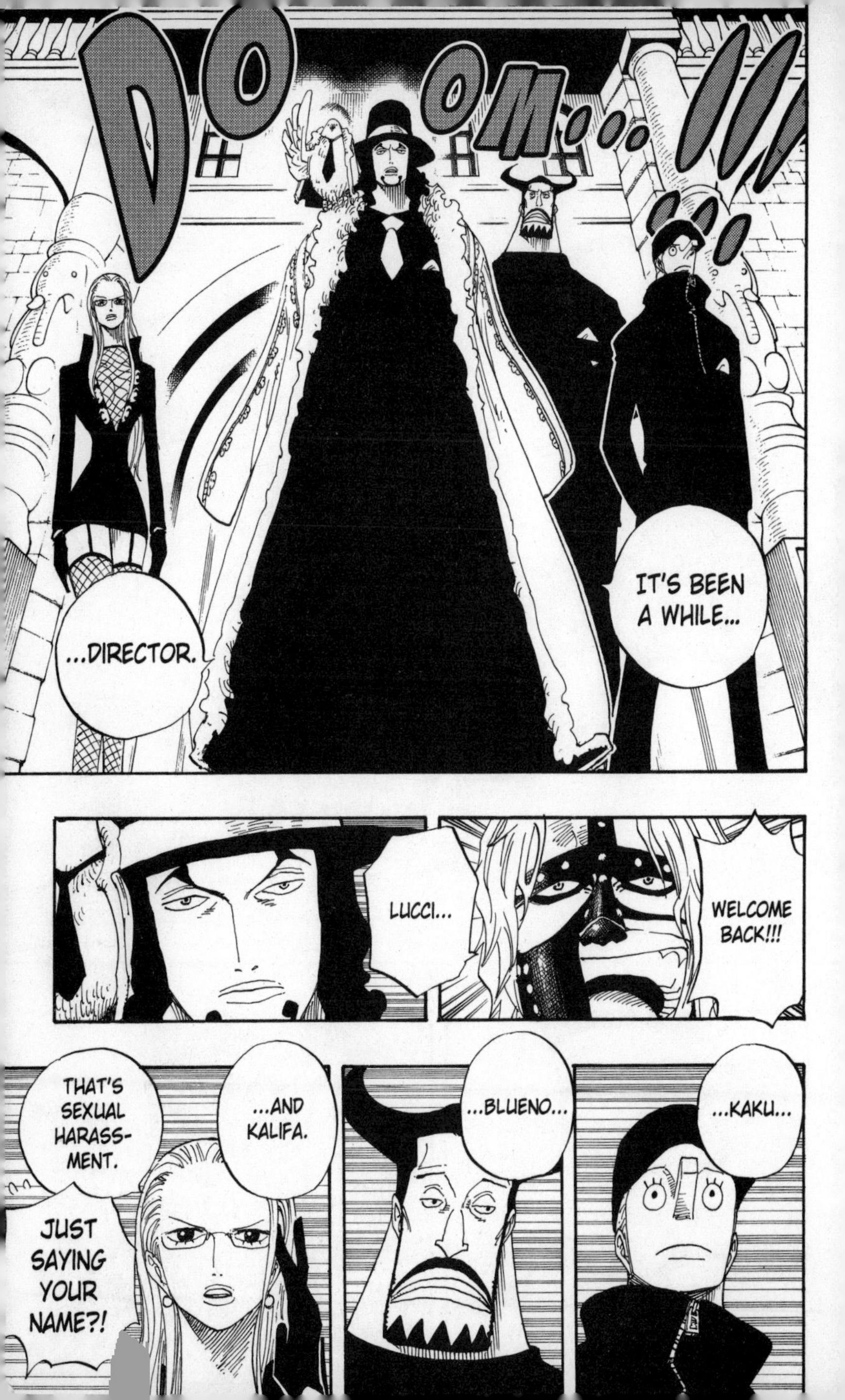
DOOM...!!!
IT'S BEEN A WHILE...
...DIRECTOR.
WELCOME BACK!!!
LUCCI...
...KAKU...
...BLUENO...
...AND KALIFA.
THAT'S SEXUAL HARASS-MENT.
JUST SAYING YOUR NAME?!

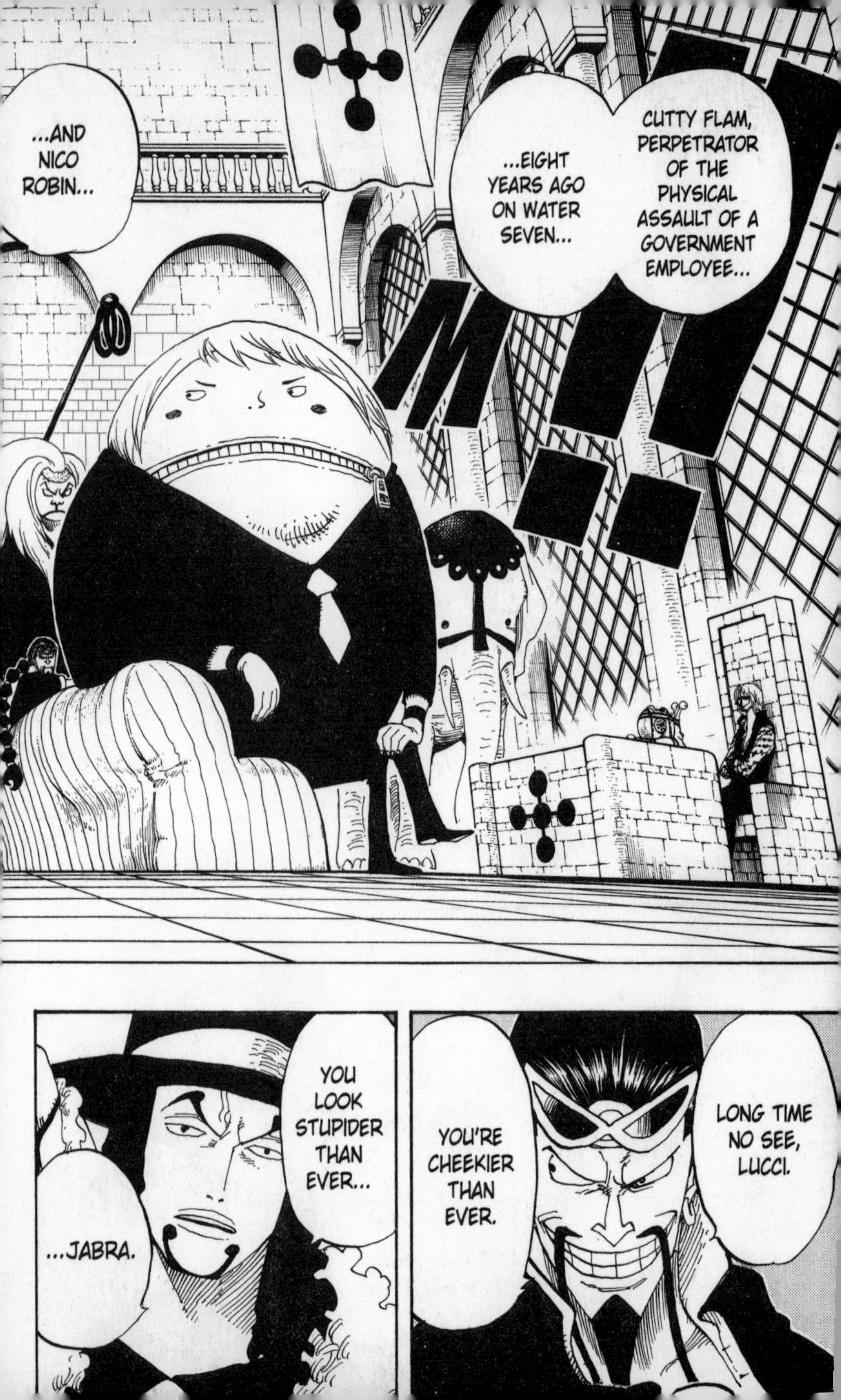
CUTTY FLAM, PERPETRATOR OF THE PHYSICAL ASSAULT OF A GOVERNMENT EMPLOYEE...
...EIGHT YEARS AGO ON WATER SEVEN...
...AND NICO ROBIN...
LONG TIME NO SEE, LUCCI.
YOU'RE CHEEKIER THAN EVER.
YOU LOOK STUPIDER THAN EVER...
...JABRA.

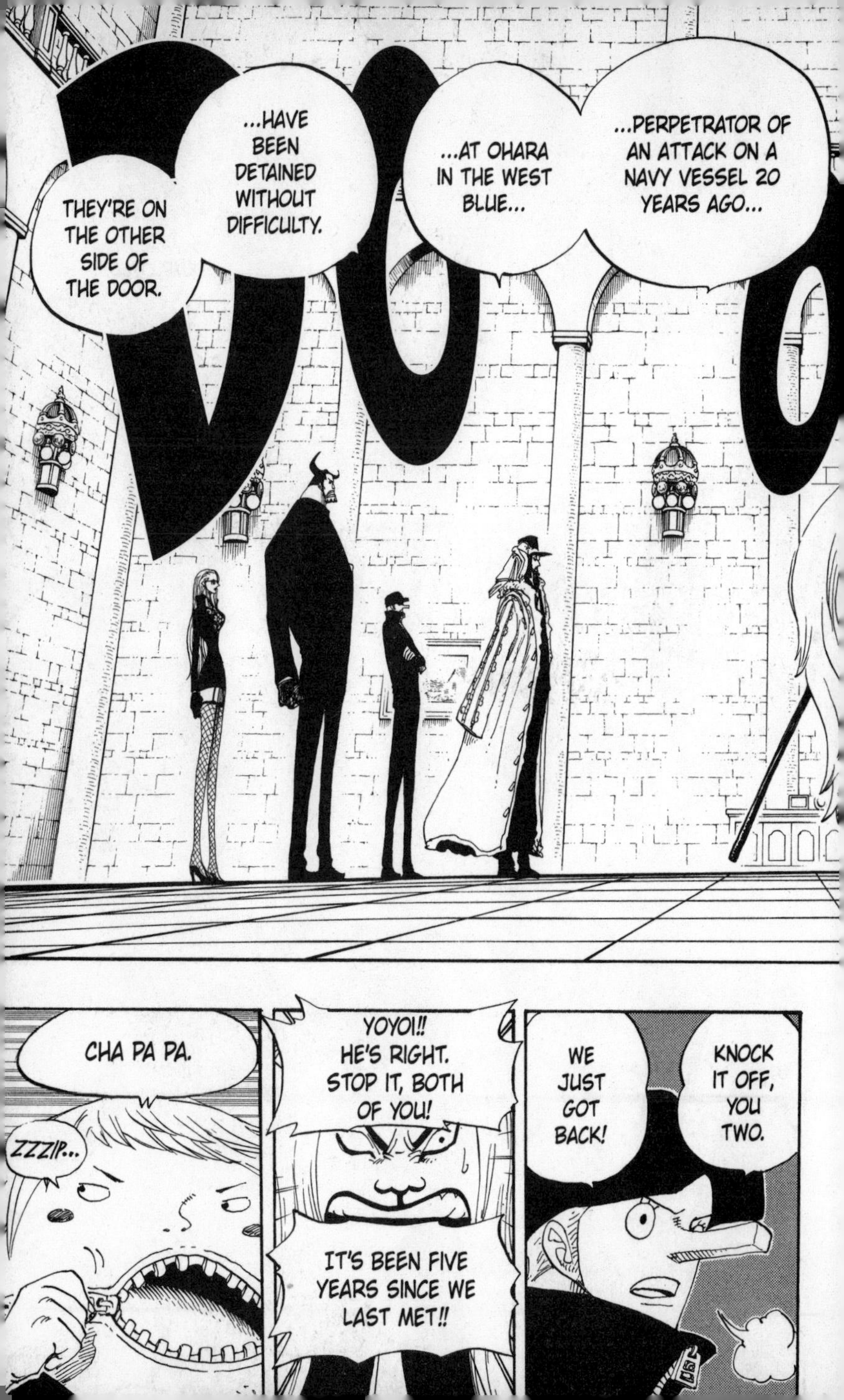
...PERPETRATOR OF AN ATTACK ON A NAVY VESSEL 20 YEARS AGO...
...AT OHARA IN THE WEST BLUE...
...HAVE BEEN DETAINED WITHOUT DIFFICULTY.
THEY'RE ON THE OTHER SIDE OF THE DOOR.
KNOCK IT OFF, YOU TWO.
WE JUST GOT BACK!
YOYOI!! HE'S RIGHT. STOP IT, BOTH OF YOU!
IT'S BEEN FIVE YEARS SINCE WE LAST MET!!
CHA PA PA.
ZZZIP...

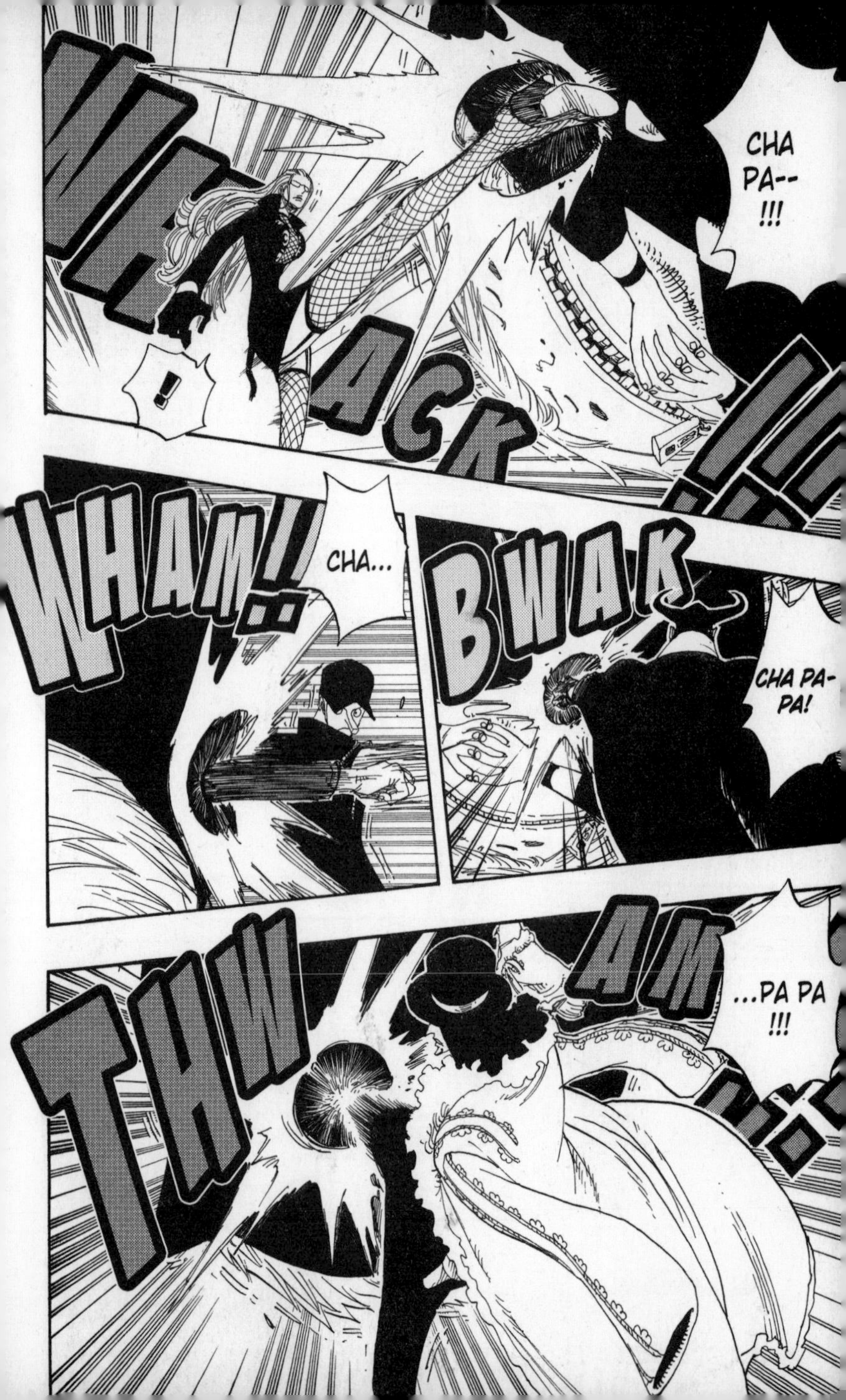
CHA PA--!!!
WHACK!!
!
BWAK
CHA PA-PA!
CHA...
WHAM!!
...PA PA !!!
THWAM

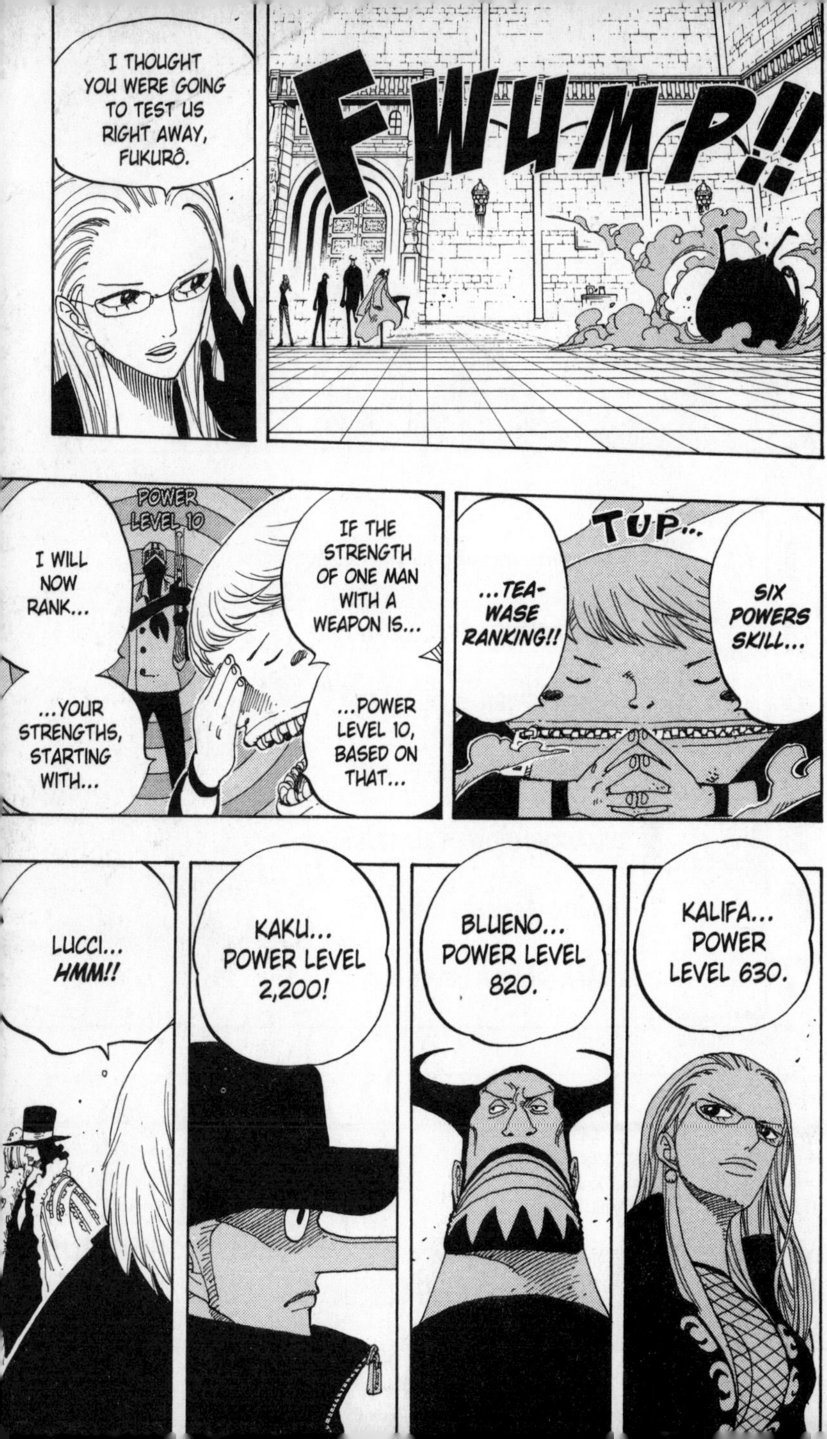
FWUMP!!
I THOUGHT YOU WERE GOING TO TEST US RIGHT AWAY, FUKURÔ.
TUP...
SIX POWERS SKILL...
...TEA-WASE RANKING!!
IF THE STRENGTH OF ONE MAN WITH A WEAPON IS...
...POWER LEVEL 10, BASED ON THAT...
POWER LEVEL 10
I WILL NOW RANK...
...YOUR STRENGTHS, STARTING WITH...
KALIFA... POWER LEVEL 630.
BLUENO... POWER LEVEL 820.
KAKU... POWER LEVEL 2,200!
LUCCI... *HMM!!*

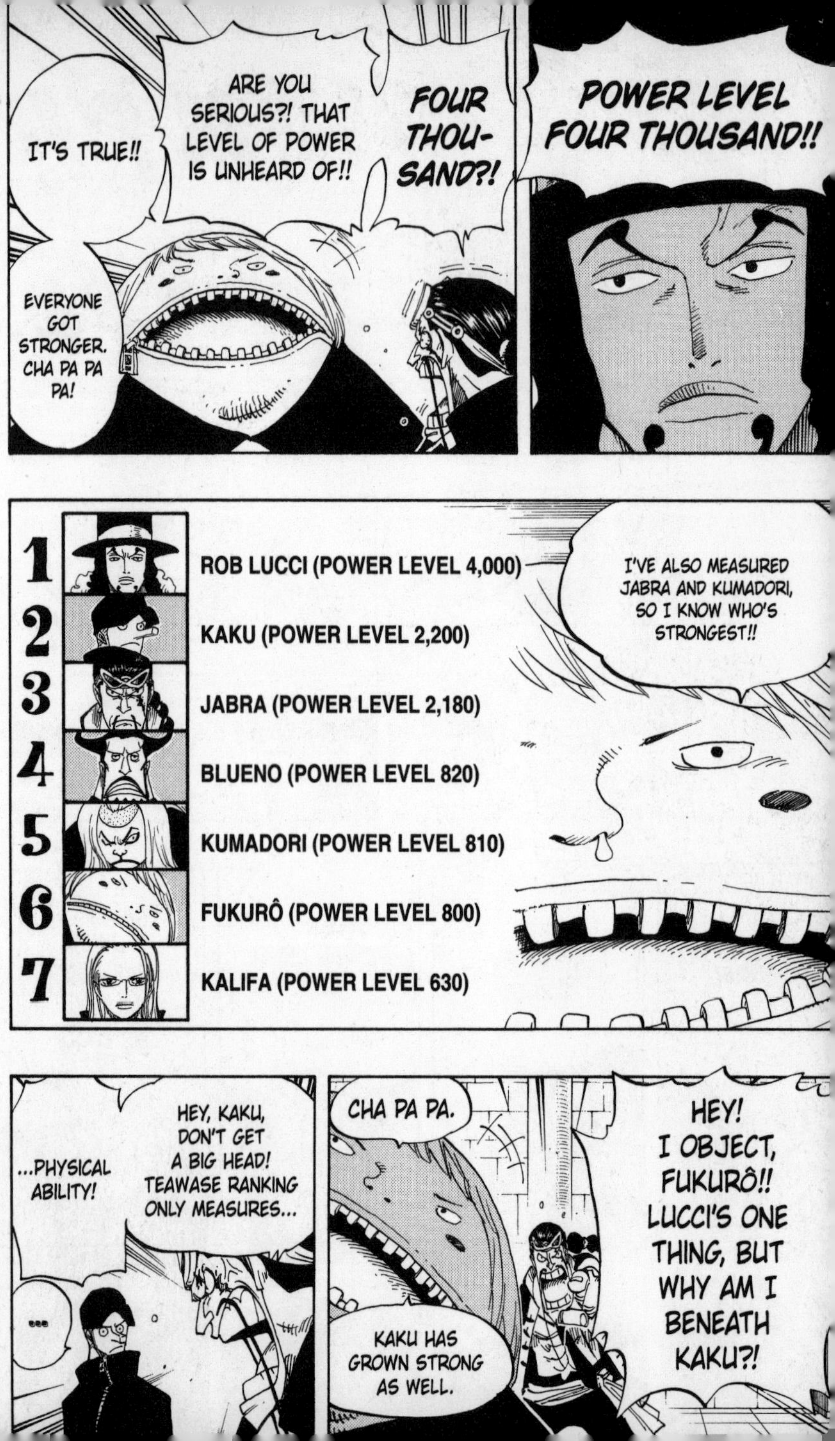

POWER LEVEL FOUR THOUSAND!!
FOUR THOUSAND?!
ARE YOU SERIOUS?! THAT LEVEL OF POWER IS UNHEARD OF!!
IT'S TRUE!!
EVERYONE GOT STRONGER. CHA PA PA PA!
I'VE ALSO MEASURED JABRA AND KUMADORI, SO I KNOW WHO'S STRONGEST!!
1 ROB LUCCI (POWER LEVEL 4,000)
2 KAKU (POWER LEVEL 2,200)
3 JABRA (POWER LEVEL 2,180)
4 BLUENO (POWER LEVEL 820)
5 KUMADORI (POWER LEVEL 810)
6 FUKURÔ (POWER LEVEL 800)
7 KALIFA (POWER LEVEL 630)
HEY! I OBJECT, FUKURÔ!! LUCCI'S ONE THING, BUT WHY AM I BENEATH KAKU?!
CHA PA PA.
KAKU HAS GROWN STRONG AS WELL.
HEY, KAKU, DON'T GET A BIG HEAD! TEAWASE RANKING ONLY MEASURES...
...PHYSICAL ABILITY!
...

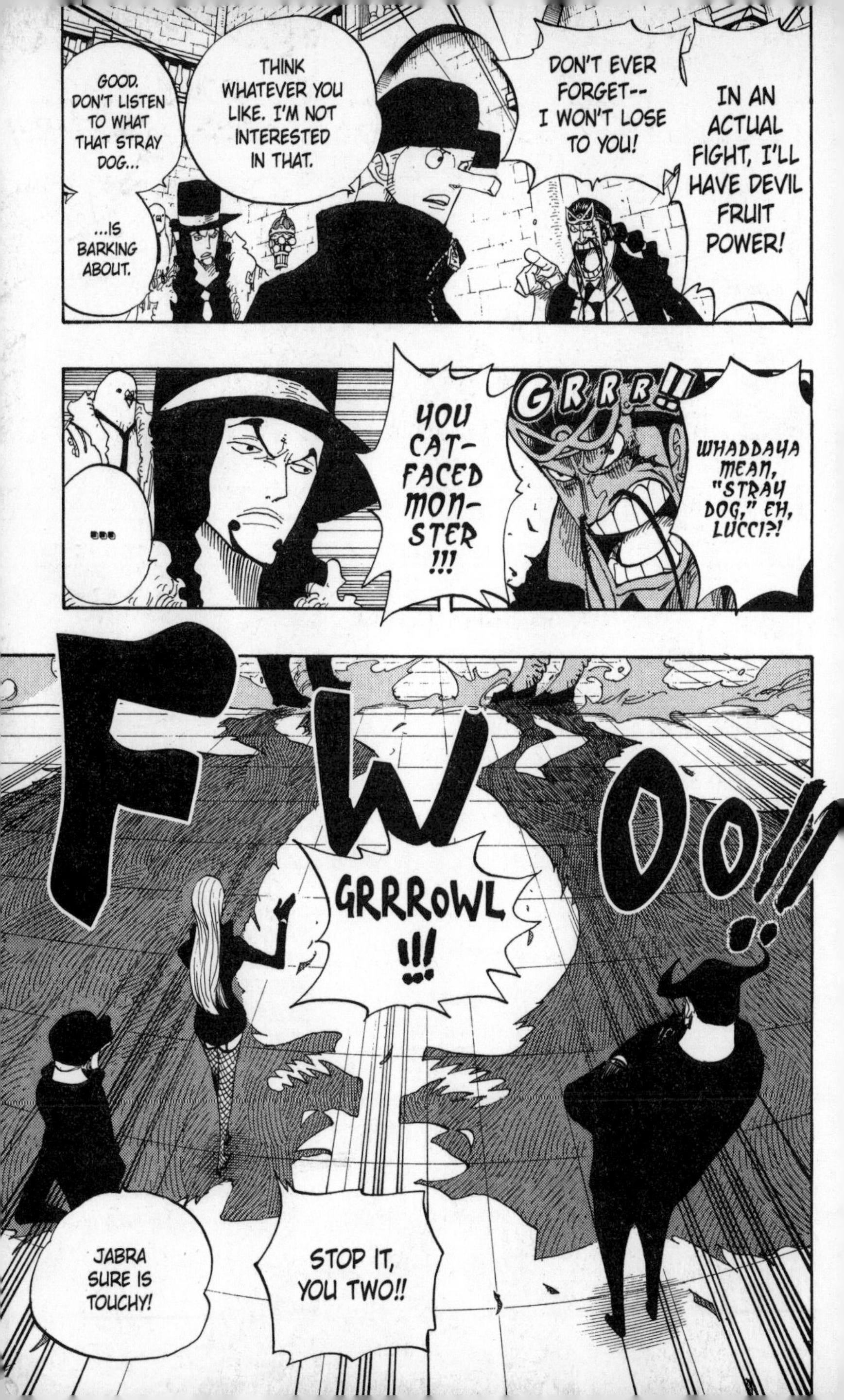

IN AN ACTUAL FIGHT, I'LL HAVE DEVIL FRUIT POWER!
DON'T EVER FORGET-- I WON'T LOSE TO YOU!
THINK WHATEVER YOU LIKE. I'M NOT INTERESTED IN THAT.
GOOD. DON'T LISTEN TO WHAT THAT STRAY DOG...
...IS BARKING ABOUT.
WHADDAYA MEAN, "STRAY DOG," EH, LUCCI?!
GRRR!!
YOU CAT-FACED MONSTER!!!
...
FWOO!!
GRRROWL!!!
STOP IT, YOU TWO!!
JABRA SURE IS TOUCHY!

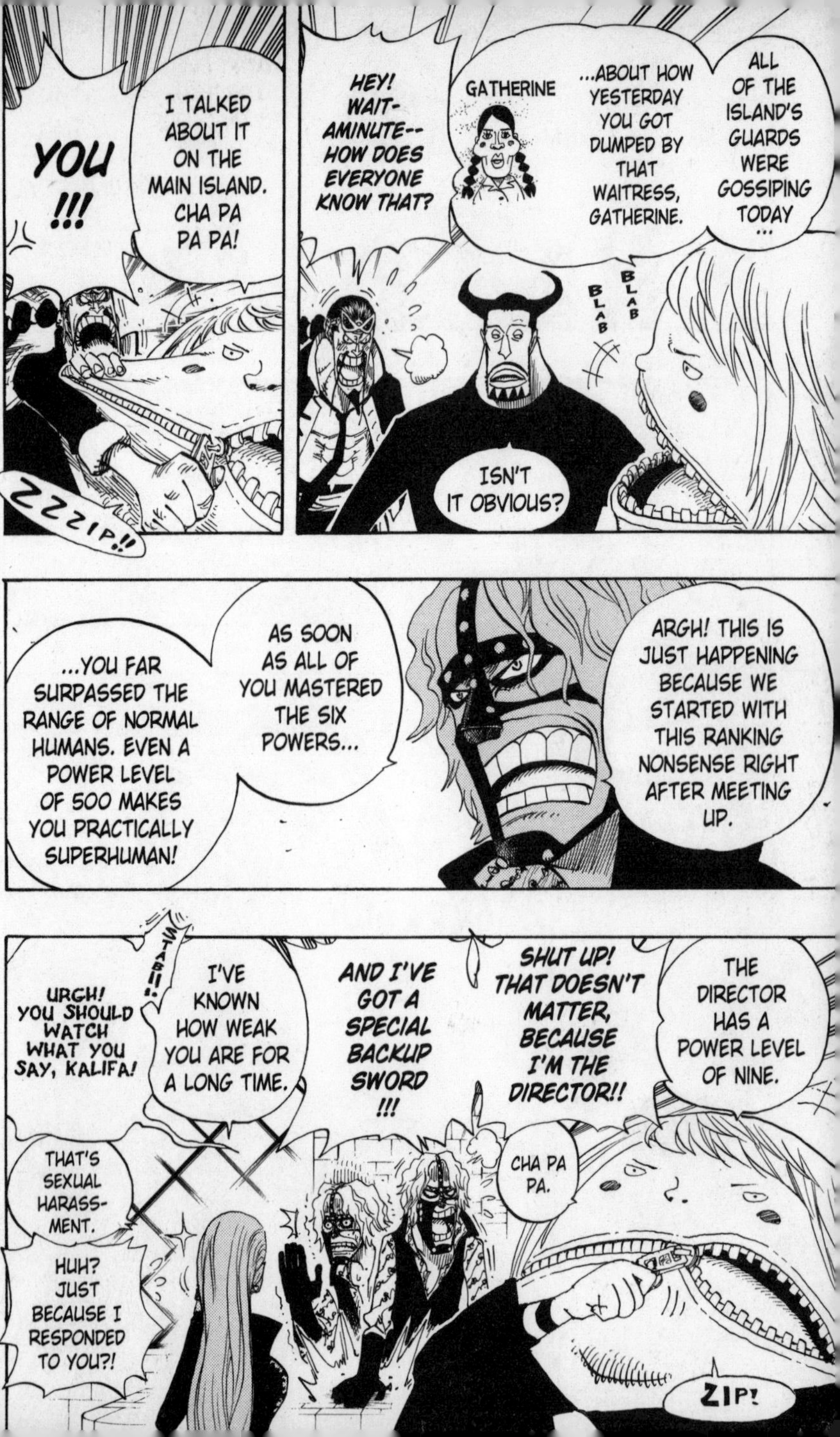
ALL OF THE ISLAND'S GUARDS WERE GOSSIPING TODAY...
...ABOUT HOW YESTERDAY YOU GOT DUMPED BY THAT WAITRESS, GATHERINE.
GATHERINE
HEY! WAIT-AMINUTE-- HOW DOES EVERYONE KNOW THAT?
BLAB BLAB
ISN'T IT OBVIOUS?
I TALKED ABOUT IT ON THE MAIN ISLAND. CHA PA PA PA!
YOU!!!
ZZZIP!!
ARGH! THIS IS JUST HAPPENING BECAUSE WE STARTED WITH THIS RANKING NONSENSE RIGHT AFTER MEETING UP.
AS SOON AS ALL OF YOU MASTERED THE SIX POWERS...
...YOU FAR SURPASSED THE RANGE OF NORMAL HUMANS. EVEN A POWER LEVEL OF 500 MAKES YOU PRACTICALLY SUPERHUMAN!
THE DIRECTOR HAS A POWER LEVEL OF NINE.
SHUT UP! THAT DOESN'T MATTER, BECAUSE I'M THE DIRECTOR!!
AND I'VE GOT A SPECIAL BACKUP SWORD!!!
I'VE KNOWN HOW WEAK YOU ARE FOR A LONG TIME.
STAB!!
URGH! YOU SHOULD WATCH WHAT YOU SAY, KALIFA!
CHA PA PA.
ZIP!
THAT'S SEXUAL HARASS-MENT.
HUH? JUST BECAUSE I RESPONDED TO YOU?!

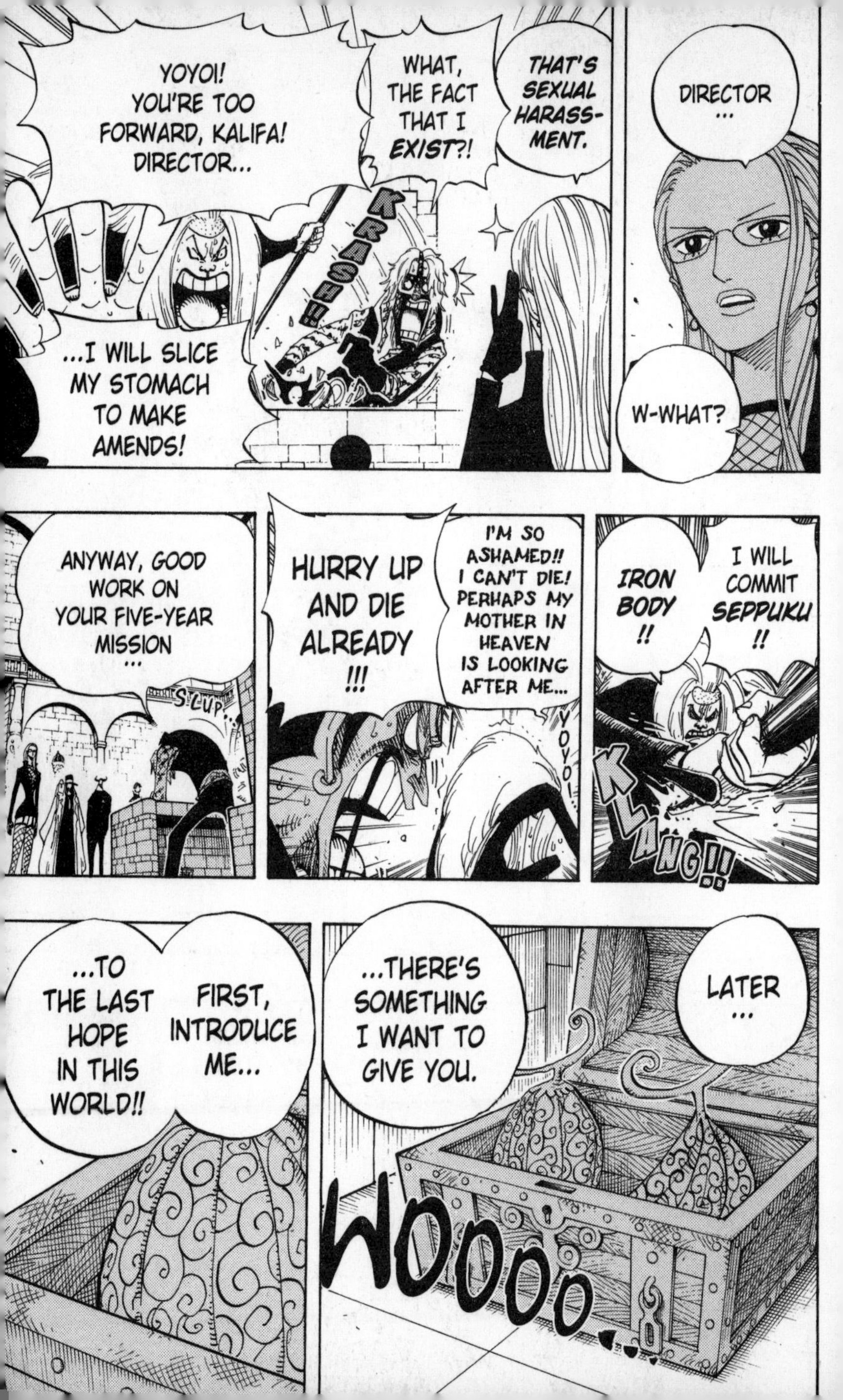
DIRECTOR ...
W-WHAT?
THAT'S SEXUAL HARASS-MENT.
WHAT, THE FACT THAT I EXIST?!
KRASH!!
YOYOI! YOU'RE TOO FORWARD, KALIFA! DIRECTOR...
...I WILL SLICE MY STOMACH TO MAKE AMENDS!
I WILL COMMIT SEPPUKU !!
IRON BODY !!
KLANG!!
I'M SO ASHAMED!! I CAN'T DIE! PERHAPS MY MOTHER IN HEAVEN IS LOOKING AFTER ME...
HURRY UP AND DIE ALREADY !!!
YOYOI!..
ANYWAY, GOOD WORK ON YOUR FIVE-YEAR MISSION ...
SLUP...
LATER ...
...THERE'S SOMETHING I WANT TO GIVE YOU.
WOOOO...
FIRST, INTRODUCE ME...
...TO THE LAST HOPE IN THIS WORLD!!

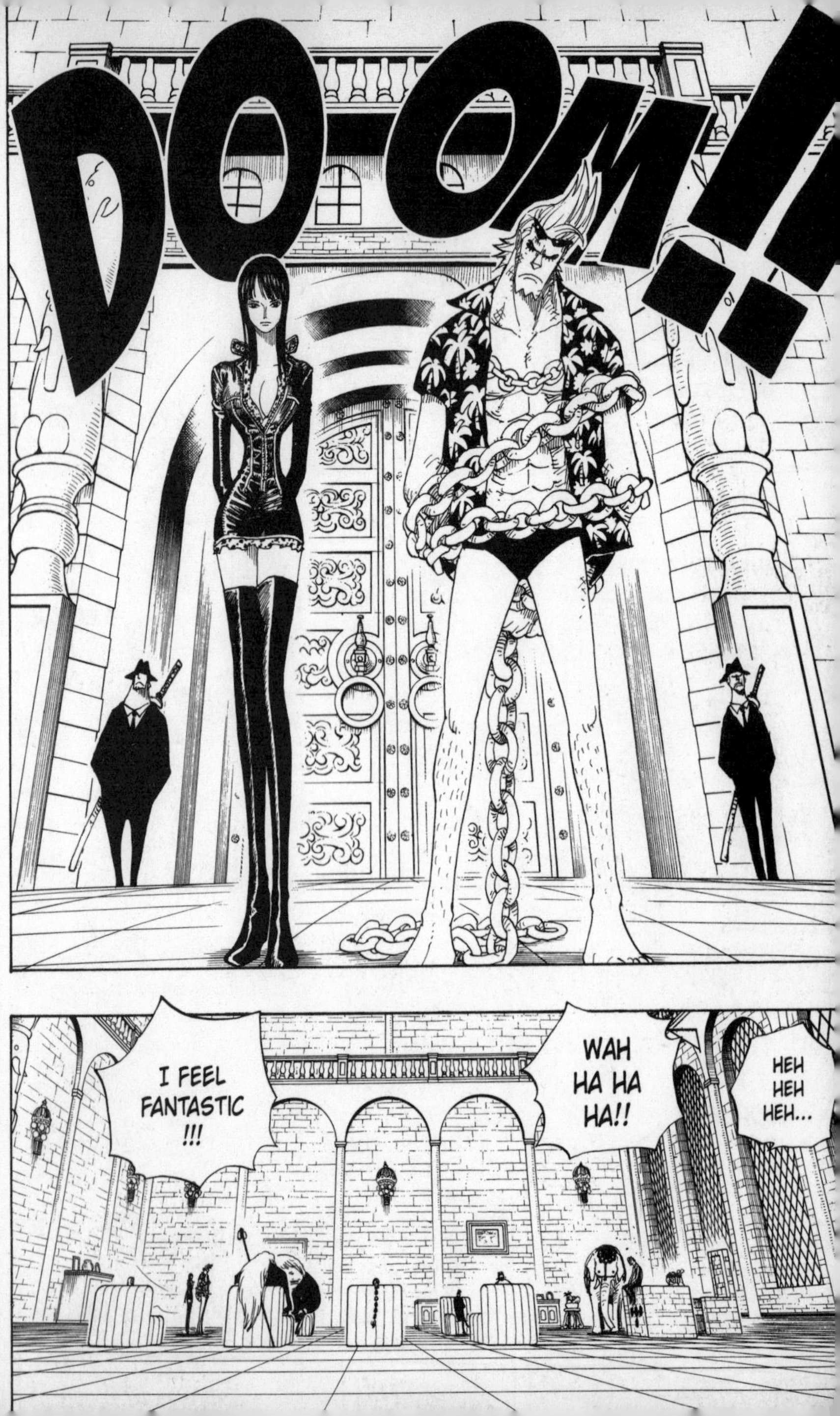
DO-OM!!
HEH HEH HEH...
WAH HA HA HA!!
I FEEL FANTASTIC !!!

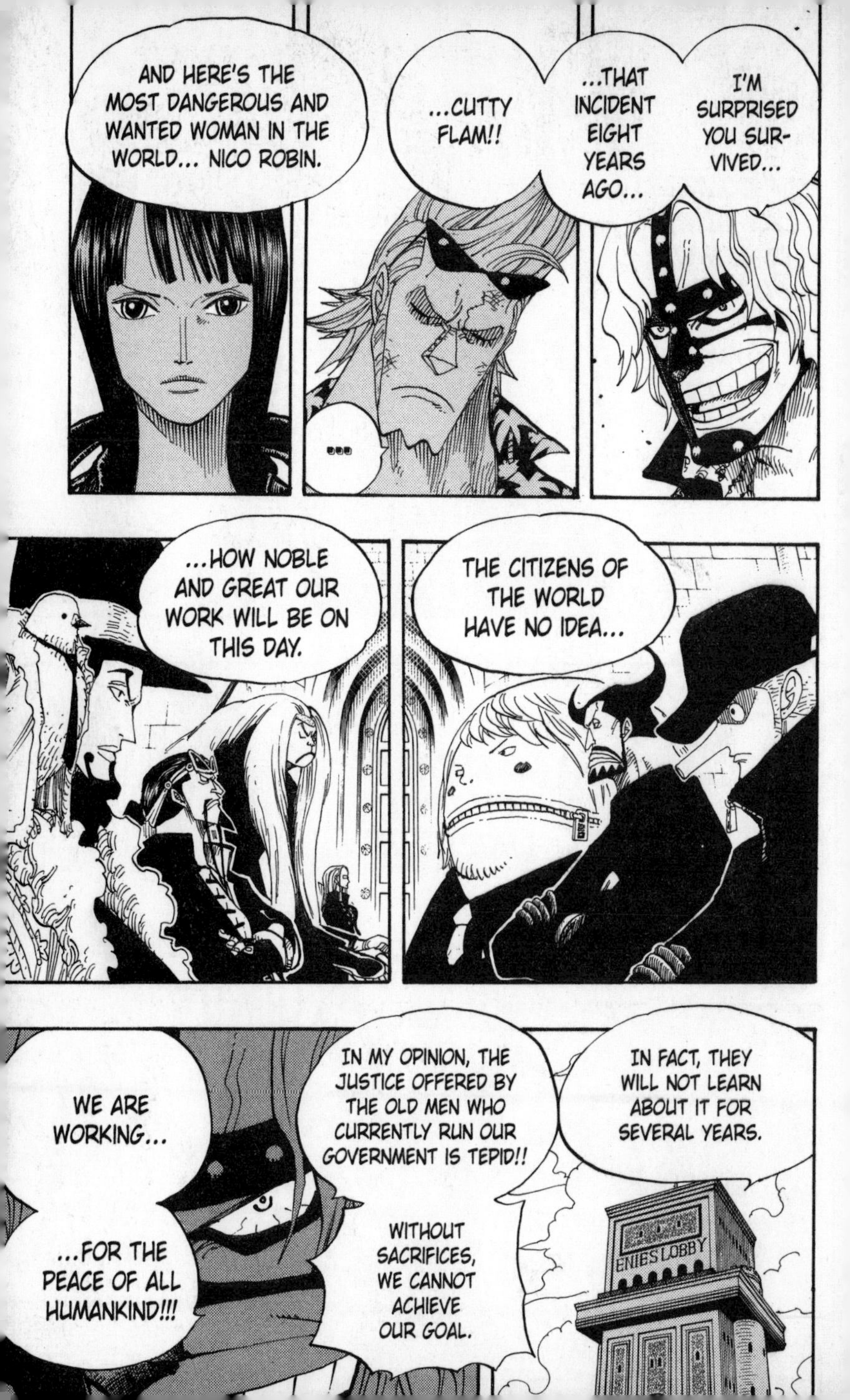
I'M SURPRISED YOU SURVIVED...
...THAT INCIDENT EIGHT YEARS AGO...
...CUTTY FLAM!!
...
AND HERE'S THE MOST DANGEROUS AND WANTED WOMAN IN THE WORLD... NICO ROBIN.
THE CITIZENS OF THE WORLD HAVE NO IDEA...
...HOW NOBLE AND GREAT OUR WORK WILL BE ON THIS DAY.
IN FACT, THEY WILL NOT LEARN ABOUT IT FOR SEVERAL YEARS.
ENIES LOBBY
IN MY OPINION, THE JUSTICE OFFERED BY THE OLD MEN WHO CURRENTLY RUN OUR GOVERNMENT IS TEPID!!
WITHOUT SACRIFICES, WE CANNOT ACHIEVE OUR GOAL.
WE ARE WORKING...
...FOR THE PEACE OF ALL HUMANKIND!!!

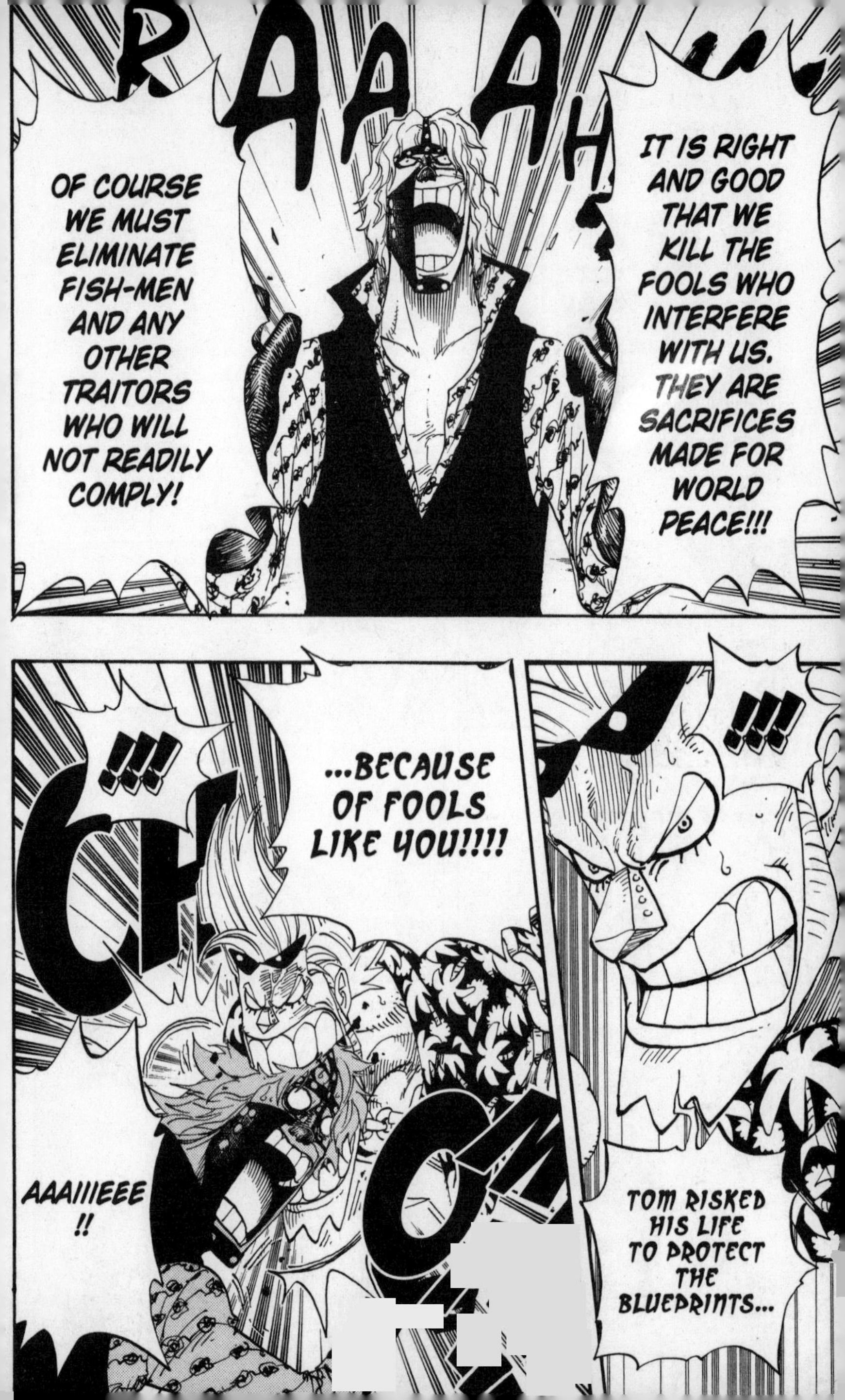
RAAAH
IT IS RIGHT AND GOOD THAT WE KILL THE FOOLS WHO INTERFERE WITH US. THEY ARE SACRIFICES MADE FOR WORLD PEACE!!!
OF COURSE WE MUST ELIMINATE FISH-MEN AND ANY OTHER TRAITORS WHO WILL NOT READILY COMPLY!
!!!
TOM RISKED HIS LIFE TO PROTECT THE BLUEPRINTS...
...BECAUSE OF FOOLS LIKE YOU!!!!
!!!
AAAIIIEEE !!

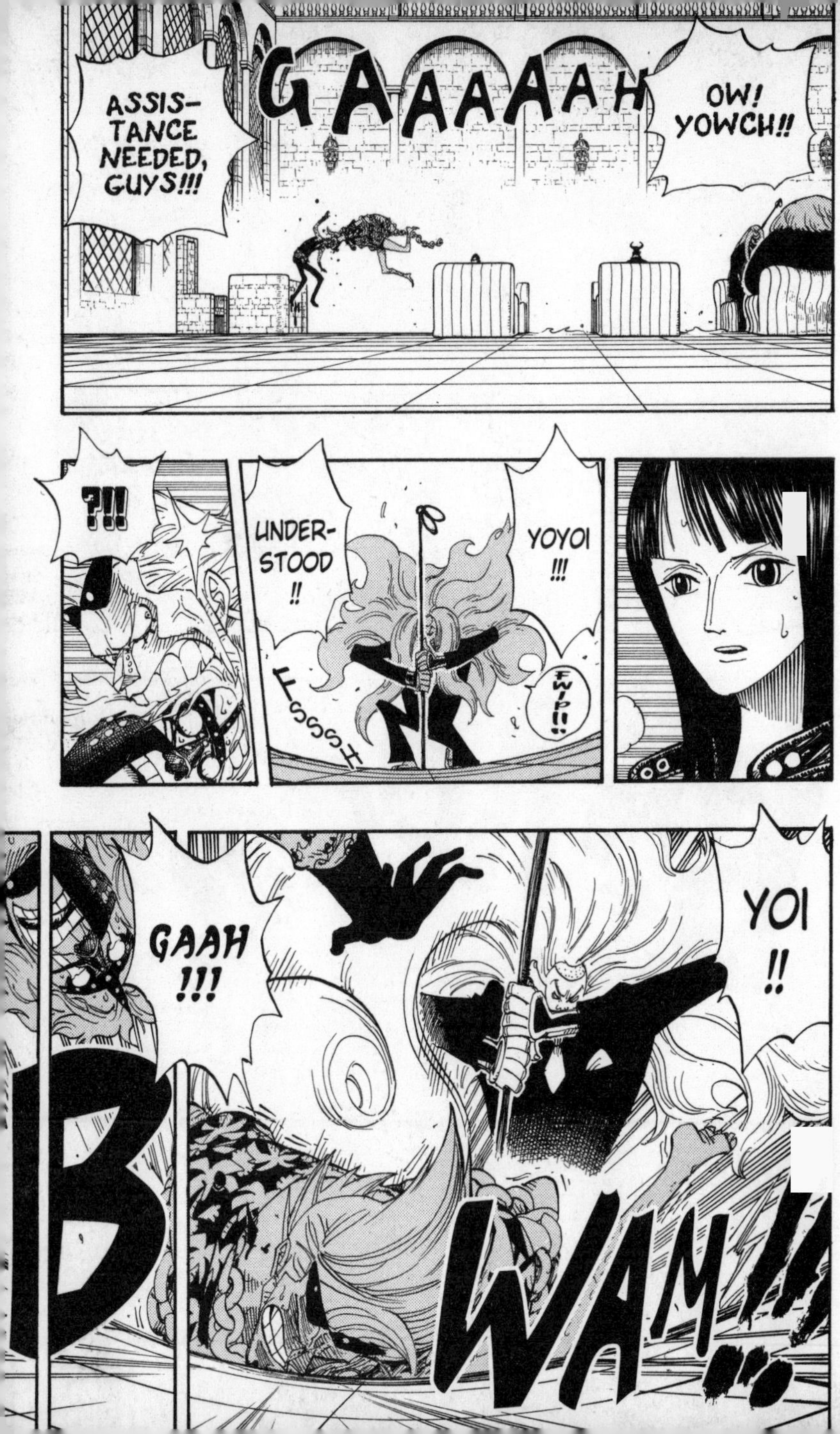
OW! YOWCH!!
GAAAAAH
ASSIS-TANCE NEEDED, GUYS!!!
YOYOI!!!
FWIP!!
UNDER-STOOD!!
FSSSH
?!!
YOI!!
GAAH!!!
BWAM!!

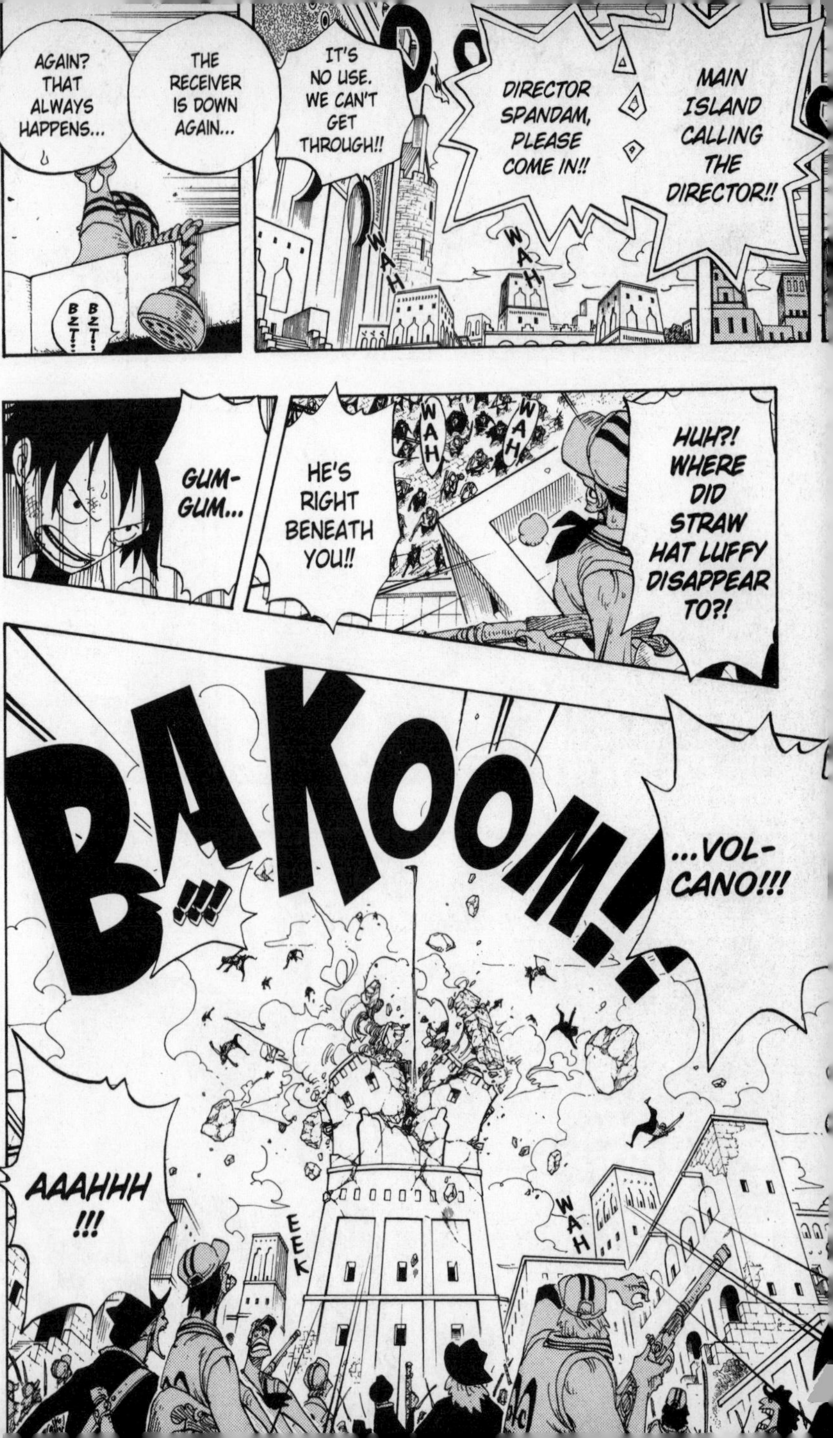
MAIN ISLAND CALLING THE DIRECTOR!!
DIRECTOR SPANDAM, PLEASE COME IN!!
WAH
WAH
IT'S NO USE. WE CAN'T GET THROUGH!!
THE RECEIVER IS DOWN AGAIN...
AGAIN? THAT ALWAYS HAPPENS...
BZT...
BZT...
HUH?! WHERE DID STRAW HAT LUFFY DISAPPEAR TO?!
WAH
WAH
HE'S RIGHT BENEATH YOU!!
GUM-GUM...
...VOL-CANO!!!
BAKOOM!!!
WAH
EEK
AAAHHH!!!

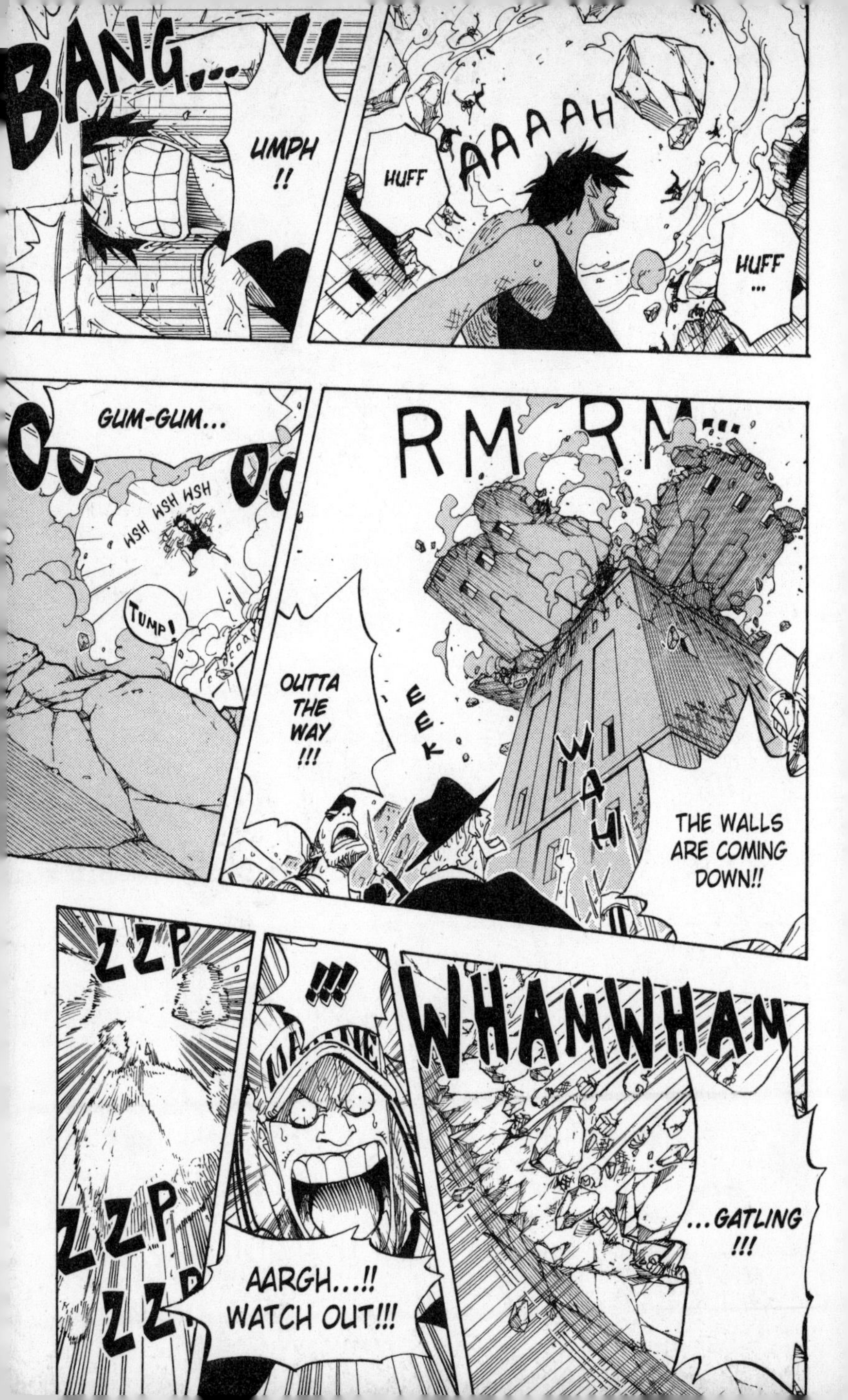
AAAAH
HUFF ...
HUFF
BANG...U
UMPH !!
RM RM...
THE WALLS ARE COMING DOWN!!
WAH
EEK
OUTTA THE WAY !!!
GUM-GUM...
OO OO
WSH WSH WSH
TUMP!
WHAMWHAM
...GATLING !!!
!!!
AARGH...!! WATCH OUT!!!
ZZP
ZZP
ZZP

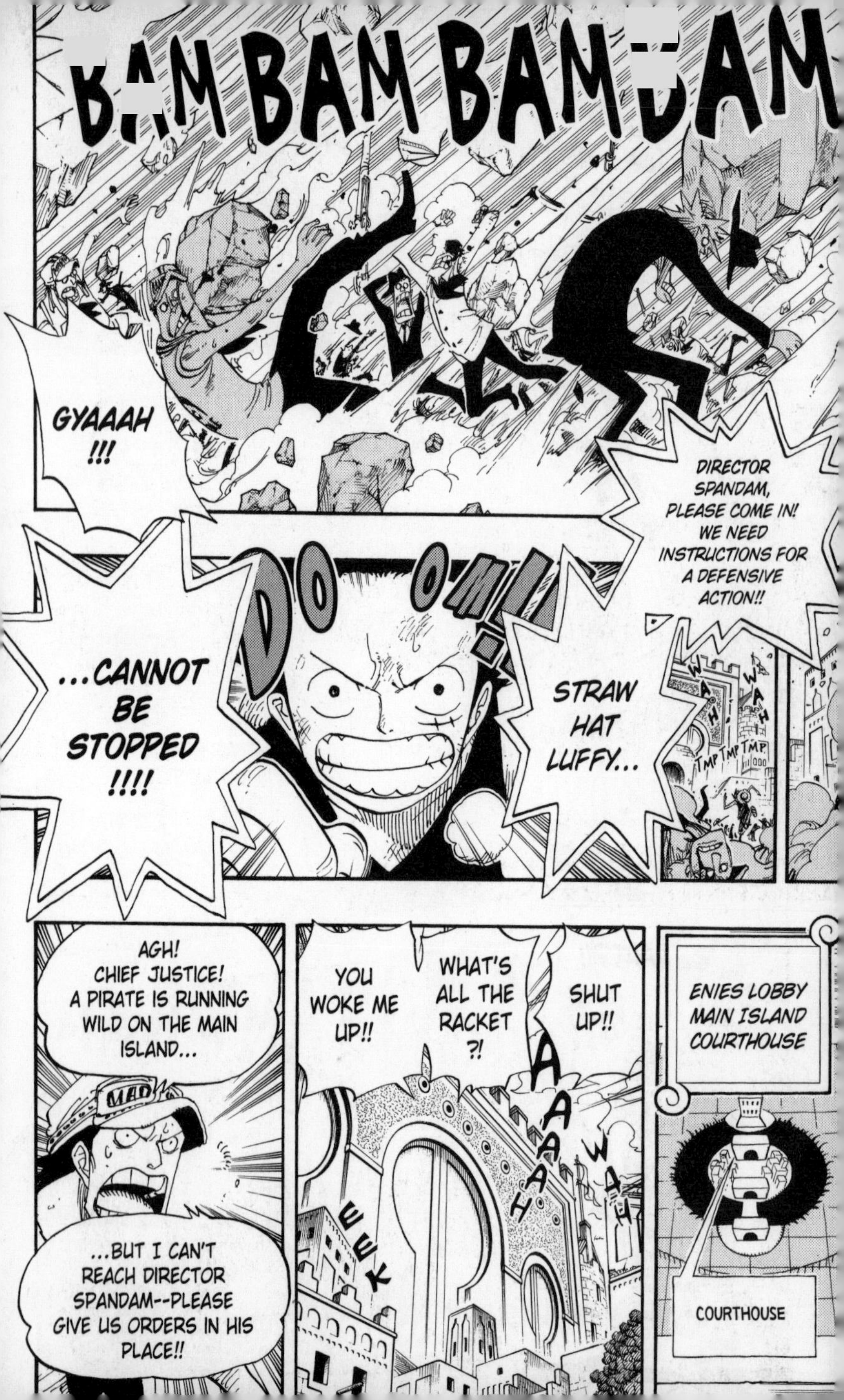

BAM BAM BAM BAM
GYAAAH!!!
DIRECTOR SPANDAM, PLEASE COME IN! WE NEED INSTRUCTIONS FOR A DEFENSIVE ACTION!!
WAH WAH
TMP TMP TMP
STRAW HAT LUFFY...
DOOM!!
...CANNOT BE STOPPED!!!!
ENIES LOBBY MAIN ISLAND COURTHOUSE
COURTHOUSE
SHUT UP!!
WHAT'S ALL THE RACKET?!
YOU WOKE ME UP!!
AAAAAH
WAH
EEEK
AGH! CHIEF JUSTICE! A PIRATE IS RUNNING WILD ON THE MAIN ISLAND...
...BUT I CAN'T REACH DIRECTOR SPANDAM--PLEASE GIVE US ORDERS IN HIS PLACE!!

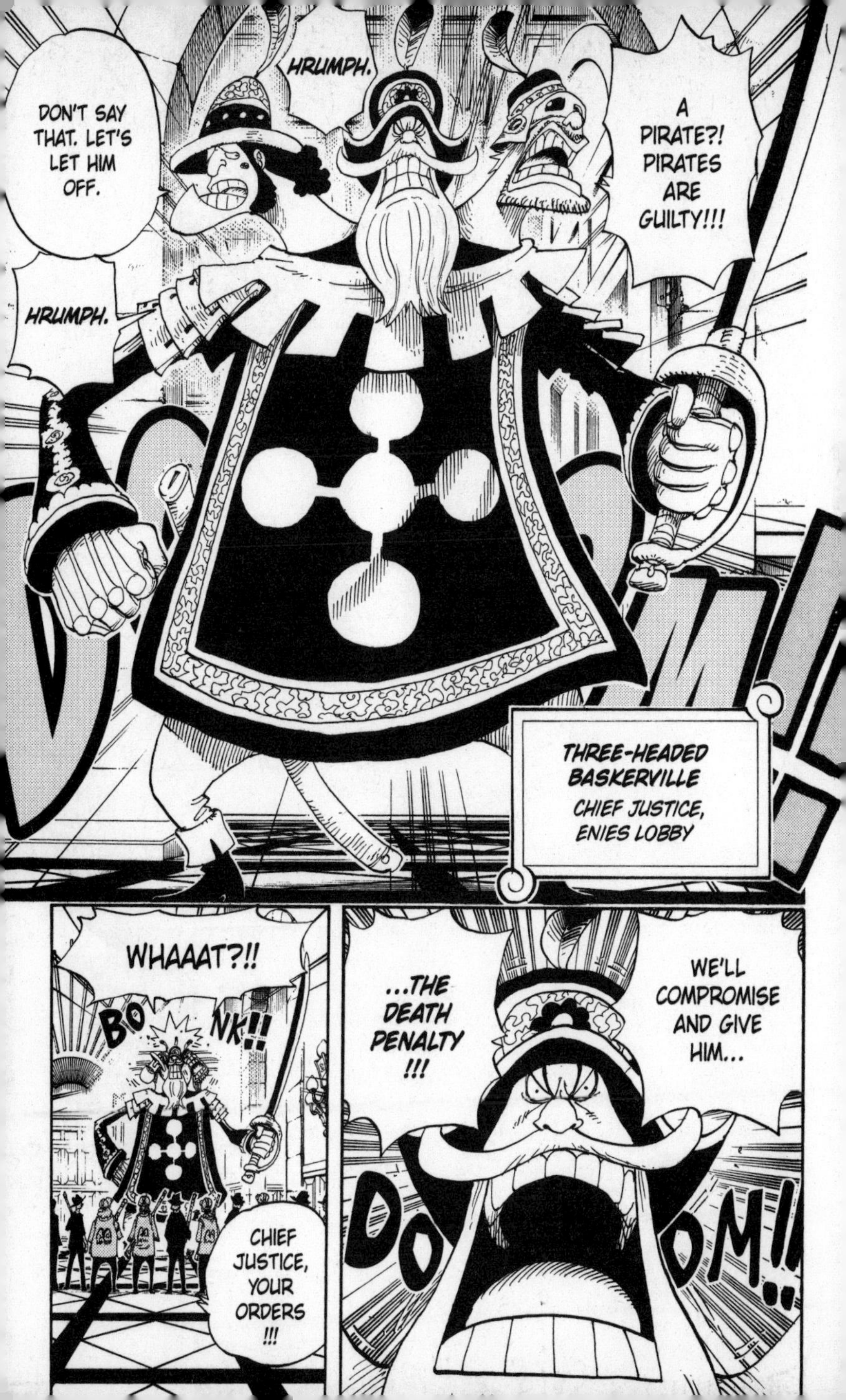

A PIRATE?! PIRATES ARE GUILTY!!!
HRUMPH.
DON'T SAY THAT. LET'S LET HIM OFF.
HRUMPH.
THREE-HEADED BASKERVILLE
CHIEF JUSTICE, ENIES LOBBY
WE'LL COMPROMISE AND GIVE HIM...
...THE DEATH PENALTY!!!
DOOM!!
WHAAAT?!!
BONK!!
CHIEF JUSTICE, YOUR ORDERS!!!

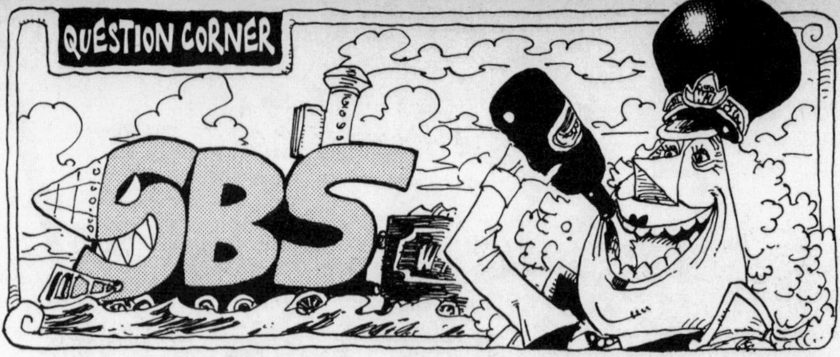
QUESTION CORNER
SBS

Reader: Hello, Oda! ♡ ♡ ♡ These days my father (50 years old) is always watching the *One Piece* anime on TV. His eyes are practically glued to the screen.☆ It's incredible that everyone from kids to old guys can enjoy *One Piece*!! (By the way, my whole family is obsessed with it.)
P.S.☆ Let's begin the Question Corner!

--Kuri

Oda: I see... Even your father is watching it. Thank y--**Aaagh!! The Question Corner has begun!!** That took me by surprise!! I thought this was just a normal fan letter!! Good! Let's move on then!

Q: Dear Oda, Some people have butt-chins, right? So what kind of chin does Franky have?

--Furedi

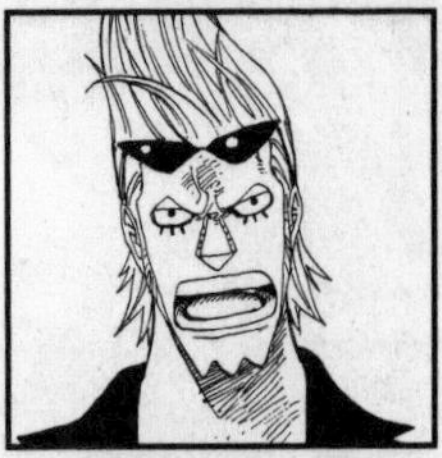

A: Hmm, it's split into three... Well, if a double-split chin is a "butt-chin," then a triple-split chin is a "butt-butt chin."

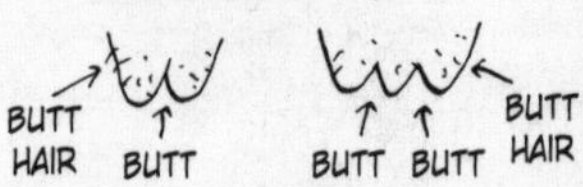
BUTT HAIR
BUTT
BUTT
BUTT
BUTT HAIR

Q: Dear Oda, Hello. Soon I'll be giving birth to my fourth child. I hope it's a girl, but if it's a boy, I want him to learn Oh Come My Way Karate like Bon Clay. Where can he learn it? Please let me know.

--Bon Clay Fan Club President

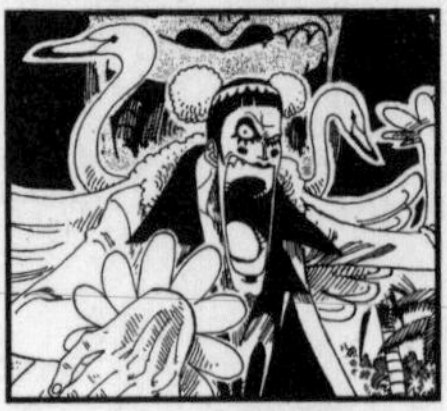

A: Have him learn ballet first, then karate, then have him work on **that kind** of practice. That's the route to take.

Chapter 380:

ENIES LOBBY MAIN ISLAND EXPRESS

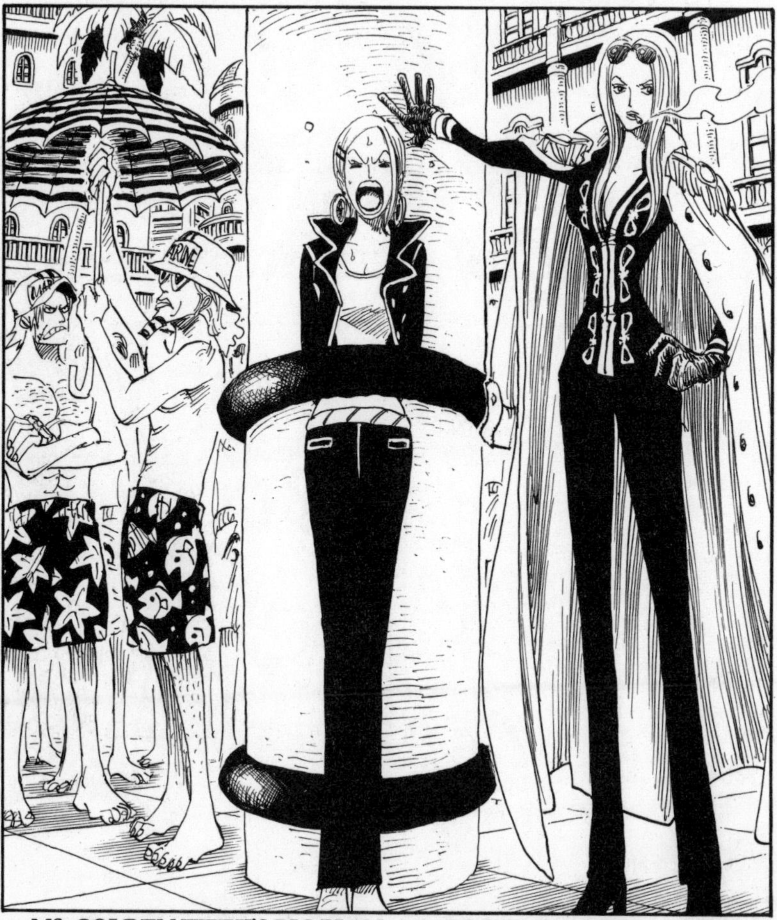
MARINE

MS. GOLDEN WEEK'S BIG PLAN, A BAROQUE REUNION, VOL. 16:
"MS. VALENTINE IS CAPTURED"

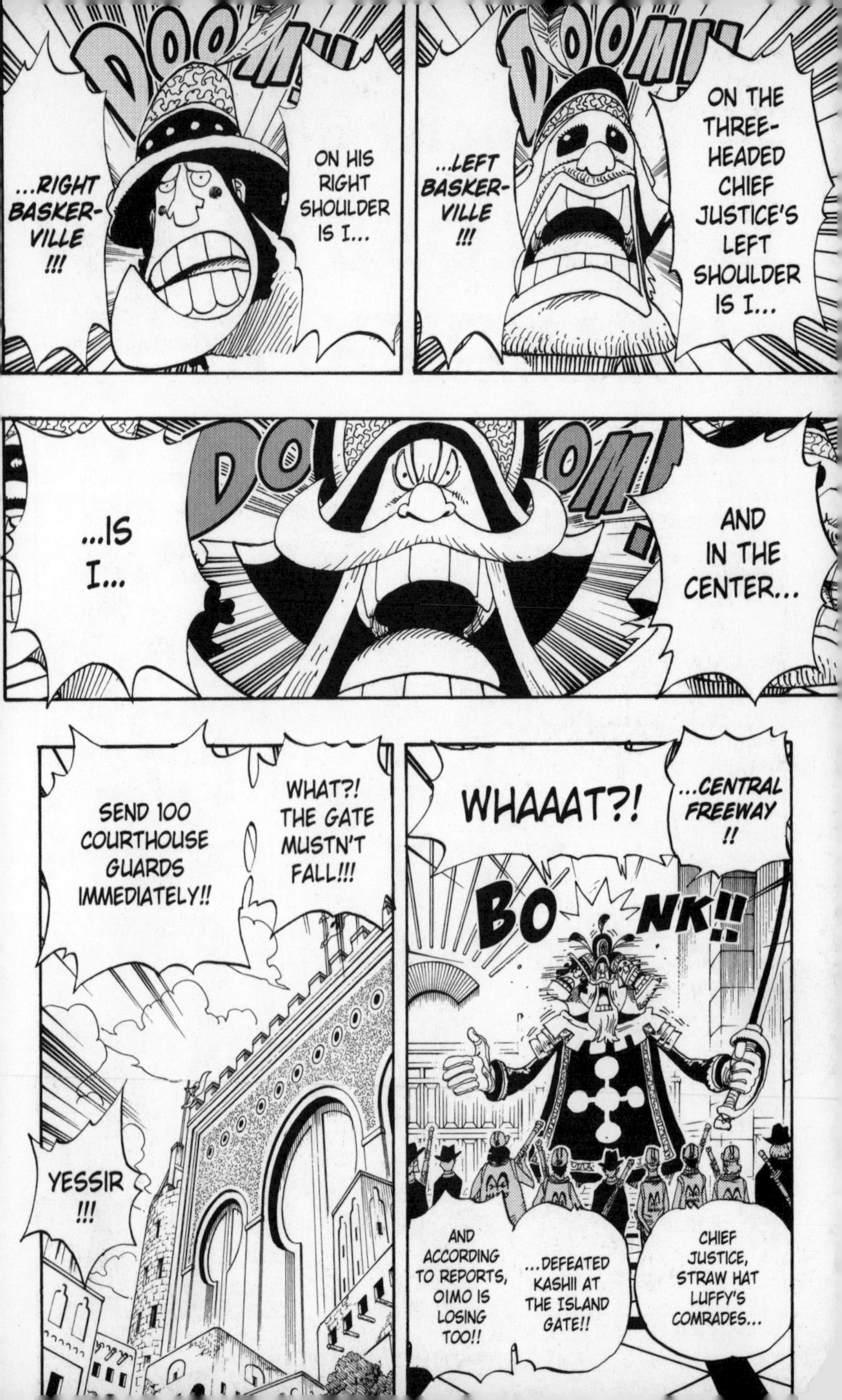
DOOM!!
ON THE THREE-HEADED CHIEF JUSTICE'S LEFT SHOULDER IS I...
...LEFT BASKERVILLE !!!
DOOM!!
ON HIS RIGHT SHOULDER IS I...
...RIGHT BASKERVILLE !!!
DOOM!!
AND IN THE CENTER...
...IS I...
...CENTRAL FREEWAY !!
WHAAAT?!
BONK!!
CHIEF JUSTICE, STRAW HAT LUFFY'S COMRADES...
...DEFEATED KASHII AT THE ISLAND GATE!!
AND ACCORDING TO REPORTS, OIMO IS LOSING TOO!!
WHAT?! THE GATE MUSTN'T FALL!!!
SEND 100 COURTHOUSE GUARDS IMMEDIATELY!!
YESSIR !!!

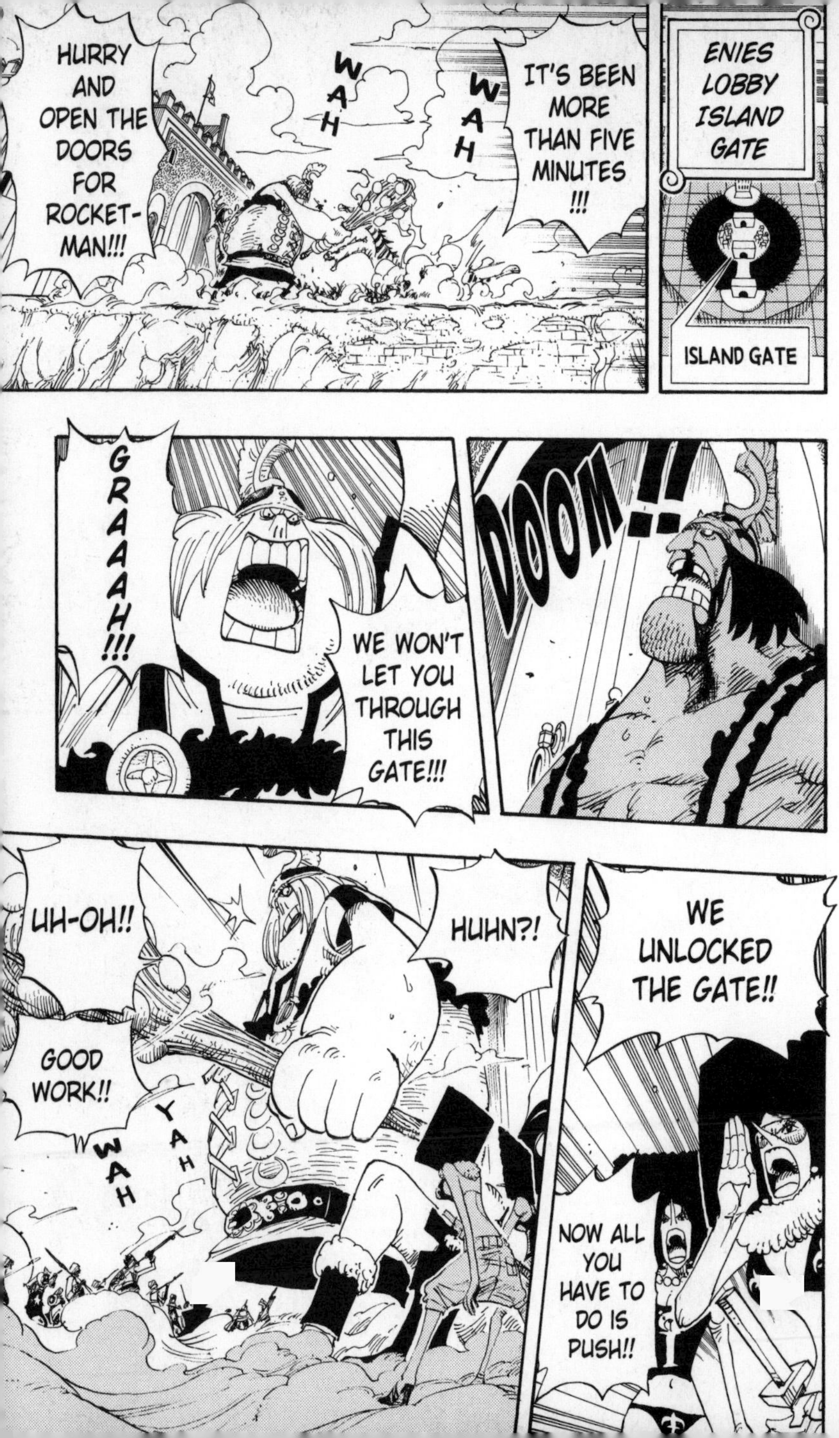
ENIES LOBBY ISLAND GATE
ISLAND GATE
IT'S BEEN MORE THAN FIVE MINUTES!!!
WAH
WAH
HURRY AND OPEN THE DOORS FOR ROCKET-MAN!!!
DOOM!!
WE WON'T LET YOU THROUGH THIS GATE!!!
GRAAAAH!!!
WE UNLOCKED THE GATE!!
NOW ALL YOU HAVE TO DO IS PUSH!!
HUHN?!
UH-OH!!
GOOD WORK!!
YAH
WAH

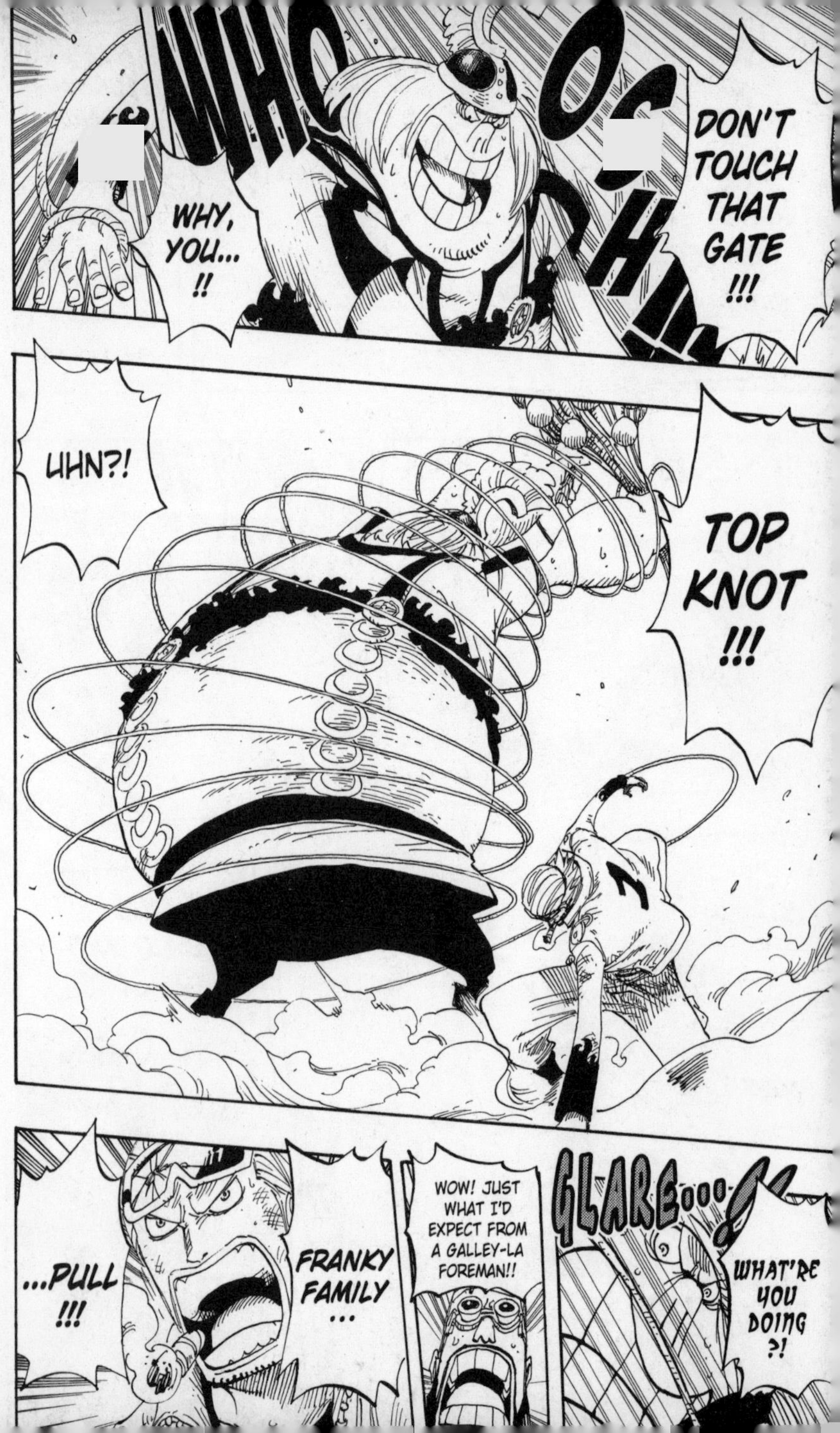
DON'T TOUCH THAT GATE!!!
WHOOSH
WHY, YOU...!!
TOP KNOT!!!
UHN?!
WHAT'RE YOU DOING?!
GLARE...
WOW! JUST WHAT I'D EXPECT FROM A GALLEY-LA FOREMAN!!
FRANKY FAMILY...
...PULL!!!

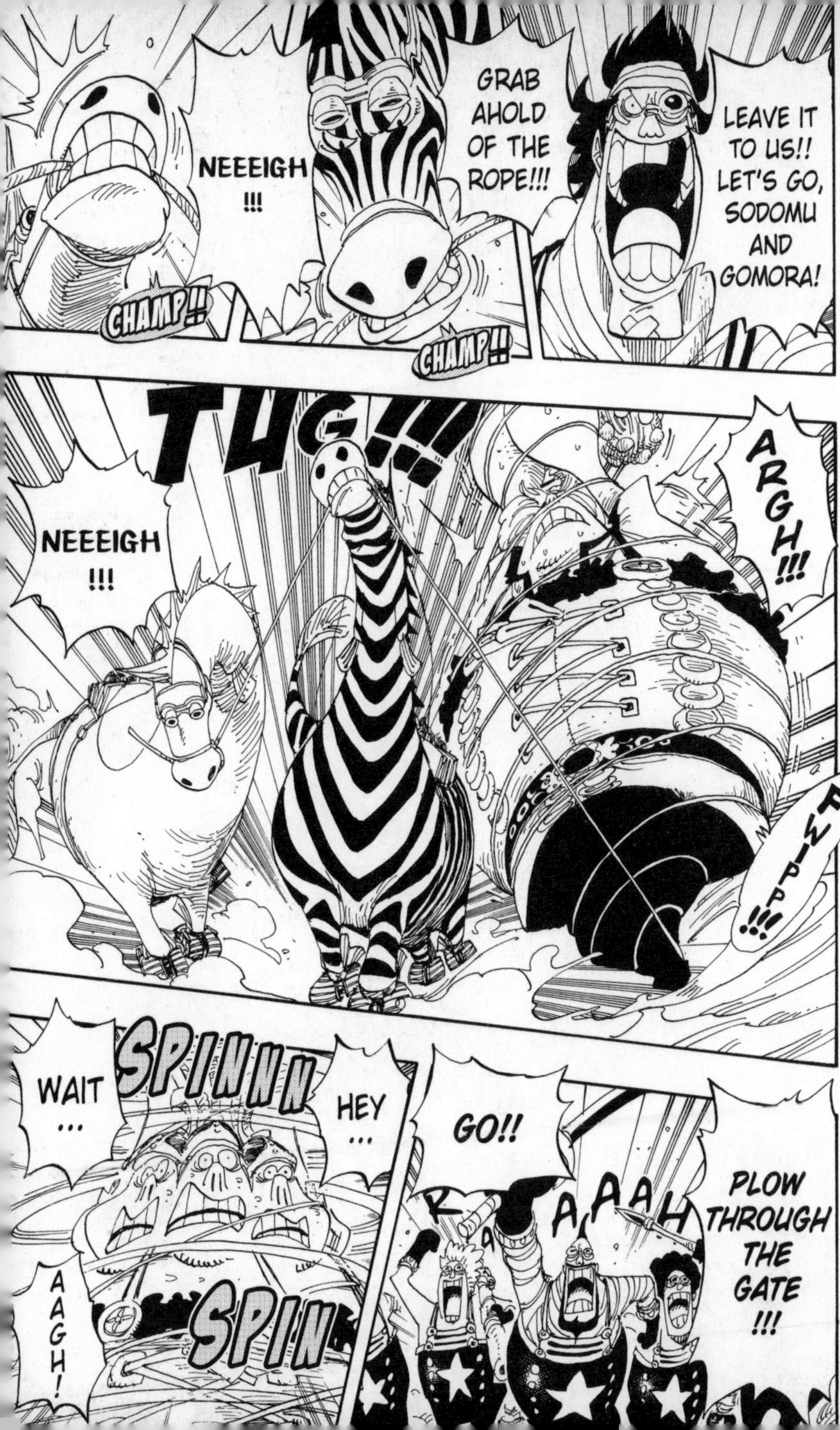
LEAVE IT TO US!! LET'S GO, SODOMU AND GOMORA!
GRAB AHOLD OF THE ROPE!!!
NEEEIGH !!!
CHAMP!!
CHAMP!!
ARGH!!!
TUG!!!
NEEEIGH !!!
FWIPP!!!
PLOW THROUGH THE GATE !!!
GO!!
RAAAAH
HEY ...
SPINNN
WAIT ...
AAGH!
SPIN

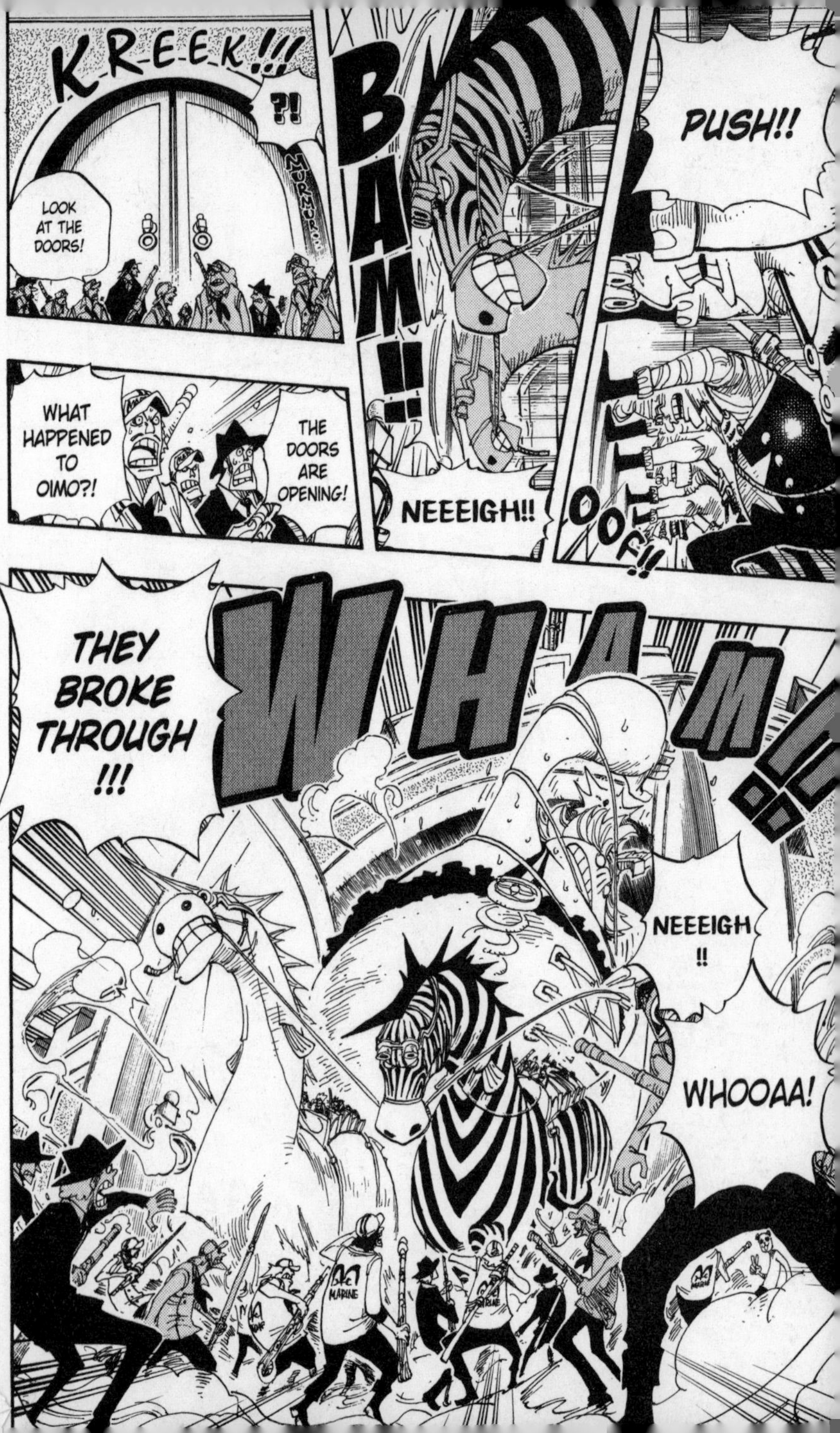
PUSH!!
OOF!!
BAM!!
NEEEIGH!!
K-R-E-E-K!!!
?!
MURMUR
LOOK AT THE DOORS!
THE DOORS ARE OPENING!
WHAT HAPPENED TO OIMO?!
WHAM!!
THEY BROKE THROUGH!!!
NEEEIGH!!
WHOOAA!

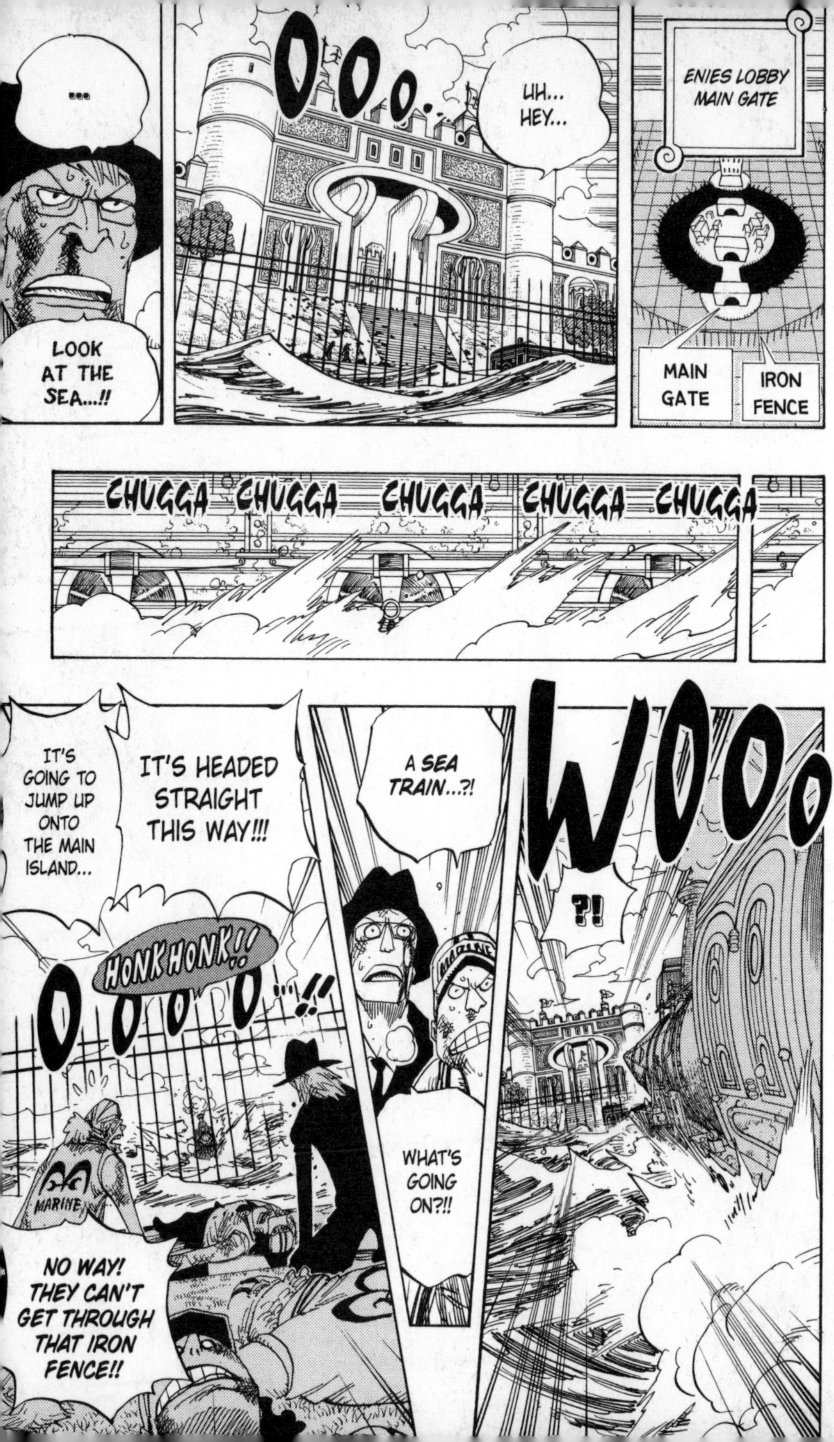
ENIES LOBBY MAIN GATE
IRON FENCE
MAIN GATE
UH... HEY...
OOO...
...
LOOK AT THE SEA...!!
CHUGGA CHUGGA CHUGGA CHUGGA CHUGGA
WOOO
?!
A SEA TRAIN...?!
WHAT'S GOING ON?!!
IT'S HEADED STRAIGHT THIS WAY!!!
IT'S GOING TO JUMP UP ONTO THE MAIN ISLAND...
HONK HONK!!
OOOO...!!
NO WAY! THEY CAN'T GET THROUGH THAT IRON FENCE!!

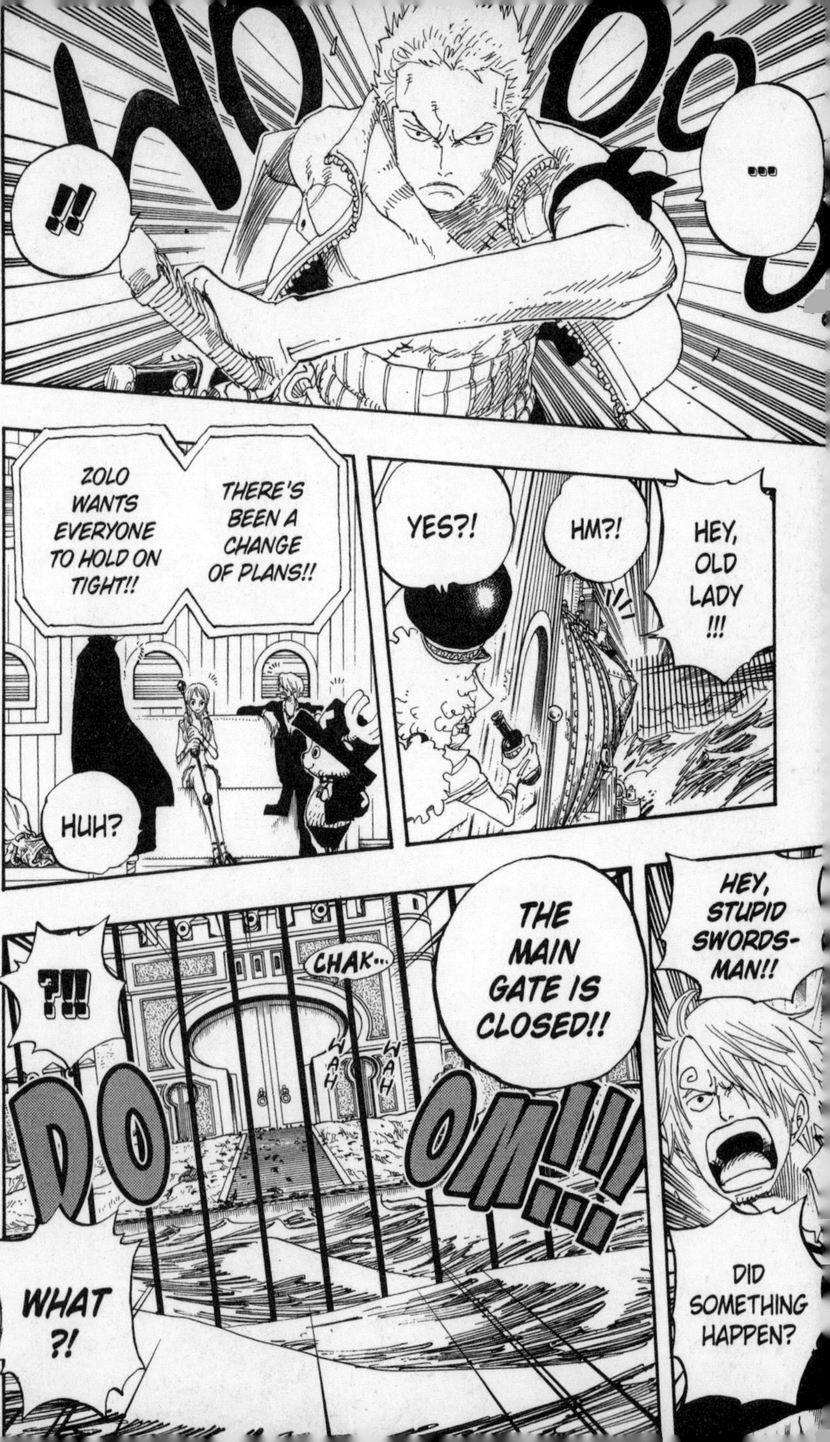
...
!!
HEY, OLD LADY!!!
HM?!
YES?!
THERE'S BEEN A CHANGE OF PLANS!!
ZOLO WANTS EVERYONE TO HOLD ON TIGHT!!
HUH?
HEY, STUPID SWORDS-MAN!!
DID SOMETHING HAPPEN?
THE MAIN GATE IS CLOSED!!
CHAK...
WAH
WAH
?!!
DOOM!!!
WHAT ?!

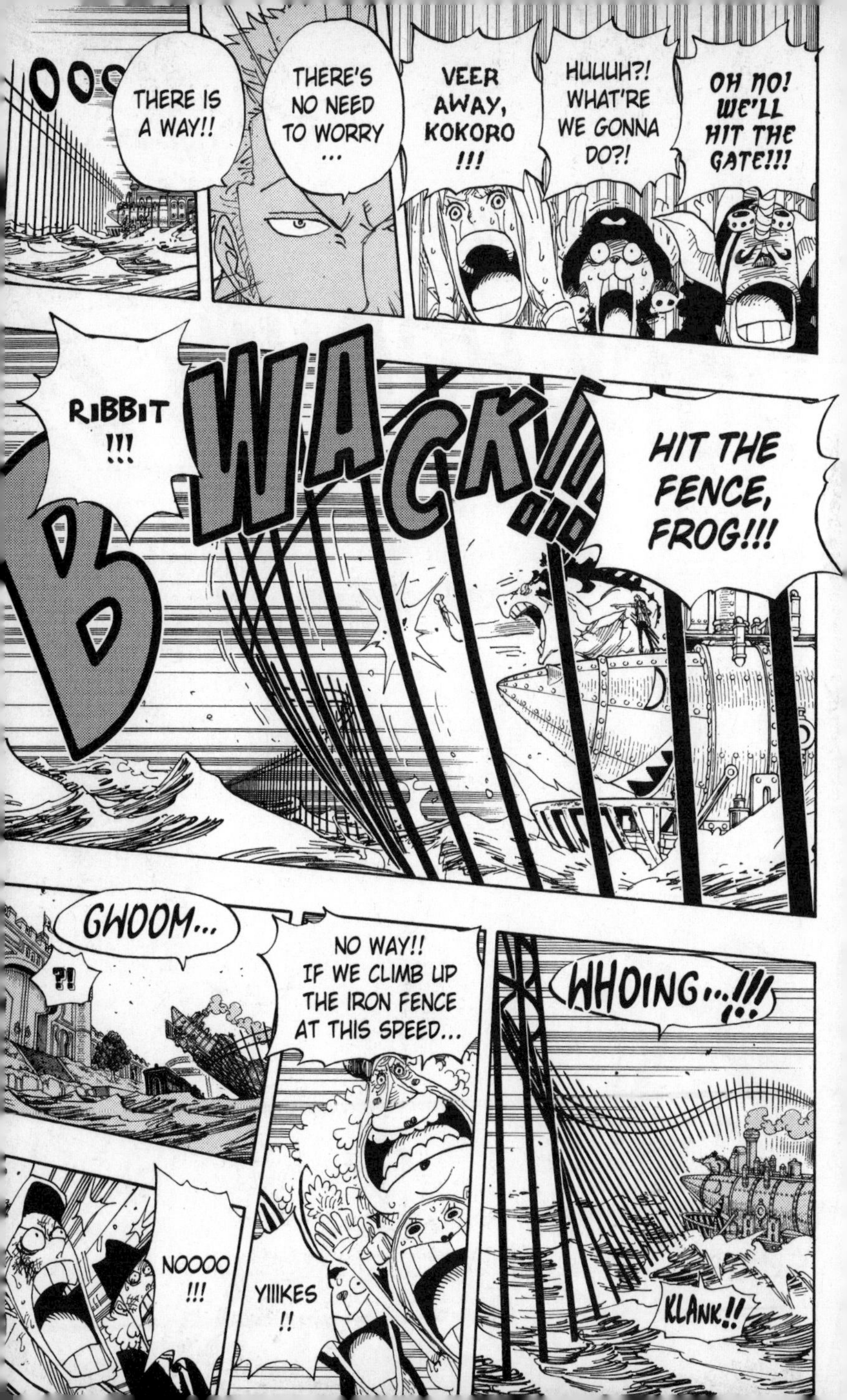
OH NO! WE'LL HIT THE GATE!!!
HUUUH?! WHAT'RE WE GONNA DO?!
VEER AWAY, KOKORO!!!
THERE'S NO NEED TO WORRY...
THERE IS A WAY!!
HIT THE FENCE, FROG!!!
BWACK!!
RIBBIT!!!
WHOING...!!!
KLANK!!
NO WAY!! IF WE CLIMB UP THE IRON FENCE AT THIS SPEED...
YIIIKES!!
GWOOM...
?!
NOOOO!!!

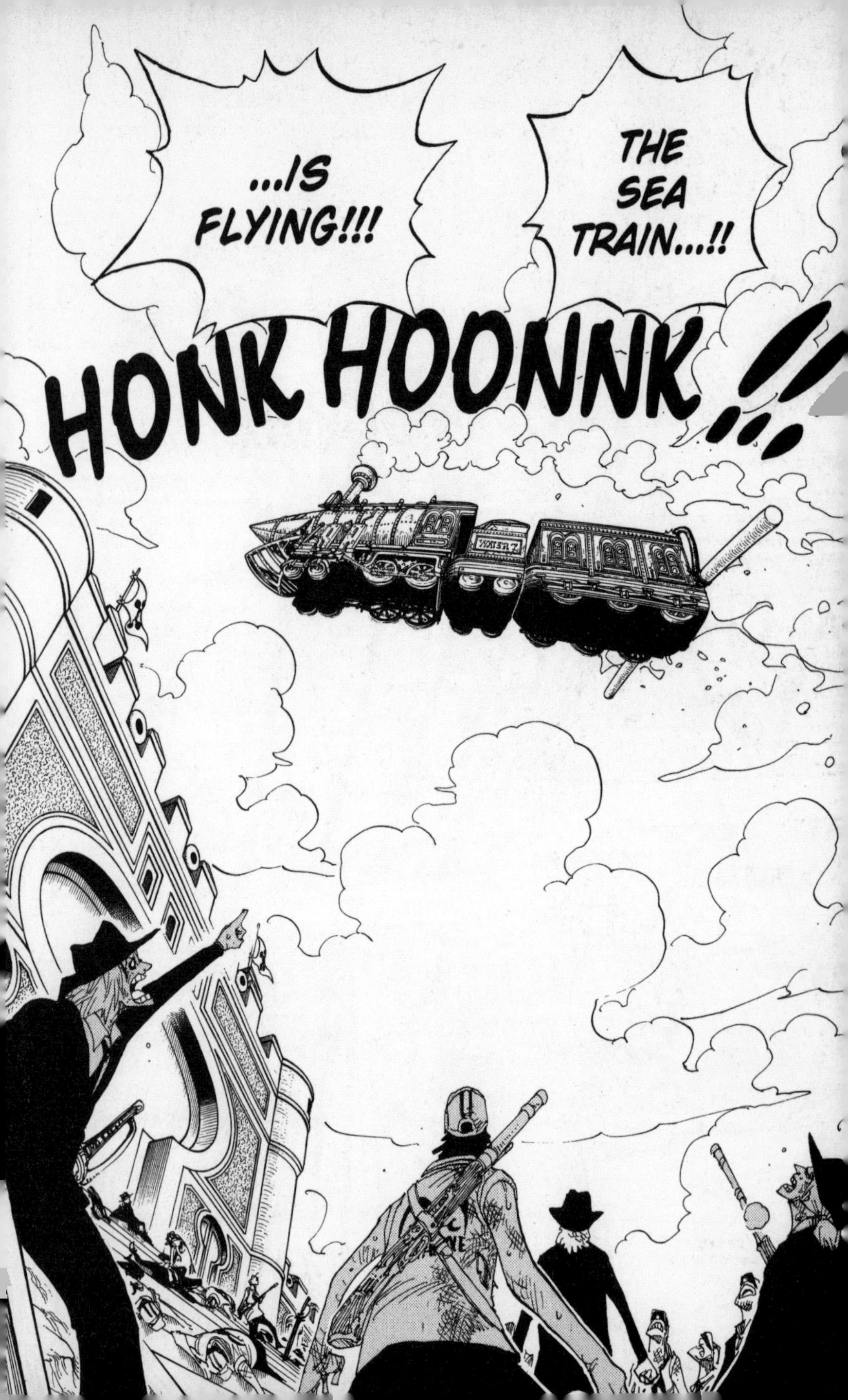
THE SEA TRAIN...!!
...IS FLYING!!!
HONK HOONNK!!

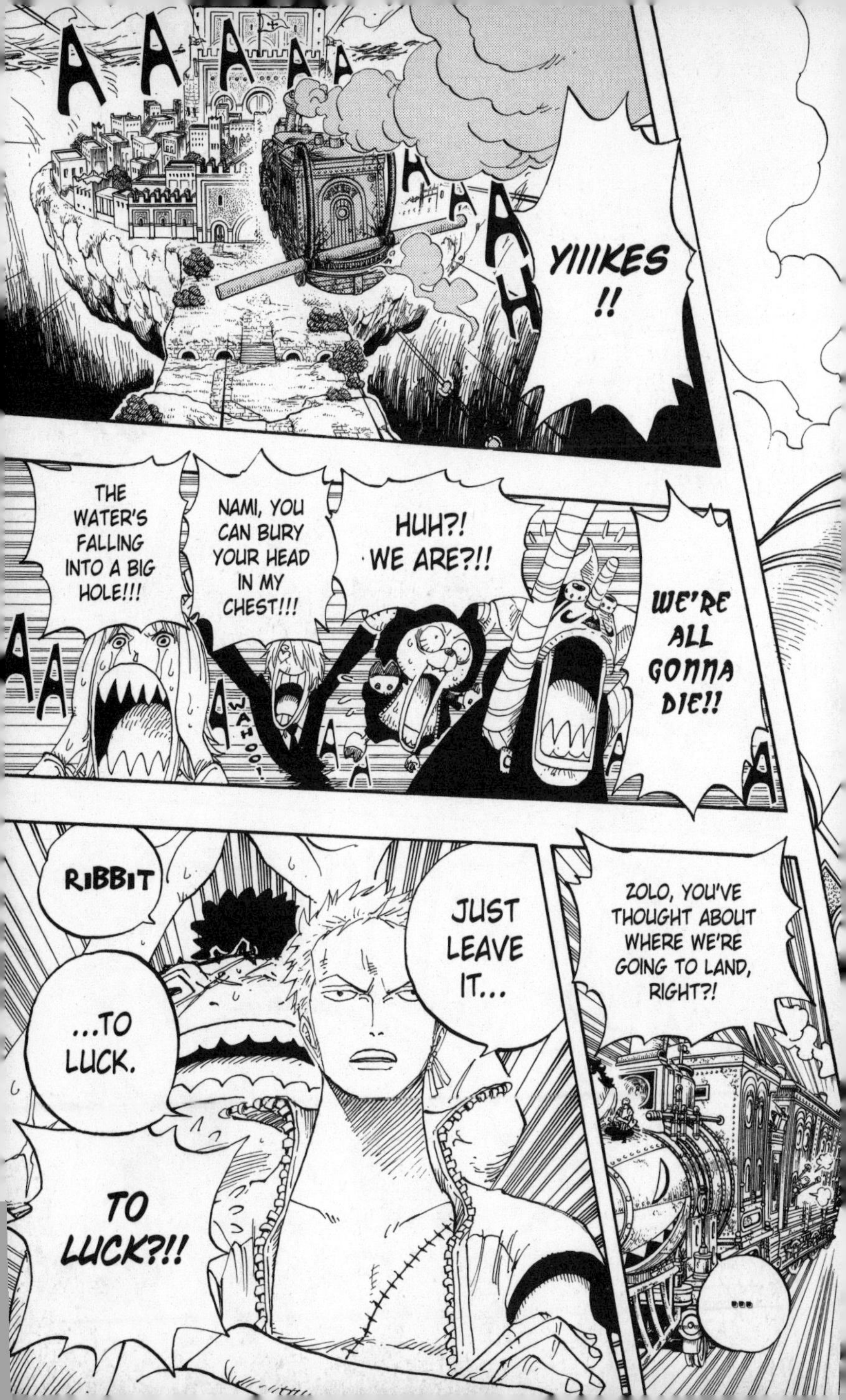
AAAAAAAAAAH
YIIIKES !!
WE'RE ALL GONNA DIE!!
HUH?! WE ARE?!!
NAMI, YOU CAN BURY YOUR HEAD IN MY CHEST!!!
WAHOO!
THE WATER'S FALLING INTO A BIG HOLE!!!
AAAAAAA
ZOLO, YOU'VE THOUGHT ABOUT WHERE WE'RE GOING TO LAND, RIGHT?!
...
JUST LEAVE IT...
RIBBIT
...TO LUCK.
TO LUCK?!!

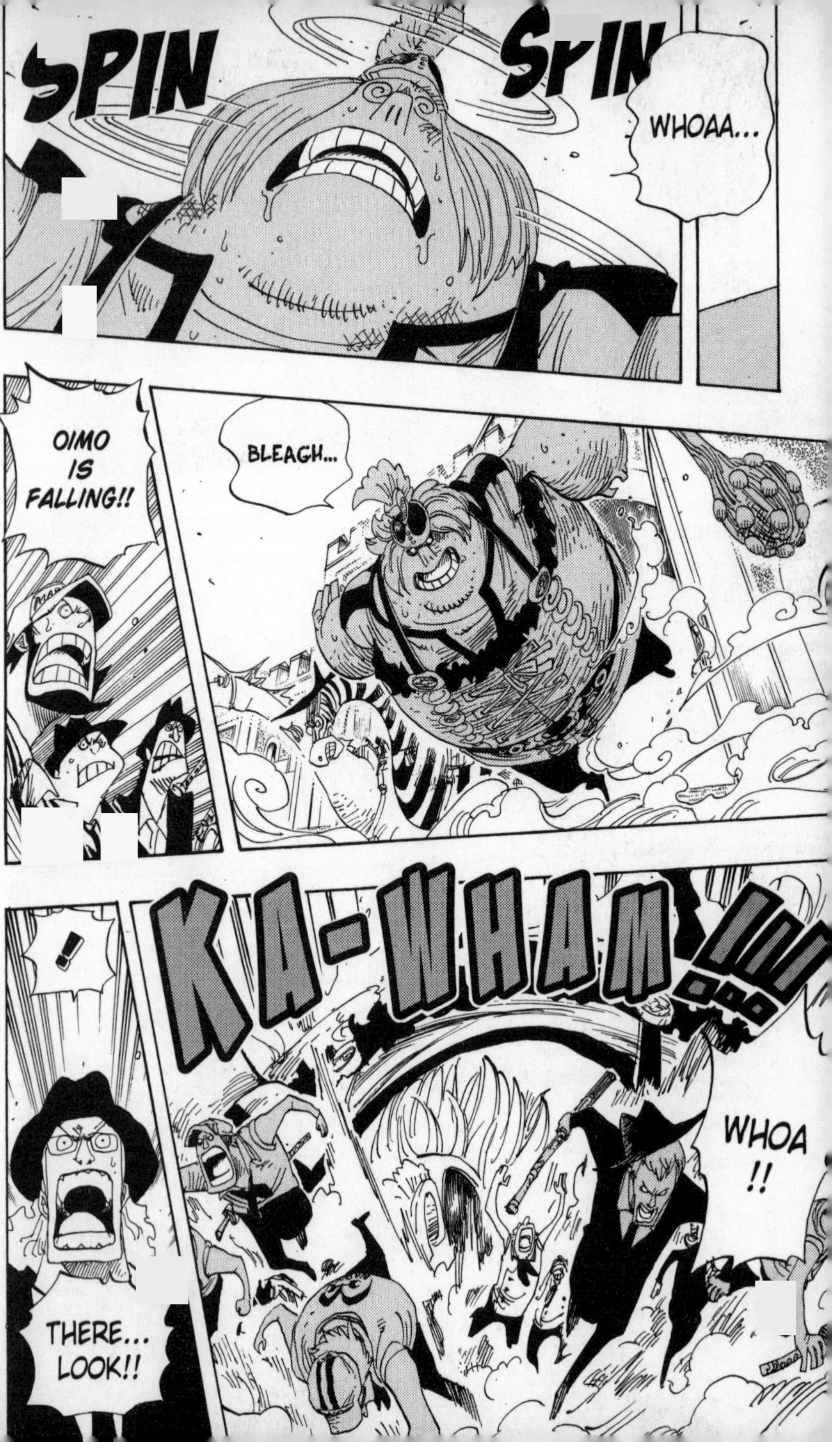
WHOAA...
SPIN
SPIN
BLEAGH...
OIMO IS FALLING!!
KA-WHAM!!!
WHOA!!
!
THERE... LOOK!!

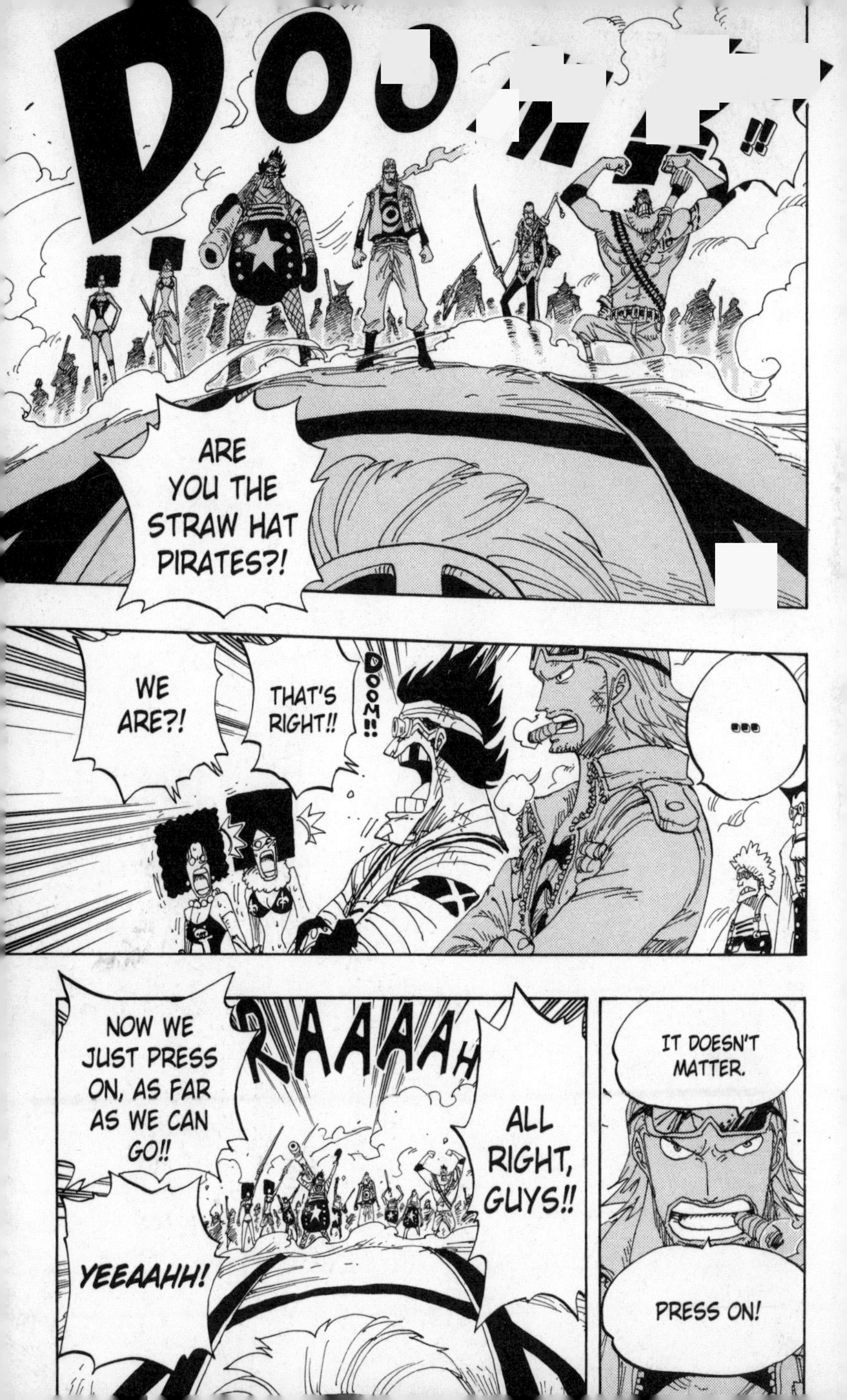
ARE YOU THE STRAW HAT PIRATES?!
...
DOOM!!
THAT'S RIGHT!!
WE ARE?!
IT DOESN'T MATTER.
PRESS ON!
ALL RIGHT, GUYS!!
RAAAAH
NOW WE JUST PRESS ON, AS FAR AS WE CAN GO!!
YEEAAHH!

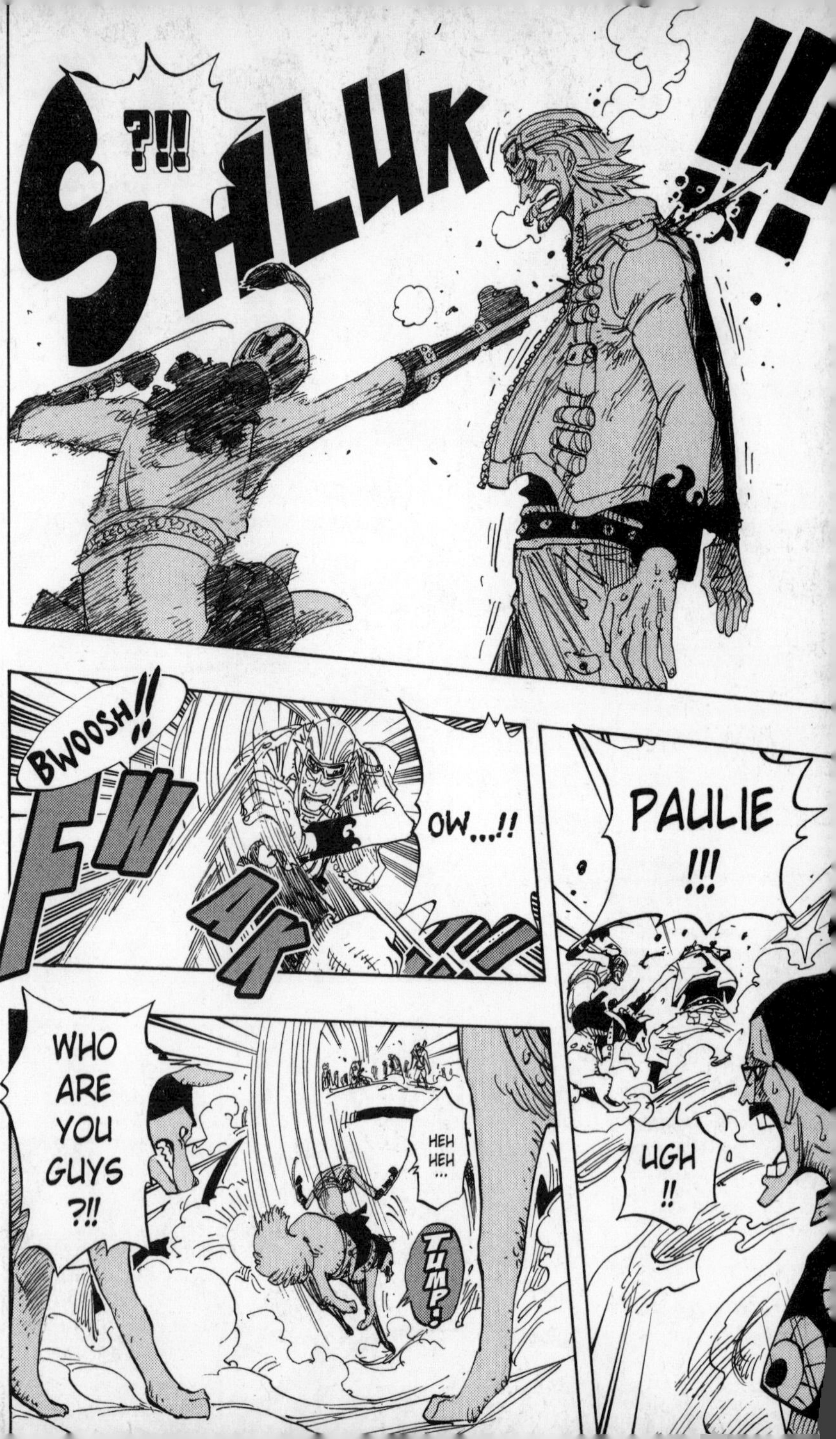
SHLUK!!!
?!!
PAULIE!!!
UGH!!
OW...!!
BWOOSH!!
FWAK!!
HEH HEH...
TUMP!
WHO ARE YOU GUYS?!!

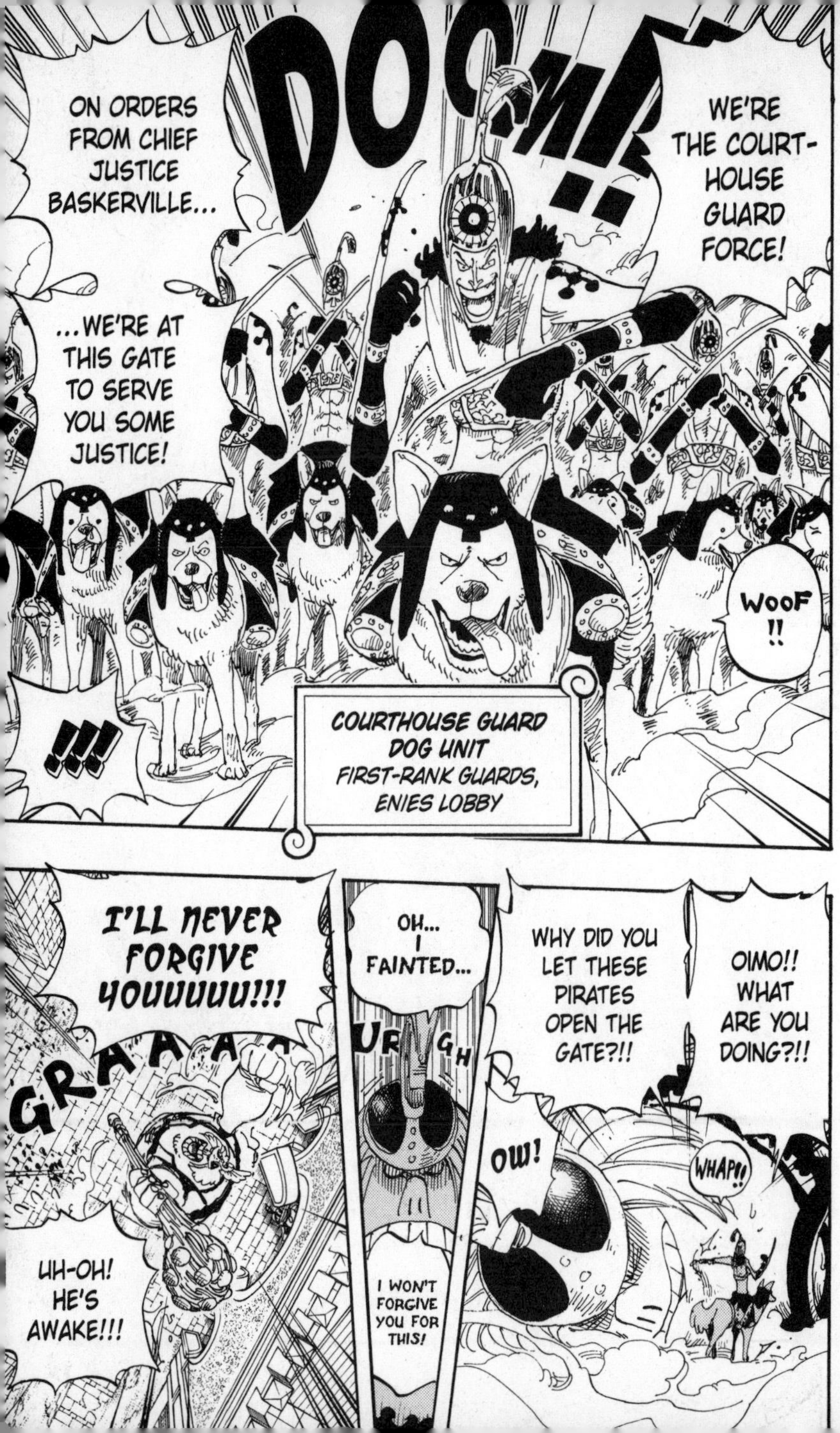
DOOM!!
WE'RE THE COURT-HOUSE GUARD FORCE!
ON ORDERS FROM CHIEF JUSTICE BASKERVILLE...
...WE'RE AT THIS GATE TO SERVE YOU SOME JUSTICE!
WOOF!!
COURTHOUSE GUARD DOG UNIT
FIRST-RANK GUARDS, ENIES LOBBY
!!!
OIMO!! WHAT ARE YOU DOING?!!
WHY DID YOU LET THESE PIRATES OPEN THE GATE?!!
WHAP!!
OW!
OH... I FAINTED...
URGH
I WON'T FORGIVE YOU FOR THIS!
I'LL NEVER FORGIVE YOUUUUU!!!
GRAAAA
UH-OH! HE'S AWAKE!!!

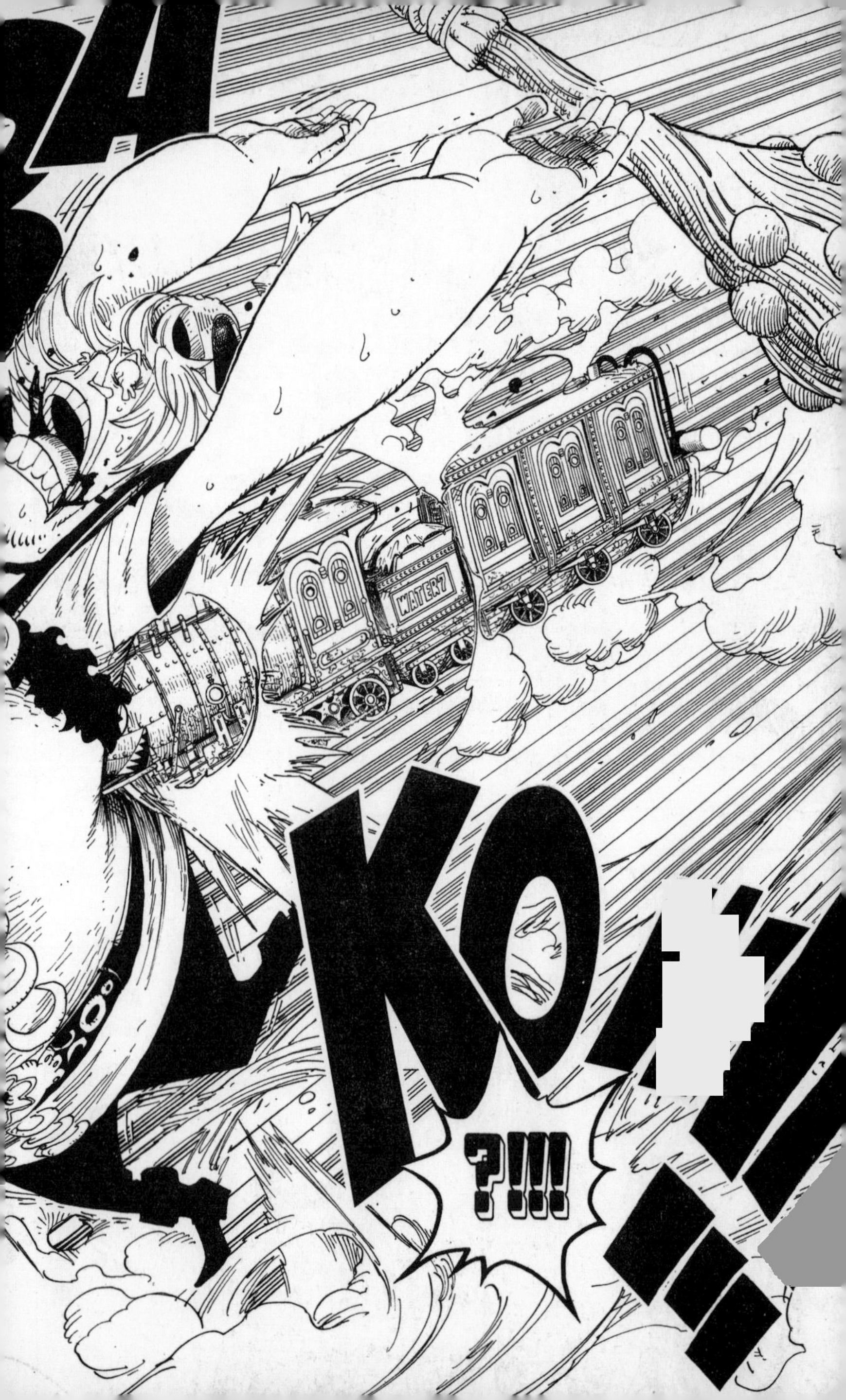
WATER7
KO
?!!!

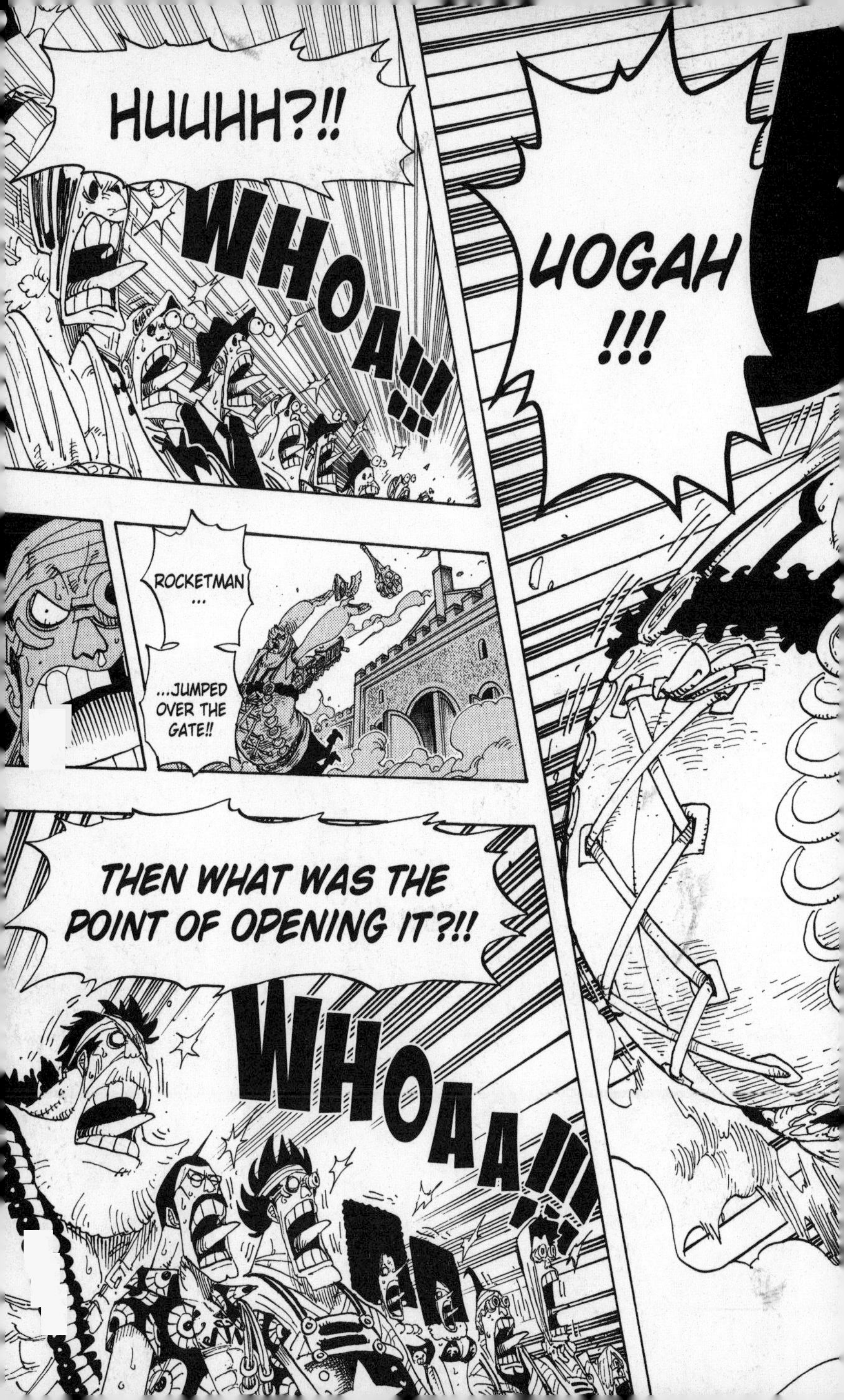
UOGAH !!!
HUUHH?!!
WHOA!!!
ROCKETMAN ...
...JUMPED OVER THE GATE!!
THEN WHAT WAS THE POINT OF OPENING IT?!!
WHOAA!!!

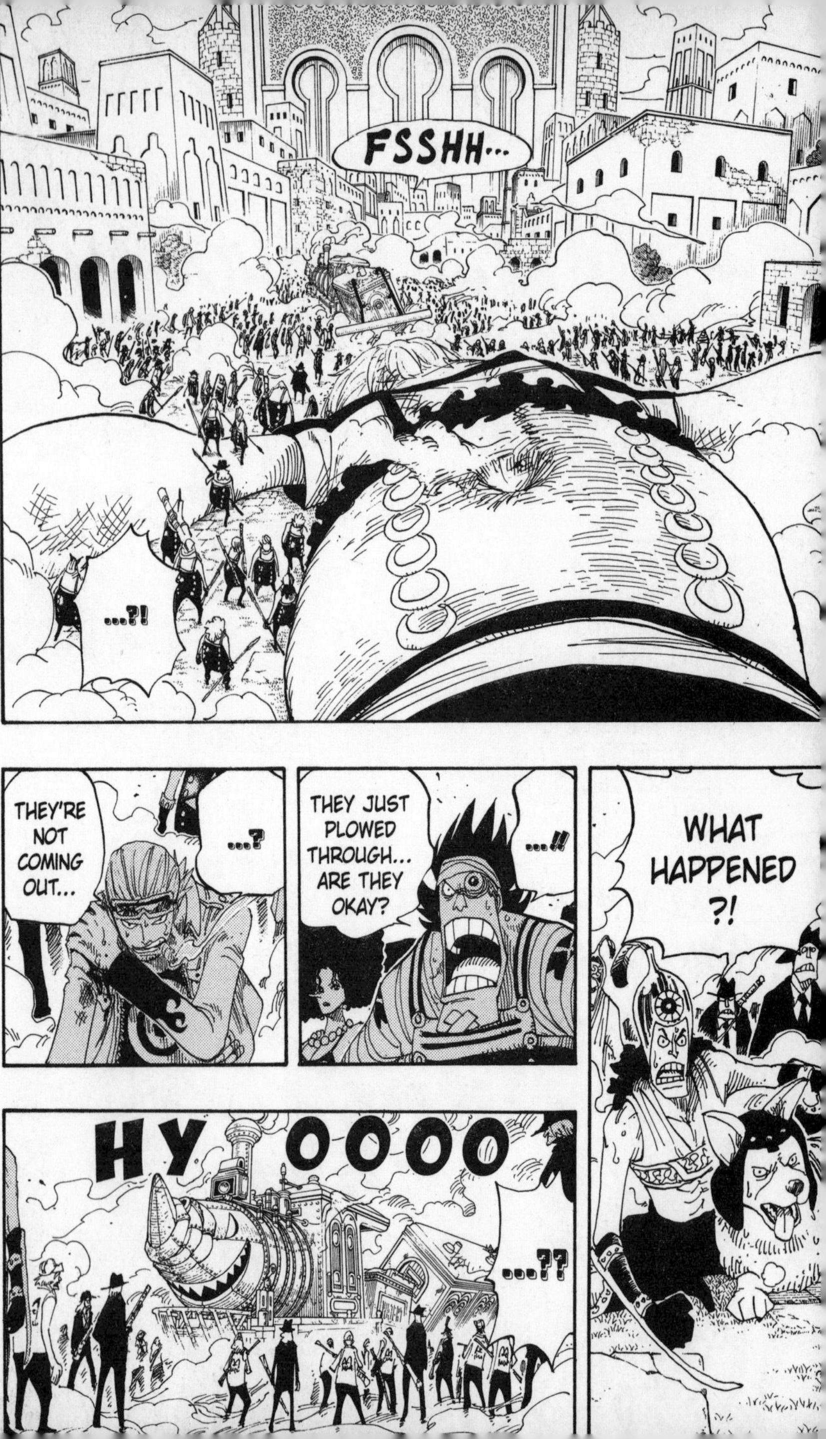
FSSHH...
...?!
WHAT HAPPENED ?!
...!!
THEY JUST PLOWED THROUGH... ARE THEY OKAY?
...?
THEY'RE NOT COMING OUT...
HYOOOO
...??

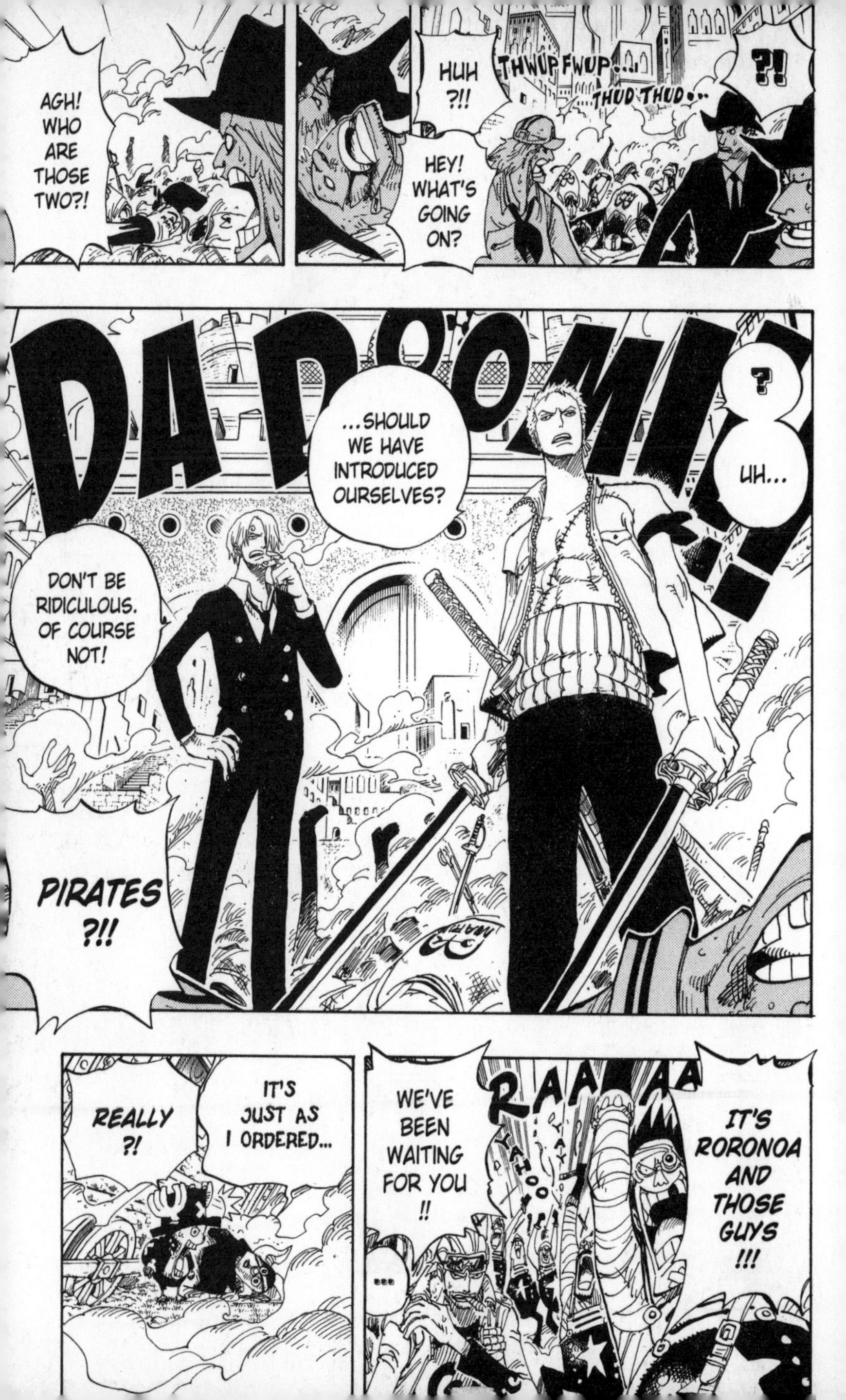
?!
THWUP FWUP...
THUD THUD...
HUH ?!!
HEY! WHAT'S GOING ON?
AGH! WHO ARE THOSE TWO?!
DA-DOOM!!
?
UH...
...SHOULD WE HAVE INTRODUCED OURSELVES?
DON'T BE RIDICULOUS. OF COURSE NOT!
PIRATES ?!!
IT'S RORONOA AND THOSE GUYS !!!
RAAAAA
YAY
YAHOO!!
WE'VE BEEN WAITING FOR YOU !!
...
IT'S JUST AS I ORDERED...
REALLY ?!

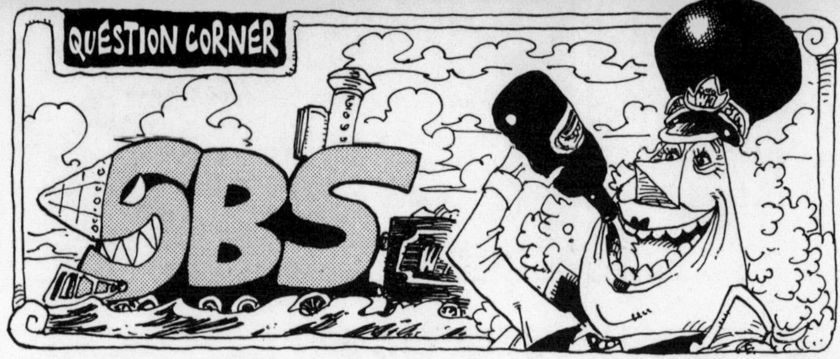
QUESTION CORNER
SBS

Q: Hello, Odacchi! Something's been bothering me, so help me out! Ever since chapter 334, Nami's been wearing a tank top with the number three on it. What does that mean?

--Hyuu

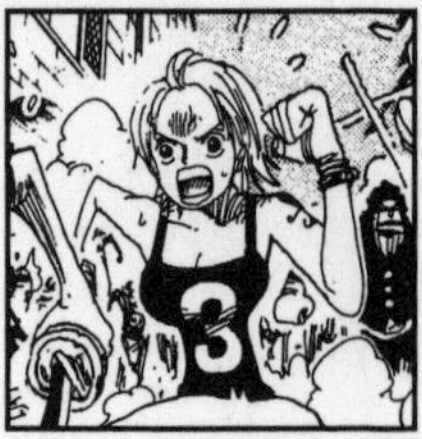

Q: Hello, Oda Sensei. If you associate each of the main characters with a particular color, please tell me.

--Daidai

Q: I've got a question!! Chopper's blue nose is so sensitive that he can tell where his comrades are by smell. How does each of the Straw Hats smell? Does Luffy smell like rubber?? Please, ask Chopper about this for me.

--Budomaru

A: Okay, okay. Three questions. I've gathered the information about the various characters below. Here are the numbers (if applicaple) and colors I associate with them and how they smell (according to Chopper).

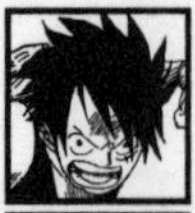

01
56 (GUM) RED
SMELLS LIKE MEAT

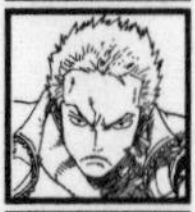

02
GREEN
SMELLS LIKE STEEL

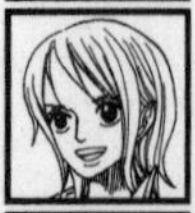

03
73 (NAMI) ORANGE
SMELLS LIKE TANGERINES (AND MONEY)

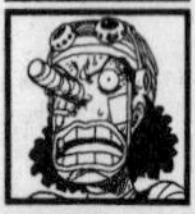

04
YELLOW
SMELLS LIKE GUNPOWDER

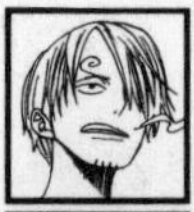

05
32 (SANJI) 59 (COOK) BLUE
SMELLS LIKE TOBACCO AND SEAFOOD

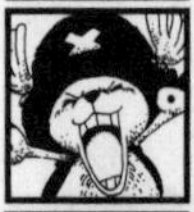

06
PINK
I DON'T KNOW HOW I SMELL!

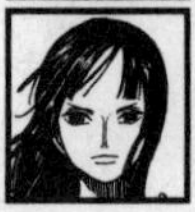

07
PURPLE
SMELLS LIKE FLOWERS

Chapter 381:
FIRED

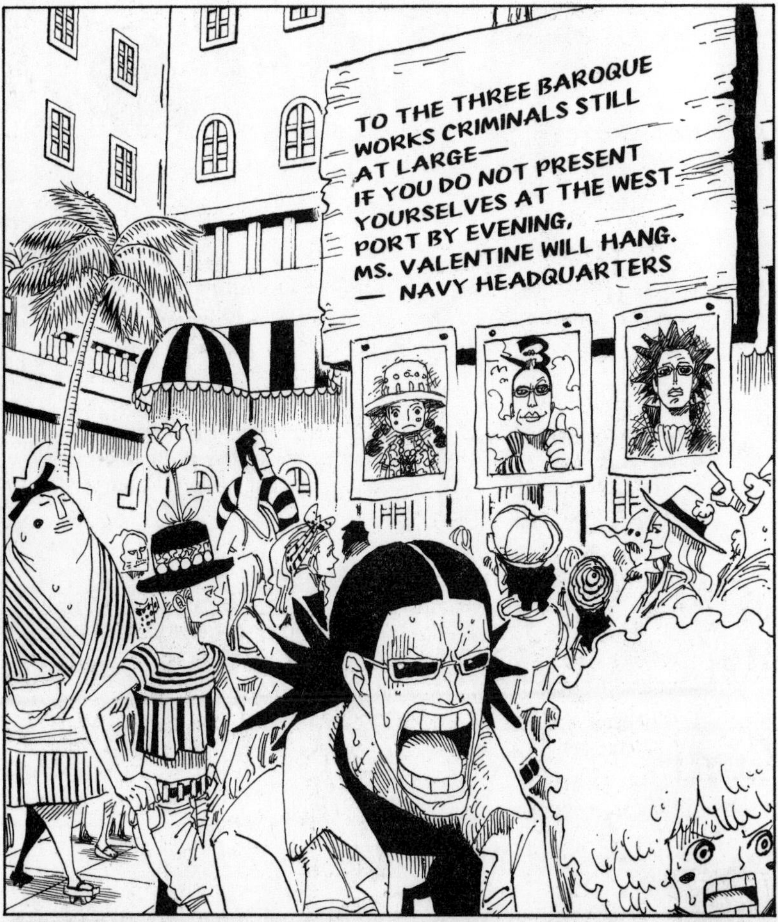
TO THE THREE BAROQUE WORKS CRIMINALS STILL AT LARGE—
IF YOU DO NOT PRESENT YOURSELVES AT THE WEST PORT BY EVENING,
MS. VALENTINE WILL HANG.
— NAVY HEADQUARTERS
3

MS. GOLDEN WEEK'S BIG PLAN, A BAROQUE REUNION, VOL. 17: "SHOW YOURSELF!!"

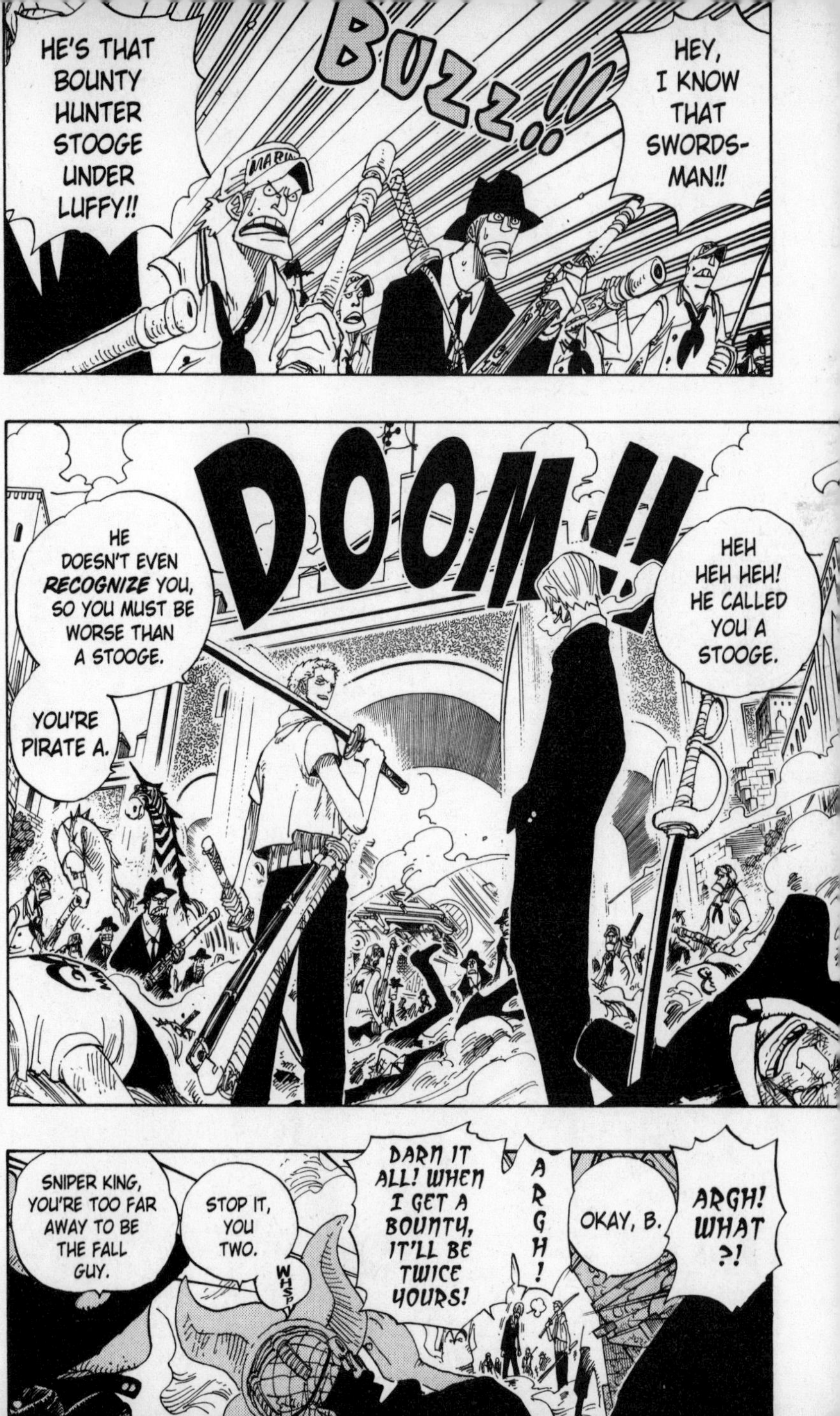
HEY, I KNOW THAT SWORDSMAN!!
BUZZ..!!
HE'S THAT BOUNTY HUNTER STOOGE UNDER LUFFY!!
DOOM!!
HEH HEH HEH! HE CALLED YOU A STOOGE.
HE DOESN'T EVEN RECOGNIZE YOU, SO YOU MUST BE WORSE THAN A STOOGE.
YOU'RE PIRATE A.
ARGH! WHAT ?!
OKAY, B.
ARGH!
DARN IT ALL! WHEN I GET A BOUNTY, IT'LL BE TWICE YOURS!
STOP IT, YOU TWO.
WHSP
SNIPER KING, YOU'RE TOO FAR AWAY TO BE THE FALL GUY.

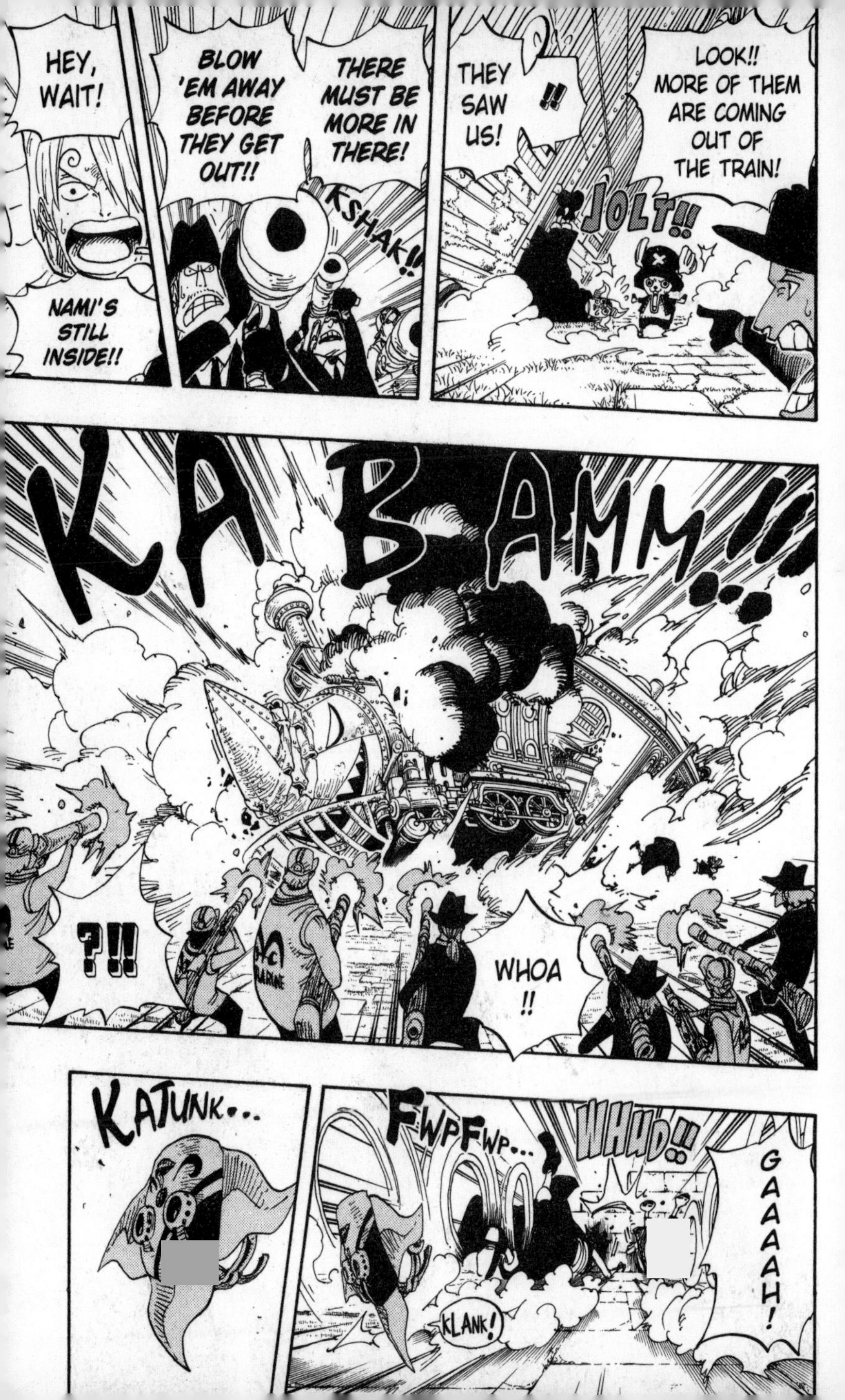
LOOK!! MORE OF THEM ARE COMING OUT OF THE TRAIN!
THEY SAW US!
!!
JOLT!!
THERE MUST BE MORE IN THERE!
BLOW 'EM AWAY BEFORE THEY GET OUT!!
KSHAK!!
HEY, WAIT!
NAMI'S STILL INSIDE!!
KABAMM!!
WHOA !!
?!!
WHUD!!
GAAAAH!
FWPFWP...
KLANK!
KATUNK...

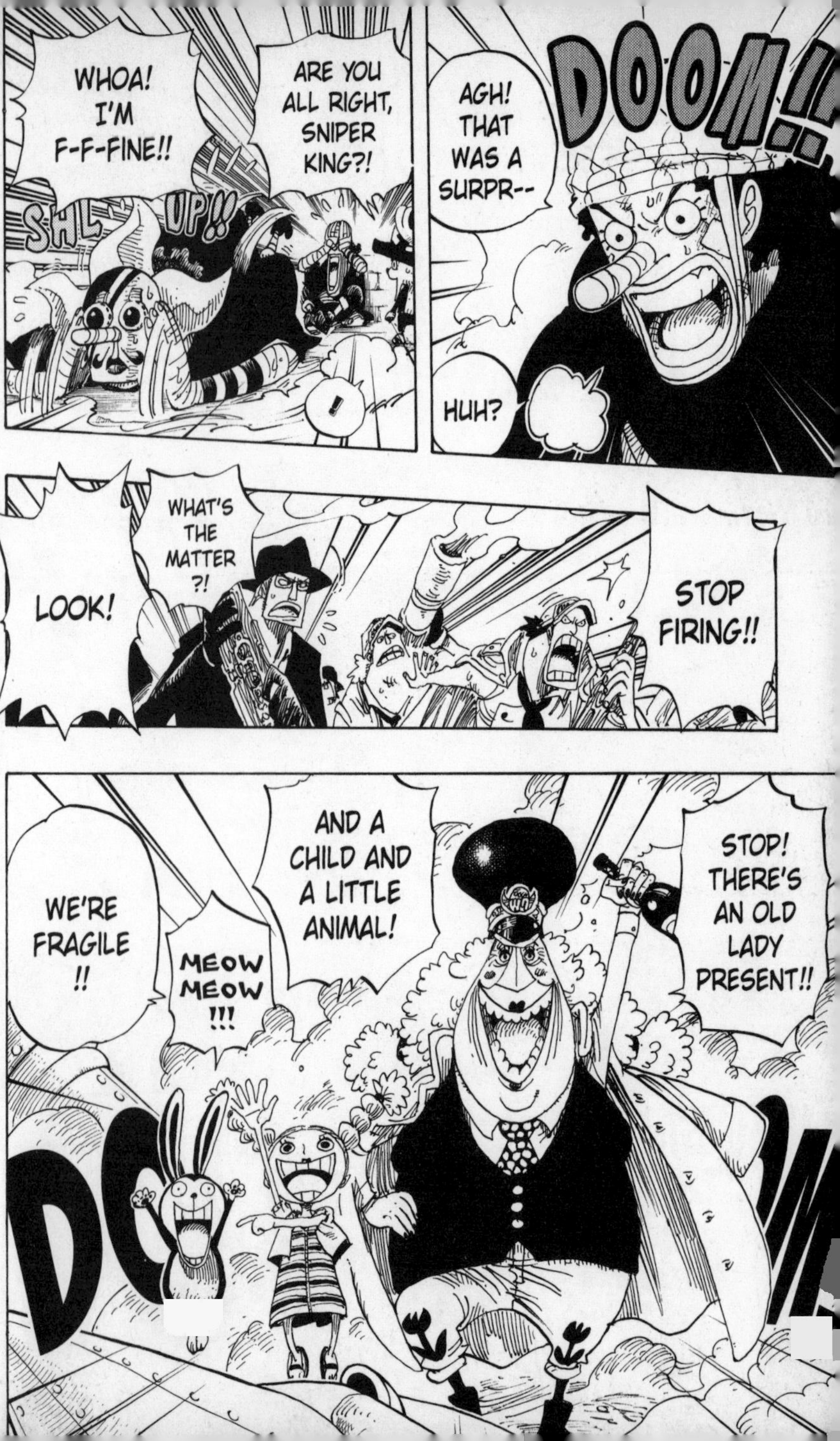
DOOM!!
AGH! THAT WAS A SURPR--
HUH?
ARE YOU ALL RIGHT, SNIPER KING?!
WHOA! I'M F-F-FINE!!
SHL UP!!
!
STOP FIRING!!
WHAT'S THE MATTER ?!
LOOK!
STOP! THERE'S AN OLD LADY PRESENT!!
AND A CHILD AND A LITTLE ANIMAL!
MEOW MEOW !!!
WE'RE FRAGILE !!

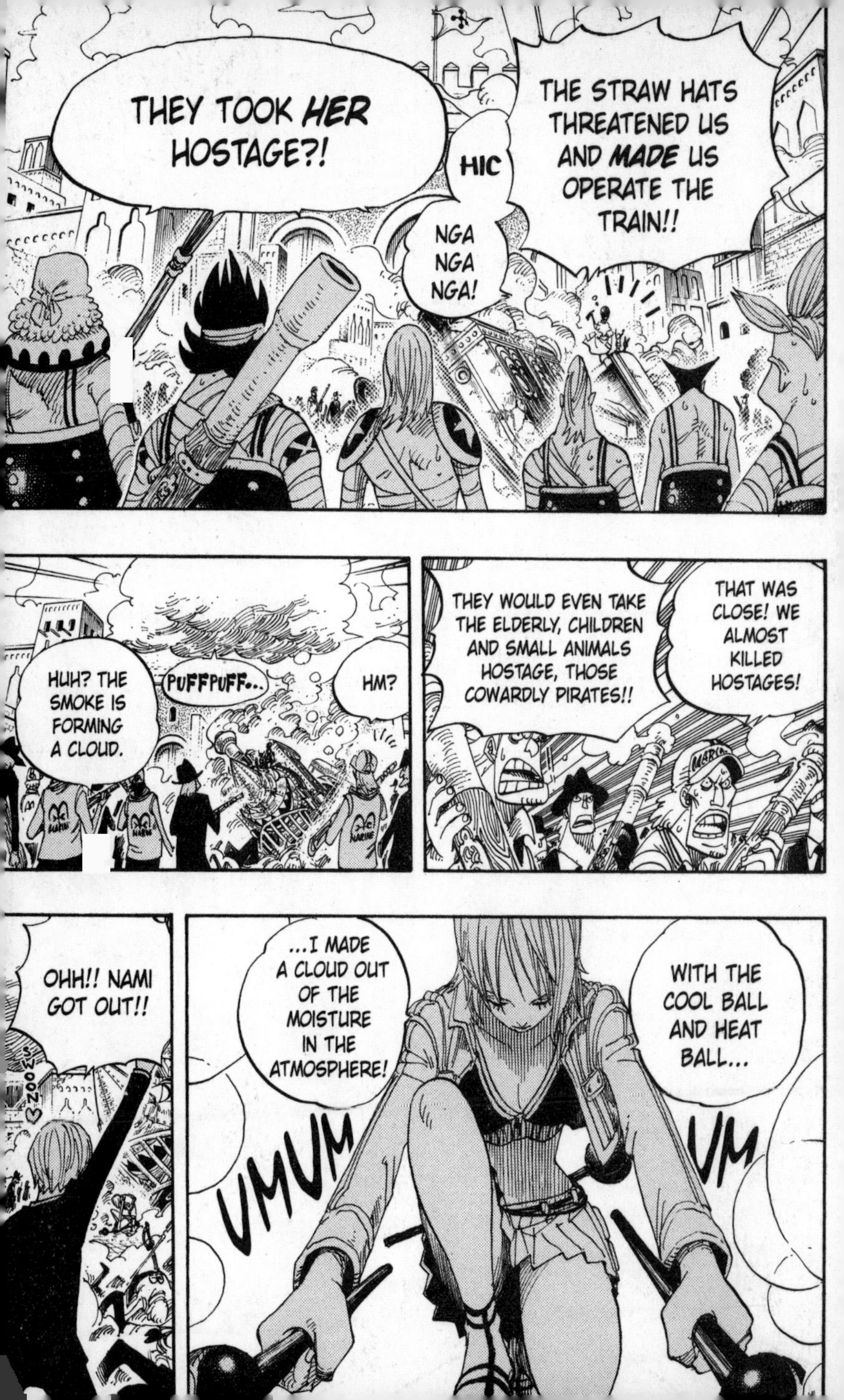
THE STRAW HATS THREATENED US AND *MADE* US OPERATE THE TRAIN!!
HIC
NGA NGA NGA!
THEY TOOK *HER* HOSTAGE?!
THAT WAS CLOSE! WE ALMOST KILLED HOSTAGES!
THEY WOULD EVEN TAKE THE ELDERLY, CHILDREN AND SMALL ANIMALS HOSTAGE, THOSE COWARDLY PIRATES!!
HM?
PUFFPUFF...
HUH? THE SMOKE IS FORMING A CLOUD.
WITH THE COOL BALL AND HEAT BALL...
UM
...I MADE A CLOUD OUT OF THE MOISTURE IN THE ATMOSPHERE!
UMUM
OHH!! NAMI GOT OUT!!
SWOON♥

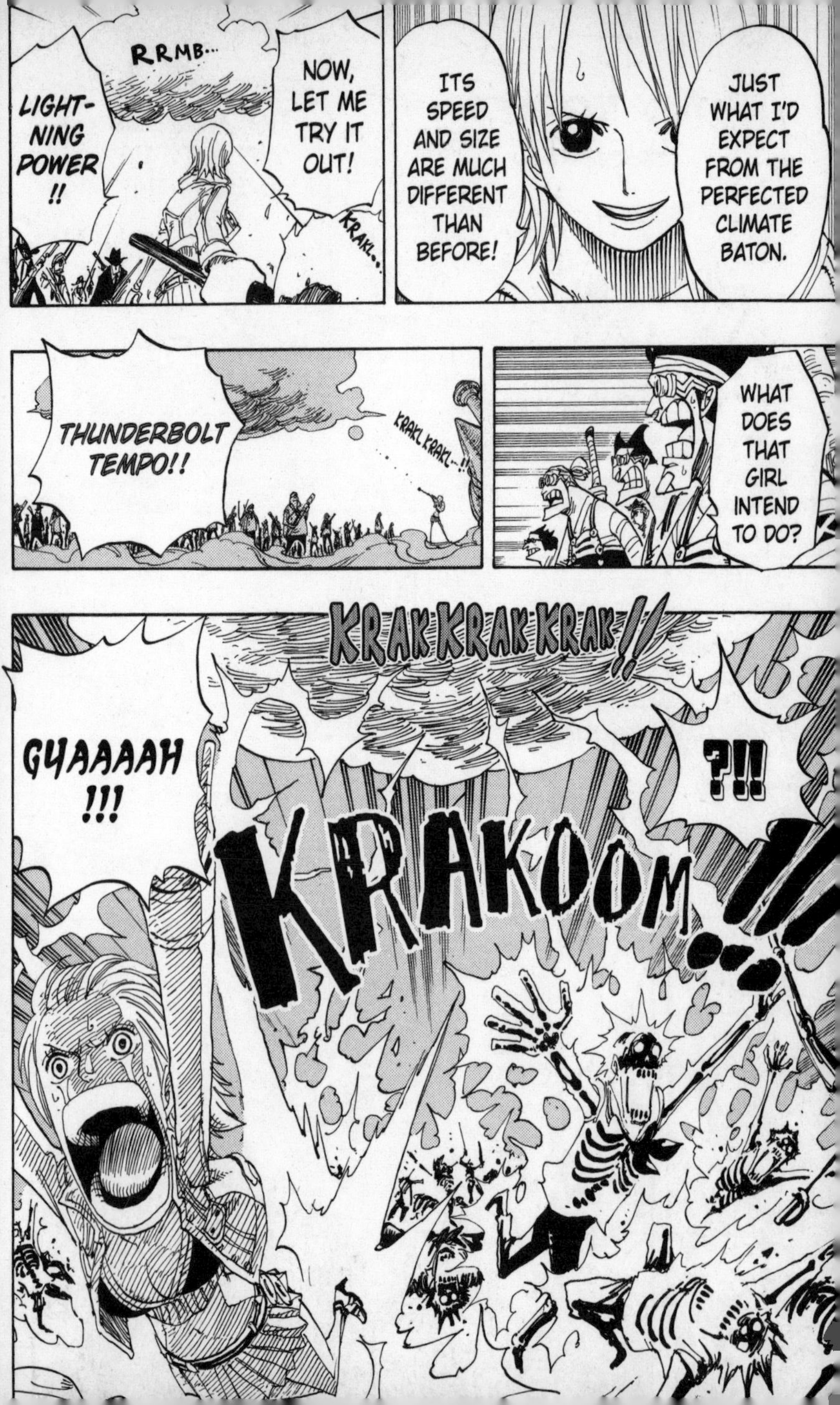
JUST WHAT I'D EXPECT FROM THE PERFECTED CLIMATE BATON.
ITS SPEED AND SIZE ARE MUCH DIFFERENT THAN BEFORE!
NOW, LET ME TRY IT OUT!
KRAKL...
RRMB...
LIGHT-NING POWER !!
WHAT DOES THAT GIRL INTEND TO DO?
KRAKL KRAKL...!!
THUNDERBOLT TEMPO!!
KRAK KRAK KRAK!!
?!!
KRAKOOM...!!
GUAAAAH !!!

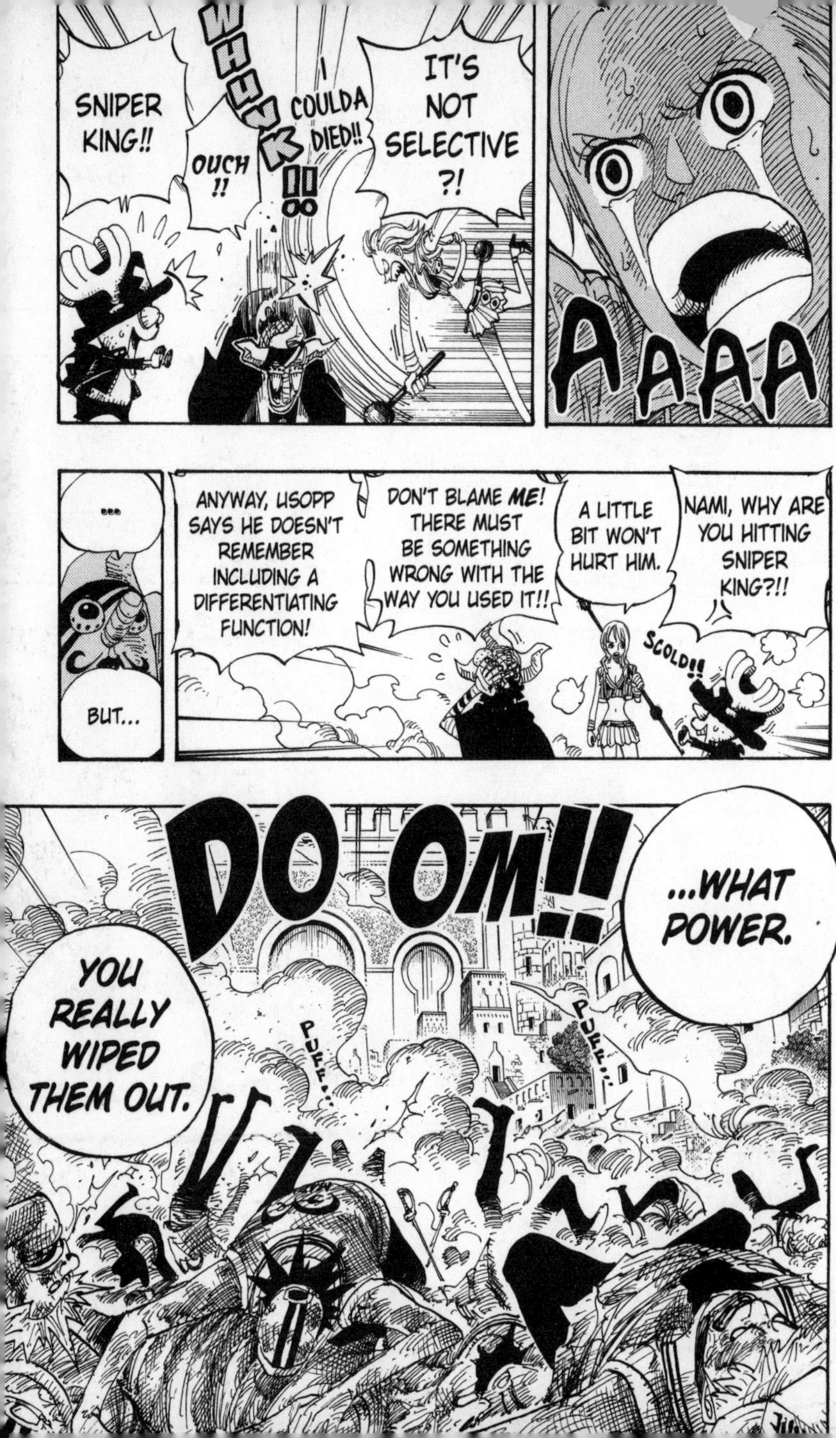
AAAA
IT'S NOT SELECTIVE ?!
I COULDA DIED!!
WHUNK!!
OUCH!!
SNIPER KING!!
NAMI, WHY ARE YOU HITTING SNIPER KING?!!
A LITTLE BIT WON'T HURT HIM.
DON'T BLAME ME! THERE MUST BE SOMETHING WRONG WITH THE WAY YOU USED IT!!
ANYWAY, USOPP SAYS HE DOESN'T REMEMBER INCLUDING A DIFFERENTIATING FUNCTION!
SCOLD!!
...
BUT...
...WHAT POWER.
DOOM!!
YOU REALLY WIPED THEM OUT.
PUFF...
PUFF...

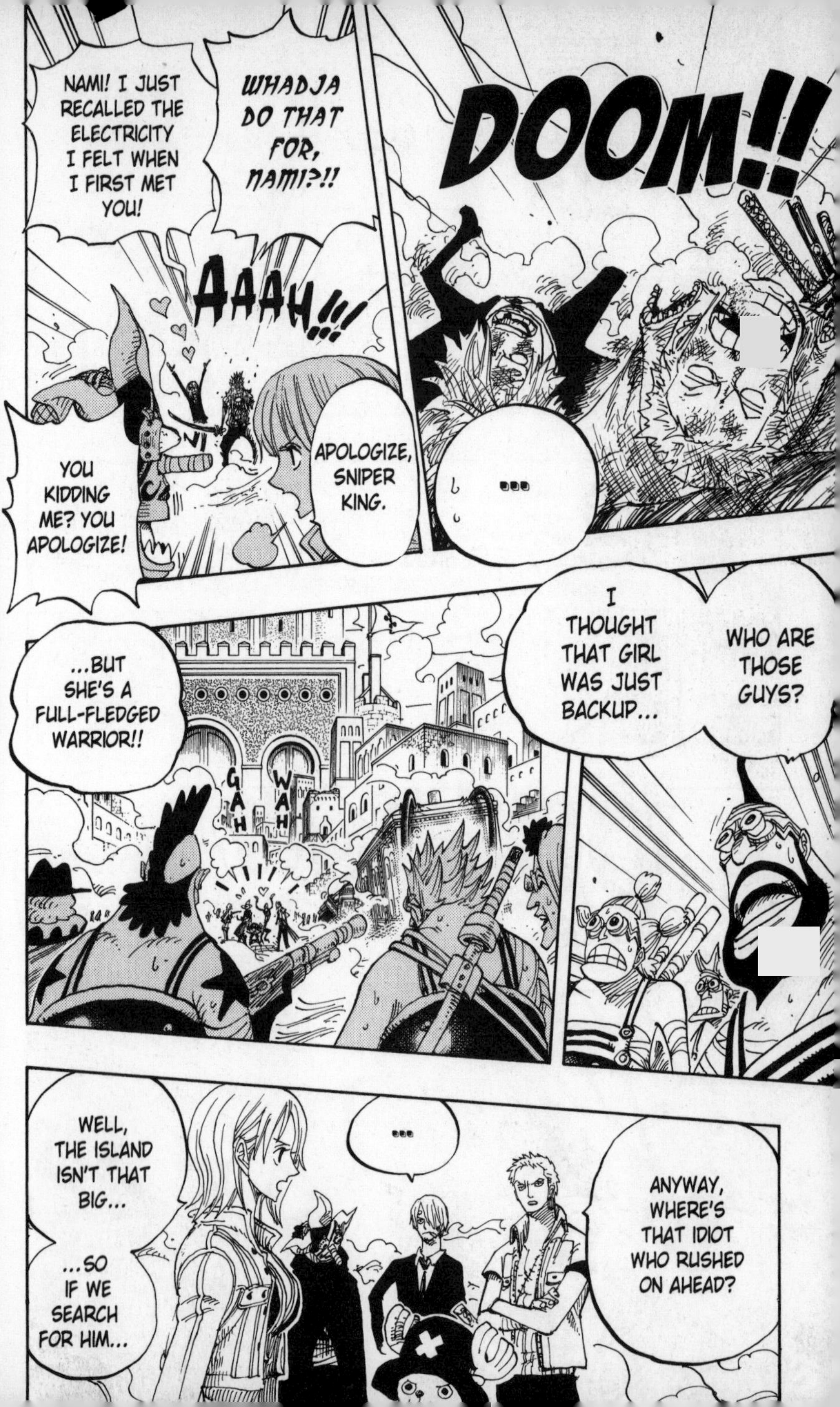
DOOM!!
...
WHADJA DO THAT FOR, NAMI?!!
NAMI! I JUST RECALLED THE ELECTRICITY I FELT WHEN I FIRST MET YOU!
AAAH!!!
APOLOGIZE, SNIPER KING.
YOU KIDDING ME? YOU APOLOGIZE!
WHO ARE THOSE GUYS?
I THOUGHT THAT GIRL WAS JUST BACKUP...
...BUT SHE'S A FULL-FLEDGED WARRIOR!!
GAH
WAH
ANYWAY, WHERE'S THAT IDIOT WHO RUSHED ON AHEAD?
...
WELL, THE ISLAND ISN'T THAT BIG...
...SO IF WE SEARCH FOR HIM...

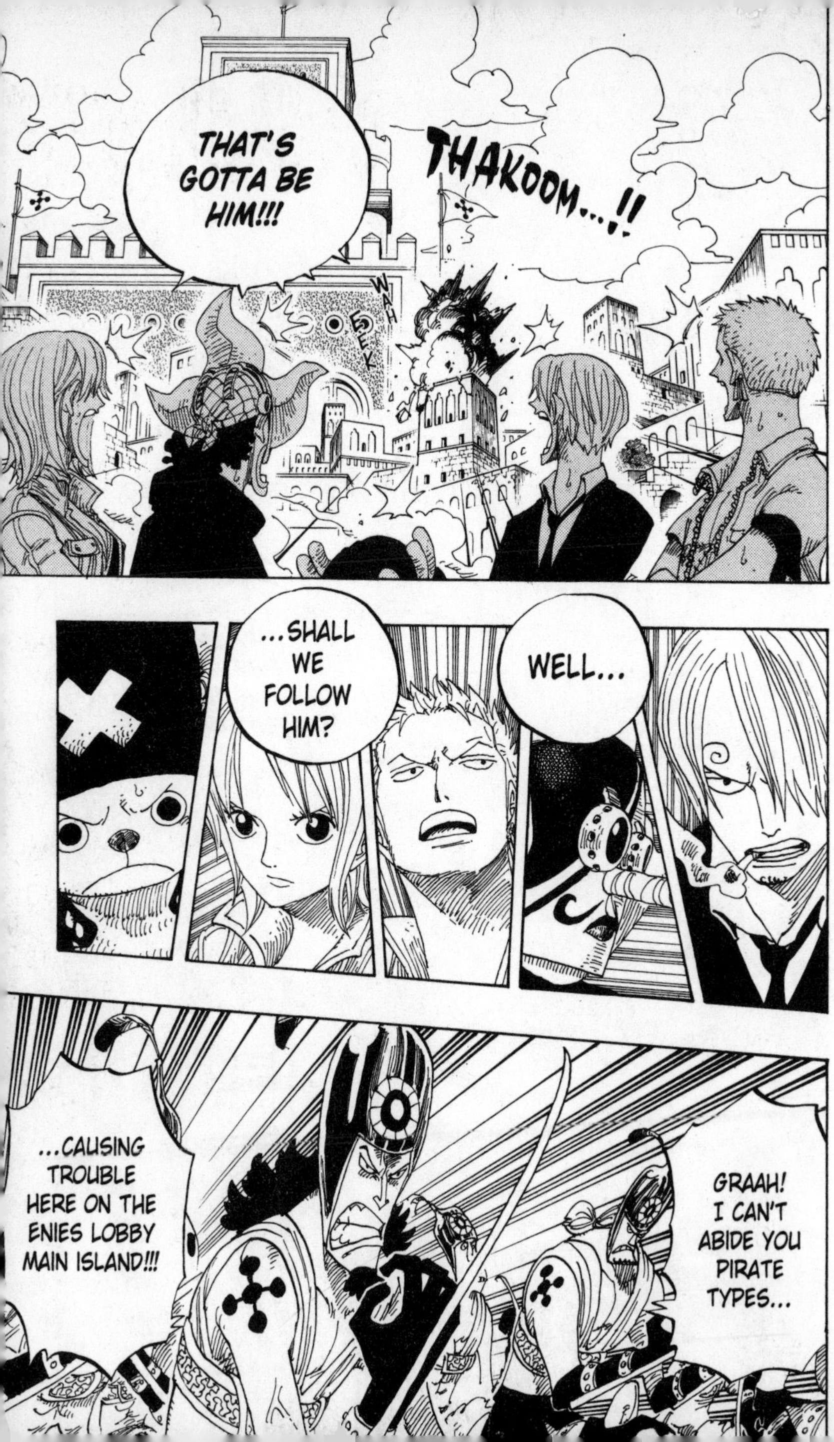
THAKOOM...!!
THAT'S GOTTA BE HIM!!!
WAH EEK
WELL...
...SHALL WE FOLLOW HIM?
GRAAH! I CAN'T ABIDE YOU PIRATE TYPES...
...CAUSING TROUBLE HERE ON THE ENIES LOBBY MAIN ISLAND!!!

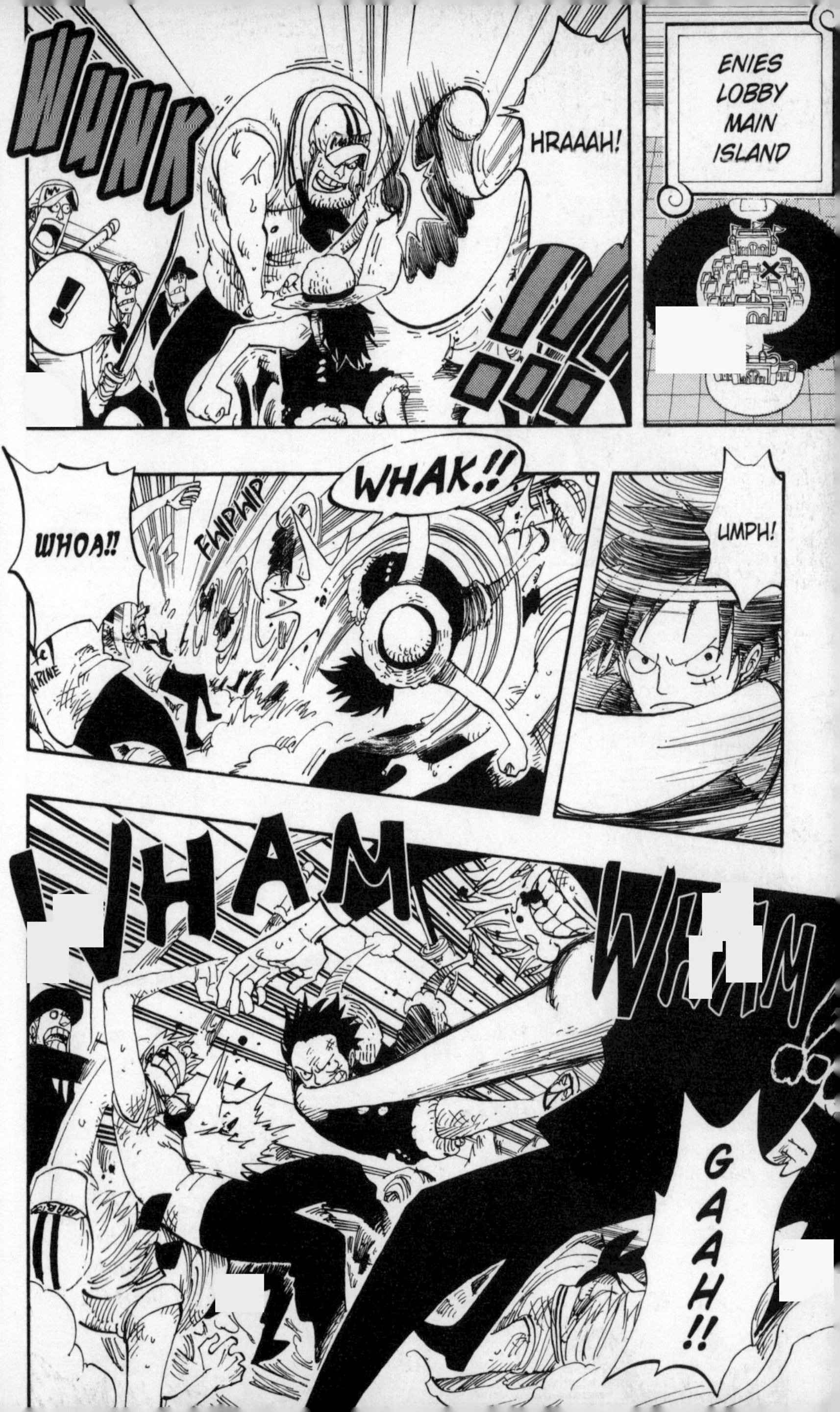
ENIES LOBBY MAIN ISLAND
HRAAAH!
WUNK
!
UMPH!
WHAK.!!
FWIPWIP
WHOA!!
WHAM
WHAM
GAAH!!

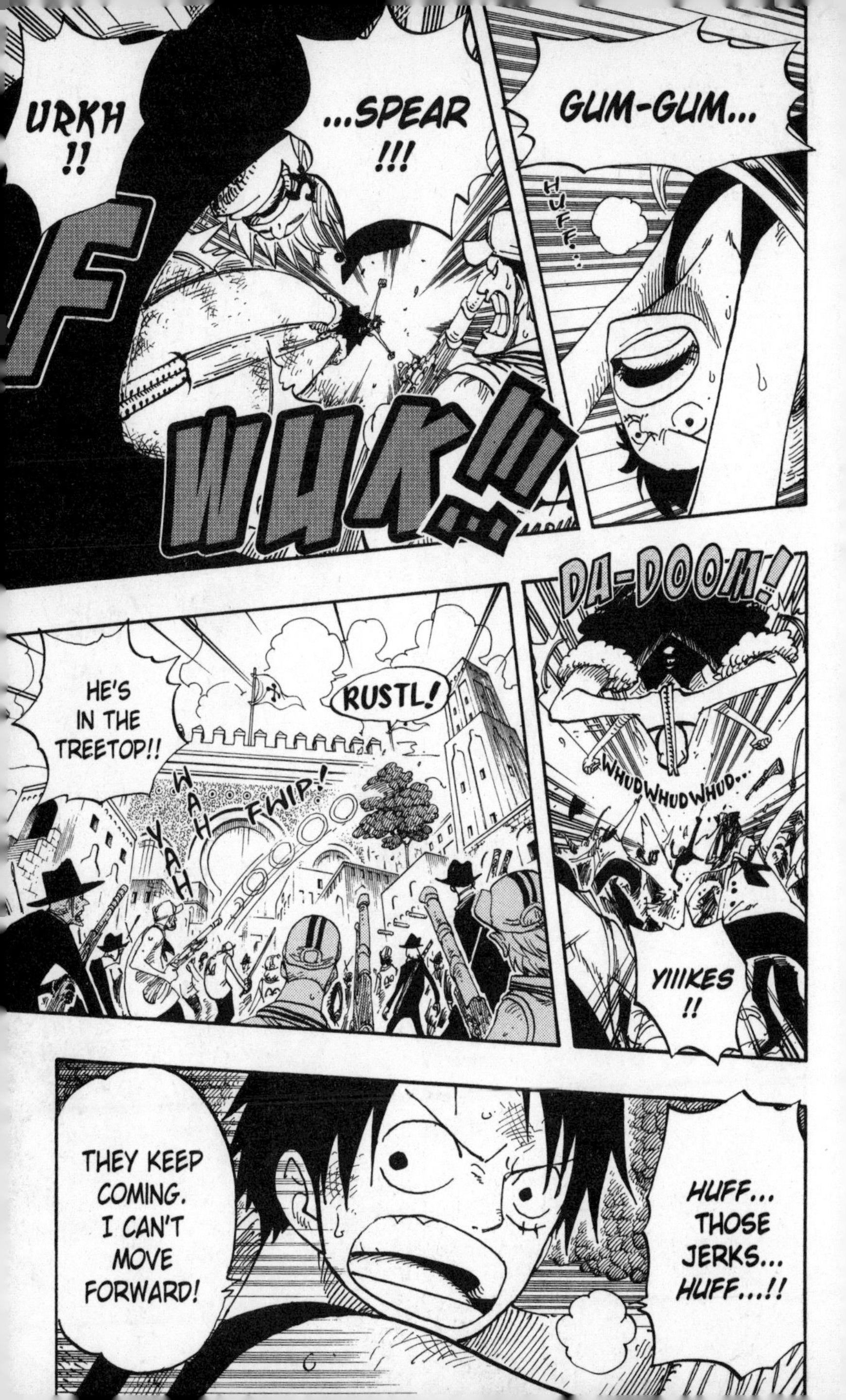
GUM-GUM...
HUFF HUFF...
...SPEAR !!!
URKH !!
WUK!!
F
DA-DOOM!
WHUDWHUDWHUD...
YIIIKES !!
RUSTL!
HE'S IN THE TREETOP!!
FWIP!
WAH
YAH
HUFF... THOSE JERKS... HUFF...!!
THEY KEEP COMING. I CAN'T MOVE FORWARD!

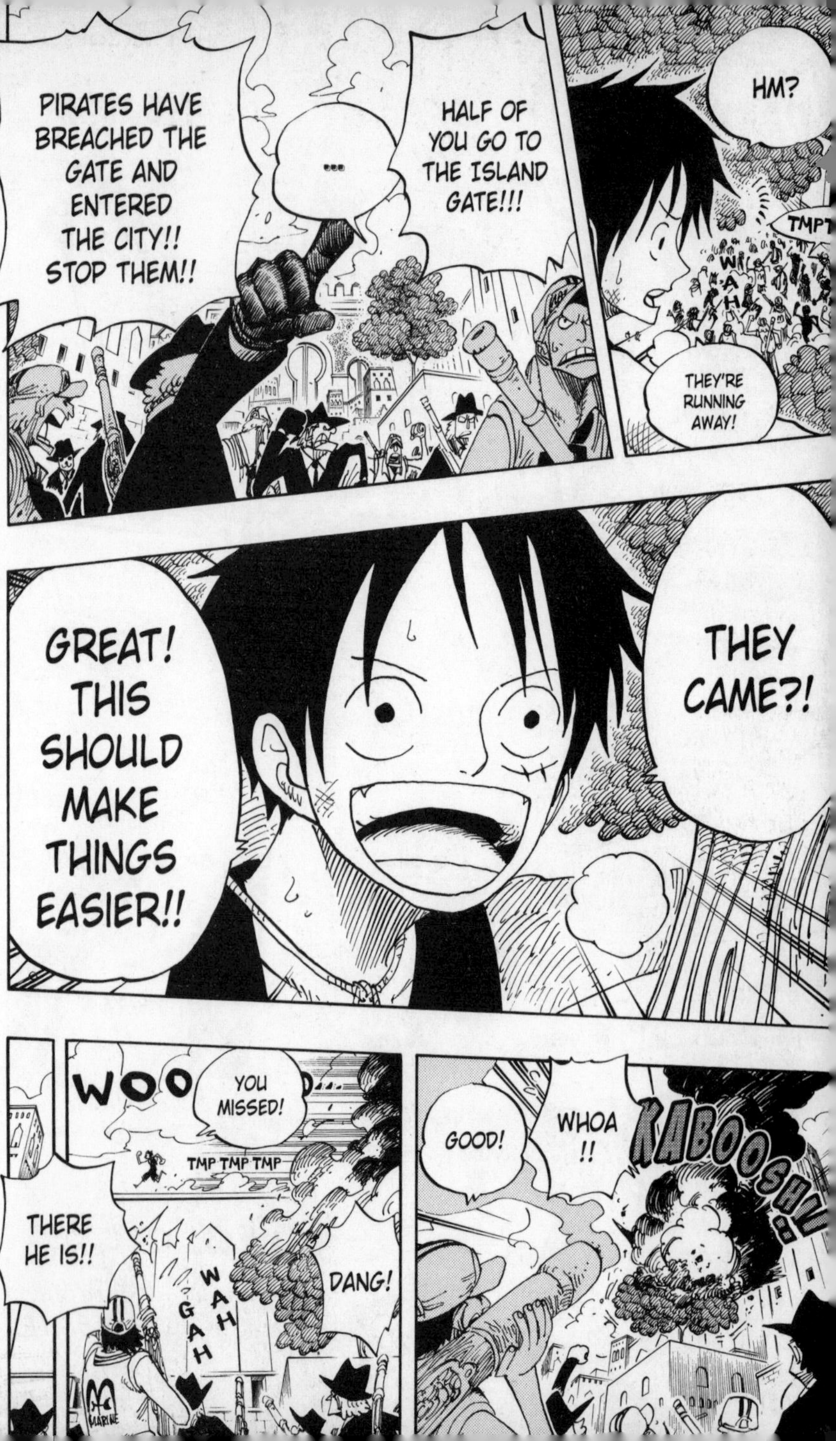
HM?
TMPT
WAH
THEY'RE RUNNING AWAY!
HALF OF YOU GO TO THE ISLAND GATE!!!
...
PIRATES HAVE BREACHED THE GATE AND ENTERED THE CITY!! STOP THEM!!
THEY CAME?!
GREAT! THIS SHOULD MAKE THINGS EASIER!!
KABOOSH
WHOA !!
GOOD!
YOU MISSED!
WOO
TMP TMP TMP
THERE HE IS!!
DANG!
WAH
GAH

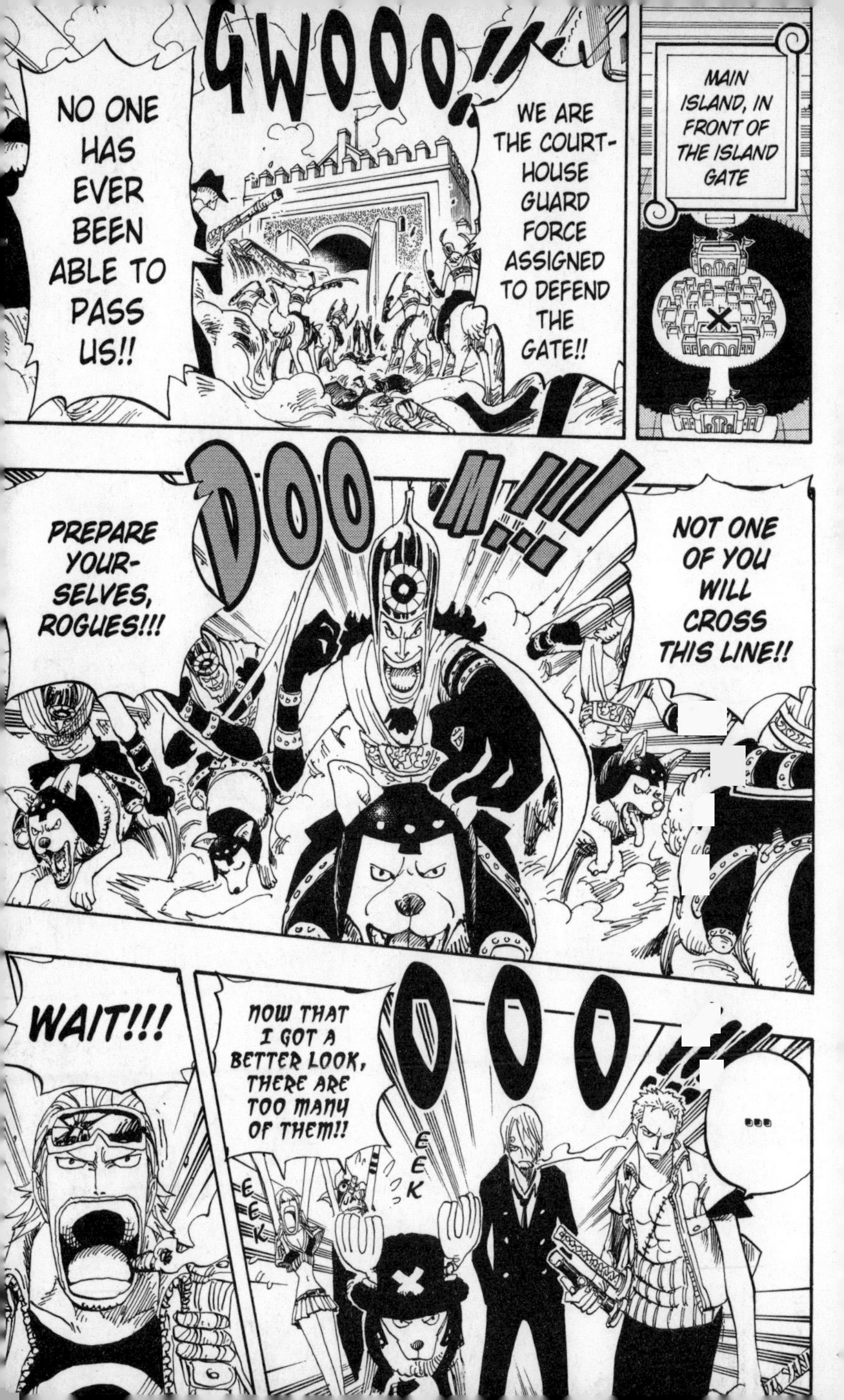

MAIN ISLAND, IN FRONT OF THE ISLAND GATE
GWOOO!!
WE ARE THE COURTHOUSE GUARD FORCE ASSIGNED TO DEFEND THE GATE!!
NO ONE HAS EVER BEEN ABLE TO PASS US!!
DOOM!!!
NOT ONE OF YOU WILL CROSS THIS LINE!!
PREPARE YOURSELVES, ROGUES!!!
OOO
...
EEK
EEK
NOW THAT I GOT A BETTER LOOK, THERE ARE TOO MANY OF THEM!!
WAIT!!!

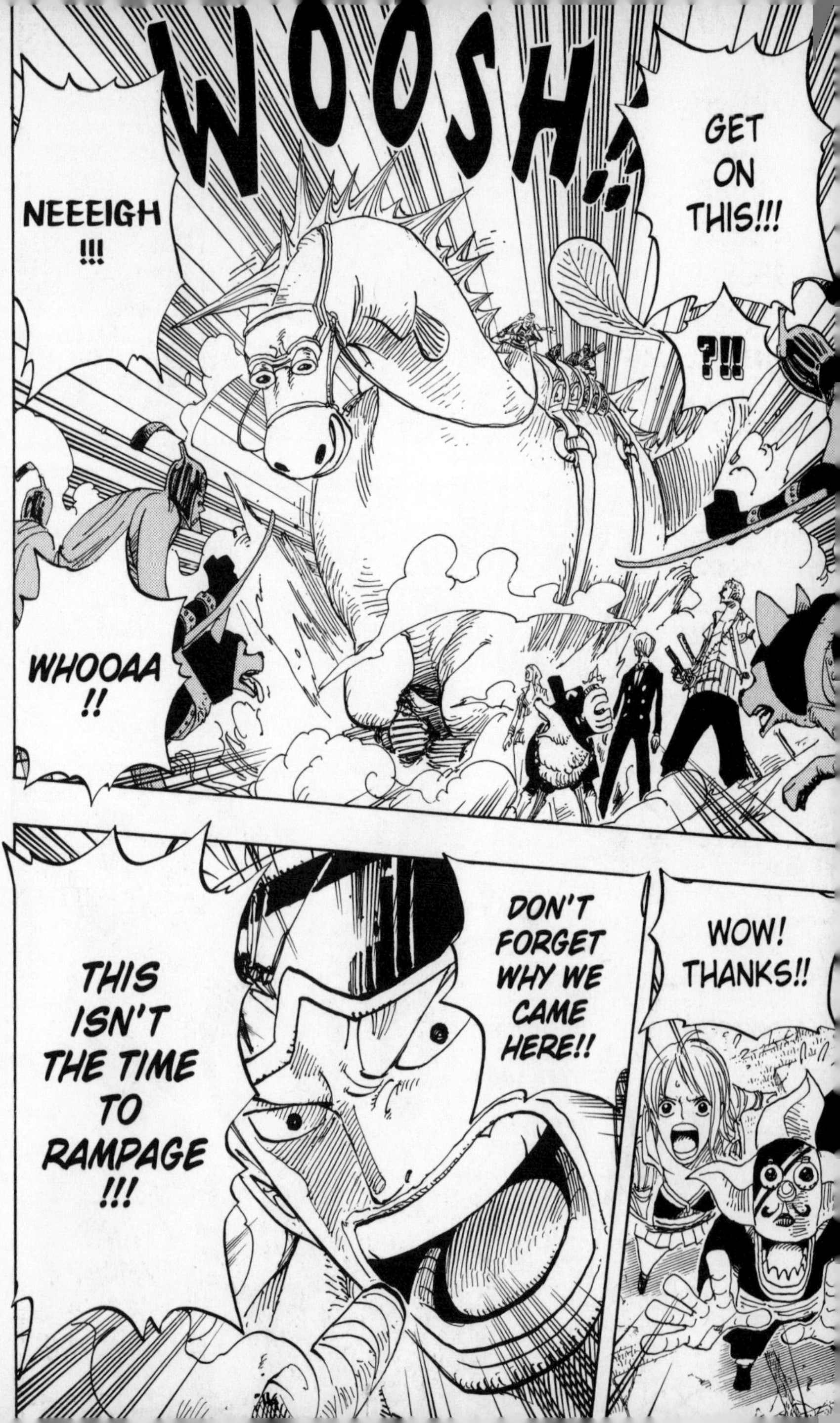
GET ON THIS!!!
WOOSH
?!!
NEEEIGH!!!
WHOOAA!!
WOW! THANKS!!
DON'T FORGET WHY WE CAME HERE!!
THIS ISN'T THE TIME TO RAMPAGE!!!

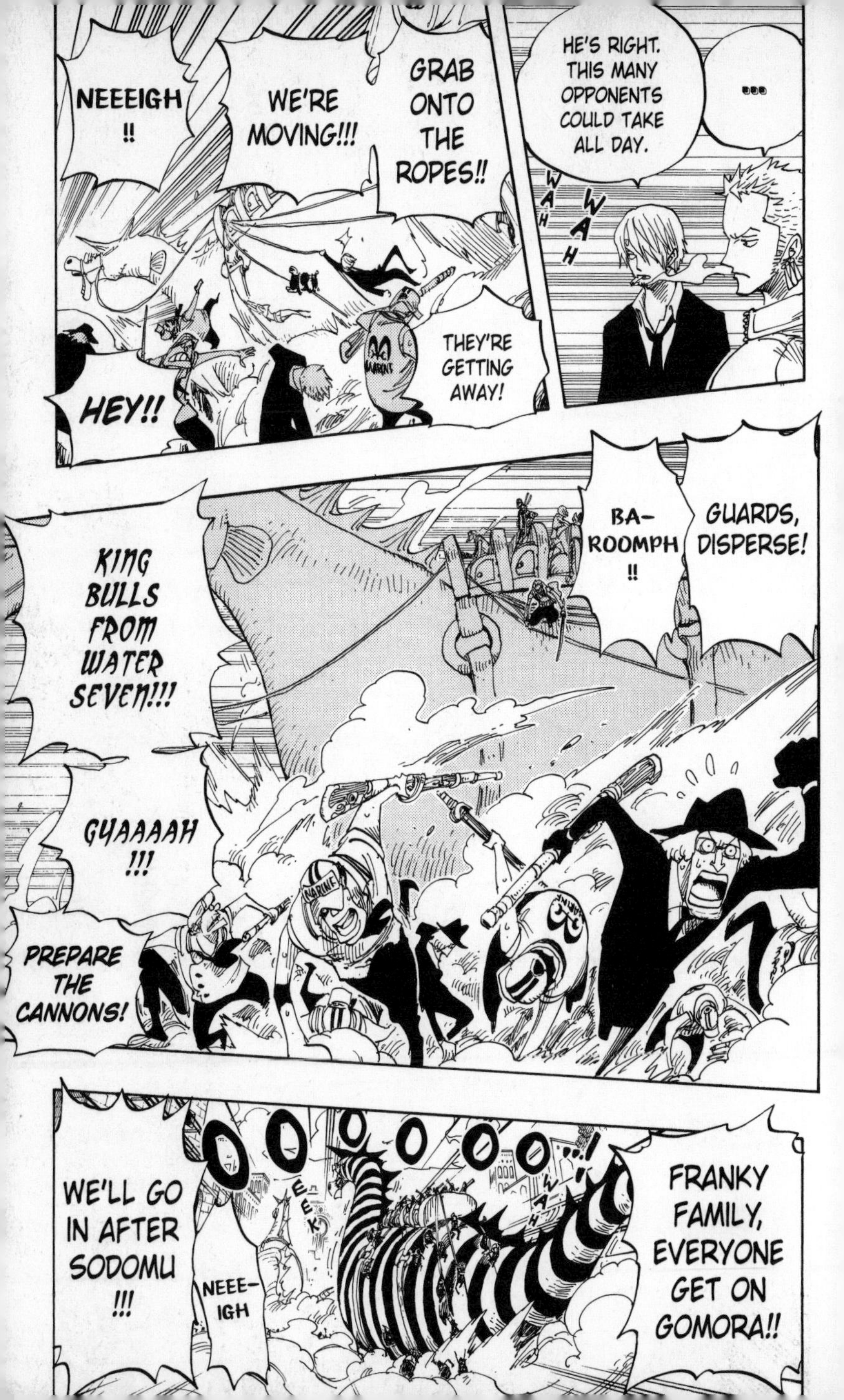
...
HE'S RIGHT. THIS MANY OPPONENTS COULD TAKE ALL DAY.
WAH
WAH
GRAB ONTO THE ROPES!!
WE'RE MOVING!!!
NEEEIGH !!
THEY'RE GETTING AWAY!
HEY!!
GUARDS, DISPERSE!
BA-ROOMPH !!
KING BULLS FROM WATER SEVEN!!!
GYAAAAH !!!
PREPARE THE CANNONS!
FRANKY FAMILY, EVERYONE GET ON GOMORA!!
OOOOOO!
WAH
EEK
NEEE-IGH
WE'LL GO IN AFTER SODOMU !!!

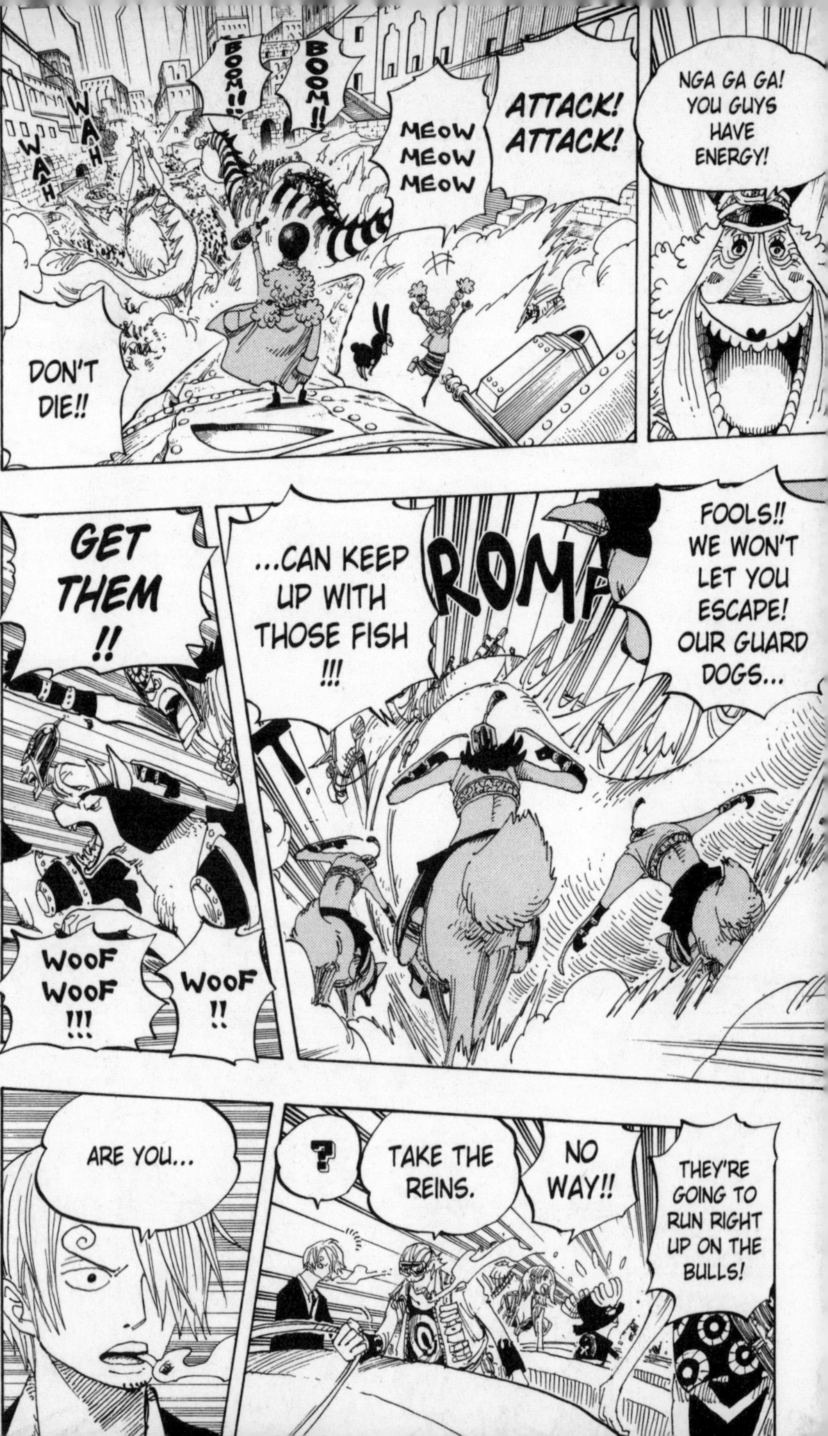
NGA GA GA! YOU GUYS HAVE ENERGY!
ATTACK! ATTACK!
MEOW MEOW MEOW
BOOM!!
BOOM!!
WAH
WAH
DON'T DIE!!
FOOLS!! WE WON'T LET YOU ESCAPE! OUR GUARD DOGS...
ROMP
...CAN KEEP UP WITH THOSE FISH!!!
GET THEM!!
WOOF!!
WOOF WOOF!!!
THEY'RE GOING TO RUN RIGHT UP ON THE BULLS!
NO WAY!!
TAKE THE REINS.
?
ARE YOU...

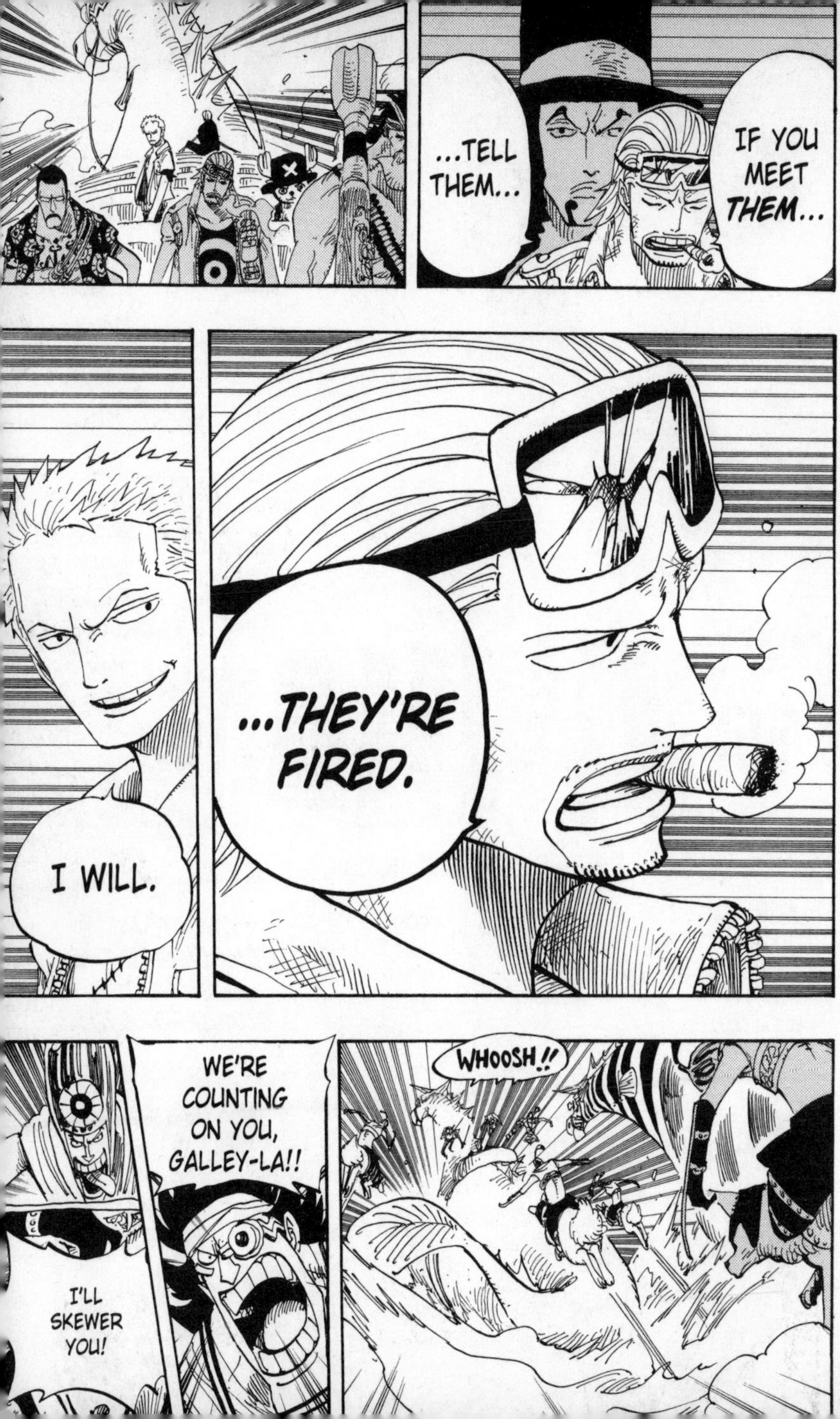
IF YOU MEET THEM...
...TELL THEM...
...THEY'RE FIRED.
I WILL.
WHOOSH!!
WE'RE COUNTING ON YOU, GALLEY-LA!!
I'LL SKEWER YOU!

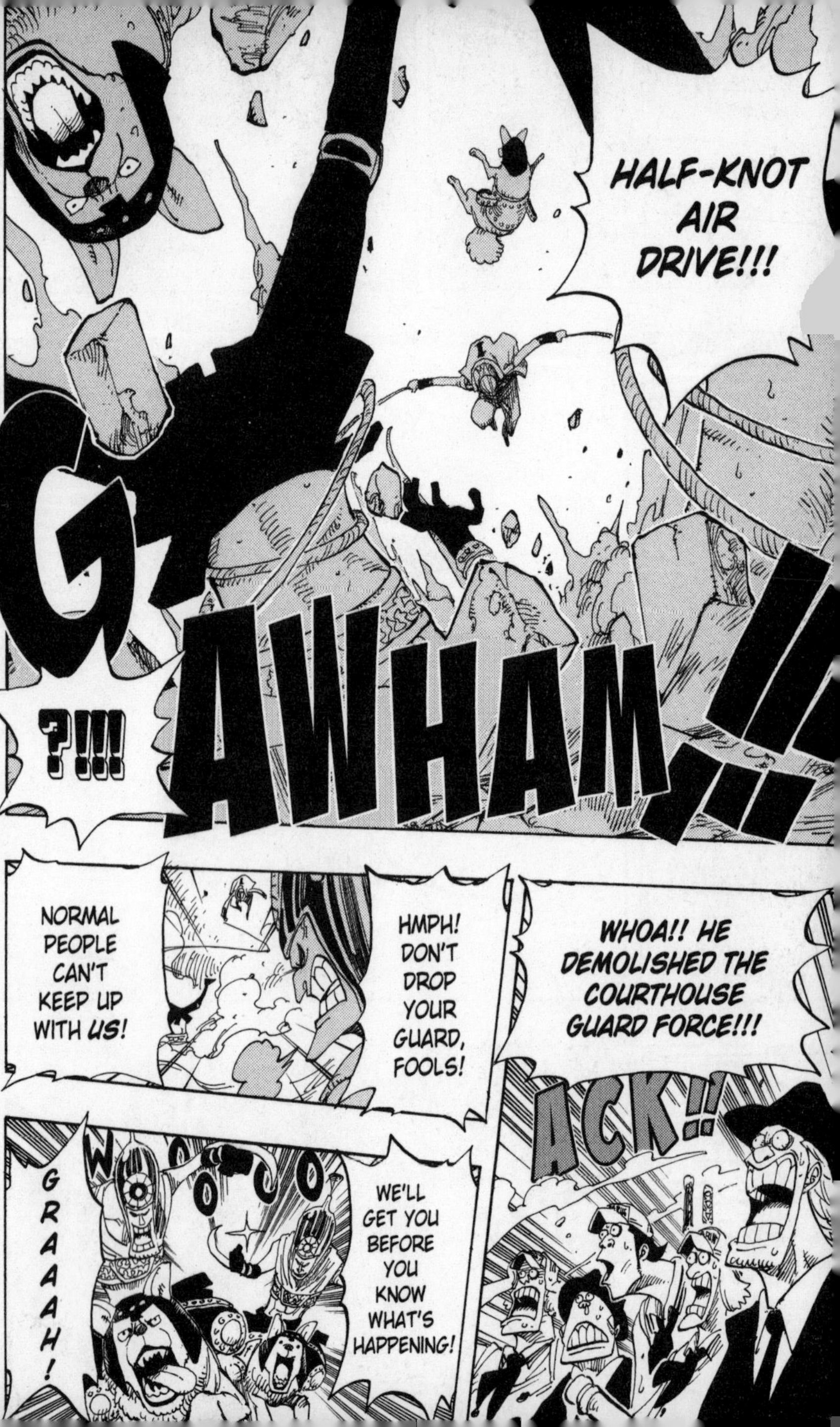

HALF-KNOT AIR DRIVE!!!
GAWHAM!!!
?!!!
WHOA!! HE DEMOLISHED THE COURTHOUSE GUARD FORCE!!!
ACK!!
HMPH! DON'T DROP YOUR GUARD, FOOLS!
NORMAL PEOPLE CAN'T KEEP UP WITH *US*!
WE'LL GET YOU BEFORE YOU KNOW WHAT'S HAPPENING!
GRAAAH!

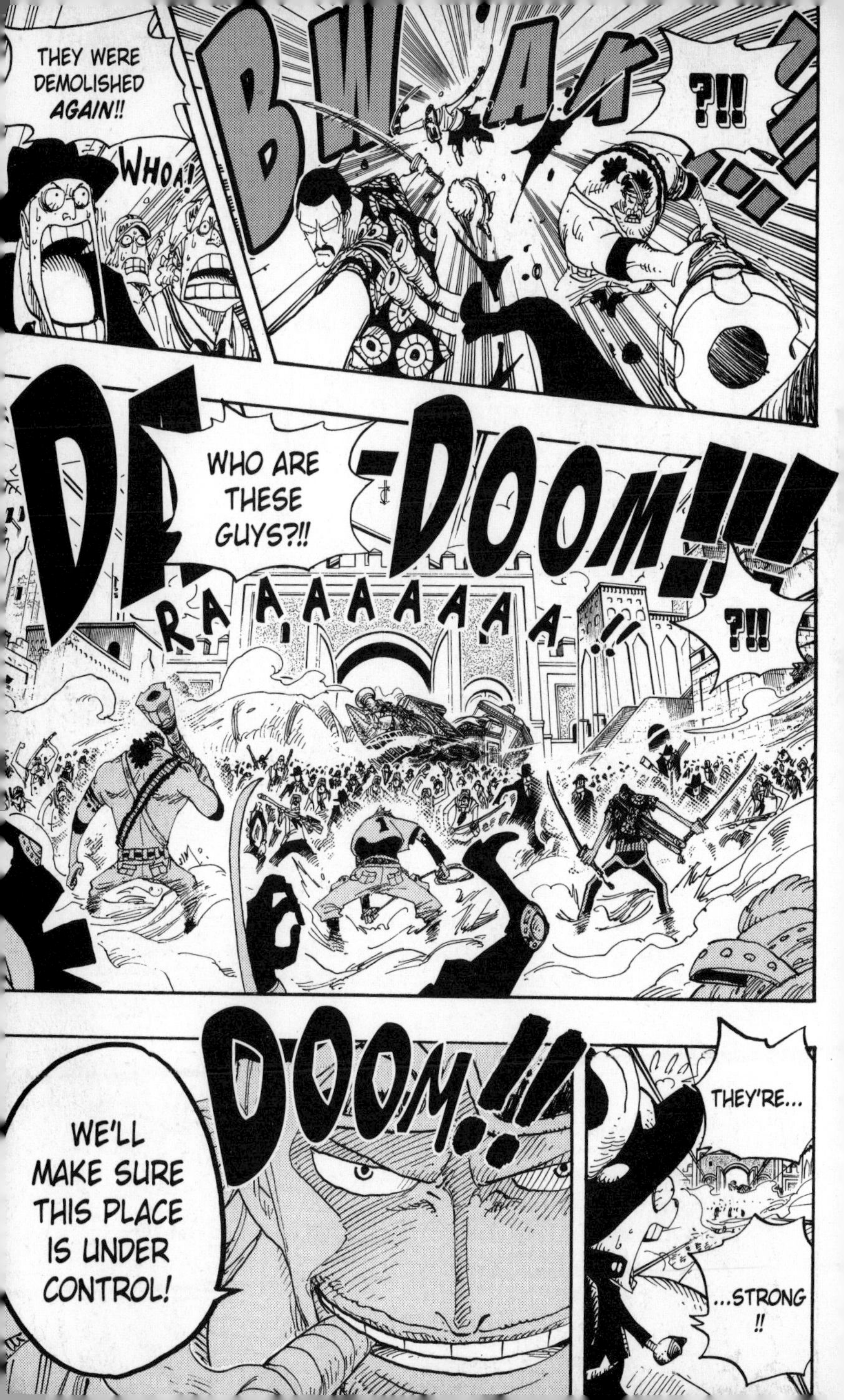

BWAA
?!!
THEY WERE DEMOLISHED AGAIN!!
WHOA!
DE-DOOM!!!
WHO ARE THESE GUYS?!!
RAAAAAAAA!!
?!!
THEY'RE...
...STRONG!!
DOOM!!
WE'LL MAKE SURE THIS PLACE IS UNDER CONTROL!

Question Corner
SBS

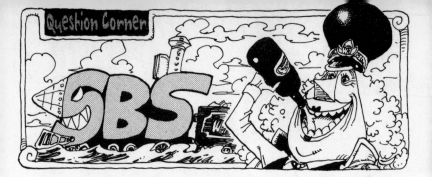

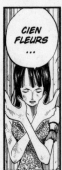

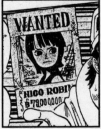

Q: ***CHAK!!!*** Busty lady lover!! (*KOFF*… Excuse me.) ***KLAK…*** ***CHAK SMAK*** ♡ (I blew you a kiss.) ***KLIK***

--Marimo

A: Whoa. This girl's getting rebellious. Well, what're you boys gonna do?! Just leave it to me! I'll say it on behalf of everyone. What are you saying?! I'm a children's manga author! **Dreams never die!!!** (I just sounded cool again.)

Q: Hello Odacchi! I always enjoy *One Piece*! But!! I always wonder what language the names of Robin's powers—like Cien Fleurs and Seis Fleurs—come from. Please let me know! ('Kay?)

--Peh

CIEN FLEURS …

A: Cien=100. Seis=6. The numbers are from Spanish. Fleur means flower in French. Some, like Clutch, are from English. It's all mixed up, but if it sounds good, it works for me.

Q: Dear Oda Sensei, aren't you going to tell us about Robin's past? Robin: "Cinco Fleurs!!"

--Namiin

WANTED
NICO ROBI

A: Yikes! I barely missed that attack by Robin. Her past? It seems like lots of readers are wondering about that. I'm working on it! Right now!! It'll be in the next volume. I'll do my best.

Chapter 382:
DEMON LAIR

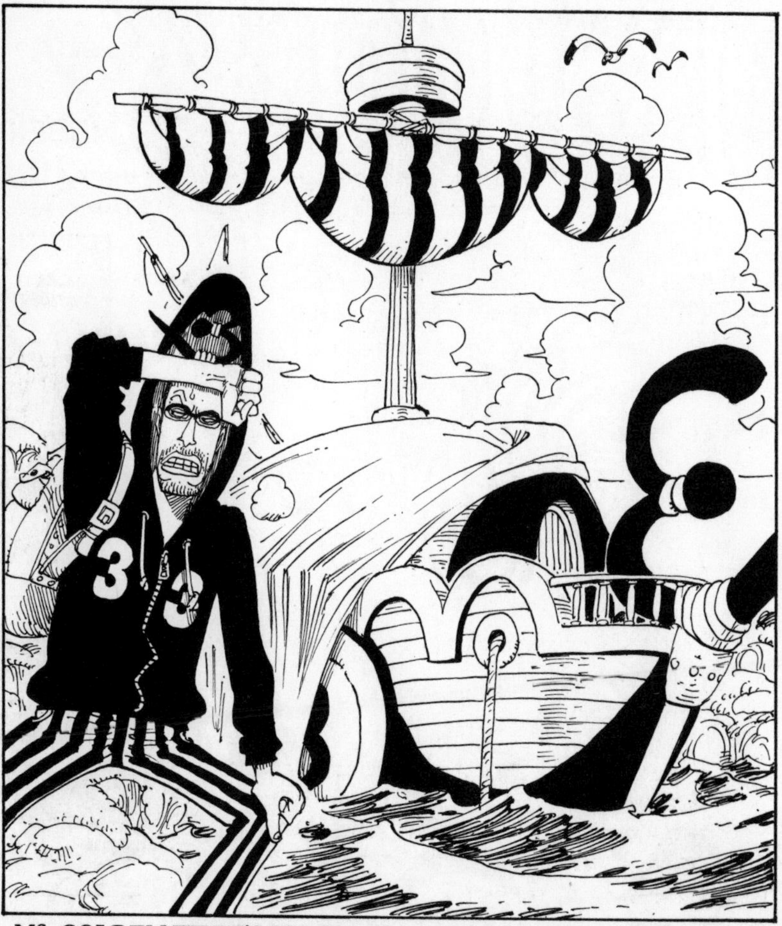

MS. GOLDEN WEEK'S BIG PLAN, A BAROQUE REUNION, VOL. 18:
"ESCAPEE FROM KYUKA ISLAND"

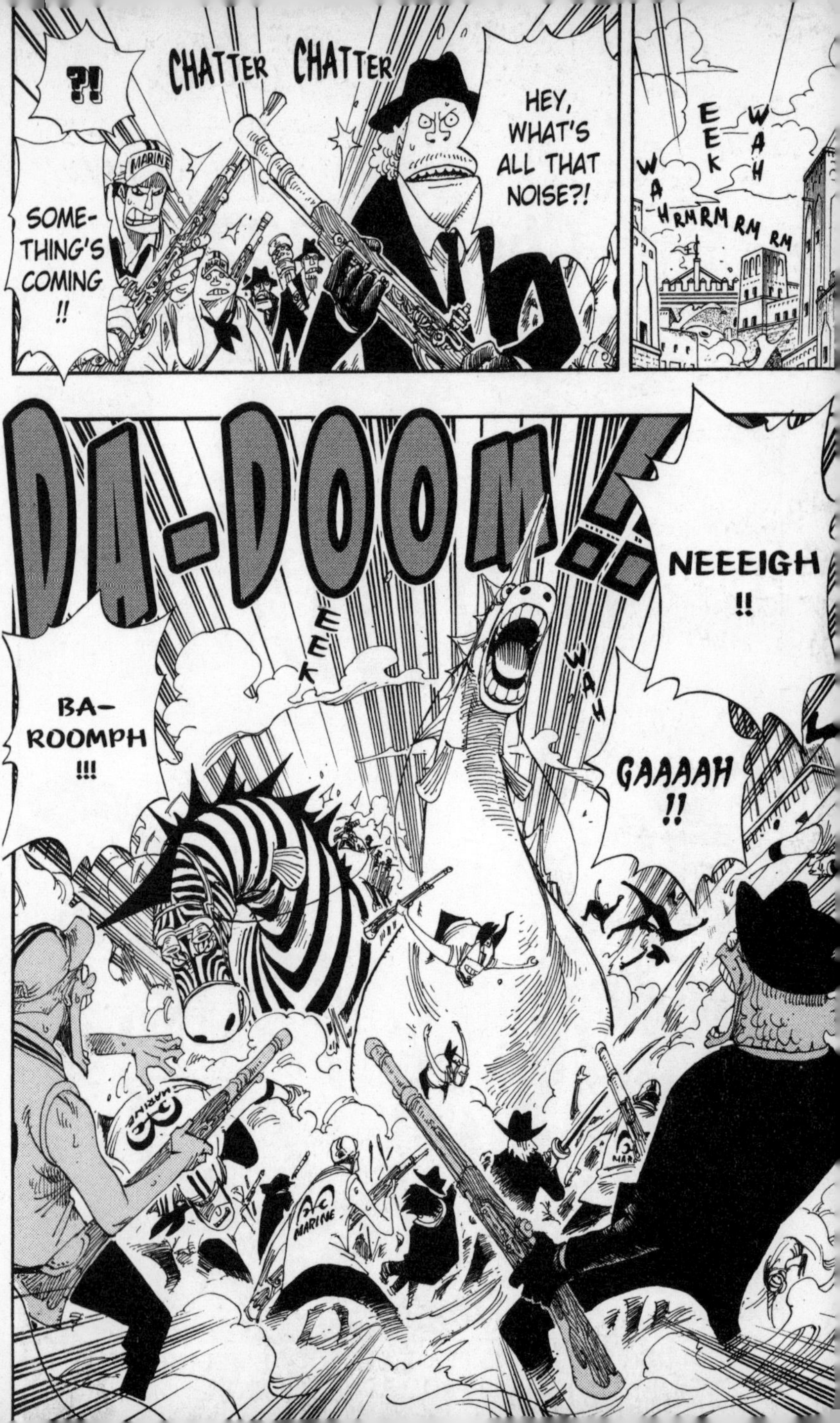
WAH
EEK
WAH
RMRM RM RM
HEY, WHAT'S ALL THAT NOISE?!
CHATTER CHATTER
?!
SOME-THING'S COMING!!
DA-DOOM!!
NEEEIGH!!
WAH
EEK
GAAAAH!!
BA-ROOMPH!!!
MARINE

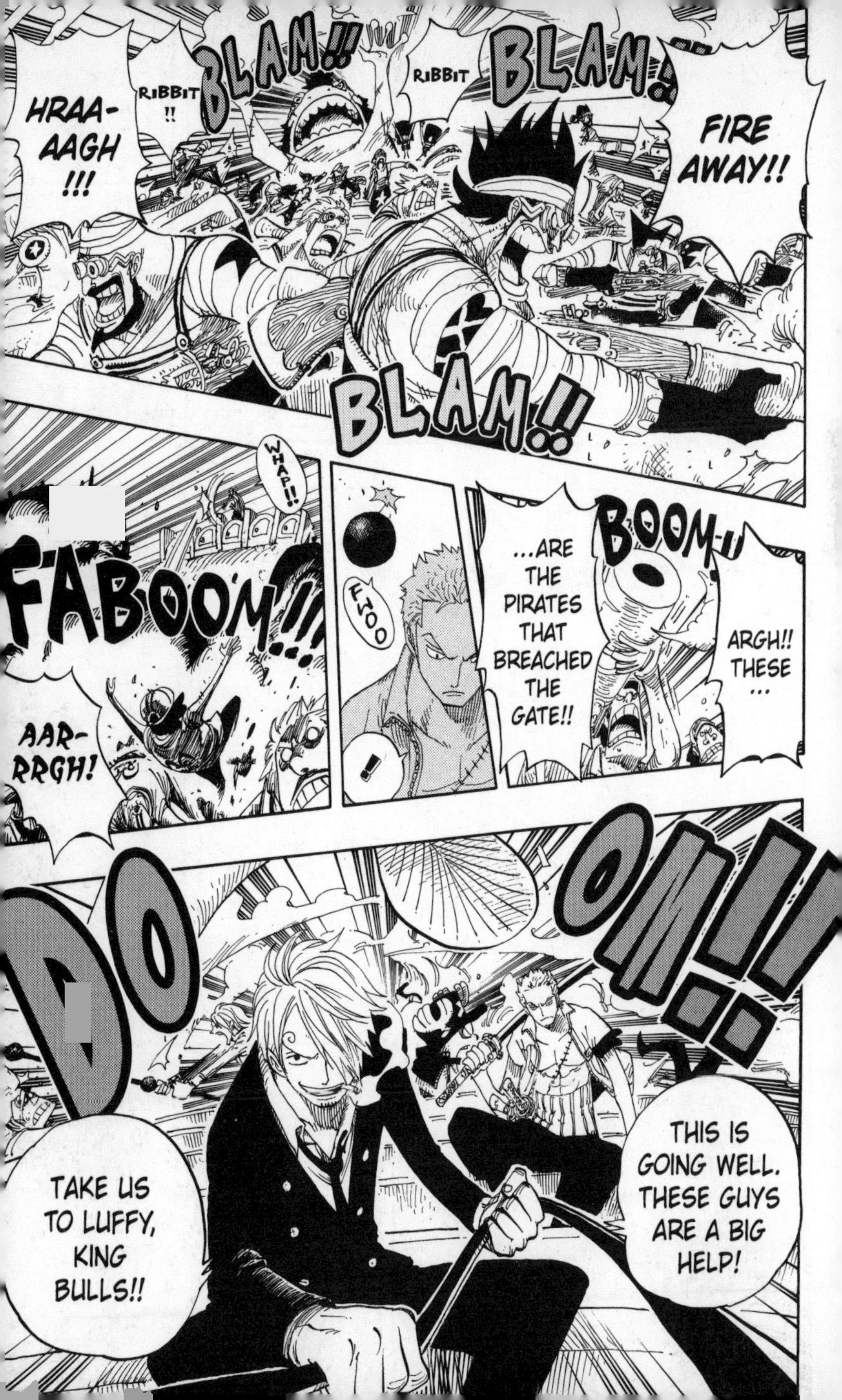
FIRE AWAY!!
BLAM!!
RIBBIT
BLAM!!
RIBBIT!!
HRAA-AAGH!!!
BLAM!!
BOOM!!
ARGH!! THESE ...
...ARE THE PIRATES THAT BREACHED THE GATE!!
FWOO
!
WHAP!!
FABOOM!!!
AAR-RRGH!
DOOM!!
THIS IS GOING WELL. THESE GUYS ARE A BIG HELP!
TAKE US TO LUFFY, KING BULLS!!

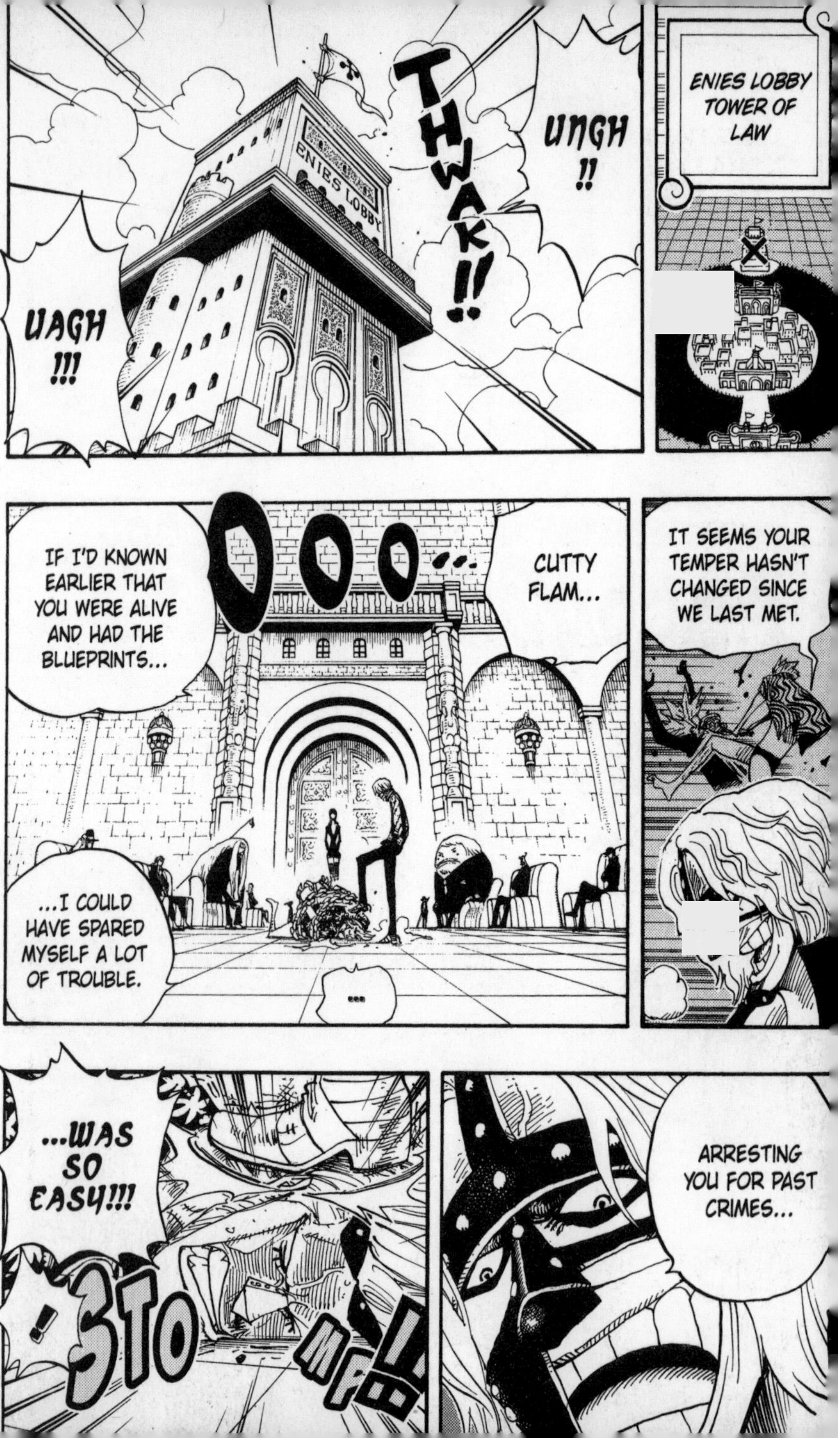
ENIES LOBBY TOWER OF LAW
ENIES LOBBY
THWAK!!
UNGH!!
UAGH!!!
IT SEEMS YOUR TEMPER HASN'T CHANGED SINCE WE LAST MET.
CUTTY FLAM...
IF I'D KNOWN EARLIER THAT YOU WERE ALIVE AND HAD THE BLUEPRINTS...
...I COULD HAVE SPARED MYSELF A LOT OF TROUBLE.
...
ARRESTING YOU FOR PAST CRIMES...
...WAS SO EASY!!!
STOMP!!

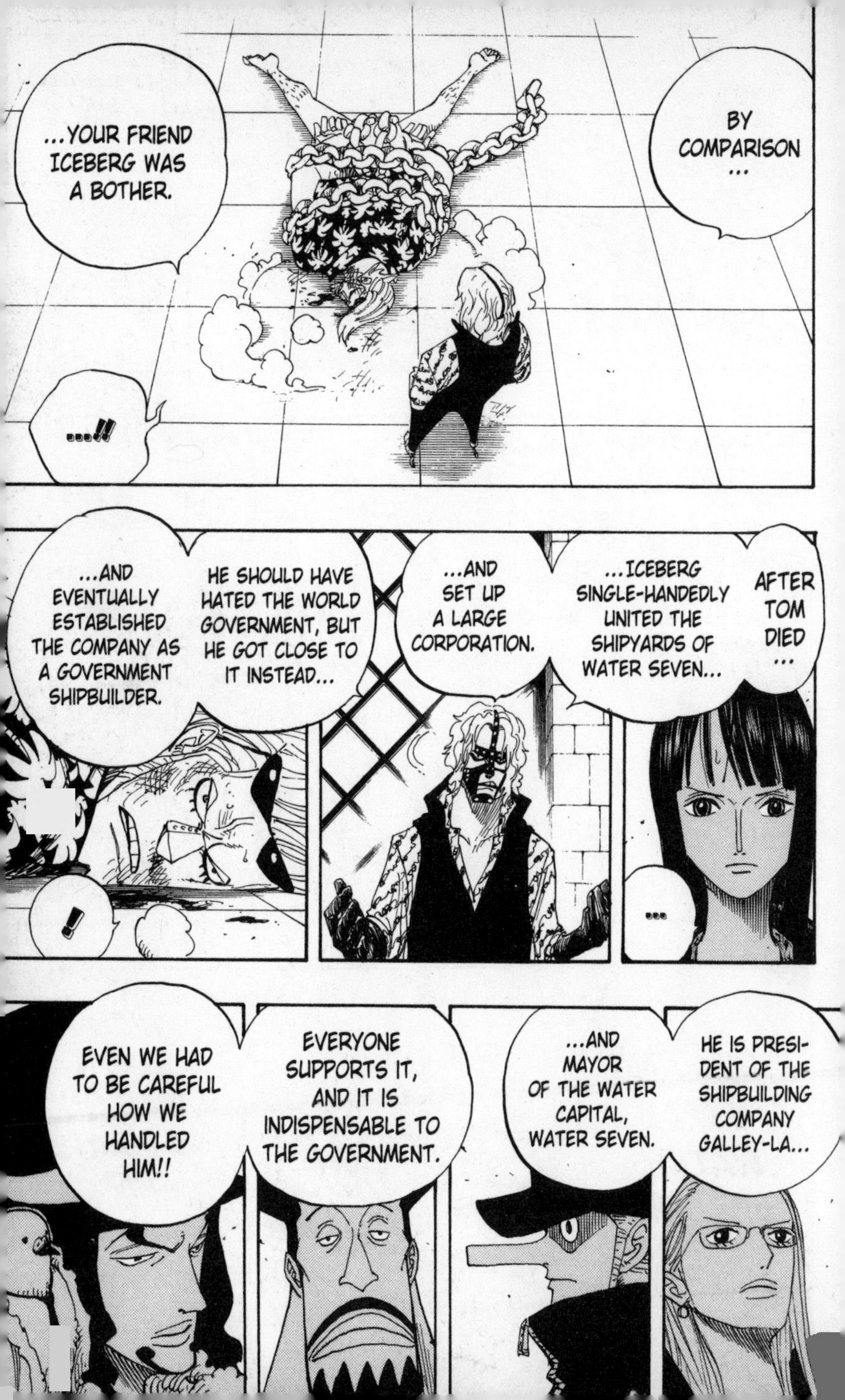
BY COMPARISON ...
...YOUR FRIEND ICEBERG WAS A BOTHER.
...!!
AFTER TOM DIED ...
...ICEBERG SINGLE-HANDEDLY UNITED THE SHIPYARDS OF WATER SEVEN...
...
...AND SET UP A LARGE CORPORATION.
HE SHOULD HAVE HATED THE WORLD GOVERNMENT, BUT HE GOT CLOSE TO IT INSTEAD...
...AND EVENTUALLY ESTABLISHED THE COMPANY AS A GOVERNMENT SHIPBUILDER.
!
HE IS PRESIDENT OF THE SHIPBUILDING COMPANY GALLEY-LA...
...AND MAYOR OF THE WATER CAPITAL, WATER SEVEN.
EVERYONE SUPPORTS IT, AND IT IS INDISPENSABLE TO THE GOVERNMENT.
EVEN WE HAD TO BE CAREFUL HOW WE HANDLED HIM!!

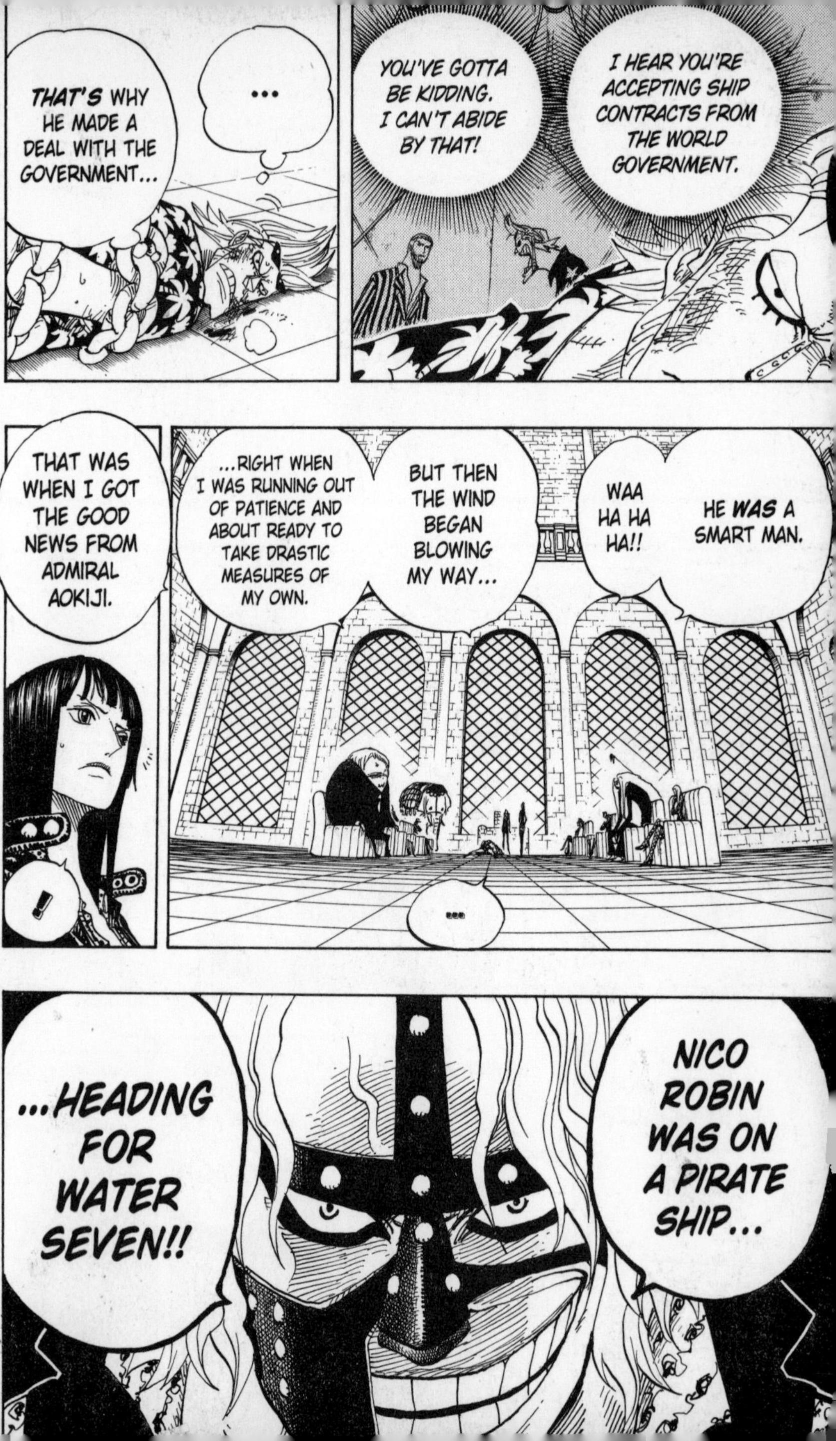
I HEAR YOU'RE ACCEPTING SHIP CONTRACTS FROM THE WORLD GOVERNMENT.
YOU'VE GOTTA BE KIDDING. I CAN'T ABIDE BY THAT!
...
THAT'S WHY HE MADE A DEAL WITH THE GOVERNMENT...
HE WAS A SMART MAN.
WAA HA HA HA!!
BUT THEN THE WIND BEGAN BLOWING MY WAY...
...RIGHT WHEN I WAS RUNNING OUT OF PATIENCE AND ABOUT READY TO TAKE DRASTIC MEASURES OF MY OWN.
...
THAT WAS WHEN I GOT THE GOOD NEWS FROM ADMIRAL AOKIJI.
!
NICO ROBIN WAS ON A PIRATE SHIP...
...HEADING FOR WATER SEVEN!!

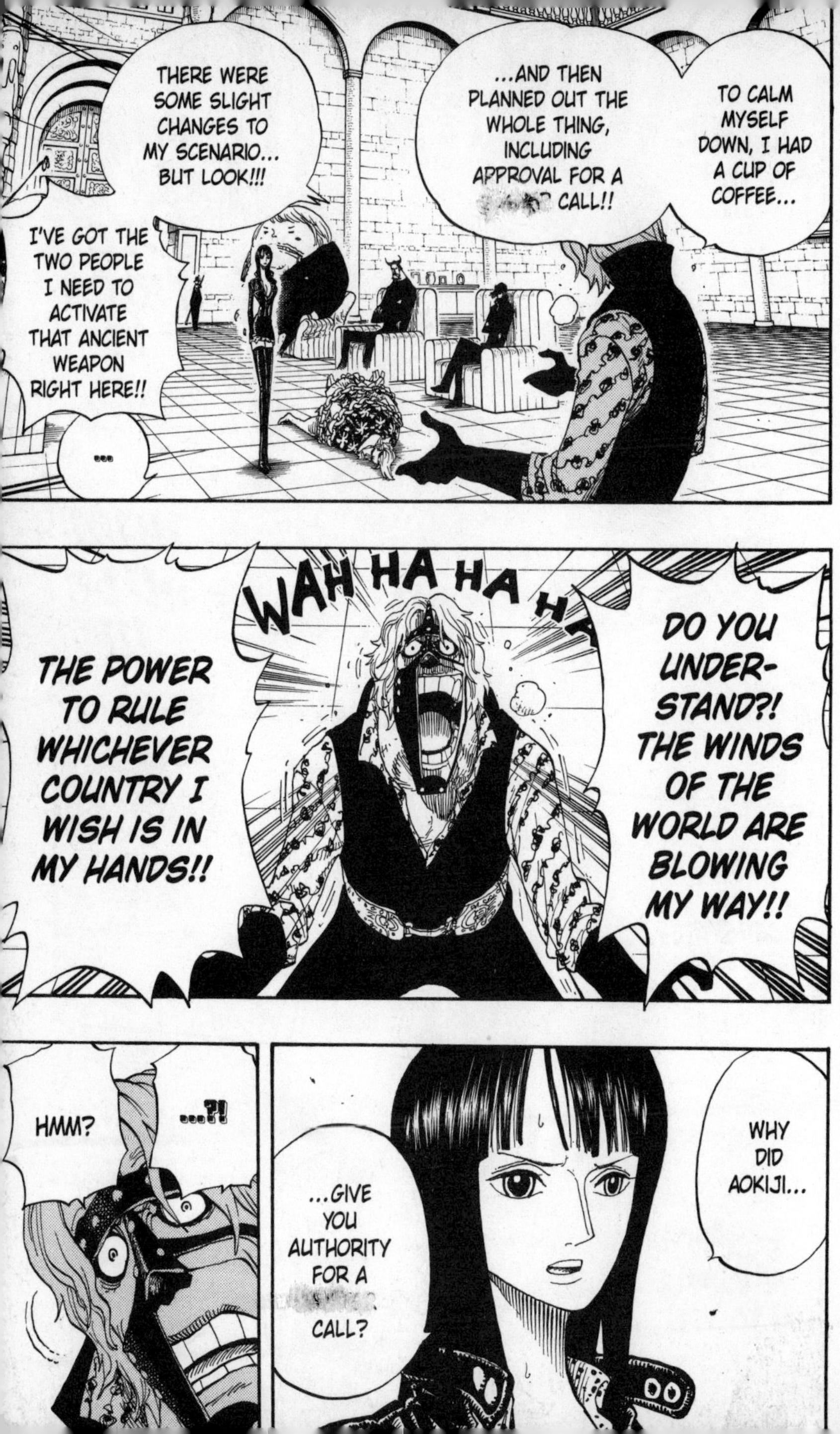
TO CALM MYSELF DOWN, I HAD A CUP OF COFFEE...
...AND THEN PLANNED OUT THE WHOLE THING, INCLUDING APPROVAL FOR A CALL!!
THERE WERE SOME SLIGHT CHANGES TO MY SCENARIO... BUT LOOK!!!
I'VE GOT THE TWO PEOPLE I NEED TO ACTIVATE THAT ANCIENT WEAPON RIGHT HERE!!
...
WAH HA HA HA
DO YOU UNDER-STAND?! THE WINDS OF THE WORLD ARE BLOWING MY WAY!!
THE POWER TO RULE WHICHEVER COUNTRY I WISH IS IN MY HANDS!!
WHY DID AOKIJI...
...GIVE YOU AUTHORITY FOR A CALL?
...?!
HMM?

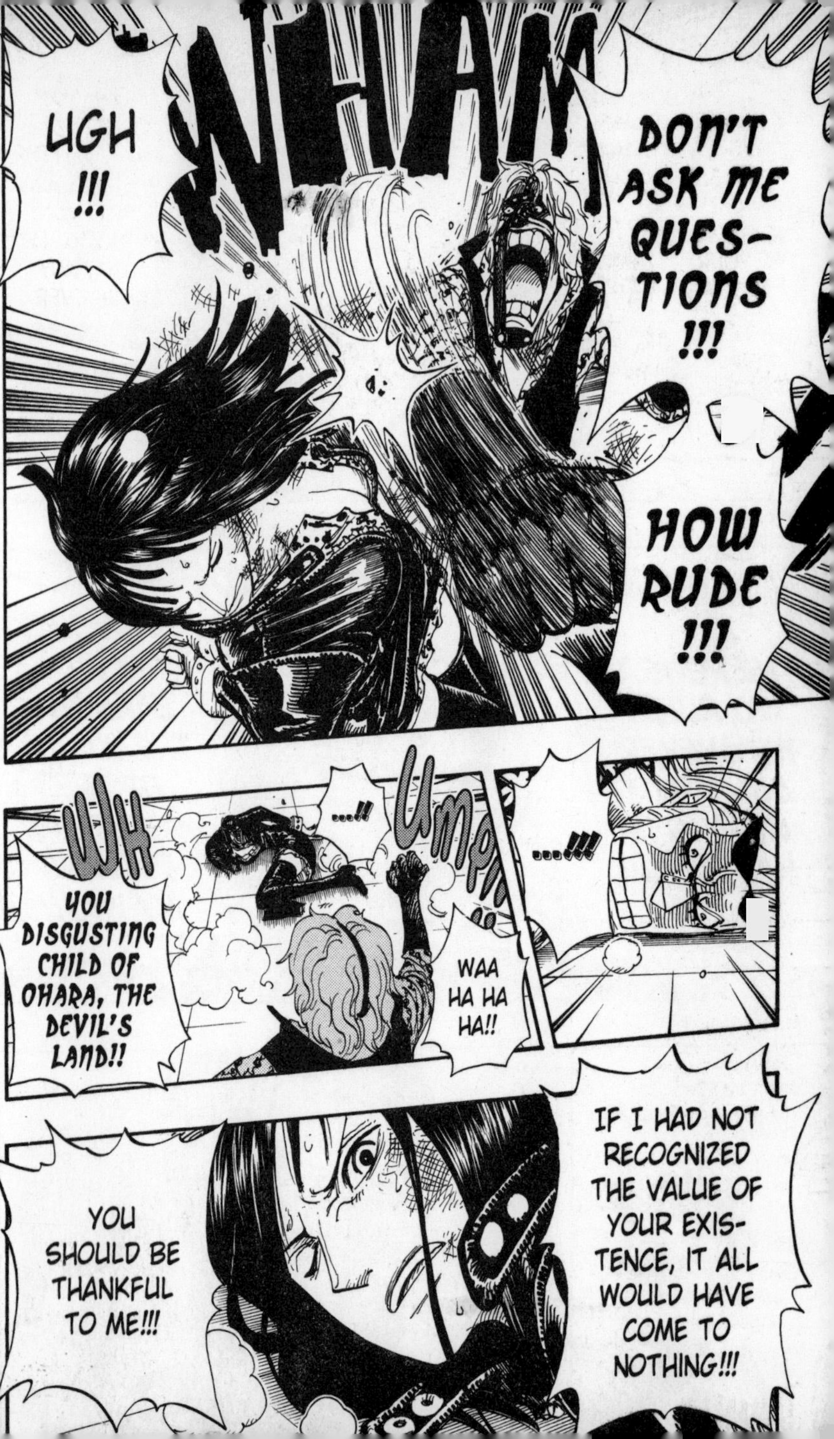
WHAM
DON'T ASK ME QUES-TIONS!!!
HOW RUDE!!!
UGH!!!
...!!!
...!!
WHUMP
WAA HA HA HA!!
YOU DISGUSTING CHILD OF OHARA, THE DEVIL'S LAND!!
IF I HAD NOT RECOGNIZED THE VALUE OF YOUR EXIS-TENCE, IT ALL WOULD HAVE COME TO NOTHING!!!
YOU SHOULD BE THANKFUL TO ME!!!

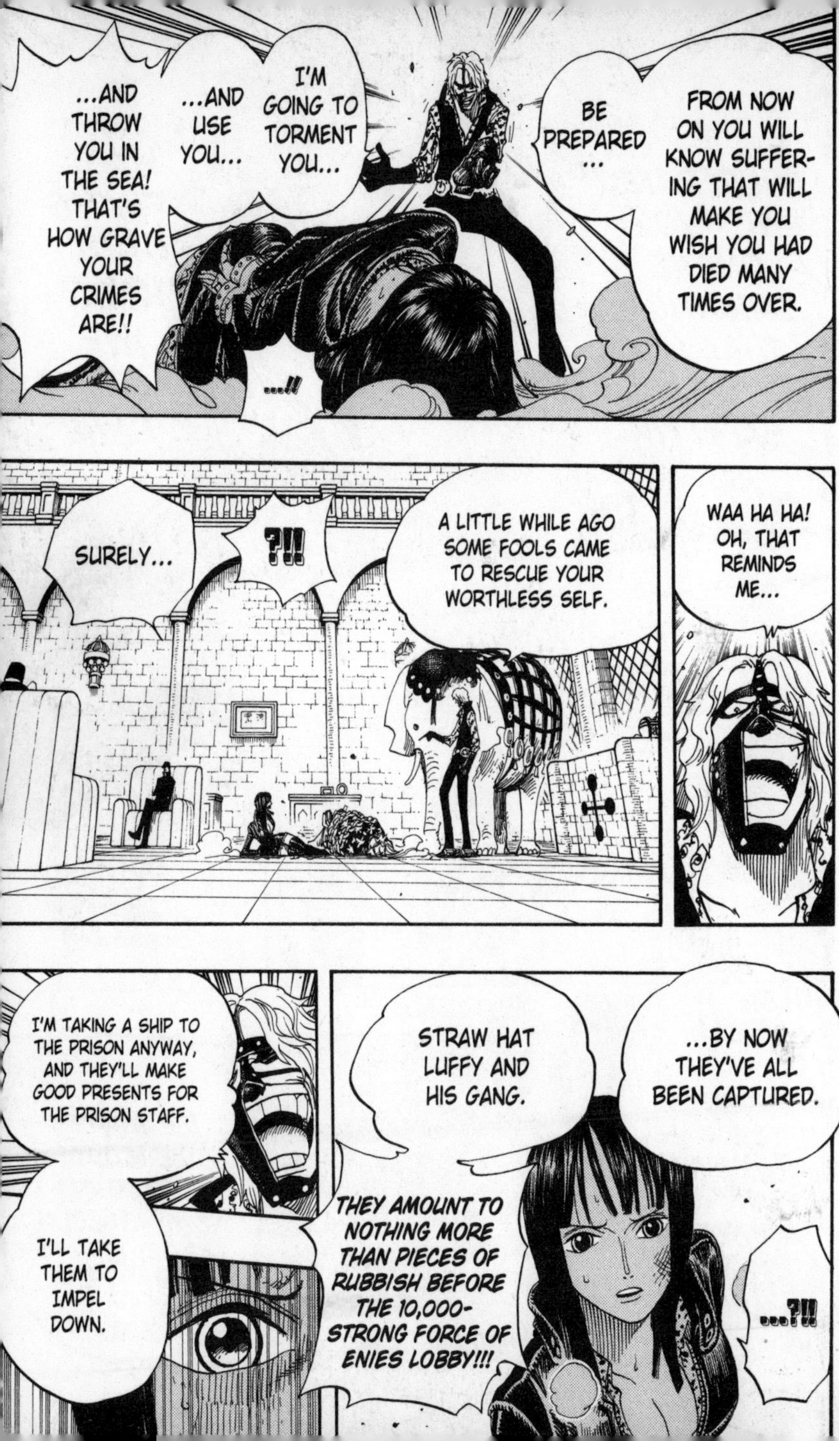
FROM NOW ON YOU WILL KNOW SUFFERING THAT WILL MAKE YOU WISH YOU HAD DIED MANY TIMES OVER.
BE PREPARED...
I'M GOING TO TORMENT YOU...
...AND USE YOU...
...AND THROW YOU IN THE SEA! THAT'S HOW GRAVE YOUR CRIMES ARE!!
...!!
WAA HA HA! OH, THAT REMINDS ME...
A LITTLE WHILE AGO SOME FOOLS CAME TO RESCUE YOUR WORTHLESS SELF.
?!!
SURELY...
...BY NOW THEY'VE ALL BEEN CAPTURED.
STRAW HAT LUFFY AND HIS GANG.
THEY AMOUNT TO NOTHING MORE THAN PIECES OF RUBBISH BEFORE THE 10,000-STRONG FORCE OF ENIES LOBBY!!!
...?!!
I'M TAKING A SHIP TO THE PRISON ANYWAY, AND THEY'LL MAKE GOOD PRESENTS FOR THE PRISON STAFF.
I'LL TAKE THEM TO IMPEL DOWN.

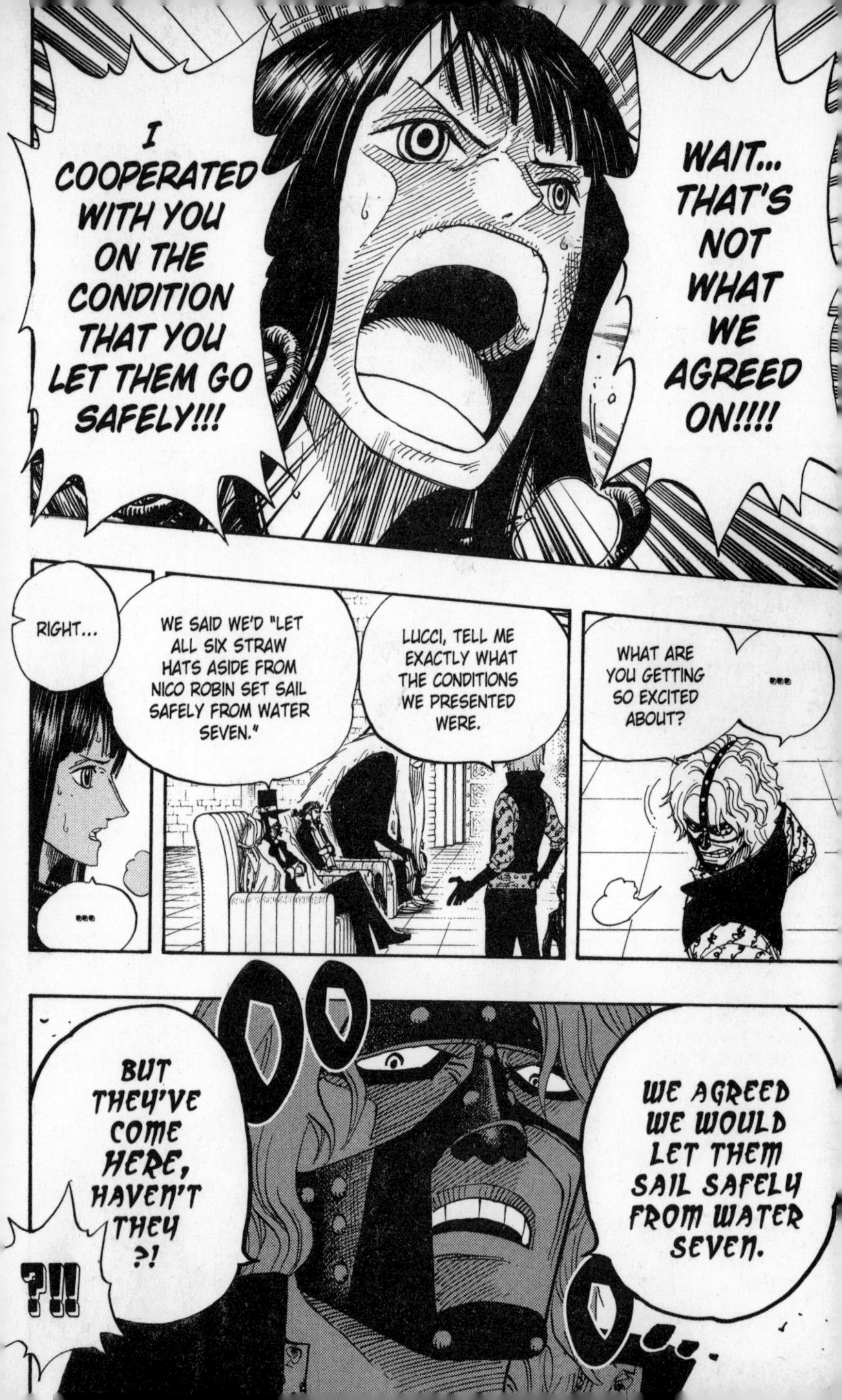
WAIT... THAT'S NOT WHAT WE AGREED ON!!!!
I COOPERATED WITH YOU ON THE CONDITION THAT YOU LET THEM GO SAFELY!!!
...
WHAT ARE YOU GETTING SO EXCITED ABOUT?
LUCCI, TELL ME EXACTLY WHAT THE CONDITIONS WE PRESENTED WERE.
RIGHT...
WE SAID WE'D "LET ALL SIX STRAW HATS ASIDE FROM NICO ROBIN SET SAIL SAFELY FROM WATER SEVEN."
...
WE AGREED WE WOULD LET THEM SAIL SAFELY FROM WATER SEVEN.
BUT THEY'VE COME HERE, HAVEN'T THEY?!
?!!

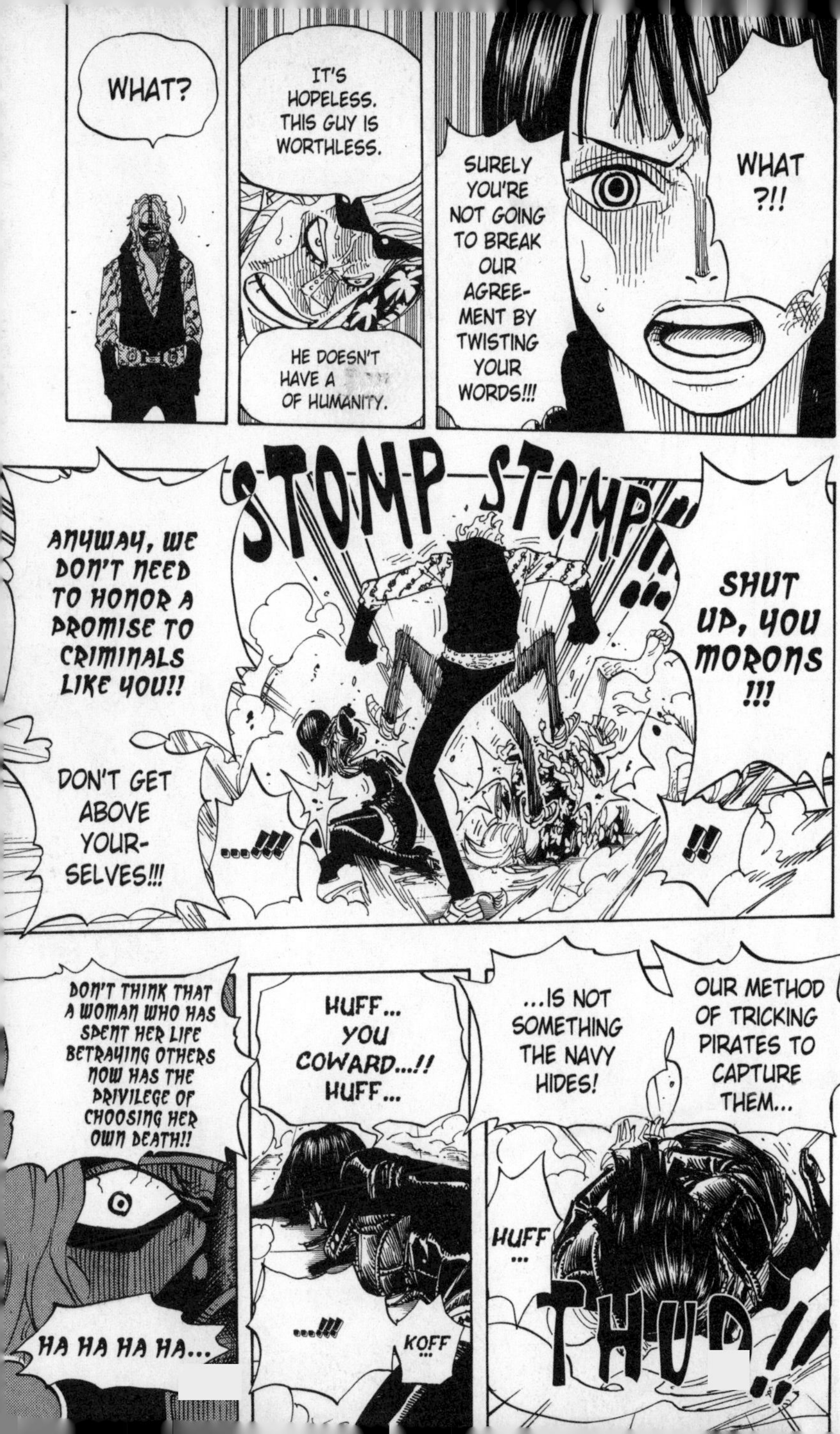
WHAT ?!!
SURELY YOU'RE NOT GOING TO BREAK OUR AGREE-MENT BY TWISTING YOUR WORDS!!!
IT'S HOPELESS. THIS GUY IS WORTHLESS.
HE DOESN'T HAVE A
OF HUMANITY.
WHAT?
STOMP STOMP
SHUT UP, YOU MORONS!!!
!!
ANYWAY, WE DON'T NEED TO HONOR A PROMISE TO CRIMINALS LIKE YOU!!
DON'T GET ABOVE YOUR-SELVES!!!
...!!!
OUR METHOD OF TRICKING PIRATES TO CAPTURE THEM...
...IS NOT SOMETHING THE NAVY HIDES!
HUFF...
THUD!!
HUFF... YOU COWARD...!! HUFF...
...!!!
KOFF...
DON'T THINK THAT A WOMAN WHO HAS SPENT HER LIFE BETRAYING OTHERS NOW HAS THE PRIVILEGE OF CHOOSING HER OWN DEATH!!
HA HA HA HA...

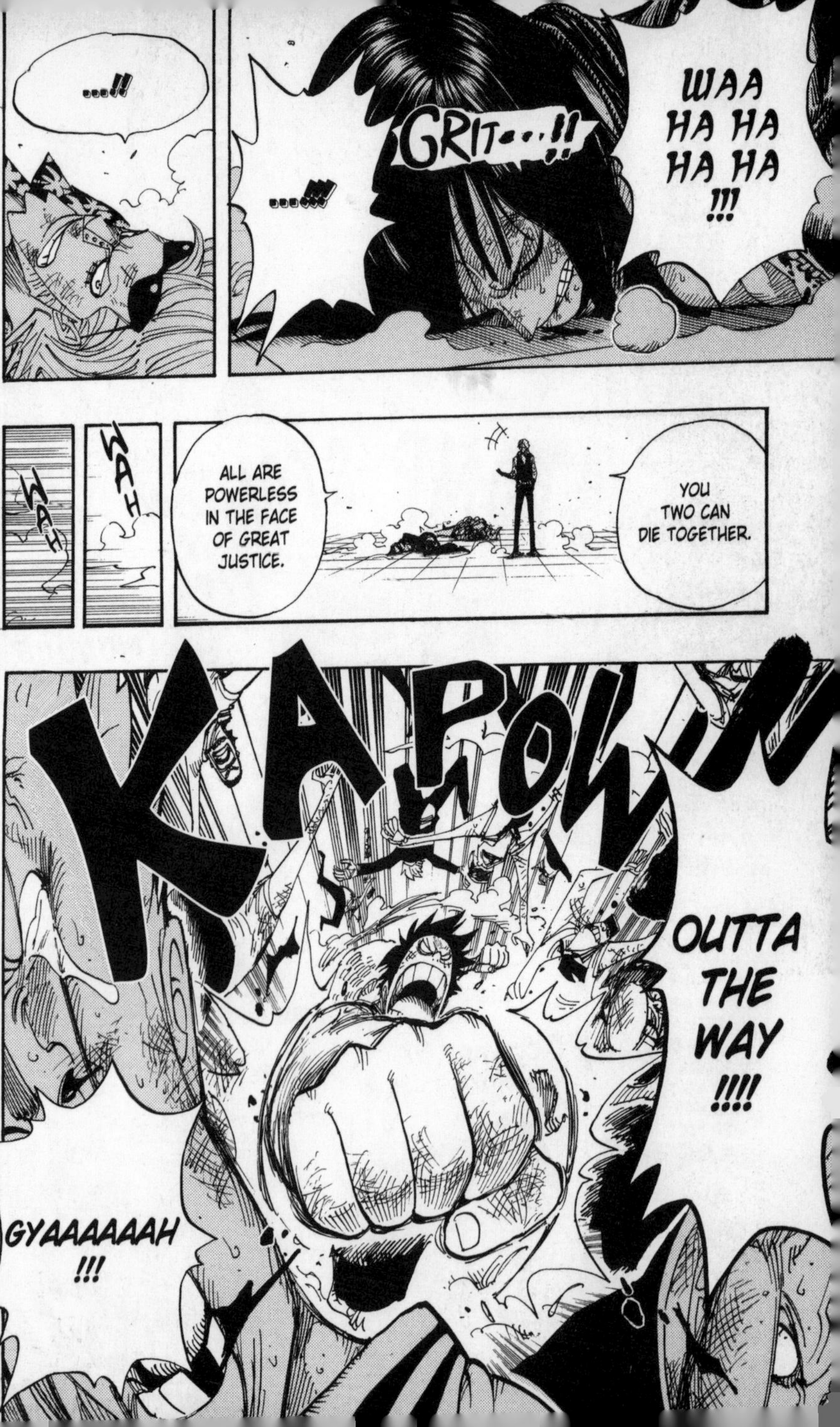
WAA HA HA HA HA !!!
GRIT...!!
...!!!
...!!
YOU TWO CAN DIE TOGETHER.
ALL ARE POWERLESS IN THE FACE OF GREAT JUSTICE.
WAH
WAH
KAPOW
OUTTA THE WAY !!!!
GYAAAAAAH !!!

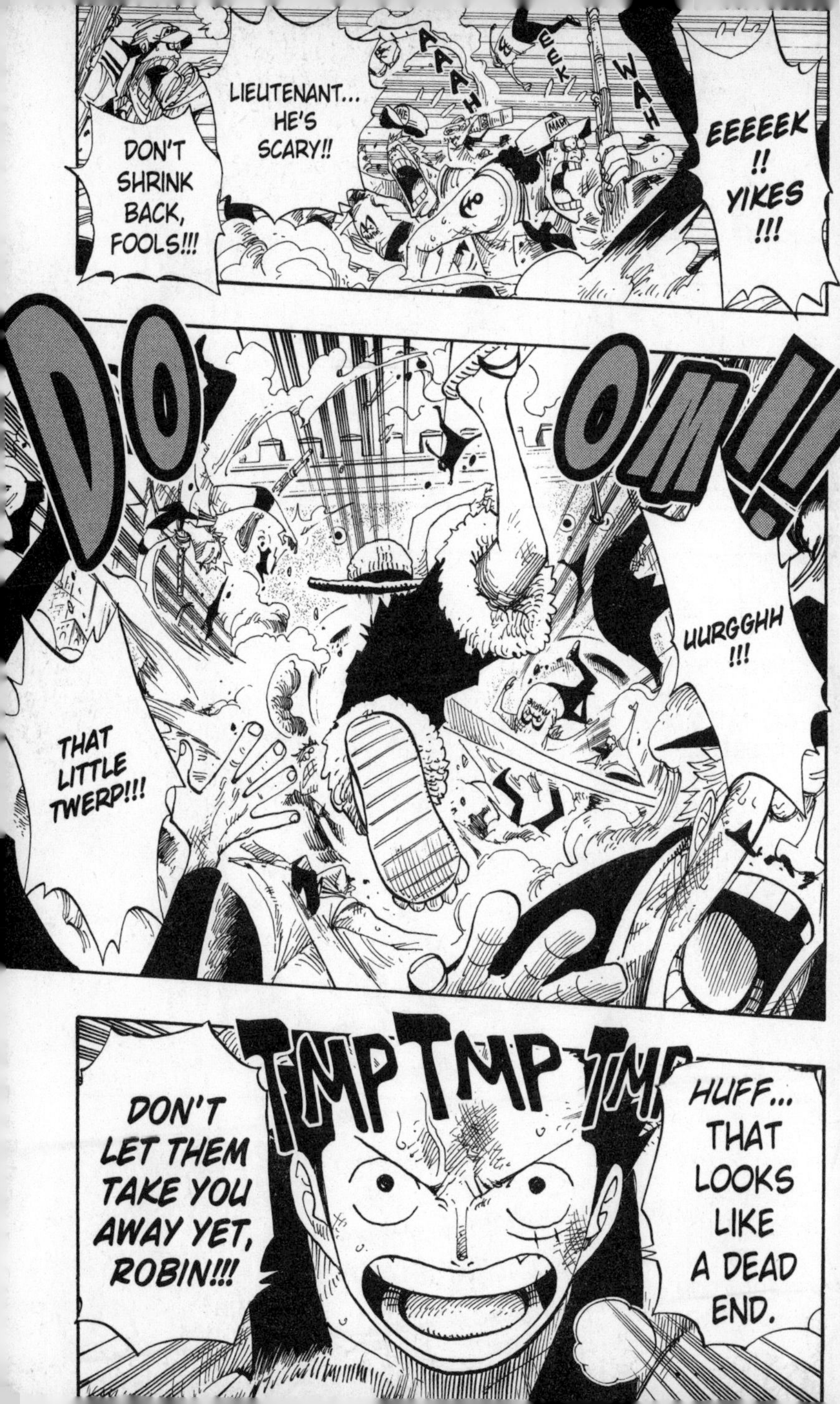
EEEEEK!! YIKES!!!
WAH
EEK
AAAH
LIEUTENANT... HE'S SCARY!!
DON'T SHRINK BACK, FOOLS!!!
DOOM!!
UURGGHH!!!
THAT LITTLE TWERP!!!
HUFF... THAT LOOKS LIKE A DEAD END.
TMP TMP TMP
DON'T LET THEM TAKE YOU AWAY YET, ROBIN!!!

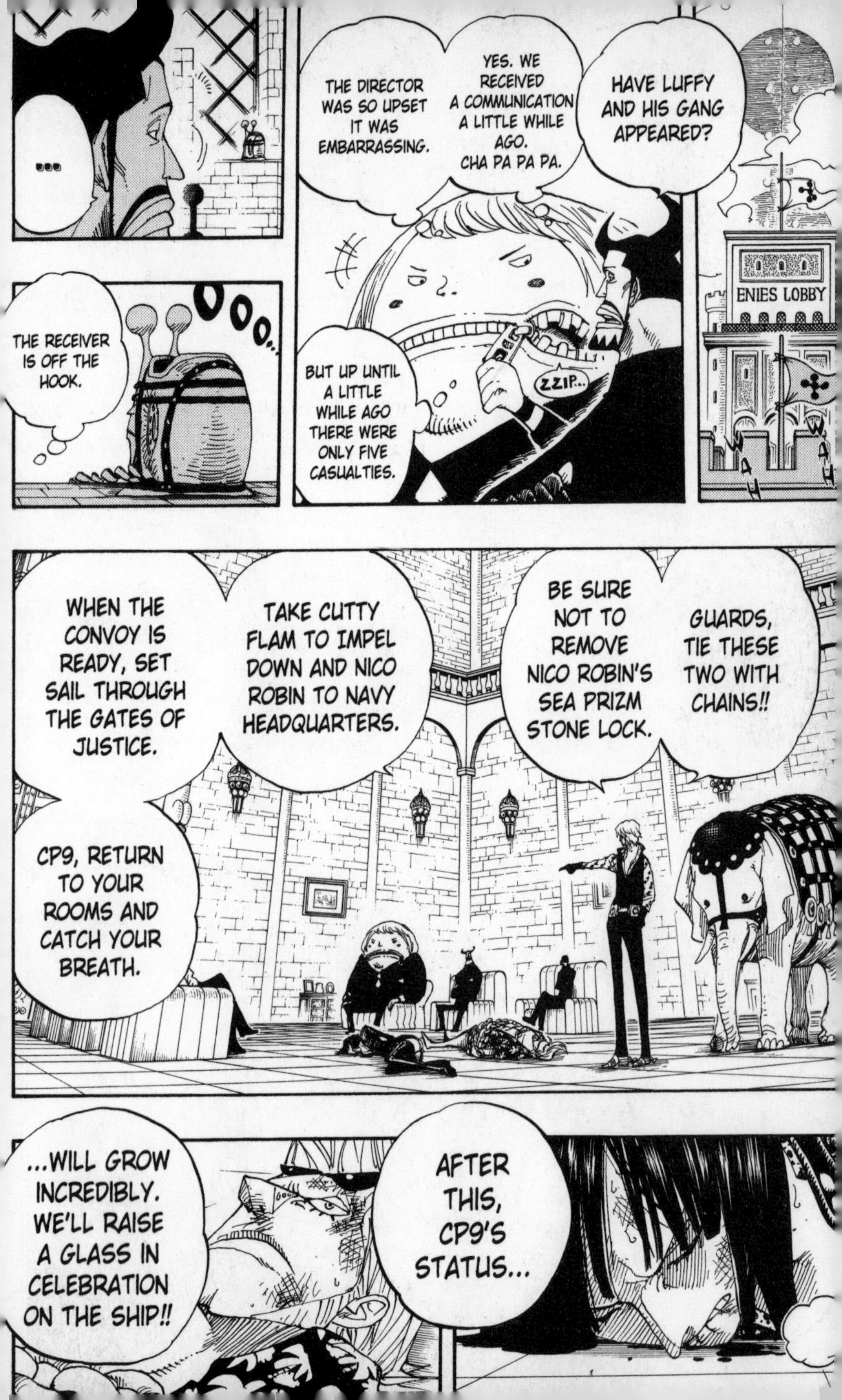
ENIES LOBBY
WAH
WAH
HAVE LUFFY AND HIS GANG APPEARED?
YES. WE RECEIVED A COMMUNICATION A LITTLE WHILE AGO. CHA PA PA PA.
THE DIRECTOR WAS SO UPSET IT WAS EMBARRASSING.
ZZIP...
BUT UP UNTIL A LITTLE WHILE AGO THERE WERE ONLY FIVE CASUALTIES.
...
OOO...
THE RECEIVER IS OFF THE HOOK.
GUARDS, TIE THESE TWO WITH CHAINS!!
BE SURE NOT TO REMOVE NICO ROBIN'S SEA PRIZM STONE LOCK.
TAKE CUTTY FLAM TO IMPEL DOWN AND NICO ROBIN TO NAVY HEADQUARTERS.
WHEN THE CONVOY IS READY, SET SAIL THROUGH THE GATES OF JUSTICE.
CP9, RETURN TO YOUR ROOMS AND CATCH YOUR BREATH.
AFTER THIS, CP9'S STATUS...
...WILL GROW INCREDIBLY. WE'LL RAISE A GLASS IN CELEBRATION ON THE SHIP!!

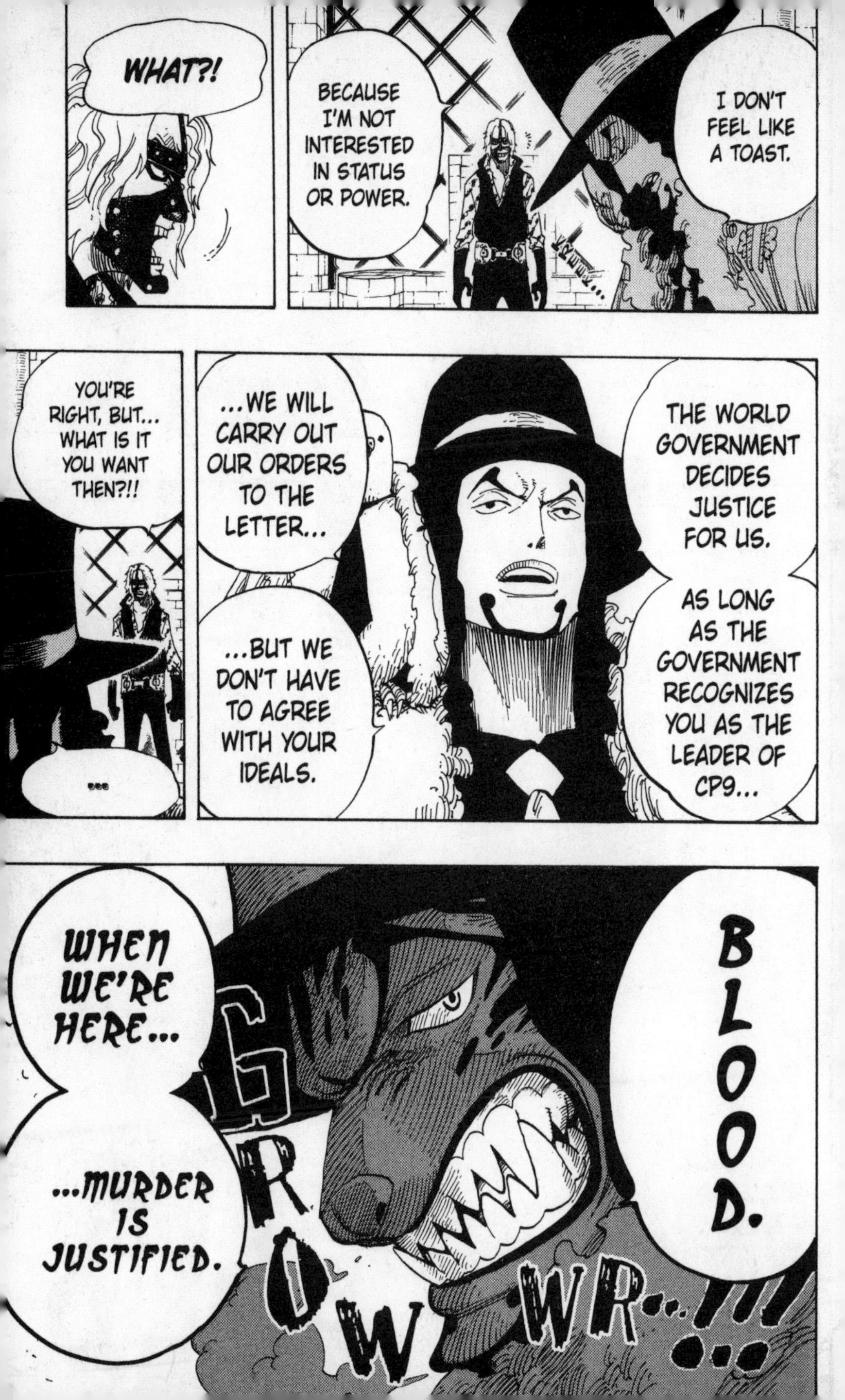
I DON'T FEEL LIKE A TOAST.
BECAUSE I'M NOT INTERESTED IN STATUS OR POWER.
WHAT?!
THE WORLD GOVERNMENT DECIDES JUSTICE FOR US.
AS LONG AS THE GOVERNMENT RECOGNIZES YOU AS THE LEADER OF CP9...
...WE WILL CARRY OUT OUR ORDERS TO THE LETTER...
...BUT WE DON'T HAVE TO AGREE WITH YOUR IDEALS.
YOU'RE RIGHT, BUT... WHAT IS IT YOU WANT THEN?!!
...
BLOOD.
WHEN WE'RE HERE...
...MURDER IS JUSTIFIED.
GROWWR...!!!

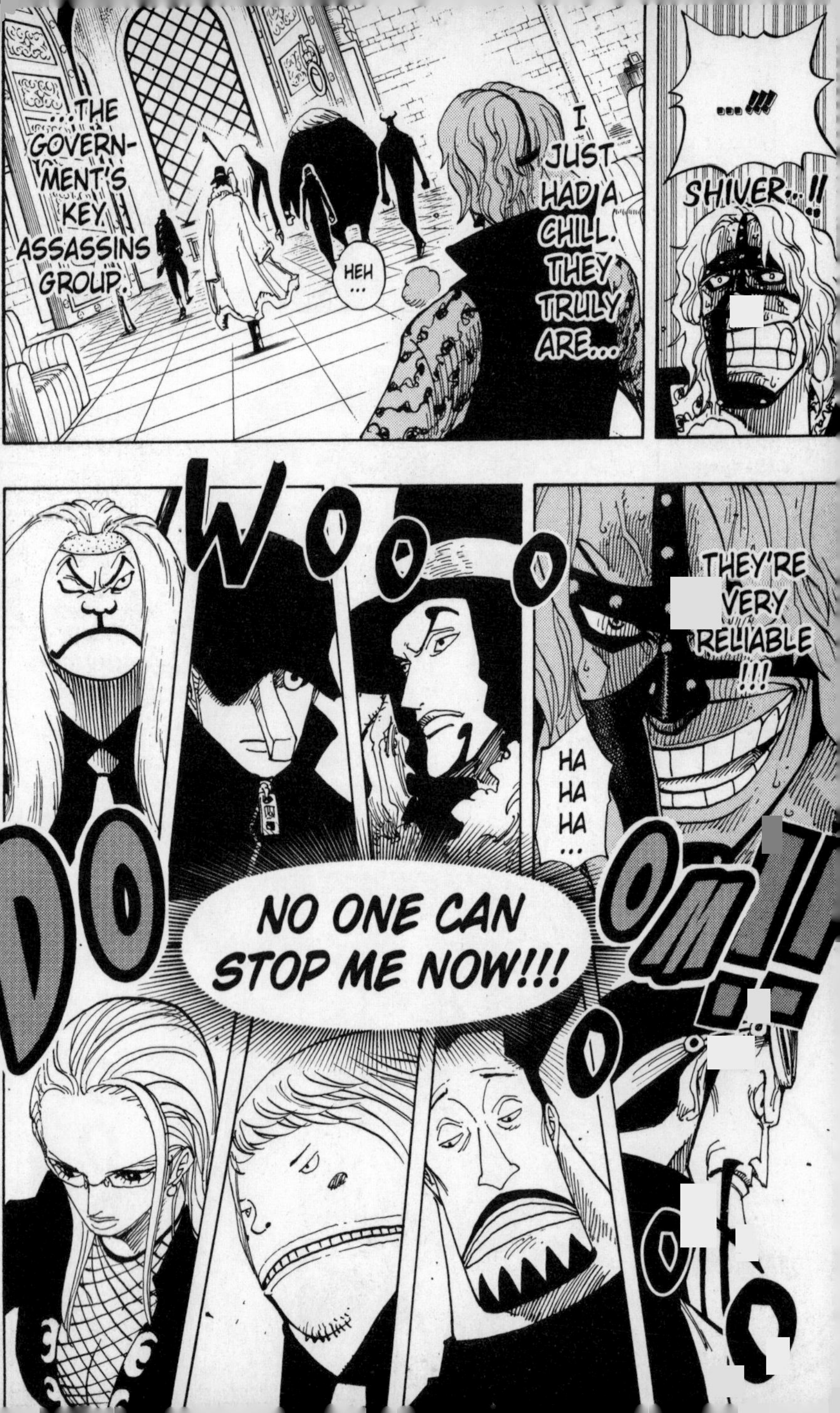

...!!!
SHIVER...!!
I JUST HAD A CHILL. THEY TRULY ARE...
HEH...
...THE GOVERNMENT'S KEY ASSASSINS GROUP.
THEY'RE VERY RELIABLE!!!
HA HA HA...
NO ONE CAN STOP ME NOW!!!

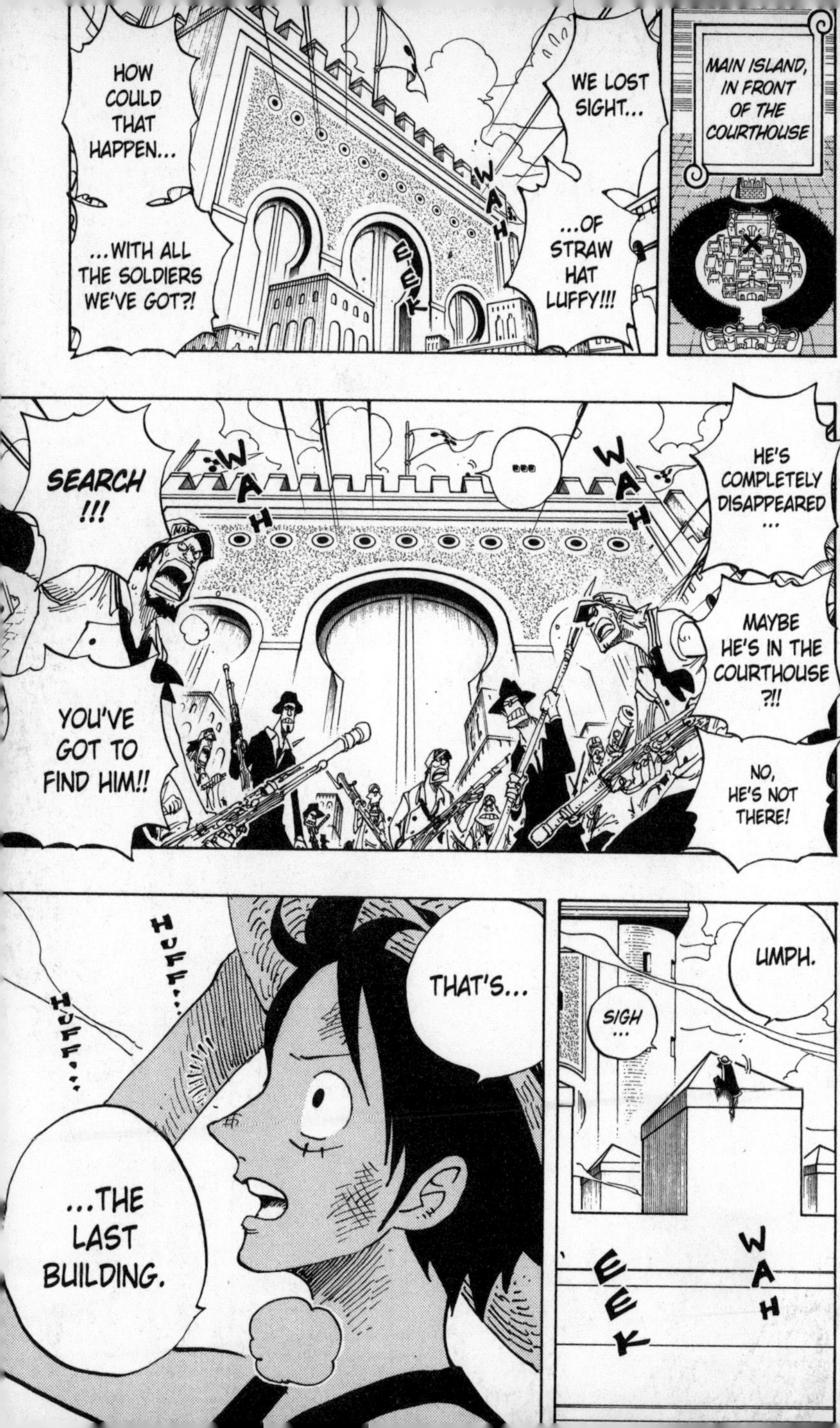
MAIN ISLAND, IN FRONT OF THE COURTHOUSE
WE LOST SIGHT...
WAH
HOW COULD THAT HAPPEN...
...OF STRAW HAT LUFFY!!!
EEK
...WITH ALL THE SOLDIERS WE'VE GOT?!
HE'S COMPLETELY DISAPPEARED...
WAH
...
WAH
SEARCH!!!
MAYBE HE'S IN THE COURTHOUSE?!!
NO, HE'S NOT THERE!
YOU'VE GOT TO FIND HIM!!
UMPH.
SIGH...
WAH
EEEK
THAT'S...
HUFF...
HUFF...
...THE LAST BUILDING.

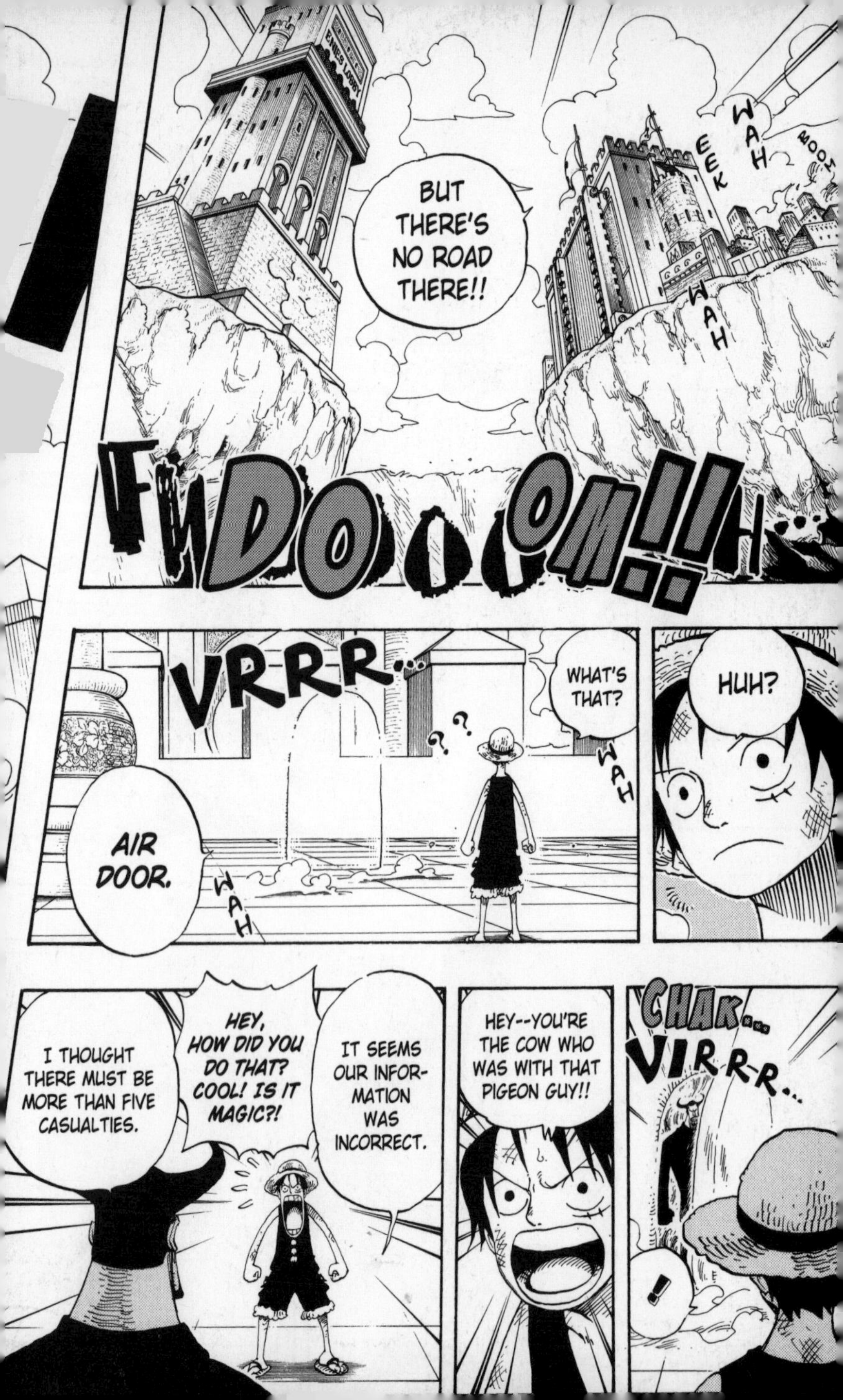
ENIES LOBBY
EEK
WAH
WAH
BUT THERE'S NO ROAD THERE!!
FWDOOOM!!
HUH?
WHAT'S THAT?
WAH
VRRR...
AIR DOOR.
WAH
CHAK...
VIRR-R-R...
!
HEY--YOU'RE THE COW WHO WAS WITH THAT PIGEON GUY!!
IT SEEMS OUR INFOR-MATION WAS INCORRECT.
HEY, HOW DID YOU DO THAT? COOL! IS IT MAGIC?!
I THOUGHT THERE MUST BE MORE THAN FIVE CASUALTIES.

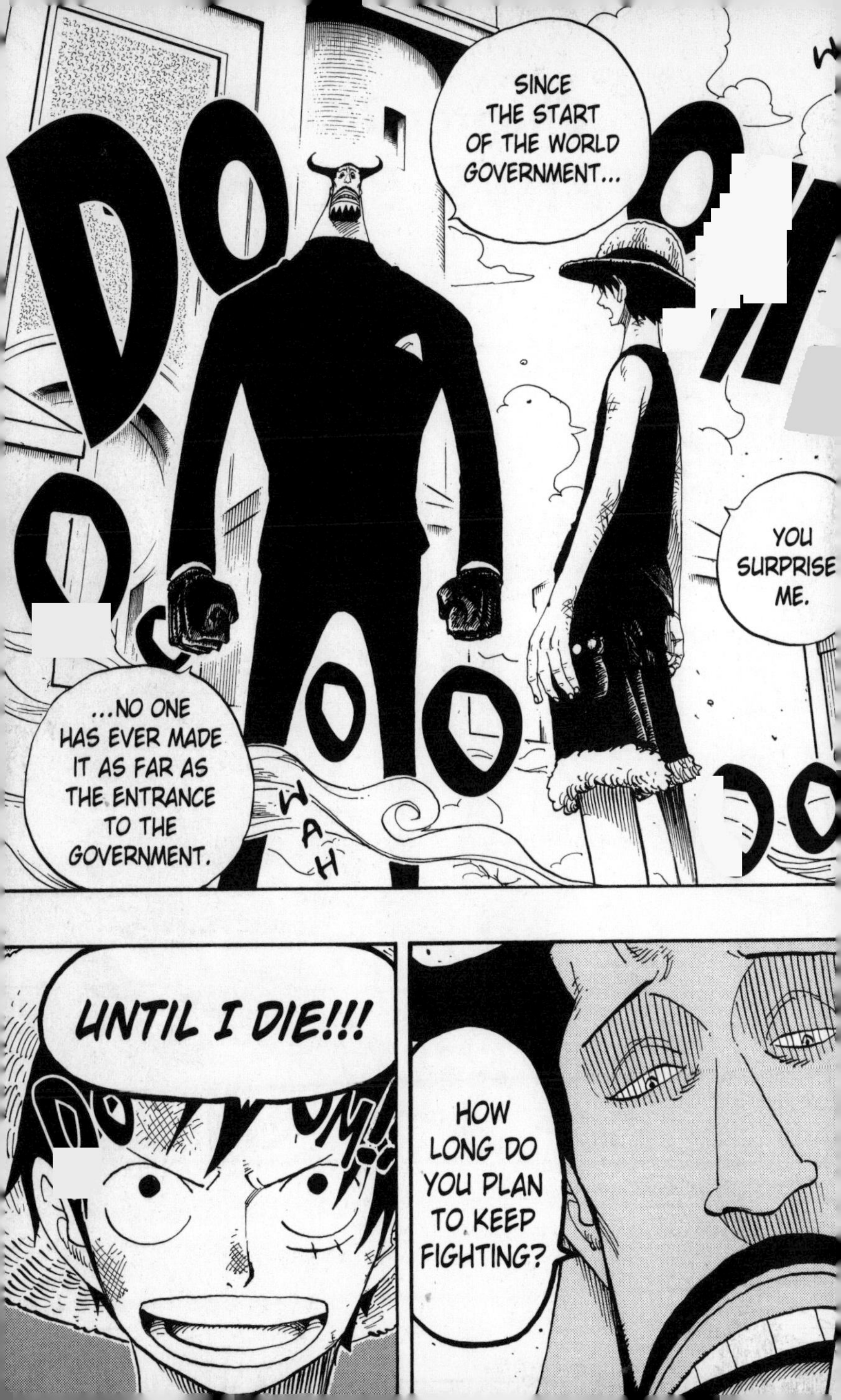

SINCE THE START OF THE WORLD GOVERNMENT...
YOU SURPRISE ME.
...NO ONE HAS EVER MADE IT AS FAR AS THE ENTRANCE TO THE GOVERNMENT.
WAH
HOW LONG DO YOU PLAN TO KEEP FIGHTING?
UNTIL I DIE!!!

Chapter 383:
LUFFY VS. BLUENO

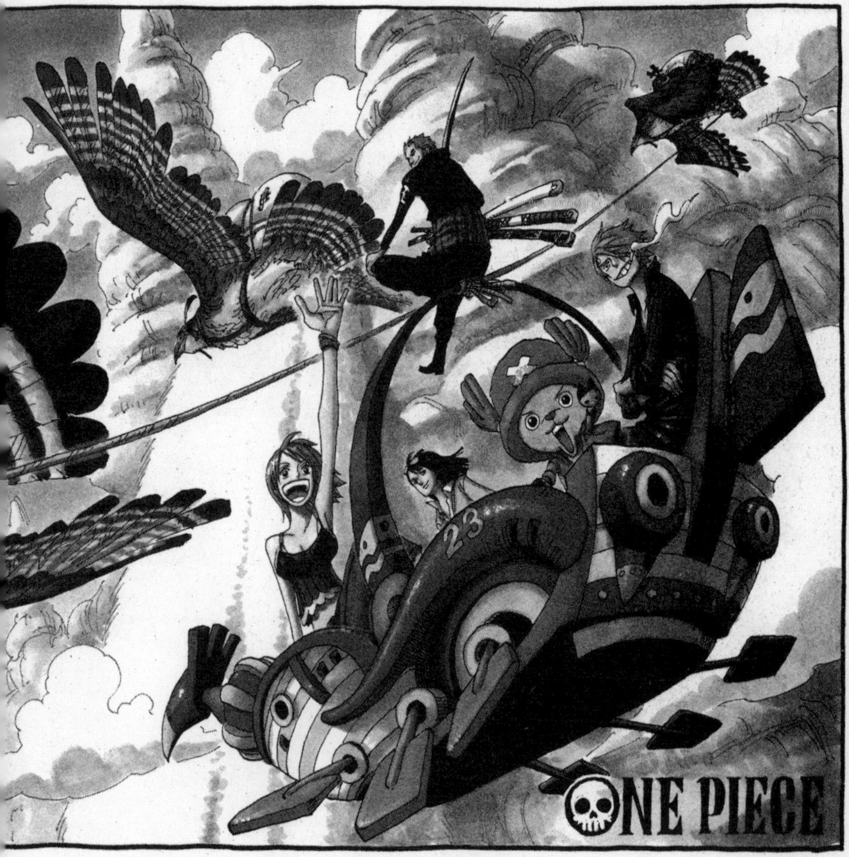
ONE PIECE

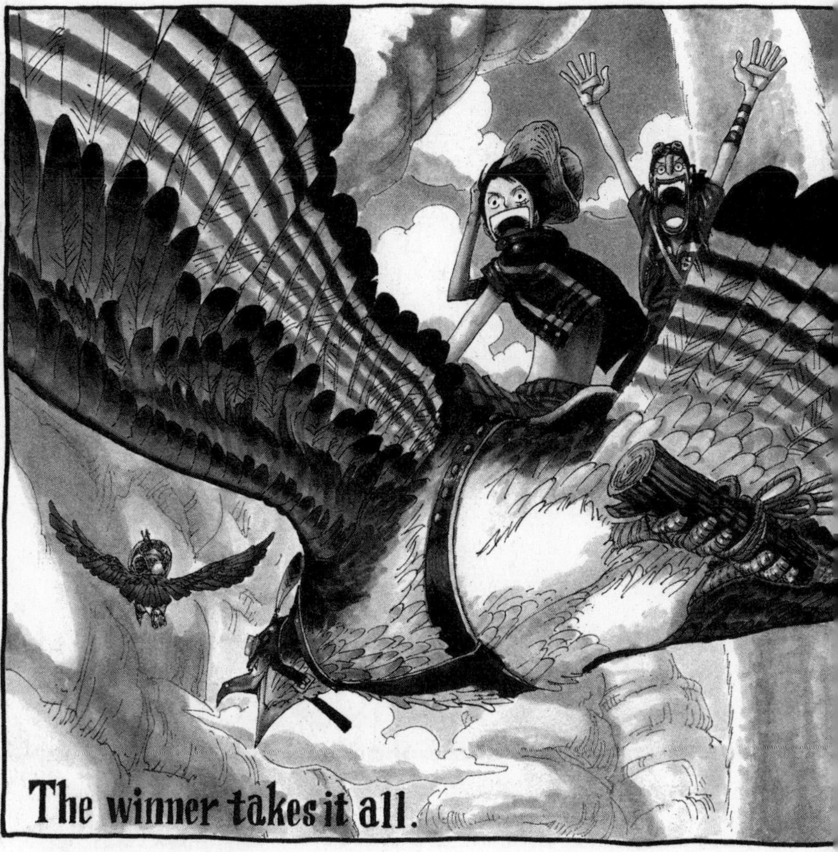
The winner takes it all.

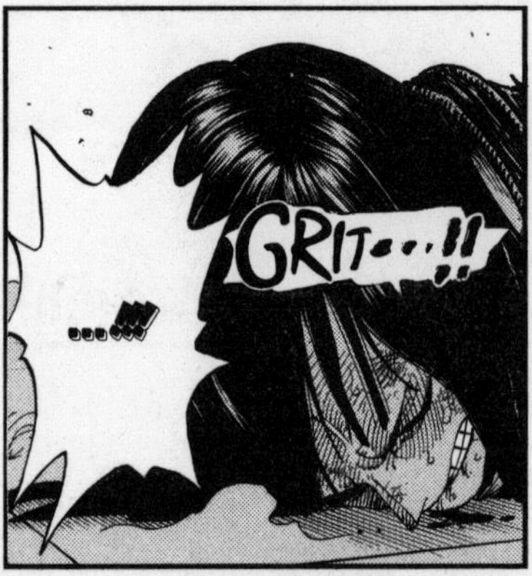

GRIT...!!
...!!!

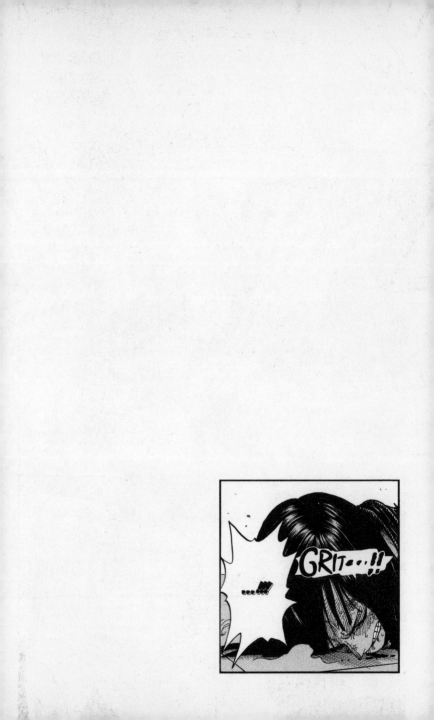

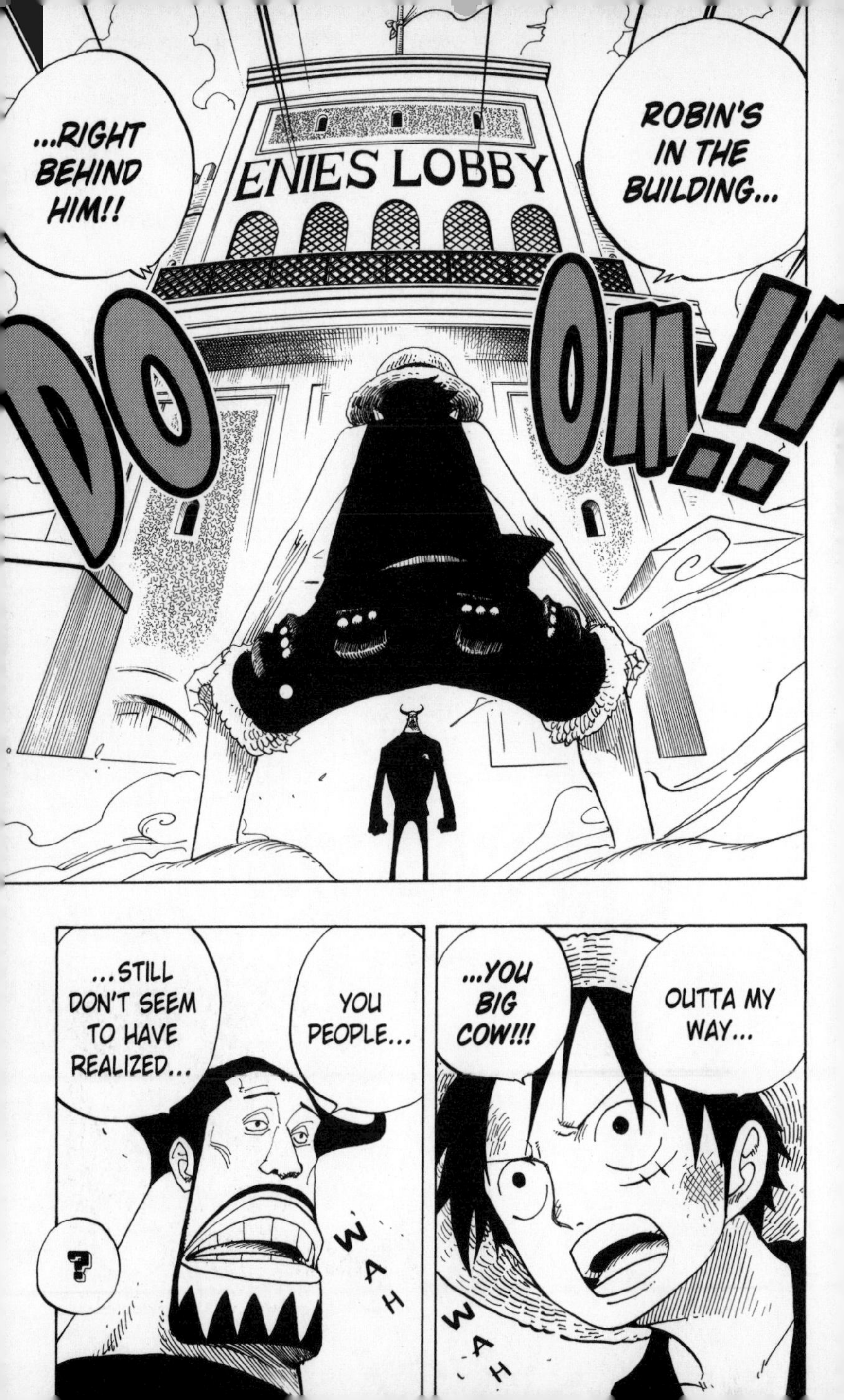
ROBIN'S IN THE BUILDING...
...RIGHT BEHIND HIM!!
ENIES LOBBY
DOOM!!
OUTTA MY WAY...
...YOU BIG COW!!!
WAH
YOU PEOPLE...
...STILL DON'T SEEM TO HAVE REALIZED...
WAH
?

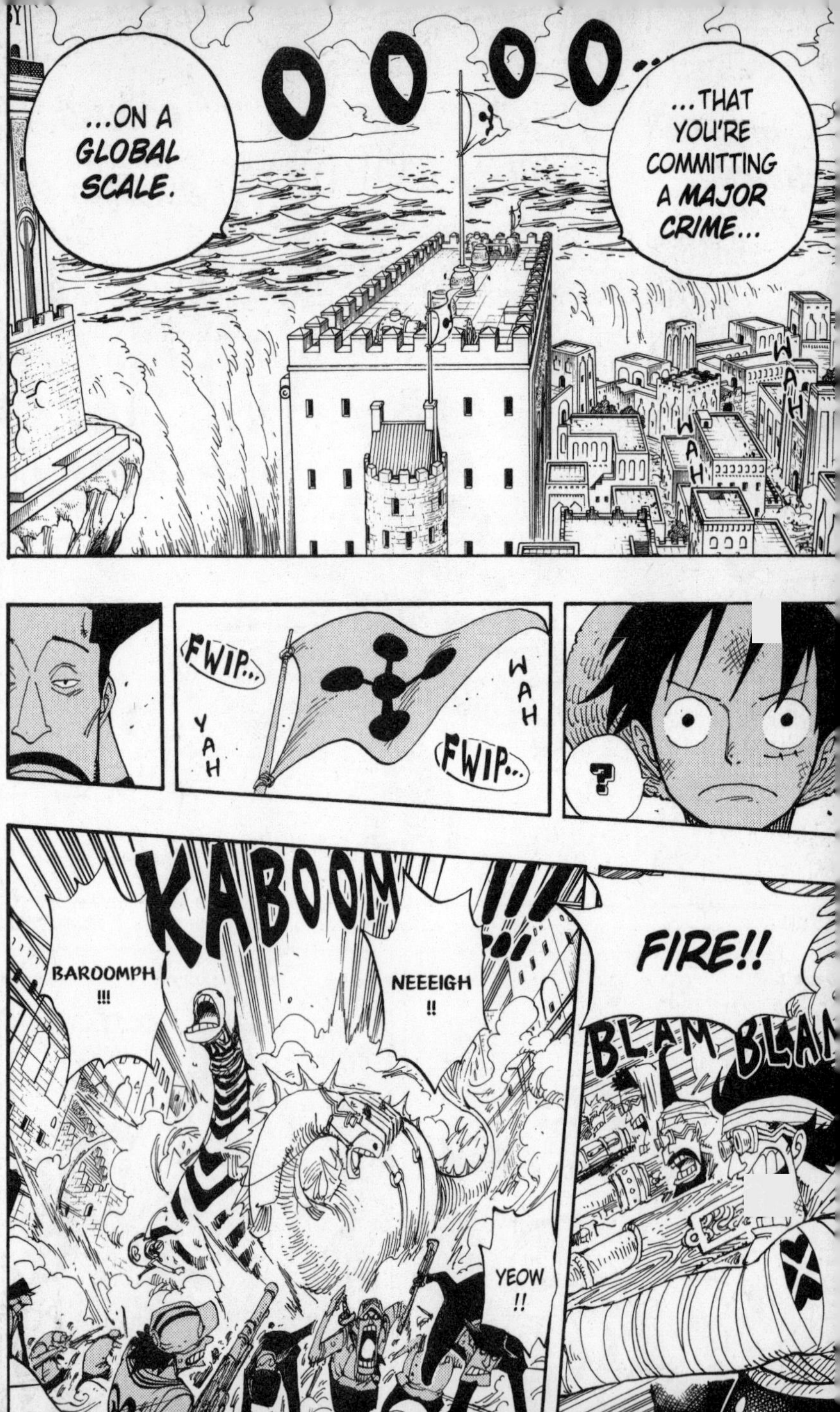

...THAT YOU'RE COMMITTING A MAJOR CRIME...
OOOO...
...ON A GLOBAL SCALE.
WAH
WAH
?
FWIP...
WAH
YAH
FWIP...
FIRE!!
BLAM BLAM
KABOOM!!
NEEEIGH!!
BAROOMPH!!!
YEOW!!

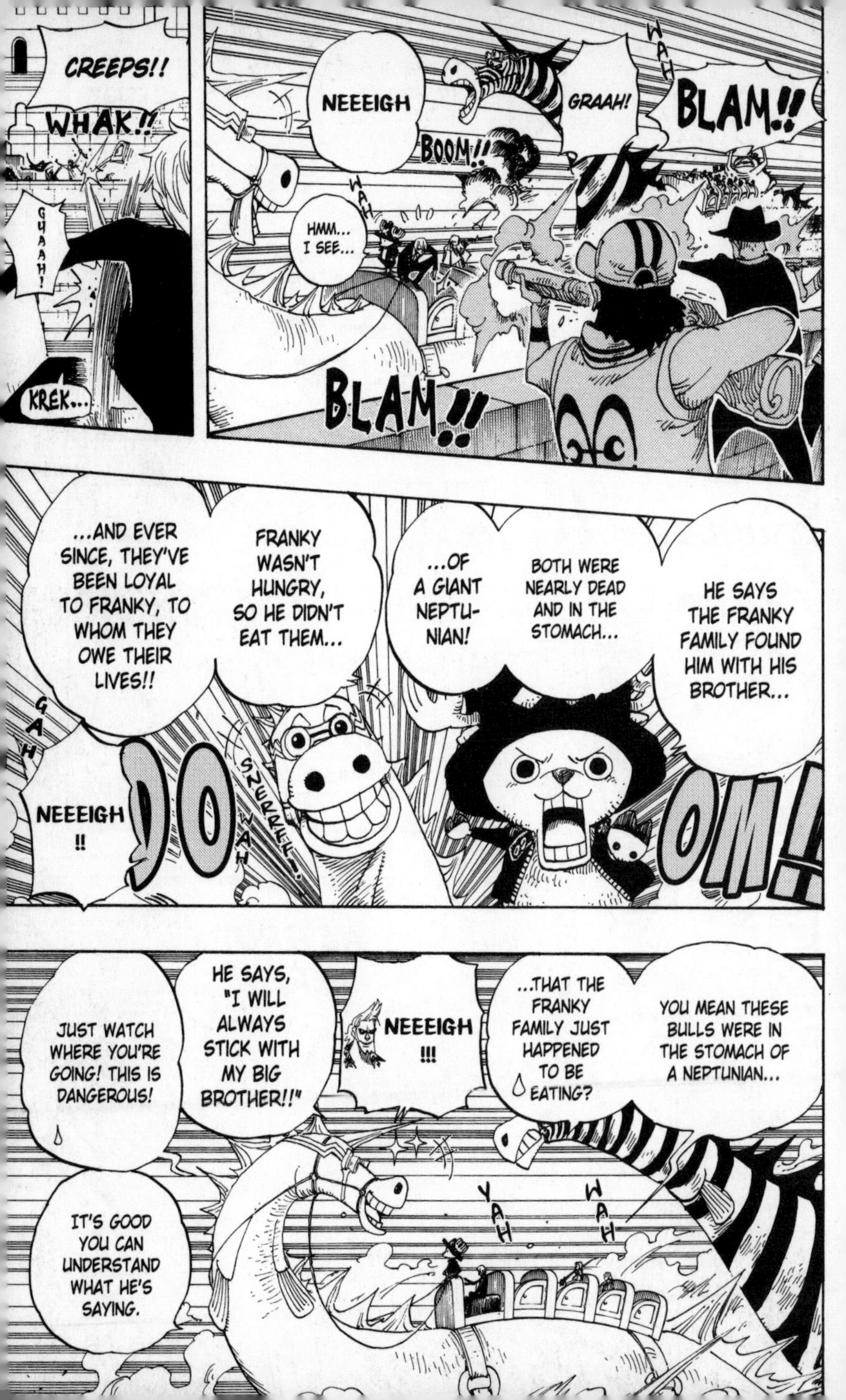
BLAM!!
WAH
GRAAH!
NEEEIGH
BOOM!!
WAH
HMM... I SEE...
BLAM!!
CREEPS!!
WHAK!!
GUAAAH!
KREK...
HE SAYS THE FRANKY FAMILY FOUND HIM WITH HIS BROTHER...
BOTH WERE NEARLY DEAD AND IN THE STOMACH...
...OF A GIANT NEPTUNIAN!
FRANKY WASN'T HUNGRY, SO HE DIDN'T EAT THEM...
...AND EVER SINCE, THEY'VE BEEN LOYAL TO FRANKY, TO WHOM THEY OWE THEIR LIVES!!
DOOM!!
SNERRFF!
WAH
GAH
NEEEIGH!!
YOU MEAN THESE BULLS WERE IN THE STOMACH OF A NEPTUNIAN...
...THAT THE FRANKY FAMILY JUST HAPPENED TO BE EATING?
NEEEIGH!!!
HE SAYS, "I WILL ALWAYS STICK WITH MY BIG BROTHER!!"
WAH
YAH
JUST WATCH WHERE YOU'RE GOING! THIS IS DANGEROUS!
IT'S GOOD YOU CAN UNDERSTAND WHAT HE'S SAYING.

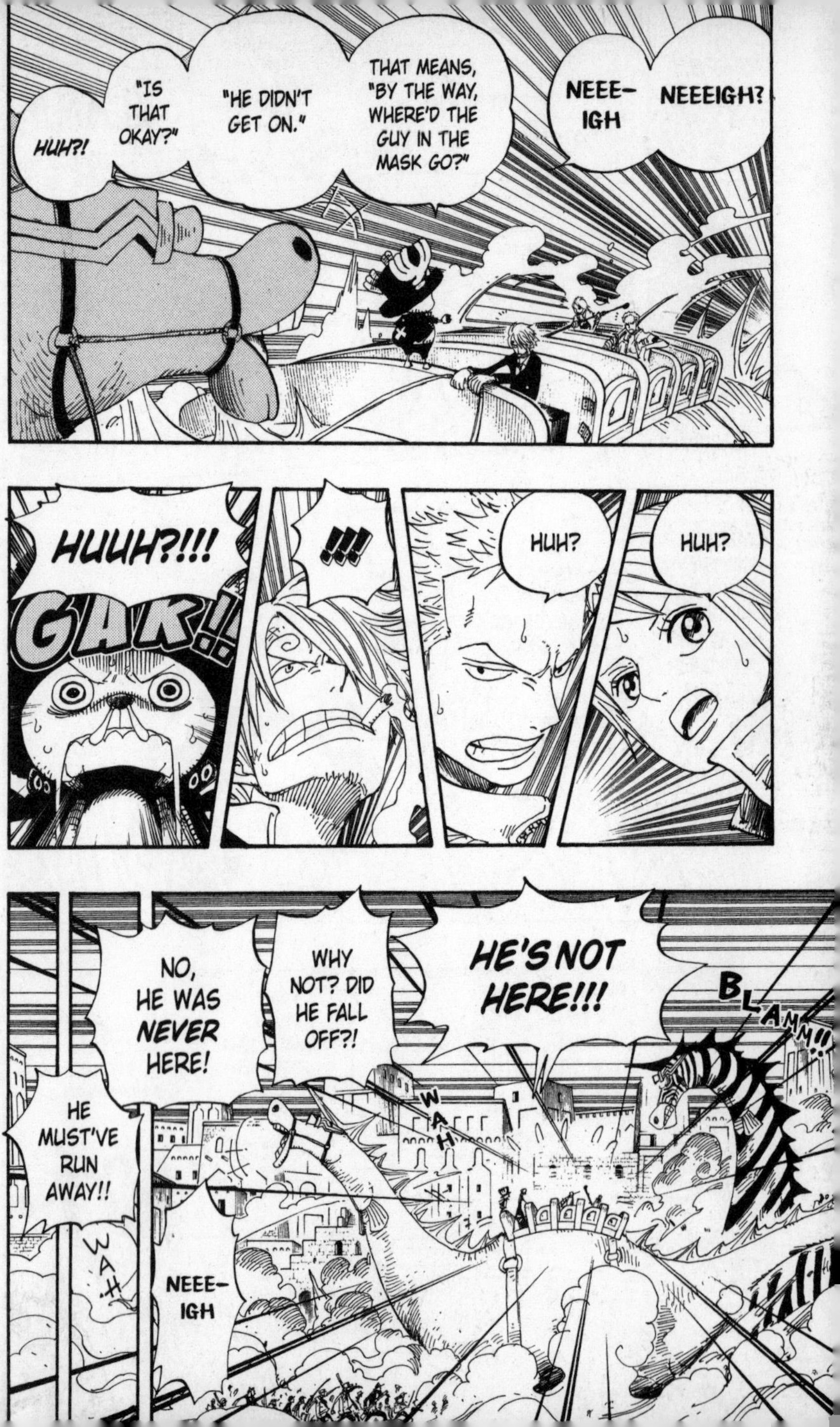
NEEEIGH?
NEEE-IGH
THAT MEANS, "BY THE WAY, WHERE'D THE GUY IN THE MASK GO?"
"HE DIDN'T GET ON."
"IS THAT OKAY?"
HUH?!
HUH?
HUH?
!!!
HUUH?!!!
GAK!!
BLAMM!!
HE'S NOT HERE!!!
WHY NOT? DID HE FALL OFF?!
NO, HE WAS NEVER HERE!
HE MUST'VE RUN AWAY!!
WAH
NEEE-IGH
WAH

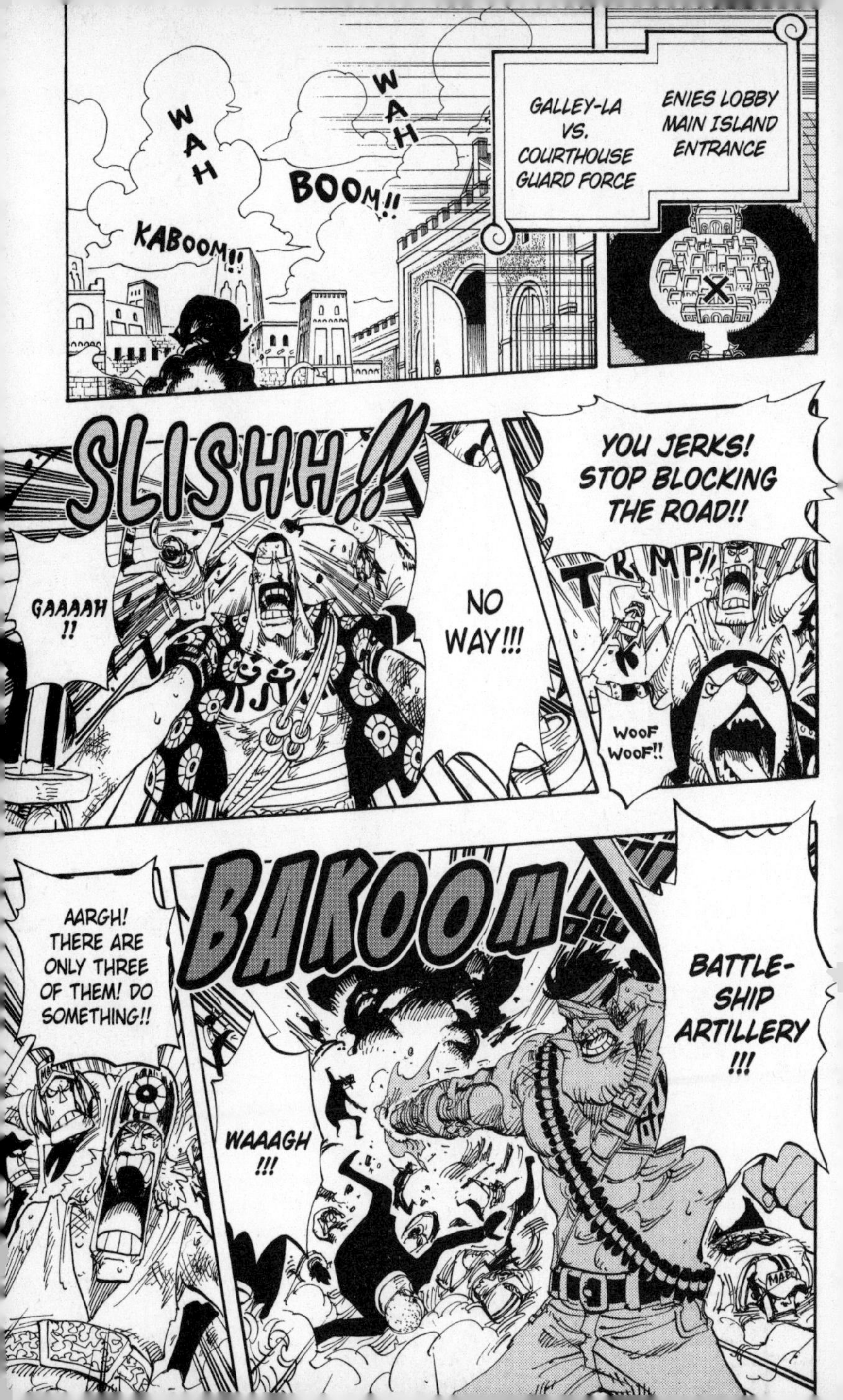
ENIES LOBBY MAIN ISLAND ENTRANCE
GALLEY-LA VS. COURTHOUSE GUARD FORCE
WAH
BOOM!!
WAH
KABOOM!!
YOU JERKS! STOP BLOCKING THE ROAD!!
TRMP!!
WOOF WOOF!!
NO WAY!!!
SLISHH!!
GAAAAH !!
BATTLE-SHIP ARTILLERY !!!
BAKOOM!!
WAAAGH !!!
AARGH! THERE ARE ONLY THREE OF THEM! DO SOMETHING!!

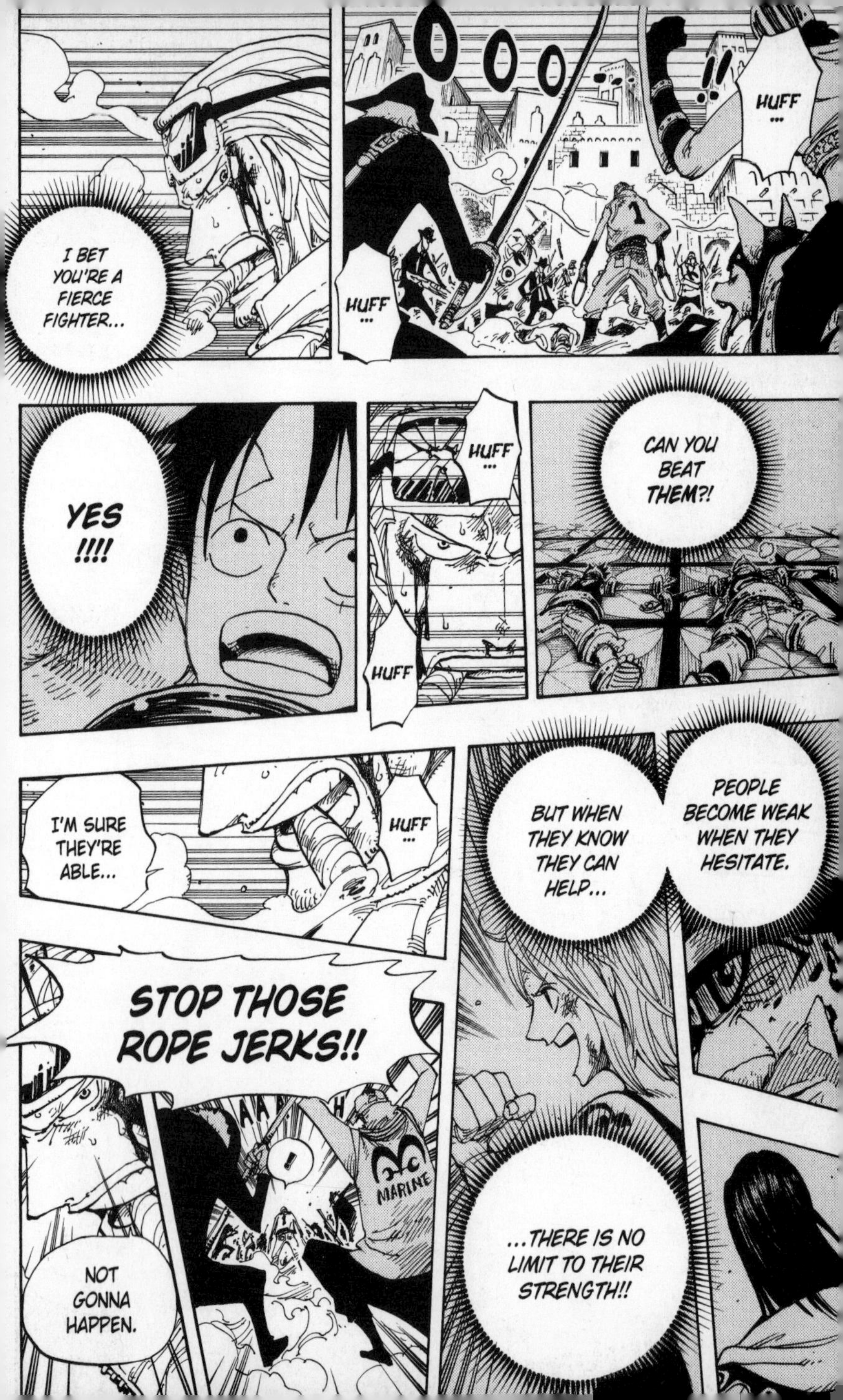
HUFF...
HUFF...
I BET YOU'RE A FIERCE FIGHTER...
CAN YOU BEAT THEM?!
HUFF...
HUFF
YES !!!!
PEOPLE BECOME WEAK WHEN THEY HESITATE.
BUT WHEN THEY KNOW THEY CAN HELP...
...THERE IS NO LIMIT TO THEIR STRENGTH!!
HUFF...
I'M SURE THEY'RE ABLE...
STOP THOSE ROPE JERKS!!
MARINE
NOT GONNA HAPPEN.

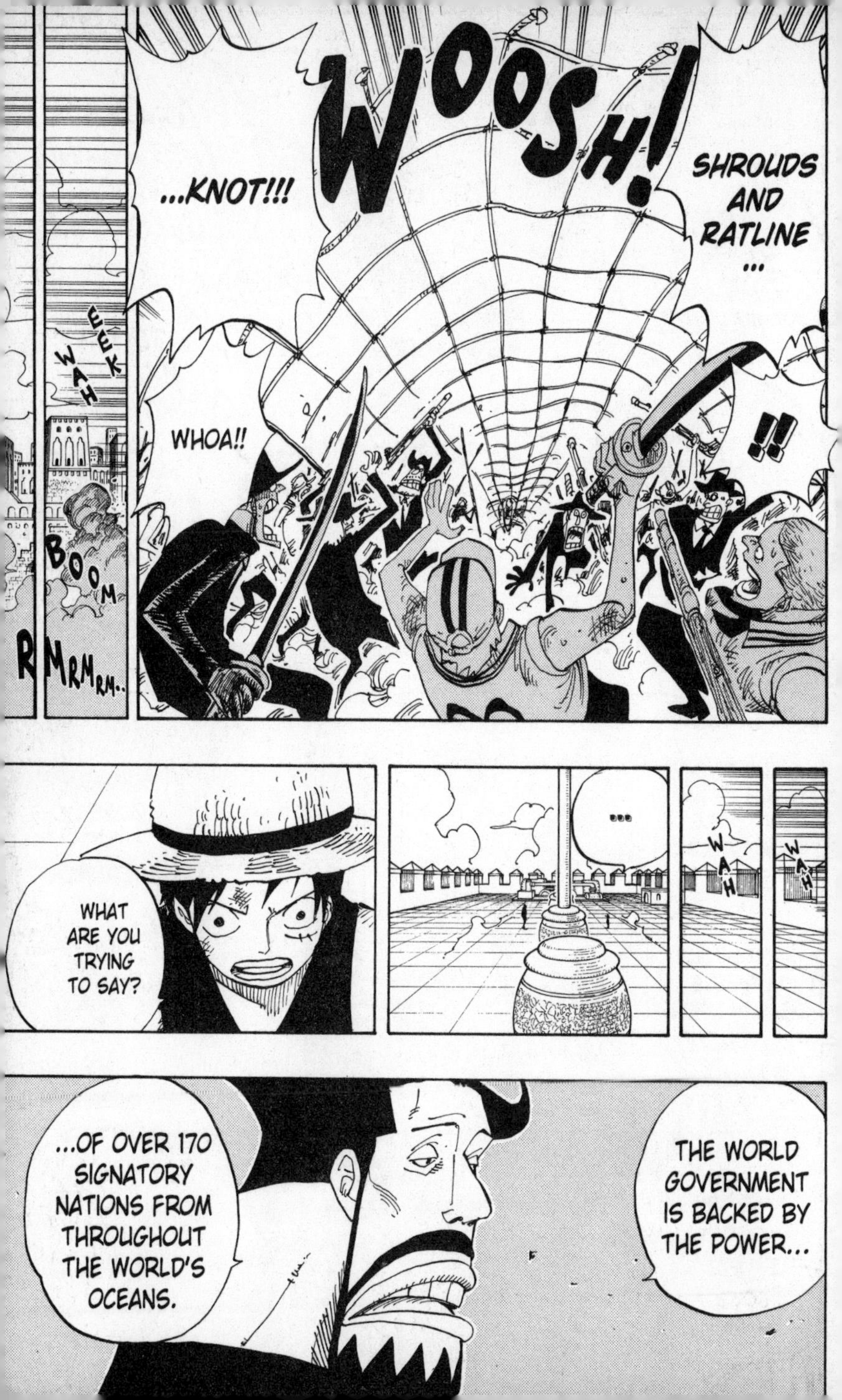
SHROUDS AND RATLINE ...
WOOSH!
...KNOT!!!
!!
WHOA!!
WAH EEK
BOOM
RMRMRM..
WAH
WAH
...
WHAT ARE YOU TRYING TO SAY?
THE WORLD GOVERNMENT IS BACKED BY THE POWER...
...OF OVER 170 SIGNATORY NATIONS FROM THROUGHOUT THE WORLD'S OCEANS.

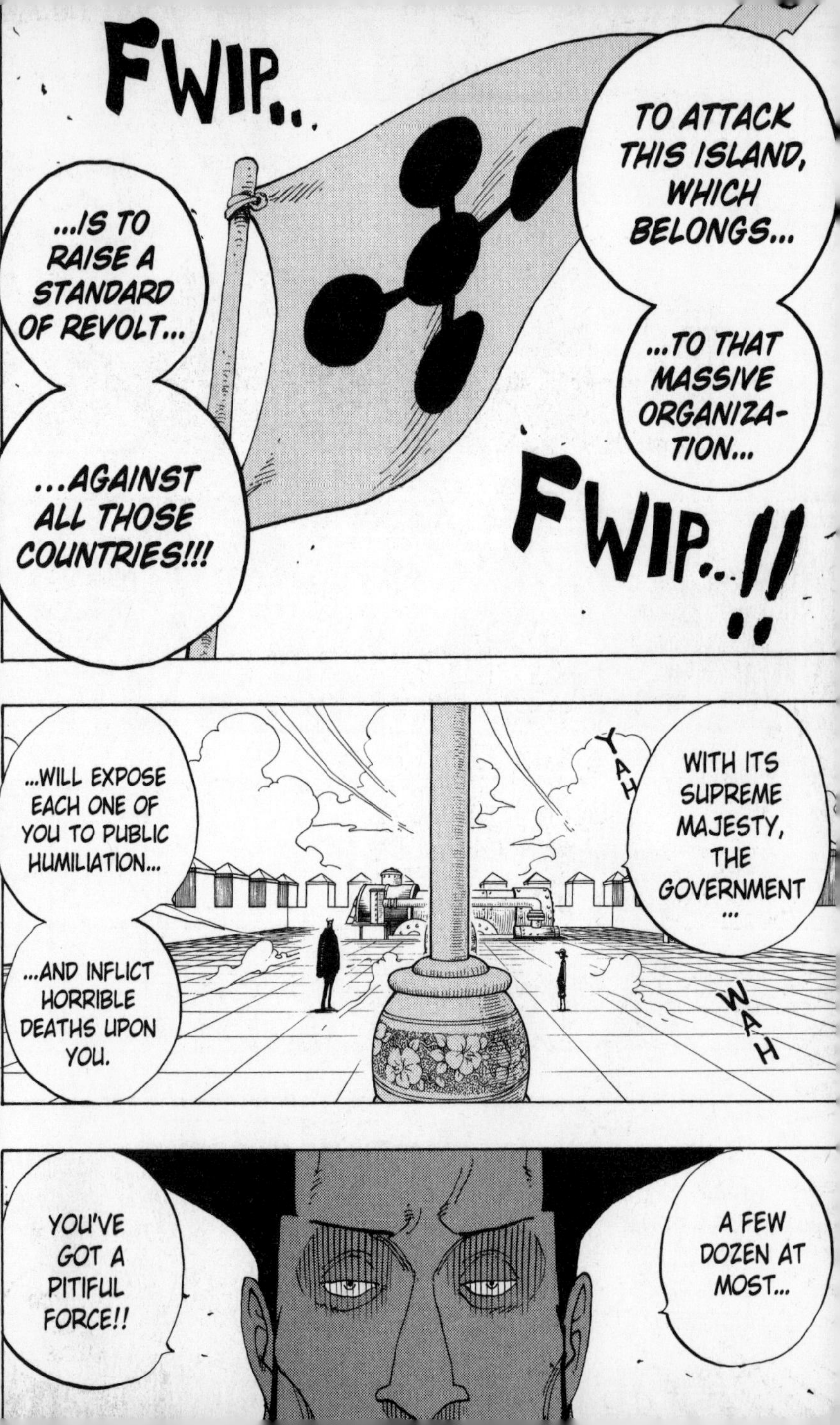

TO ATTACK THIS ISLAND, WHICH BELONGS...
...TO THAT MASSIVE ORGANIZATION...
FWIP...
...IS TO RAISE A STANDARD OF REVOLT...
...AGAINST ALL THOSE COUNTRIES!!!
FWIP...!!
YAH
WITH ITS SUPREME MAJESTY, THE GOVERNMENT ...
WAH
...WILL EXPOSE EACH ONE OF YOU TO PUBLIC HUMILIATION...
...AND INFLICT HORRIBLE DEATHS UPON YOU.
A FEW DOZEN AT MOST...
YOU'VE GOT A PITIFUL FORCE!!

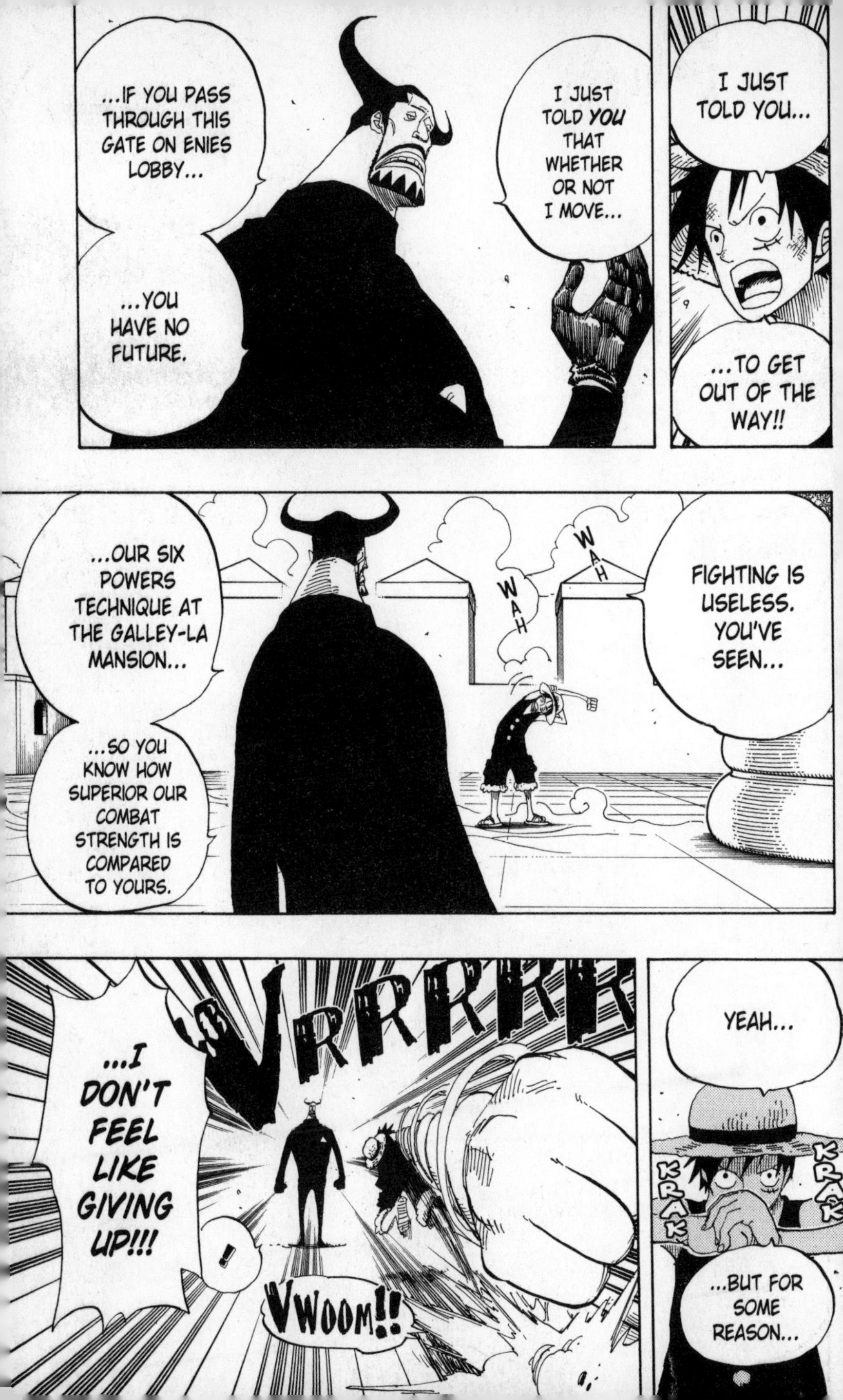
I JUST TOLD YOU...
...TO GET OUT OF THE WAY!!
I JUST TOLD YOU THAT WHETHER OR NOT I MOVE...
...IF YOU PASS THROUGH THIS GATE ON ENIES LOBBY...
...YOU HAVE NO FUTURE.
FIGHTING IS USELESS. YOU'VE SEEN...
WAH
WAH
...OUR SIX POWERS TECHNIQUE AT THE GALLEY-LA MANSION...
...SO YOU KNOW HOW SUPERIOR OUR COMBAT STRENGTH IS COMPARED TO YOURS.
YEAH...
KRAK
KRAK
...BUT FOR SOME REASON...
VRRRRRR
...I DON'T FEEL LIKE GIVING UP!!!
!
VWOOM!!

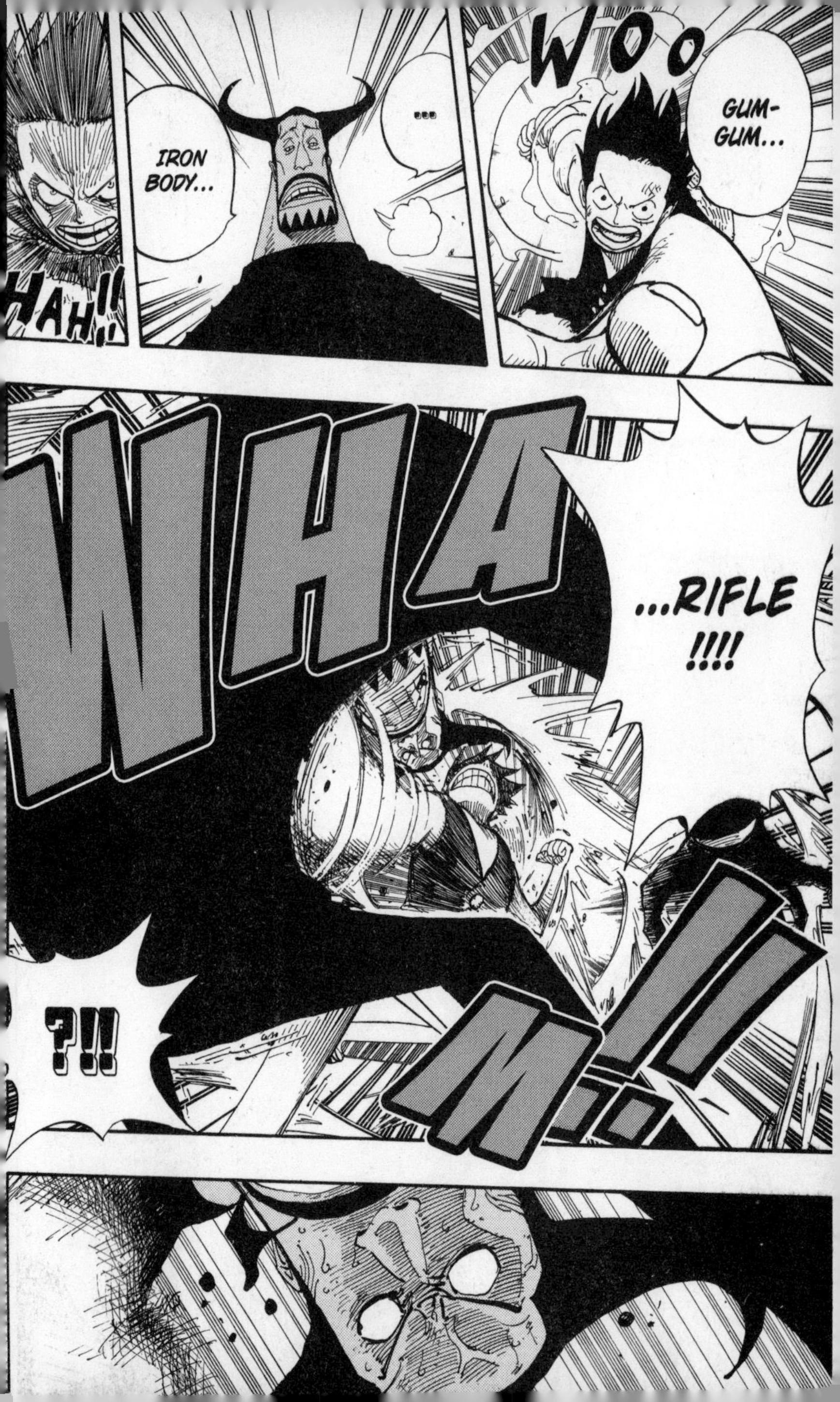
WOO
GUM-GUM...
...
IRON BODY...
HAH!!
WHA
...RIFLE !!!!
M..!!
?!!

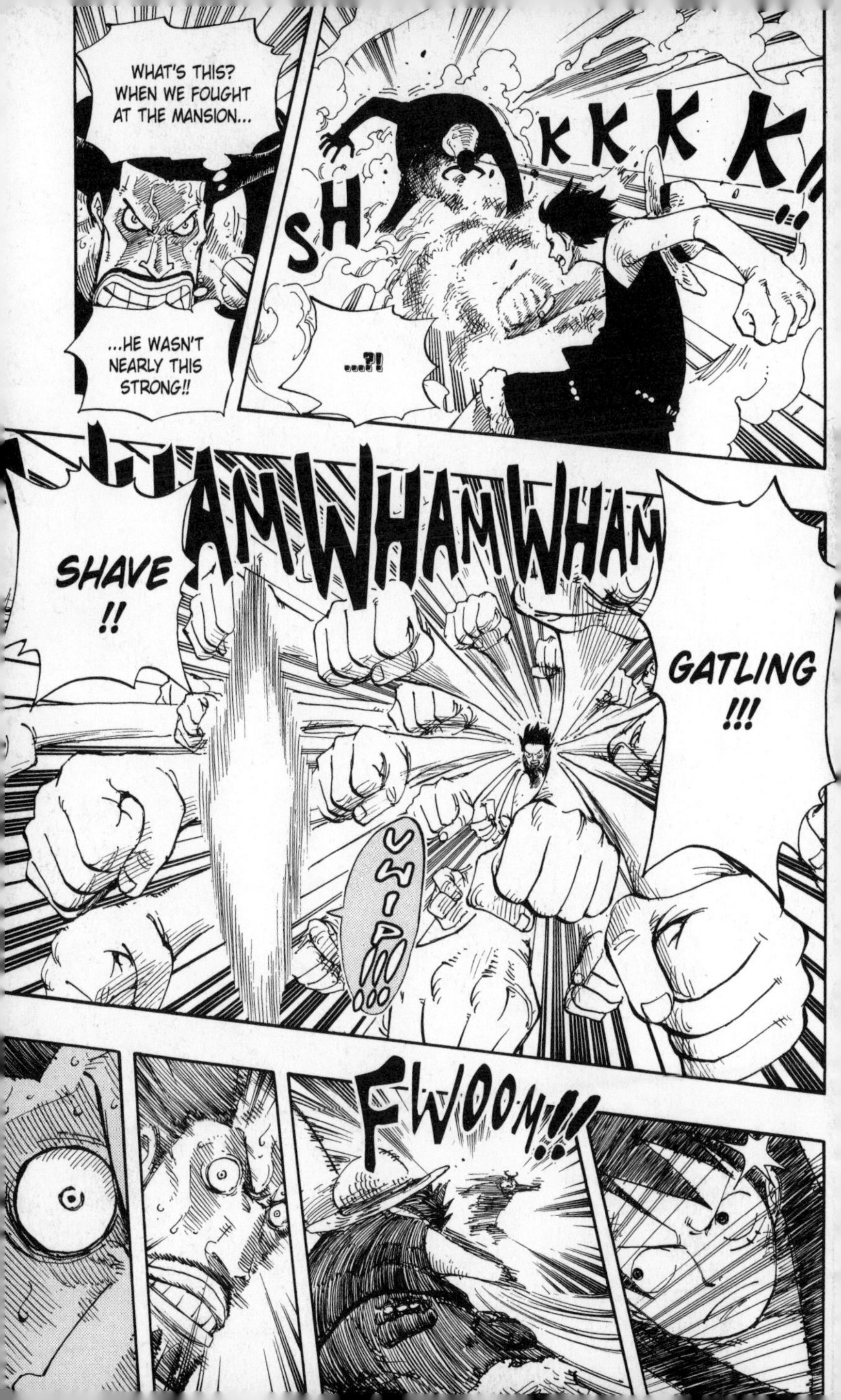
SHKKKKK!!
...?!
WHAT'S THIS? WHEN WE FOUGHT AT THE MANSION...
...HE WASN'T NEARLY THIS STRONG!!
GATLING !!!
WHAM WHAM WHAM
SHAVE !!
WHIP!!
FWOOM!!

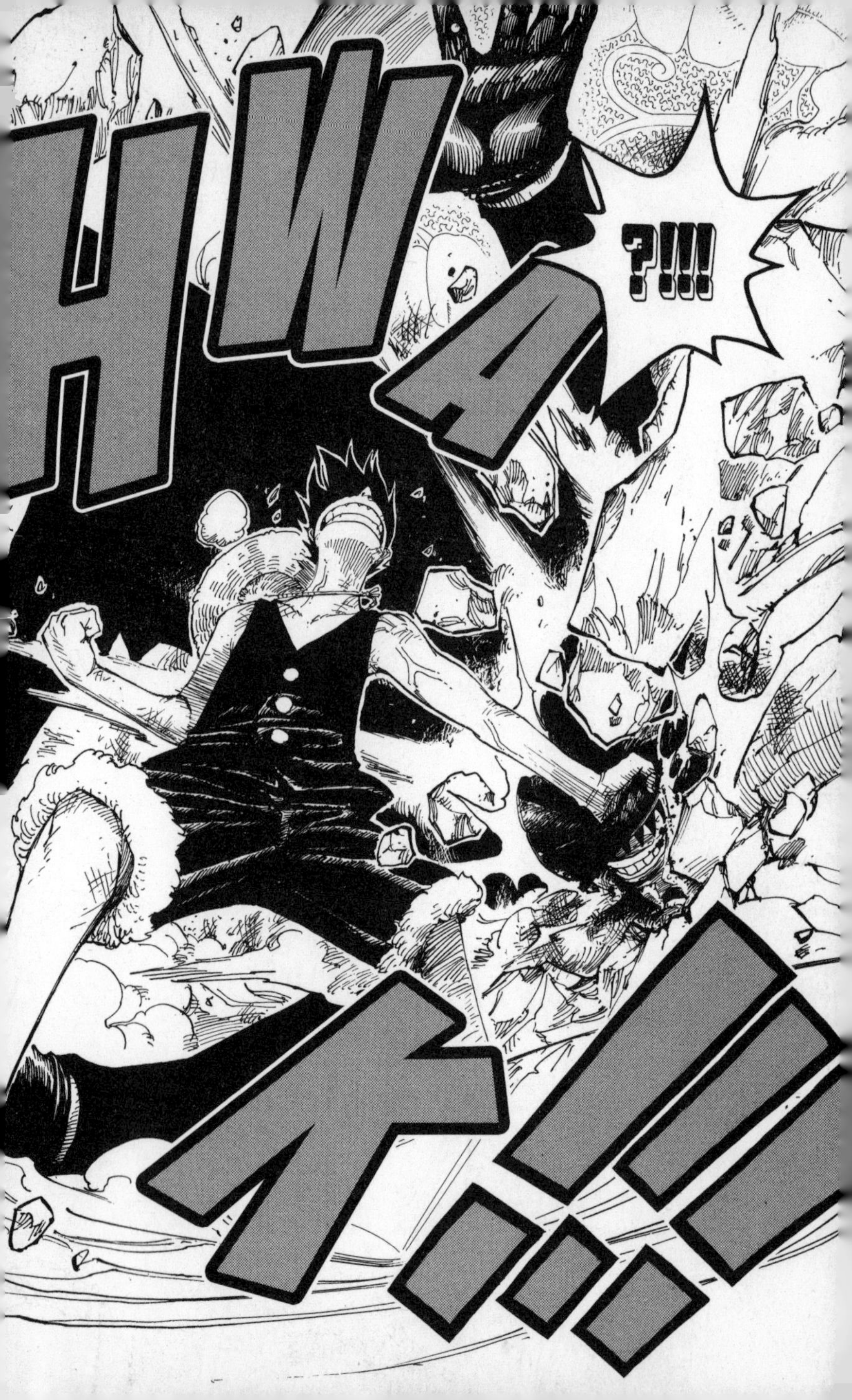
?!!!

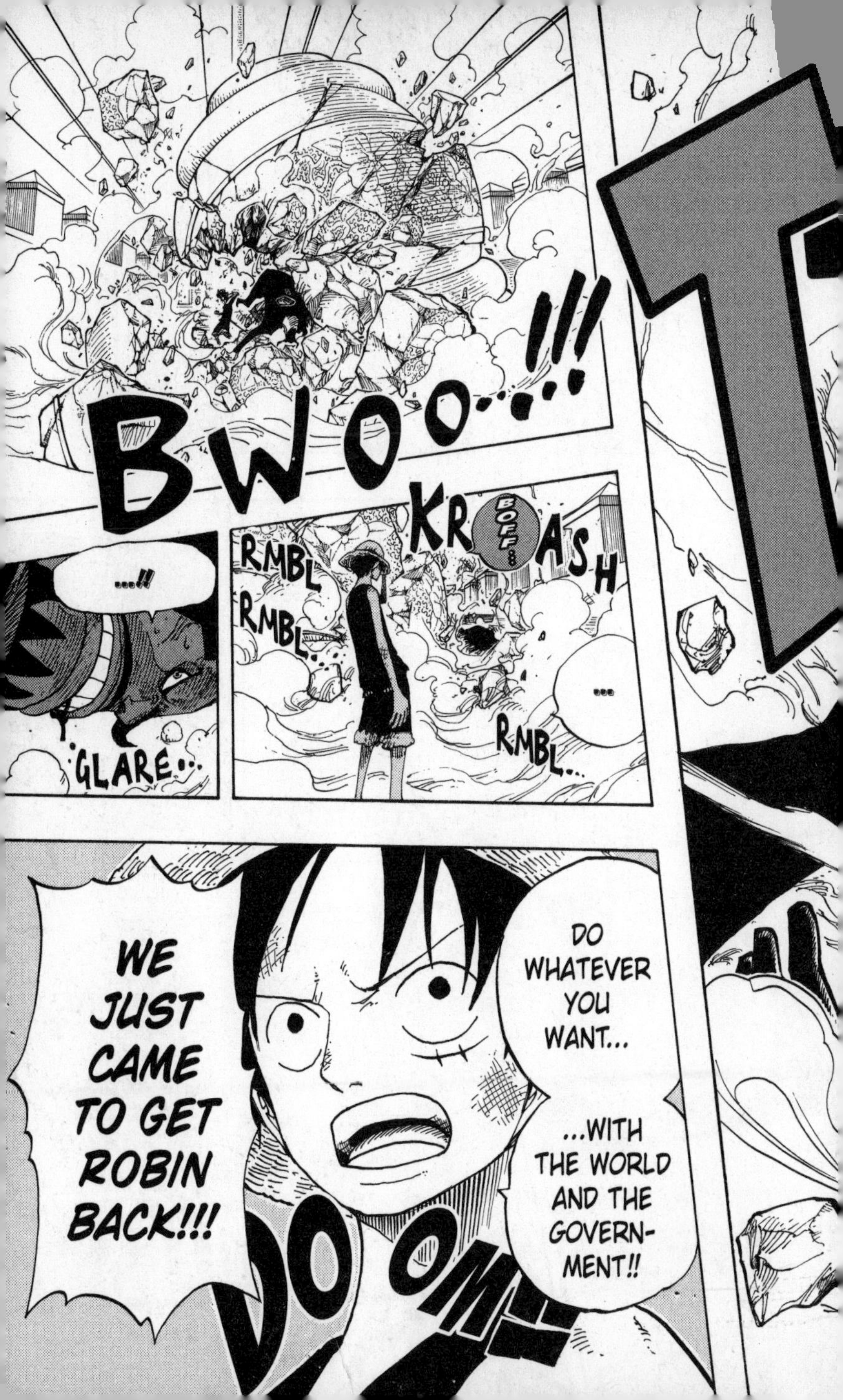
BWOO...!!!
KRASH
BOFF
RMBL
RMBL...
...
RMBL...
...!!
GLARE...
DO WHATEVER YOU WANT...
...WITH THE WORLD AND THE GOVERNMENT!!
WE JUST CAME TO GET ROBIN BACK!!!
DOOM

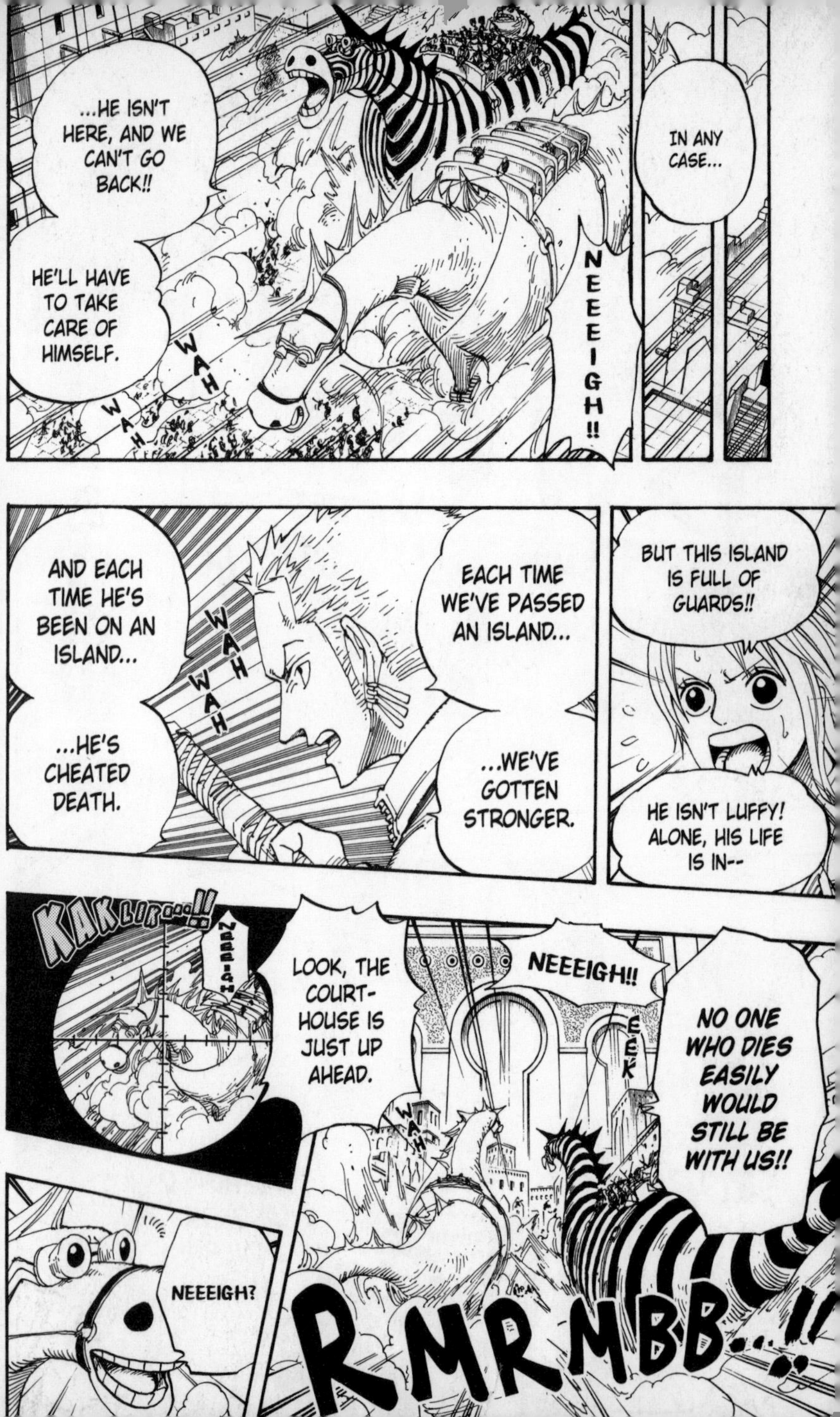

IN ANY CASE...
NEEEIGH!!
...HE ISN'T HERE, AND WE CAN'T GO BACK!!
HE'LL HAVE TO TAKE CARE OF HIMSELF.
WAH
WAH
BUT THIS ISLAND IS FULL OF GUARDS!!
HE ISN'T LUFFY! ALONE, HIS LIFE IS IN--
EACH TIME WE'VE PASSED AN ISLAND...
...WE'VE GOTTEN STRONGER.
WAH
WAH
AND EACH TIME HE'S BEEN ON AN ISLAND...
...HE'S CHEATED DEATH.
NO ONE WHO DIES EASILY WOULD STILL BE WITH US!!
EEK
NEEEIGH!!
LOOK, THE COURT-HOUSE IS JUST UP AHEAD.
WAH
RMRMBB...!!
KAKLIK...!!
NEEEIGH
NEEEIGH?

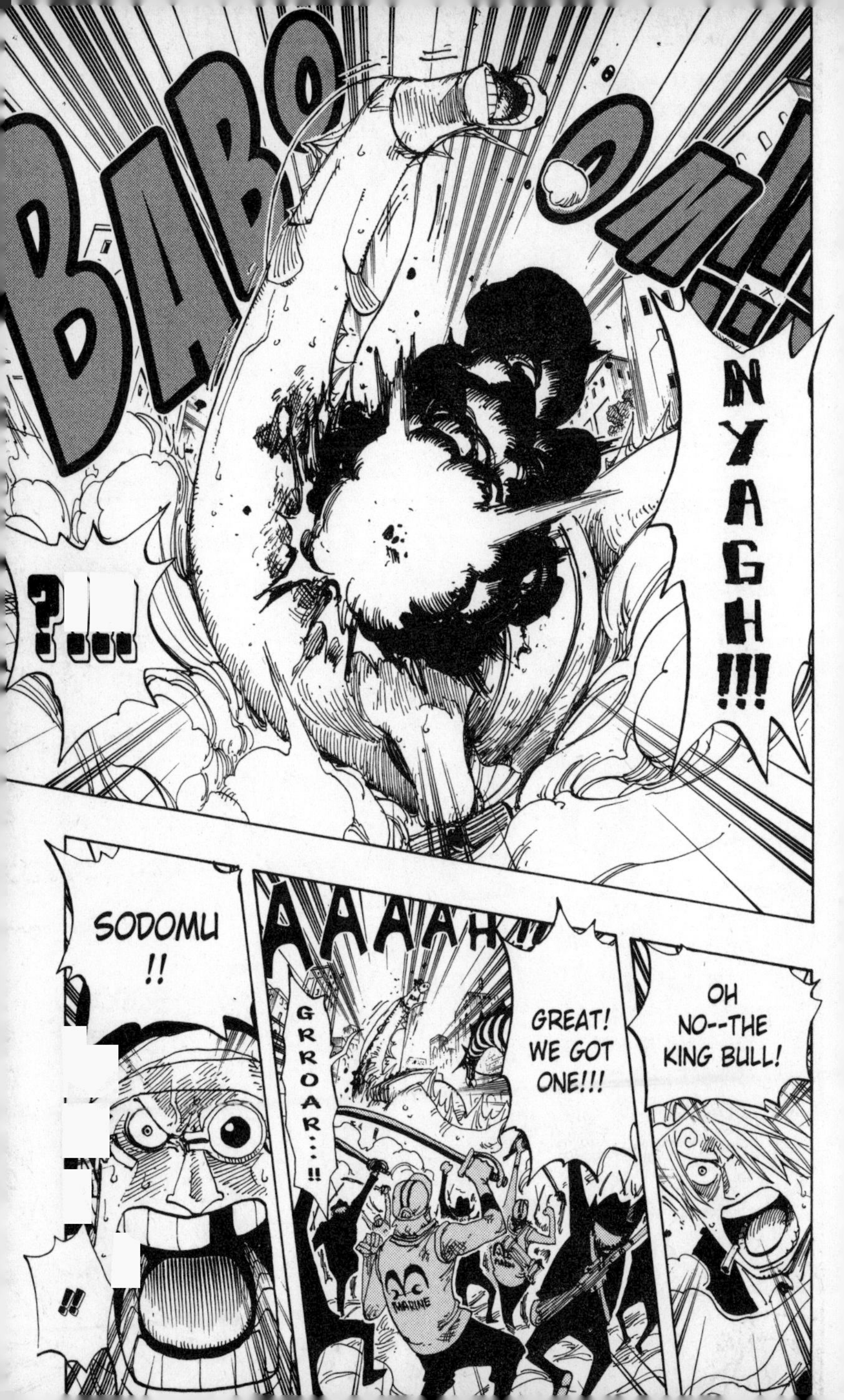
BABOOM!!
NYAGH!!!
?...
OH NO--THE KING BULL!
GREAT! WE GOT ONE!!!
AAAAH!!
GRRROAR...!!
SODOMU !!
!!

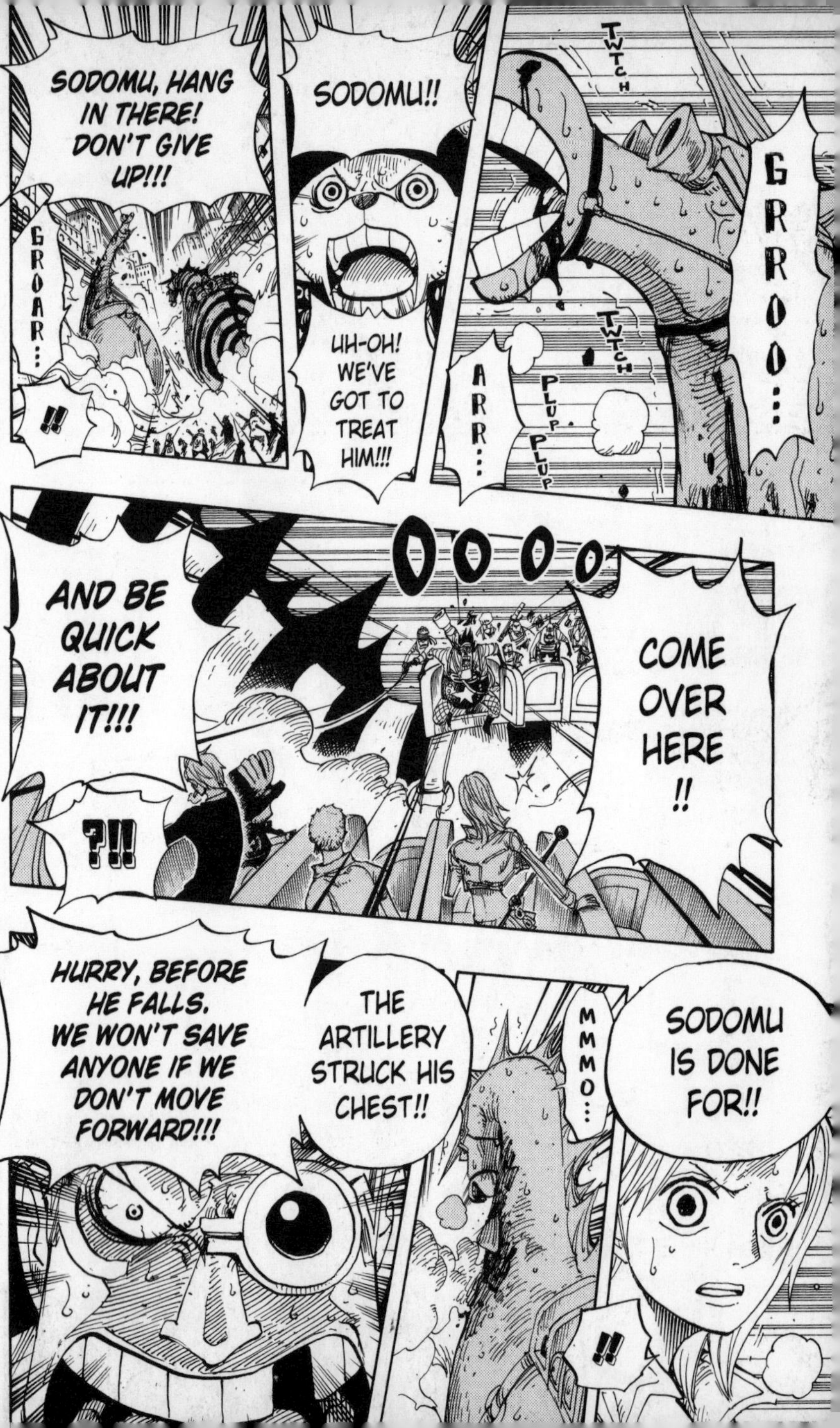
GRROO...
TWTCH
TWTCH
ARR...
PLUP
PLUP
SODOMU!!
UH-OH! WE'VE GOT TO TREAT HIM!!!
SODOMU, HANG IN THERE! DON'T GIVE UP!!!
GROAR...
!!
OOOO
COME OVER HERE!!
AND BE QUICK ABOUT IT!!!
?!!
SODOMU IS DONE FOR!!
MMMO...
!!
THE ARTILLERY STRUCK HIS CHEST!!
HURRY, BEFORE HE FALLS. WE WON'T SAVE ANYONE IF WE DON'T MOVE FORWARD!!!

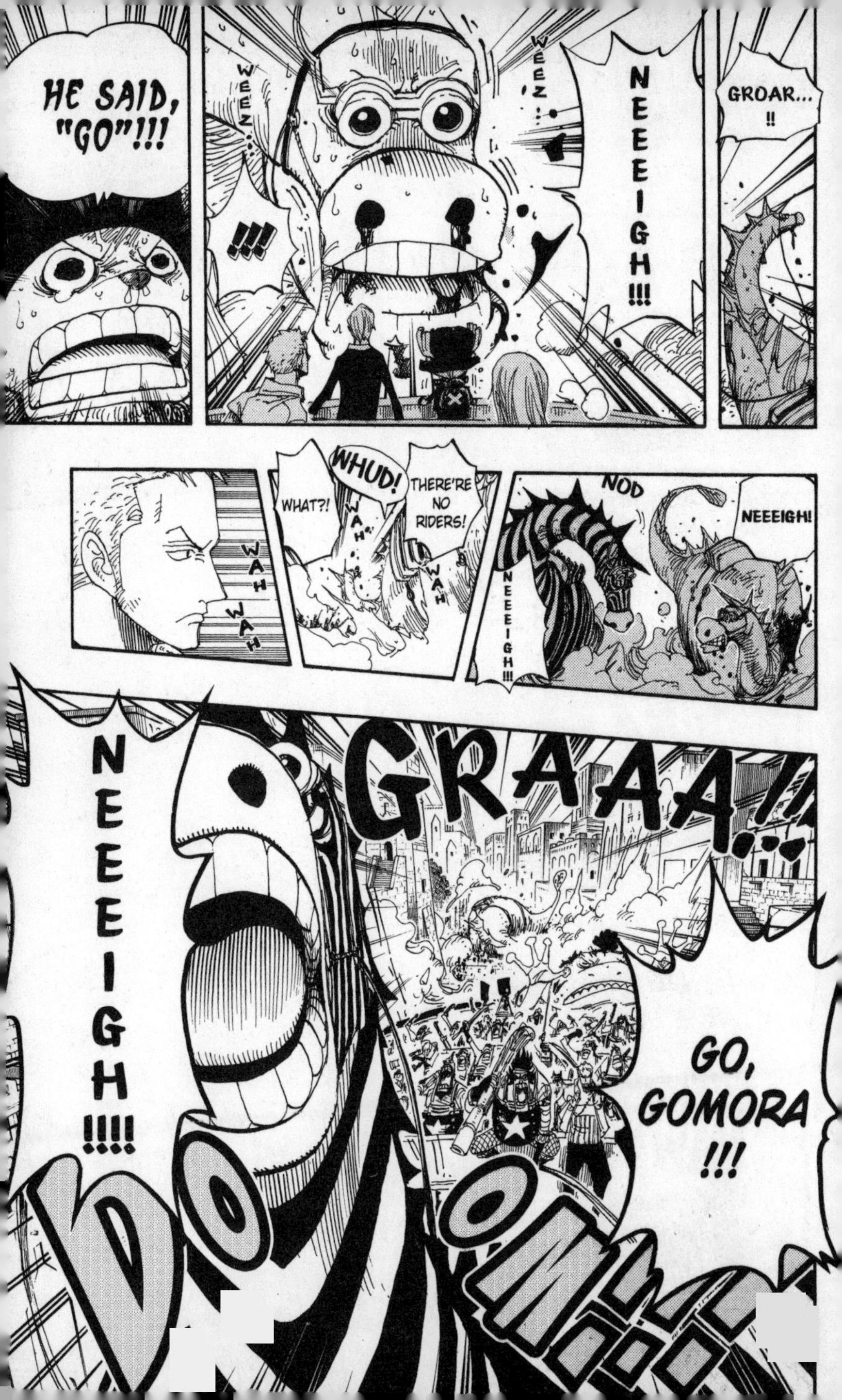
GROAR...
!!
W E E Z !!
NEEEEIGH!!!
W E E Z
!!!
HE SAID, "GO"!!!
NEEEIGH!
NOD
NEEEEIGH!!!
THERE'RE NO RIDERS!
WHUD!
WHAT?!
WAH
WAH
WAH
WAH
WAH
GRAAA!!
NEEEEIGH!!!!
GO, GOMORA!!!
DOOMMM

CONTINUED FROM VOL. 39

The first *One Piece*

"FAN FAVORITE MOVES" CONTEST RESULTS!

FIRE FIST

FOURTH PLACE (1,340 VOTES)

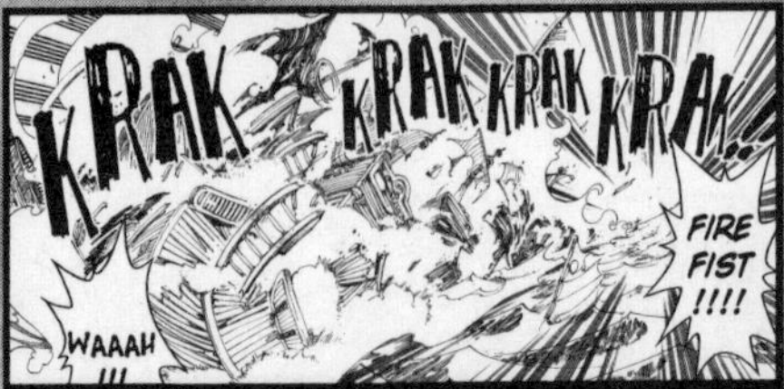

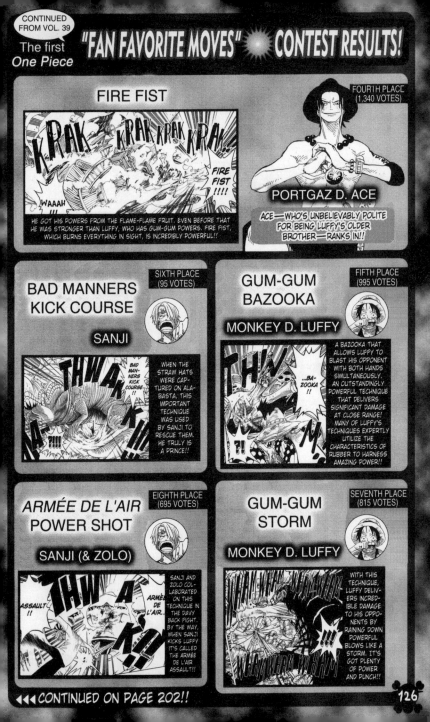

KRAK
KRAK KRAK KRAK...
FIRE FIST !!!!
WAAAH !!!

HE GOT HIS POWERS FROM THE FLAME-FLAME FRUIT. EVEN BEFORE THAT HE WAS STRONGER THAN LUFFY, WHO HAS GUM-GUM POWERS. FIRE FIST, WHICH BURNS EVERYTHING IN SIGHT, IS INCREDIBLY POWERFUL!!

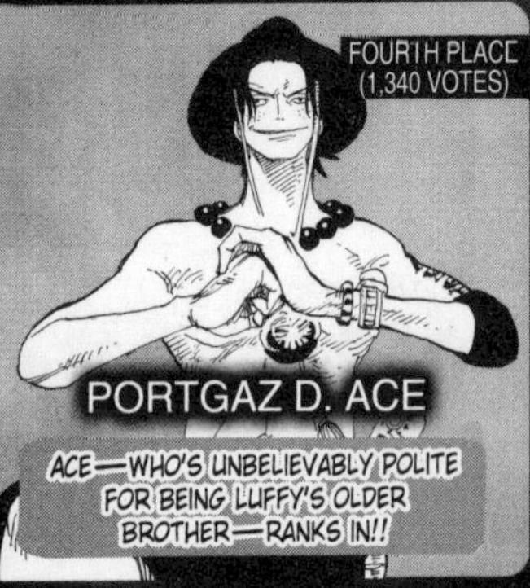

PORTGAZ D. ACE

ACE—WHO'S UNBELIEVABLY POLITE FOR BEING LUFFY'S OLDER BROTHER—RANKS IN!!

BAD MANNERS KICK COURSE

SIXTH PLACE (95 VOTES)

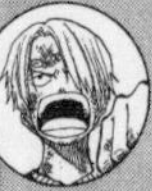

SANJI

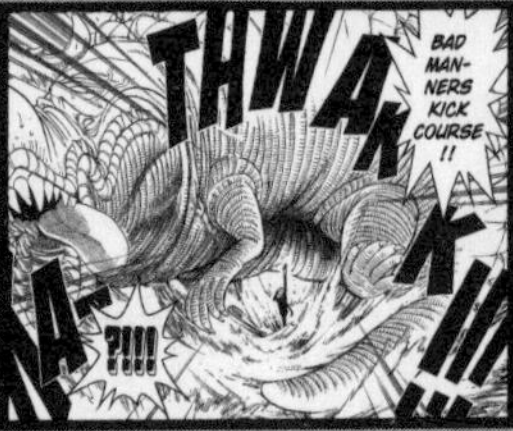

THWAKK!!!
BAD MANNERS KICK COURSE !!
A-?!!!

WHEN THE STRAW HATS WERE CAPTURED ON ALABASTA, THIS IMPORTANT TECHNIQUE WAS USED BY SANJI TO RESCUE THEM. HE TRULY IS A PRINCE!!

GUM-GUM BAZOOKA

FIFTH PLACE (995 VOTES)

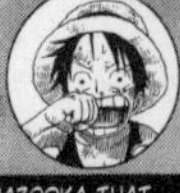

MONKEY D. LUFFY

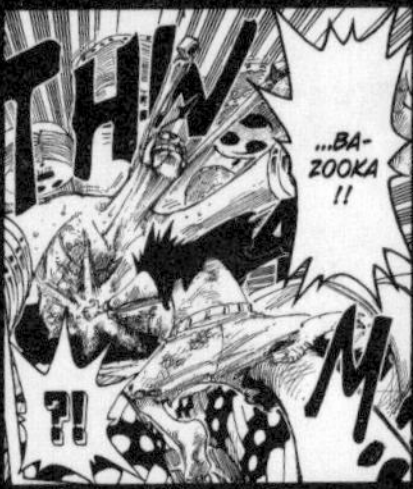

THWM!
...BAZOOKA !!
?!

A BAZOOKA THAT ALLOWS LUFFY TO BLAST HIS OPPONENT WITH BOTH HANDS SIMULTANEOUSLY. AN OUTSTANDINGLY POWERFUL TECHNIQUE THAT DELIVERS SIGNIFICANT DAMAGE AT CLOSE RANGE! MANY OF LUFFY'S TECHNIQUES EXPERTLY UTILIZE THE CHARACTERISTICS OF RUBBER TO HARNESS AMAZING POWER!!

ARMÉE DE L'AIR POWER SHOT

EIGHTH PLACE (695 VOTES)

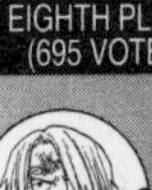

SANJI (& ZOLO)

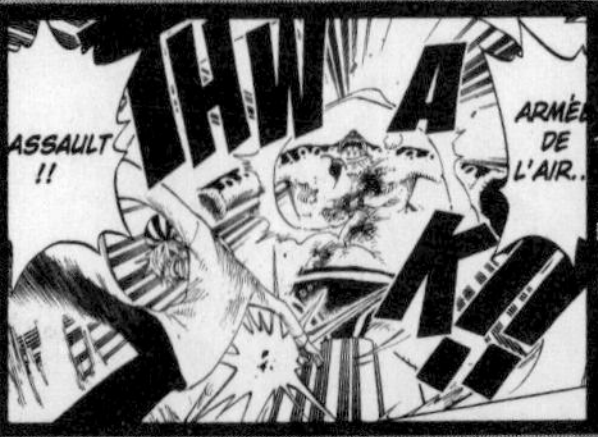

THWAK!!
ARMÉE DE L'AIR..
ASSAULT !!

SANJI AND ZOLO COLLABORATED ON THIS TECHNIQUE IN THE DAVY BACK FIGHT. BY THE WAY, WHEN SANJI KICKS LUFFY IT'S CALLED THE ARMÉE DE L'AIR ASSAULT!!

GUM-GUM STORM

SEVENTH PLACE (815 VOTES)

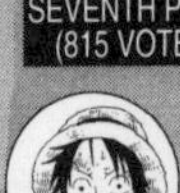

MONKEY D. LUFFY

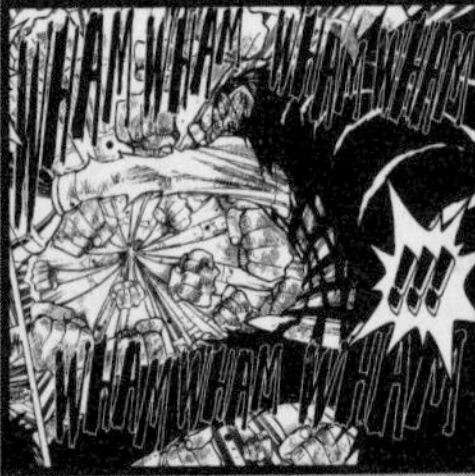

WHAM WHAM WHAM WHAM
!!!
WHAM WHAM WHAM

WITH THIS TECHNIQUE, LUFFY DELIVERS INCREDIBLE DAMAGE TO HIS OPPONENTS BY RAINING DOWN POWERFUL BLOWS LIKE A STORM. IT'S GOT PLENTY OF POWER AND PUNCH!!

◀◀◀ CONTINUED ON PAGE 202!!

Chapter 384:
SIGNAL THE COUNTERATTACK

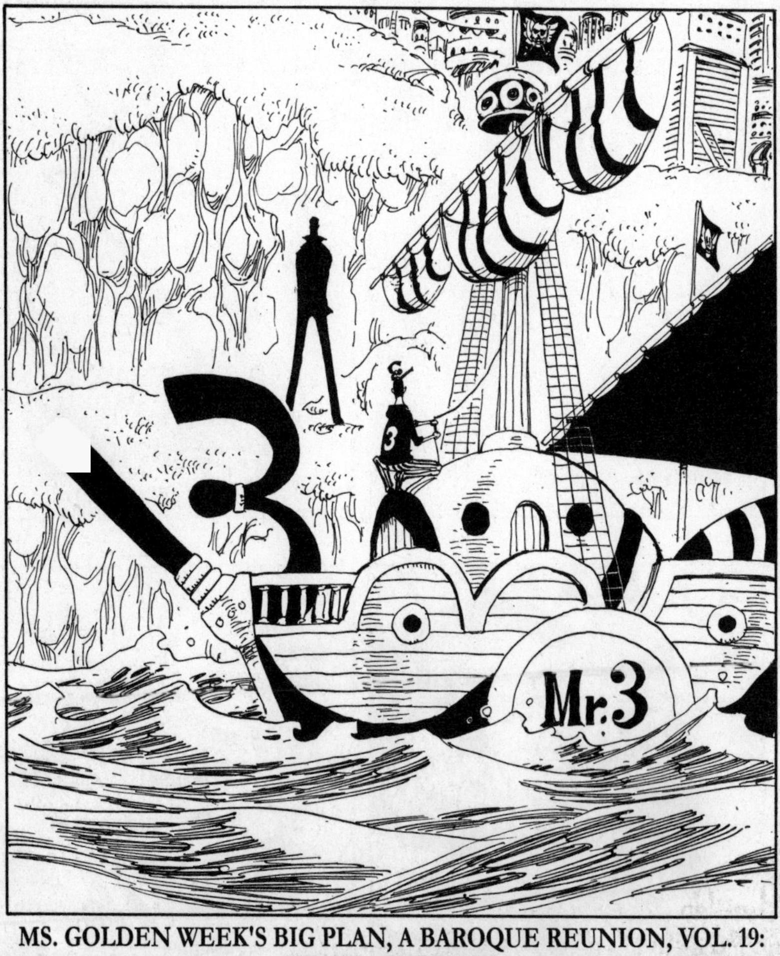

3
Mr.3

MS. GOLDEN WEEK'S BIG PLAN, A BAROQUE REUNION, VOL. 19:
"WAIT A SECOND"

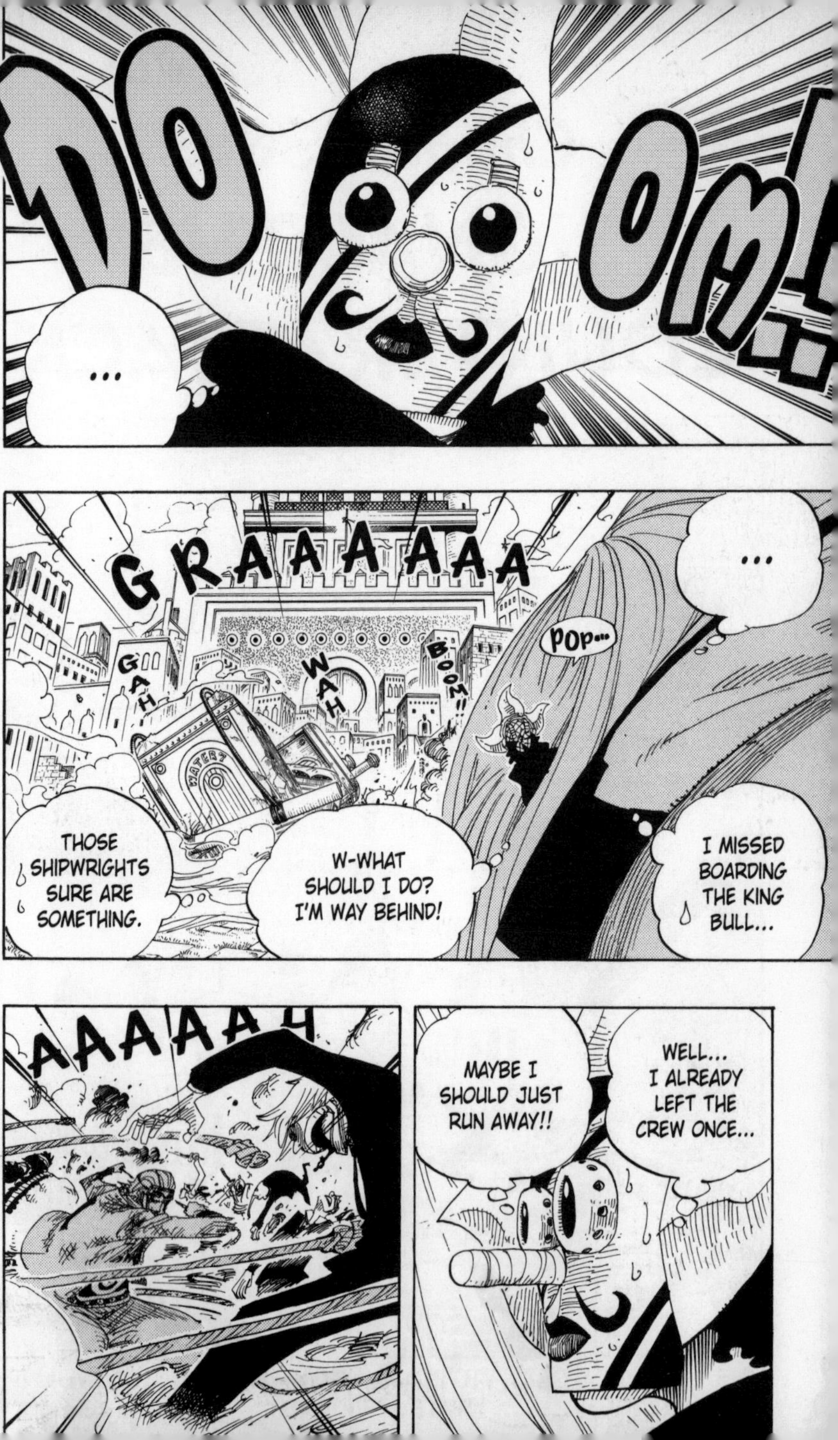
DOOM!
...
...
POP...
I MISSED BOARDING THE KING BULL...
BOOM!!
WAH
GAH
GRAAAAAAA
W-WHAT SHOULD I DO? I'M WAY BEHIND!
THOSE SHIPWRIGHTS SURE ARE SOMETHING.
WELL... I ALREADY LEFT THE CREW ONCE...
MAYBE I SHOULD JUST RUN AWAY!!
AAAAAA

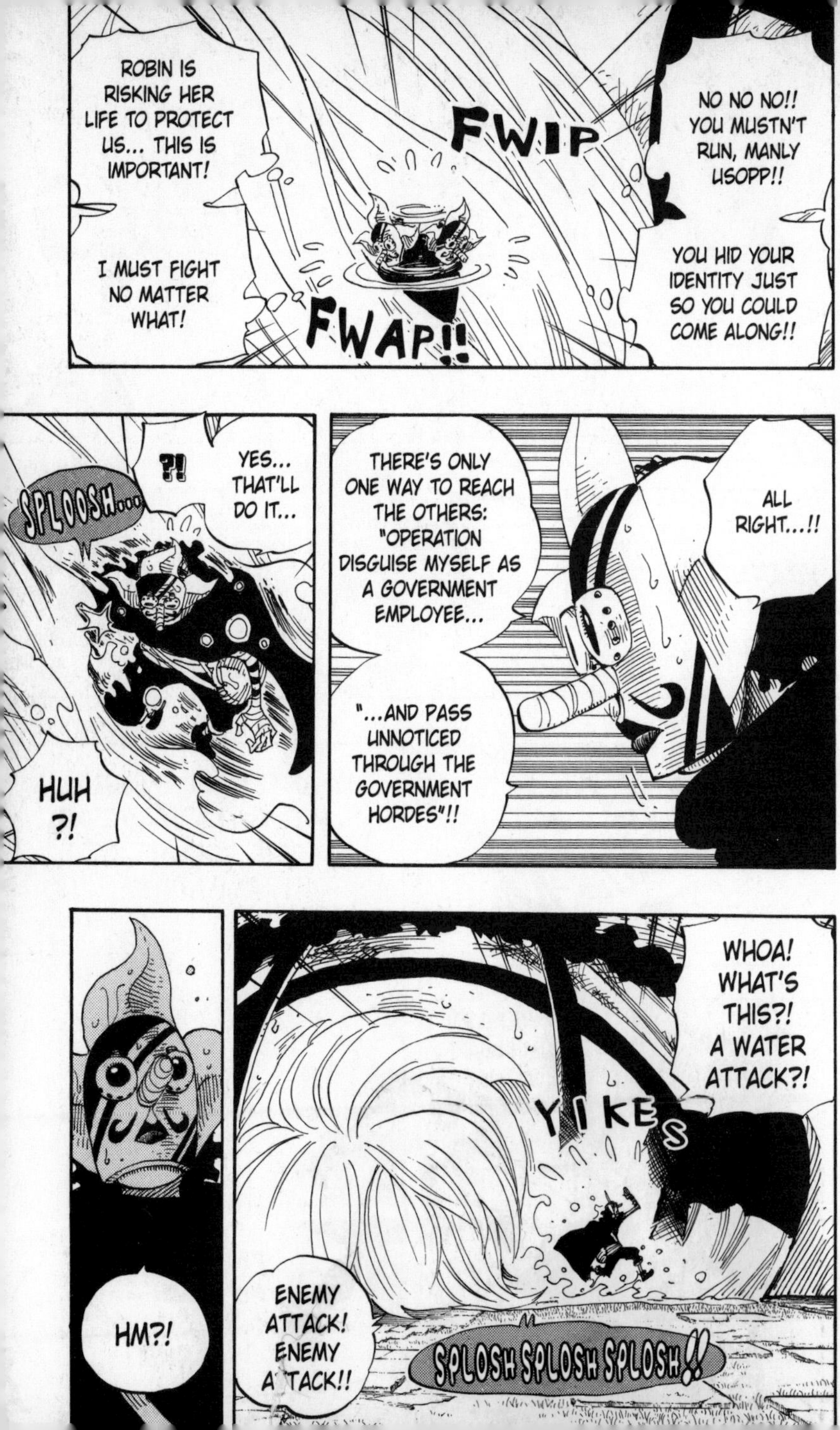
NO NO NO!! YOU MUSTN'T RUN, MANLY USOPP!!
FWIP
ROBIN IS RISKING HER LIFE TO PROTECT US... THIS IS IMPORTANT!
YOU HID YOUR IDENTITY JUST SO YOU COULD COME ALONG!!
I MUST FIGHT NO MATTER WHAT!
FWAP!!
ALL RIGHT...!!
THERE'S ONLY ONE WAY TO REACH THE OTHERS: "OPERATION DISGUISE MYSELF AS A GOVERNMENT EMPLOYEE...
"...AND PASS UNNOTICED THROUGH THE GOVERNMENT HORDES"!!
YES... THAT'LL DO IT...
?!
SPLOOSH...
HUH ?!
WHOA! WHAT'S THIS?! A WATER ATTACK?!
YIKES
ENEMY ATTACK! ENEMY ATTACK!!
SPLOSH SPLOSH SPLOSH!!
HM?!

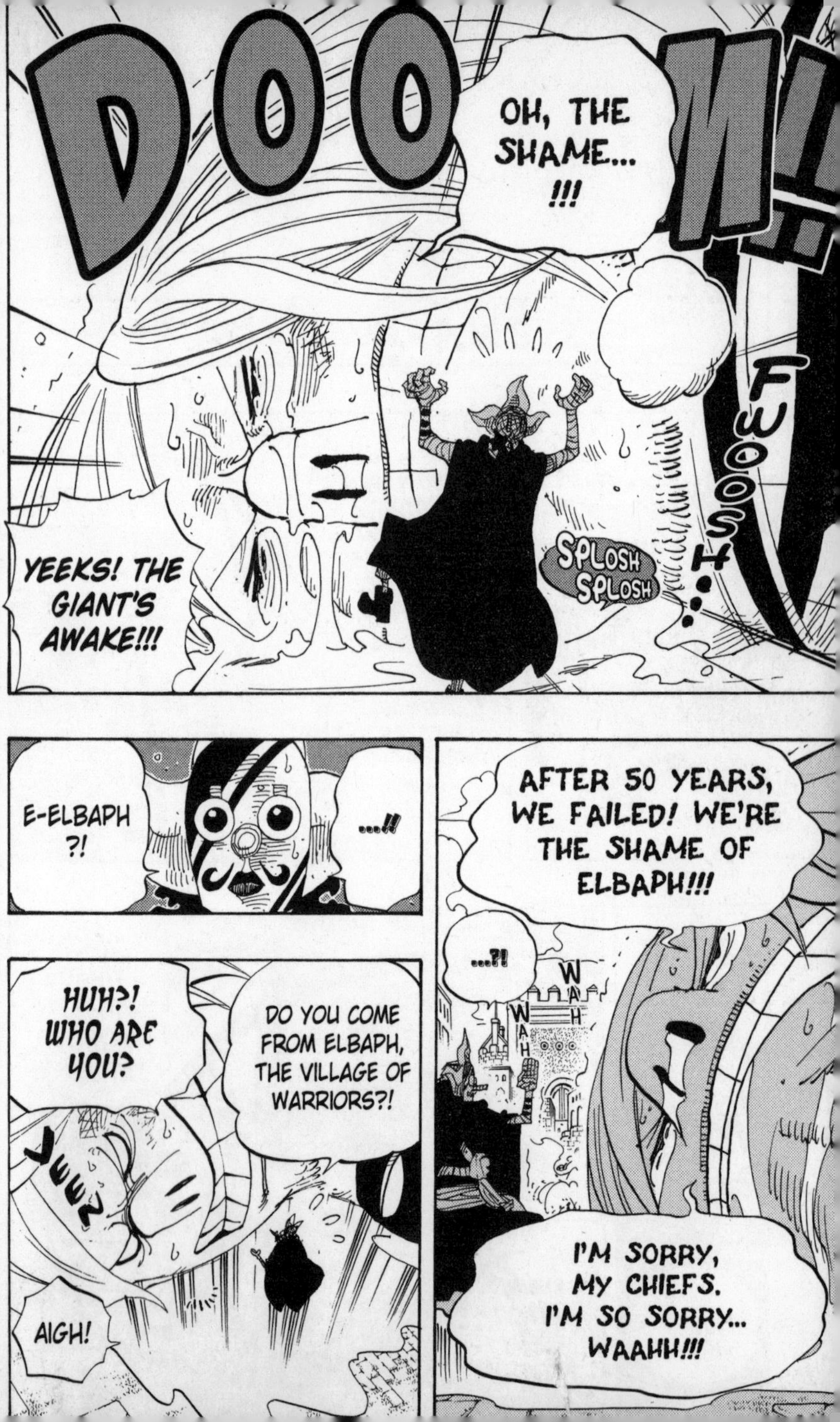
DOOM!!
OH, THE SHAME... !!!
FWOOOSH...
SPLOSH SPLOSH
YEEKS! THE GIANT'S AWAKE!!!
AFTER 50 YEARS, WE FAILED! WE'RE THE SHAME OF ELBAPH!!!
...?!
WAH WAH WAH
I'M SORRY, MY CHIEFS. I'M SO SORRY... WAAHH!!!
...!!
E-ELBAPH ?!
DO YOU COME FROM ELBAPH, THE VILLAGE OF WARRIORS?!
HUH?! WHO ARE YOU?
AIGH!

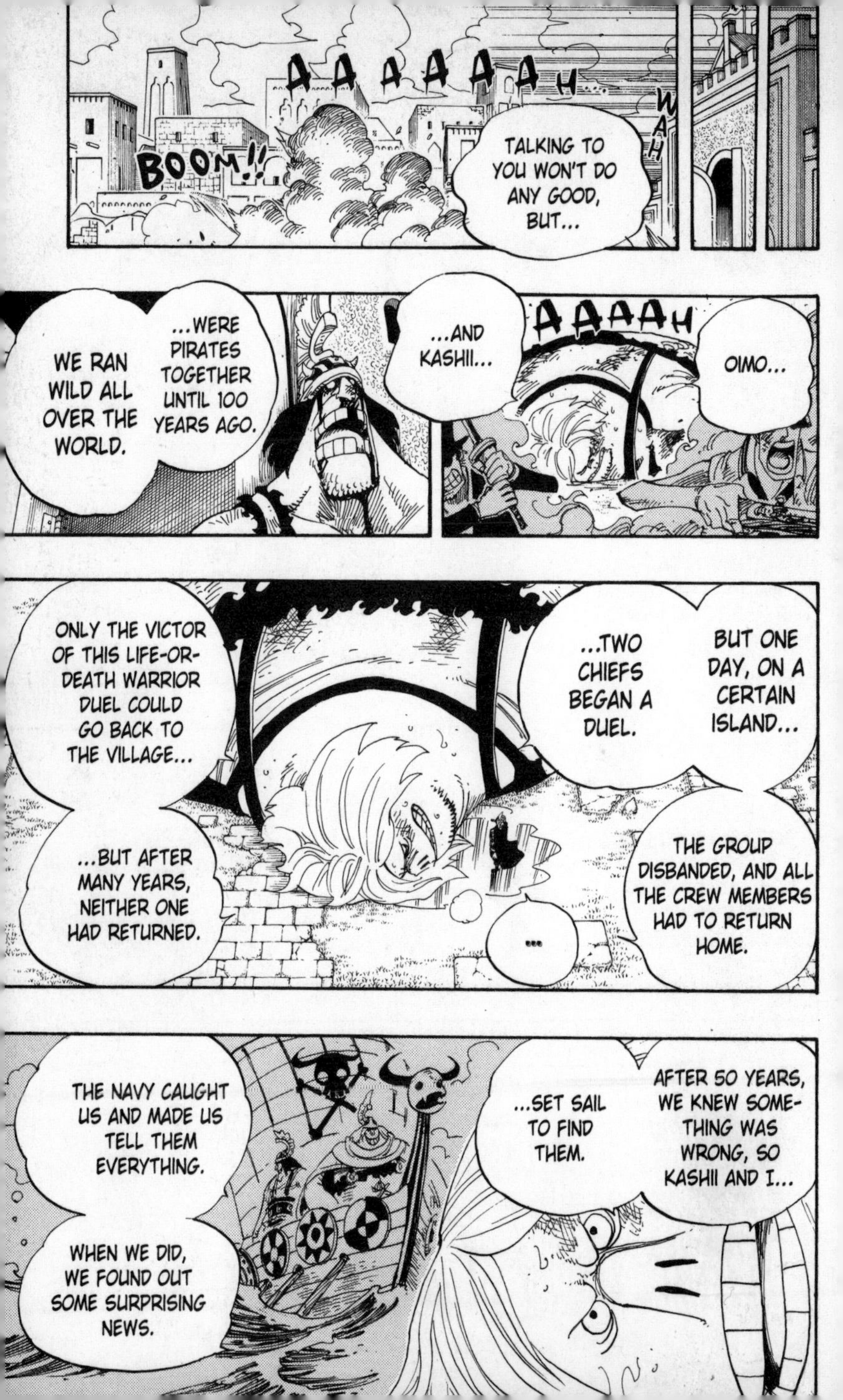
AAAAAAH...
WAH
TALKING TO YOU WON'T DO ANY GOOD, BUT...
BOOM!!
AAAAH
OIMO...
...AND KASHII...
...WERE PIRATES TOGETHER UNTIL 100 YEARS AGO.
WE RAN WILD ALL OVER THE WORLD.
BUT ONE DAY, ON A CERTAIN ISLAND...
...TWO CHIEFS BEGAN A DUEL.
THE GROUP DISBANDED, AND ALL THE CREW MEMBERS HAD TO RETURN HOME.
...
ONLY THE VICTOR OF THIS LIFE-OR-DEATH WARRIOR DUEL COULD GO BACK TO THE VILLAGE...
...BUT AFTER MANY YEARS, NEITHER ONE HAD RETURNED.
AFTER 50 YEARS, WE KNEW SOME-THING WAS WRONG, SO KASHII AND I...
...SET SAIL TO FIND THEM.
THE NAVY CAUGHT US AND MADE US TELL THEM EVERYTHING.
WHEN WE DID, WE FOUND OUT SOME SURPRISING NEWS.

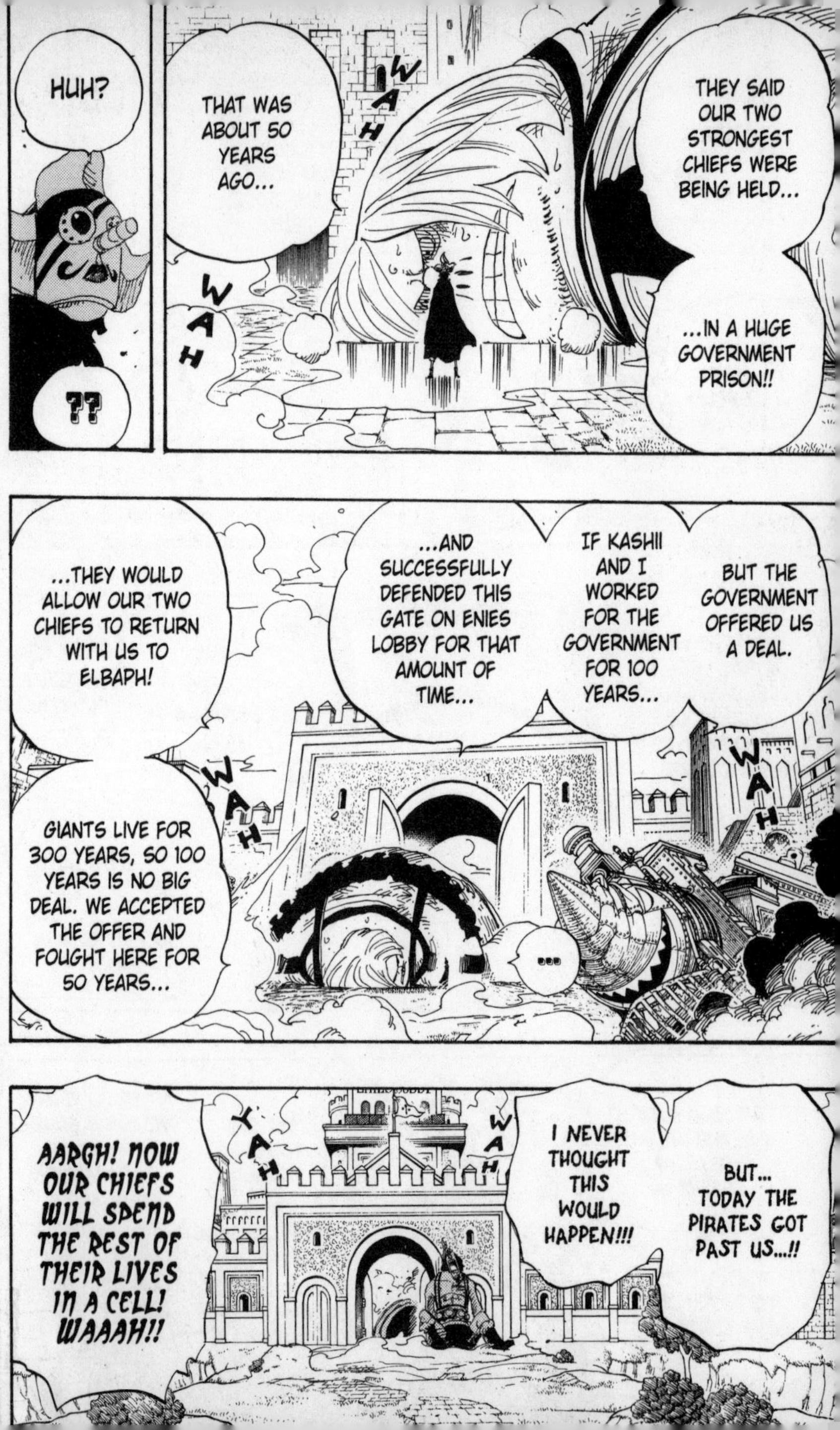
THEY SAID OUR TWO STRONGEST CHIEFS WERE BEING HELD...
...IN A HUGE GOVERNMENT PRISON!!
WAH
THAT WAS ABOUT 50 YEARS AGO...
WAH
HUH?
??
BUT THE GOVERNMENT OFFERED US A DEAL.
IF KASHII AND I WORKED FOR THE GOVERNMENT FOR 100 YEARS...
...AND SUCCESSFULLY DEFENDED THIS GATE ON ENIES LOBBY FOR THAT AMOUNT OF TIME...
WAH
...THEY WOULD ALLOW OUR TWO CHIEFS TO RETURN WITH US TO ELBAPH!
...
WAH
GIANTS LIVE FOR 300 YEARS, SO 100 YEARS IS NO BIG DEAL. WE ACCEPTED THE OFFER AND FOUGHT HERE FOR 50 YEARS...
BUT... TODAY THE PIRATES GOT PAST US...!!
I NEVER THOUGHT THIS WOULD HAPPEN!!!
WAH
YAH
AARGH! NOW OUR CHIEFS WILL SPEND THE REST OF THEIR LIVES IN A CELL! WAAAH!!

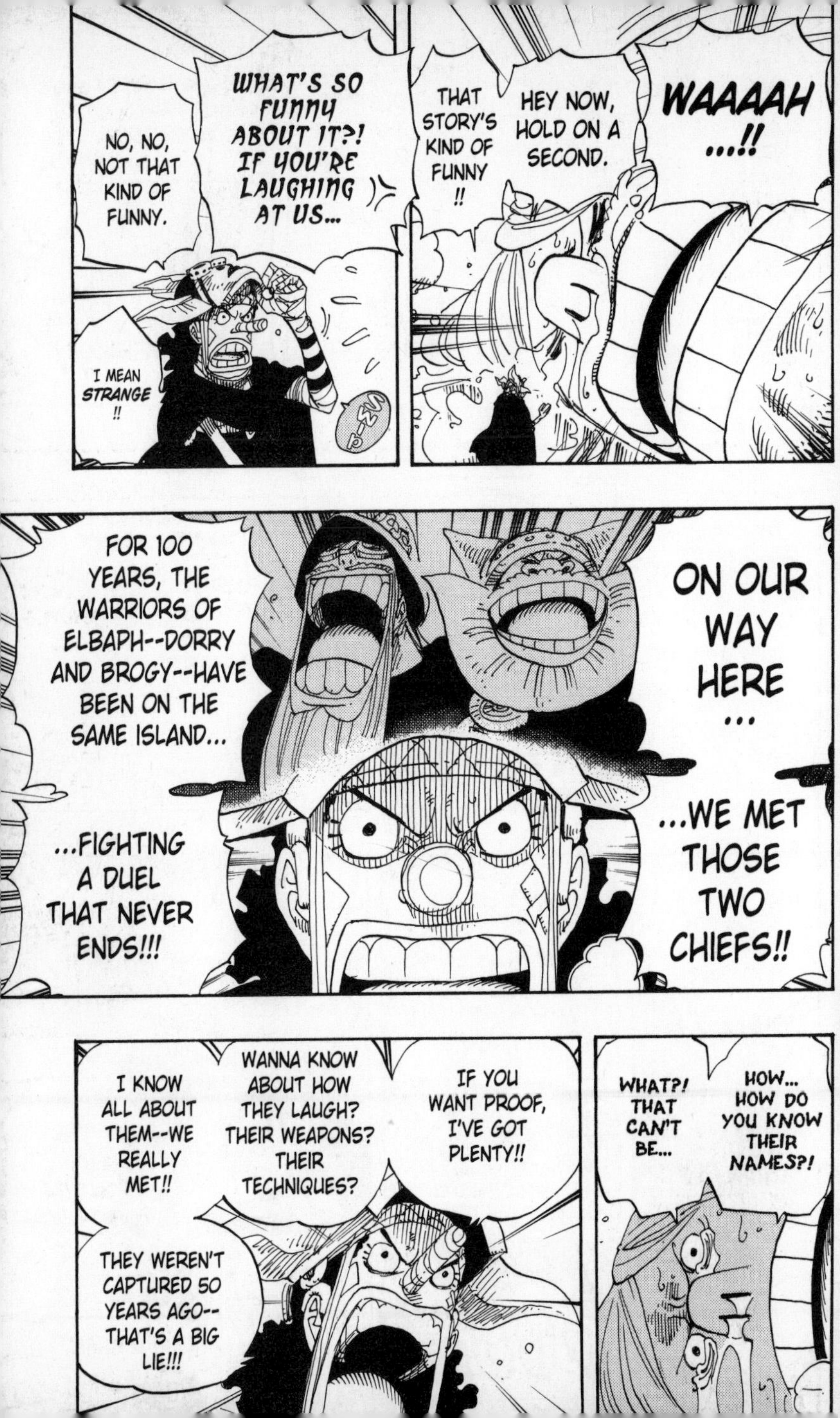
WAAAAH ...!!
HEY NOW, HOLD ON A SECOND.
THAT STORY'S KIND OF FUNNY !!
WHAT'S SO FUNNY ABOUT IT?! IF YOU'RE LAUGHING AT US...
NO, NO, NOT THAT KIND OF FUNNY.
I MEAN STRANGE !!
SWIP
ON OUR WAY HERE ...
...WE MET THOSE TWO CHIEFS!!
FOR 100 YEARS, THE WARRIORS OF ELBAPH--DORRY AND BROGY--HAVE BEEN ON THE SAME ISLAND...
...FIGHTING A DUEL THAT NEVER ENDS!!!
HOW... HOW DO YOU KNOW THEIR NAMES?!
WHAT?! THAT CAN'T BE...
IF YOU WANT PROOF, I'VE GOT PLENTY!!
WANNA KNOW ABOUT HOW THEY LAUGH? THEIR WEAPONS? THEIR TECHNIQUES?
I KNOW ALL ABOUT THEM--WE REALLY MET!!
THEY WEREN'T CAPTURED 50 YEARS AGO--THAT'S A BIG LIE!!!

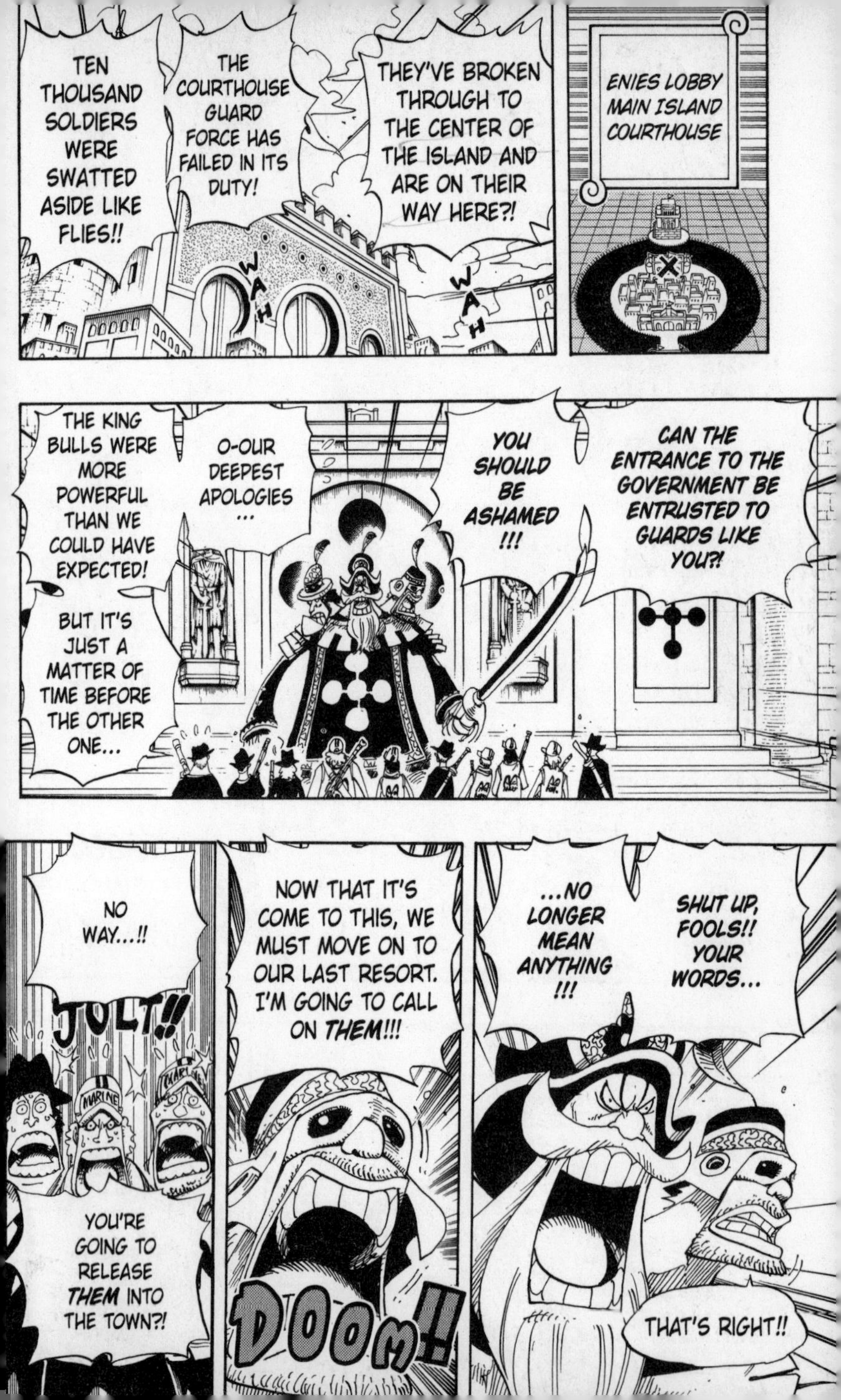
ENIES LOBBY MAIN ISLAND COURTHOUSE
THEY'VE BROKEN THROUGH TO THE CENTER OF THE ISLAND AND ARE ON THEIR WAY HERE?!
THE COURTHOUSE GUARD FORCE HAS FAILED IN ITS DUTY!
TEN THOUSAND SOLDIERS WERE SWATTED ASIDE LIKE FLIES!!
WAH
WAH
CAN THE ENTRANCE TO THE GOVERNMENT BE ENTRUSTED TO GUARDS LIKE YOU?!
YOU SHOULD BE ASHAMED!!!
O-OUR DEEPEST APOLOGIES...
THE KING BULLS WERE MORE POWERFUL THAN WE COULD HAVE EXPECTED!
BUT IT'S JUST A MATTER OF TIME BEFORE THE OTHER ONE...
SHUT UP, FOOLS!! YOUR WORDS...
...NO LONGER MEAN ANYTHING!!!
THAT'S RIGHT!!
NOW THAT IT'S COME TO THIS, WE MUST MOVE ON TO OUR LAST RESORT. I'M GOING TO CALL ON *THEM*!!!
DOOM!!
NO WAY...!!
JOLT!!
YOU'RE GOING TO RELEASE *THEM* INTO THE TOWN?!

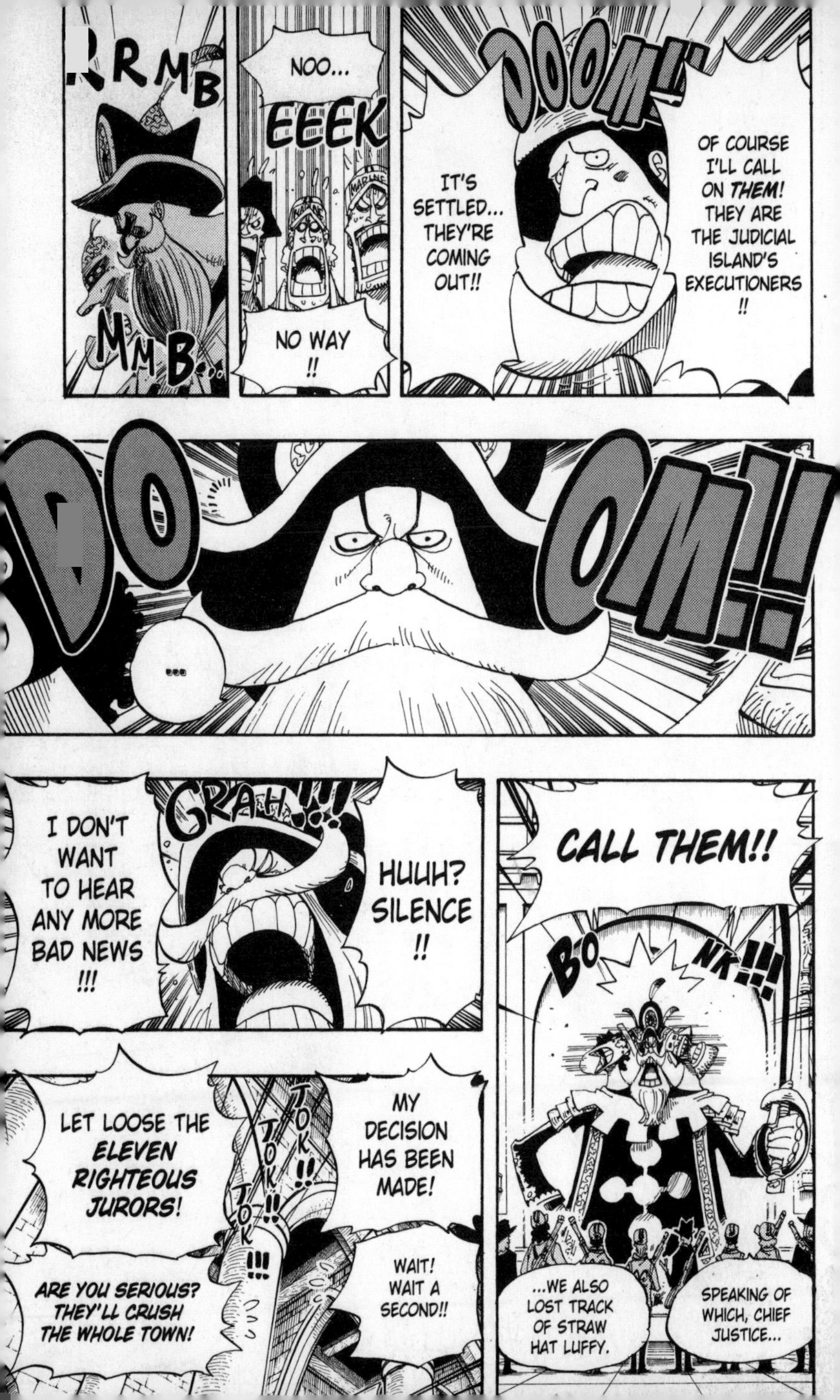
DOOM!!
OF COURSE I'LL CALL ON *THEM*! THEY ARE THE JUDICIAL ISLAND'S EXECUTIONERS!!
IT'S SETTLED... THEY'RE COMING OUT!!
NOO...
EEEK
NO WAY!!
RRMB
MMB
DOOM!!
...
CALL THEM!!
BONK!!!
SPEAKING OF WHICH, CHIEF JUSTICE...
...WE ALSO LOST TRACK OF STRAW HAT LUFFY.
GRAH!!!
HUUH? SILENCE!!
I DON'T WANT TO HEAR ANY MORE BAD NEWS!!!
MY DECISION HAS BEEN MADE!
TOK!!
TOK!!
TOK!!!
LET LOOSE THE *ELEVEN RIGHTEOUS JURORS!*
WAIT! WAIT A SECOND!!
ARE YOU SERIOUS? THEY'LL CRUSH THE WHOLE TOWN!

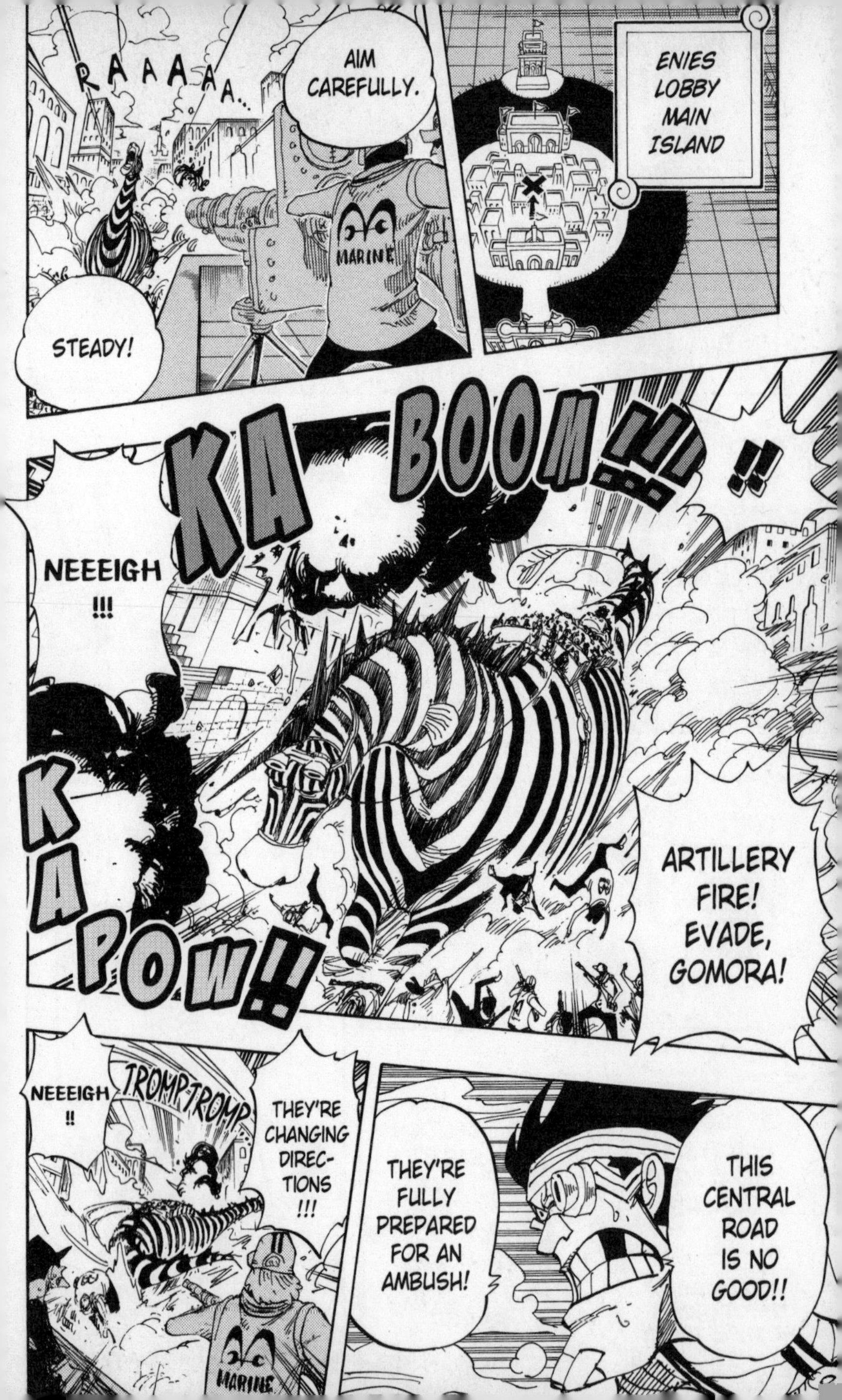
ENIES LOBBY MAIN ISLAND
AIM CAREFULLY.
RAAAAAA...
MARINE
STEADY!
KA-BOOM!!!!!
ARTILLERY FIRE! EVADE, GOMORA!
NEEEIGH!!!
KAPOW!!
THIS CENTRAL ROAD IS NO GOOD!!
THEY'RE FULLY PREPARED FOR AN AMBUSH!
THEY'RE CHANGING DIREC-TIONS!!!
TROMP TROMP
NEEEIGH!!
MARINE

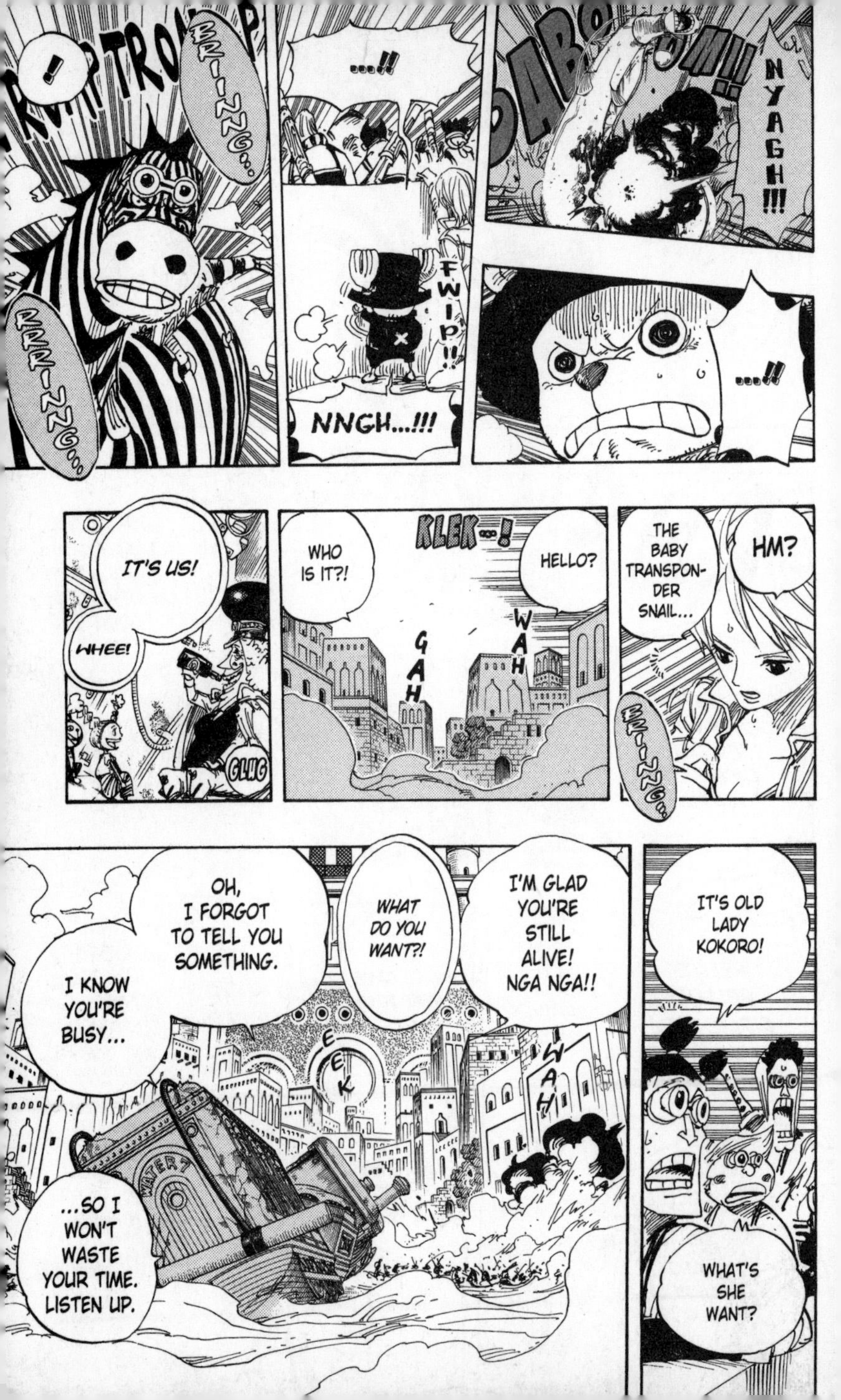

DABOOM!!
NYAGH!!!
...!!
...!!
FWIP!!
NNGH...!!!
!
BRRIIING...
RRRIIINNG...
HM?
THE BABY TRANSPONDER SNAIL...
BRIIING...
KLEK...!
HELLO?
WHO IS IT?!
WAH
GAH
IT'S US!
WHEE!
GLUG
IT'S OLD LADY KOKORO!
WHAT'S SHE WANT?
I'M GLAD YOU'RE STILL ALIVE! NGA NGA!!
WHAT DO YOU WANT?!
OH, I FORGOT TO TELL YOU SOMETHING.
I KNOW YOU'RE BUSY...
WAH
EEK
...SO I WON'T WASTE YOUR TIME. LISTEN UP.

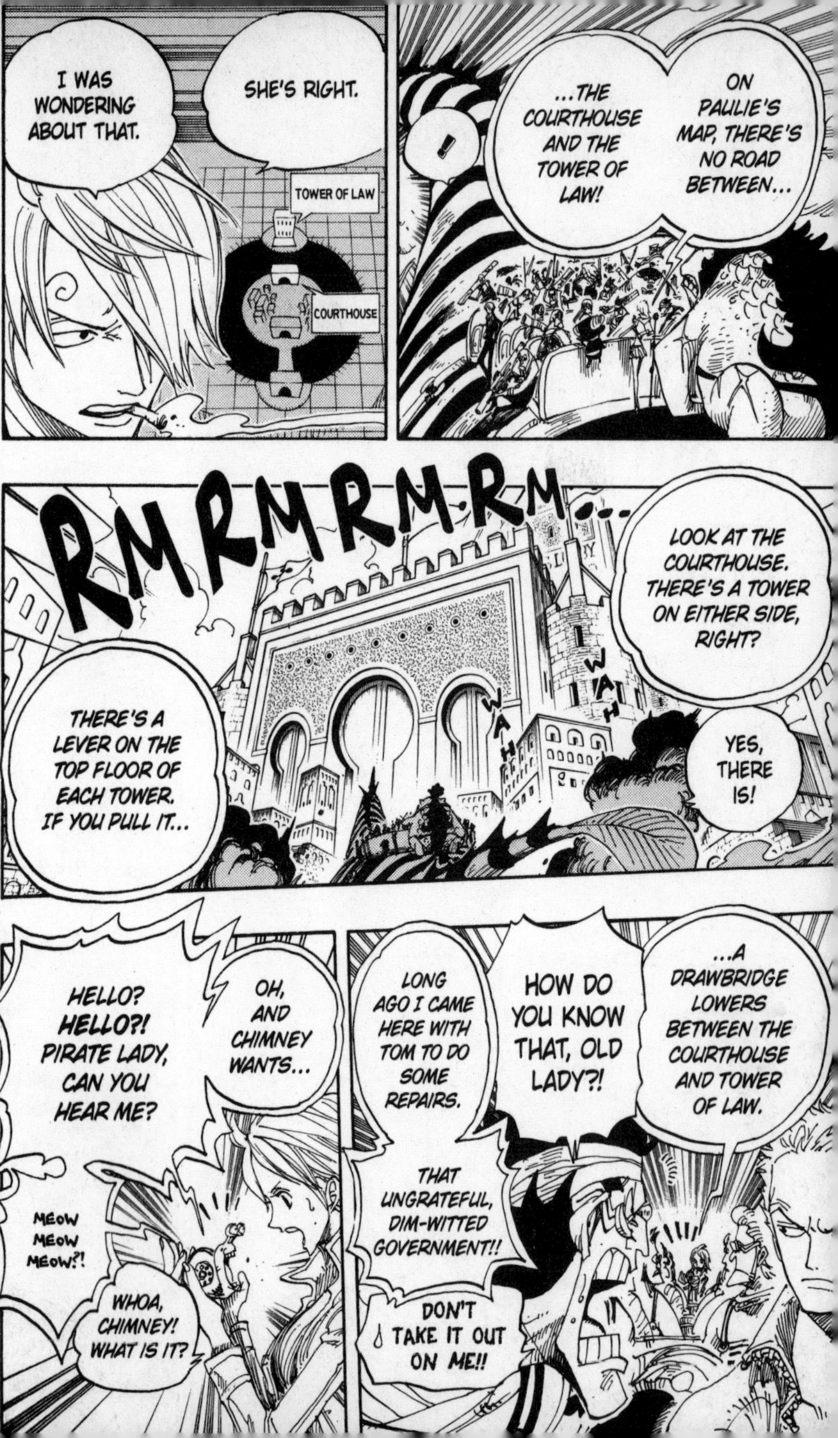
!
ON PAULIE'S MAP, THERE'S NO ROAD BETWEEN...
...THE COURTHOUSE AND THE TOWER OF LAW!
SHE'S RIGHT.
I WAS WONDERING ABOUT THAT.
TOWER OF LAW
COURTHOUSE
RMRMRMRM...
LOOK AT THE COURTHOUSE. THERE'S A TOWER ON EITHER SIDE, RIGHT?
YES, THERE IS!
WAH
WAH
THERE'S A LEVER ON THE TOP FLOOR OF EACH TOWER. IF YOU PULL IT...
...A DRAWBRIDGE LOWERS BETWEEN THE COURTHOUSE AND TOWER OF LAW.
HOW DO YOU KNOW THAT, OLD LADY?!
LONG AGO I CAME HERE WITH TOM TO DO SOME REPAIRS.
THAT UNGRATEFUL, DIM-WITTED GOVERNMENT!!
DON'T TAKE IT OUT ON ME!!
OH, AND CHIMNEY WANTS...
HELLO? HELLO?! PIRATE LADY, CAN YOU HEAR ME?
MEOW MEOW MEOW?!
WHOA, CHIMNEY! WHAT IS IT?

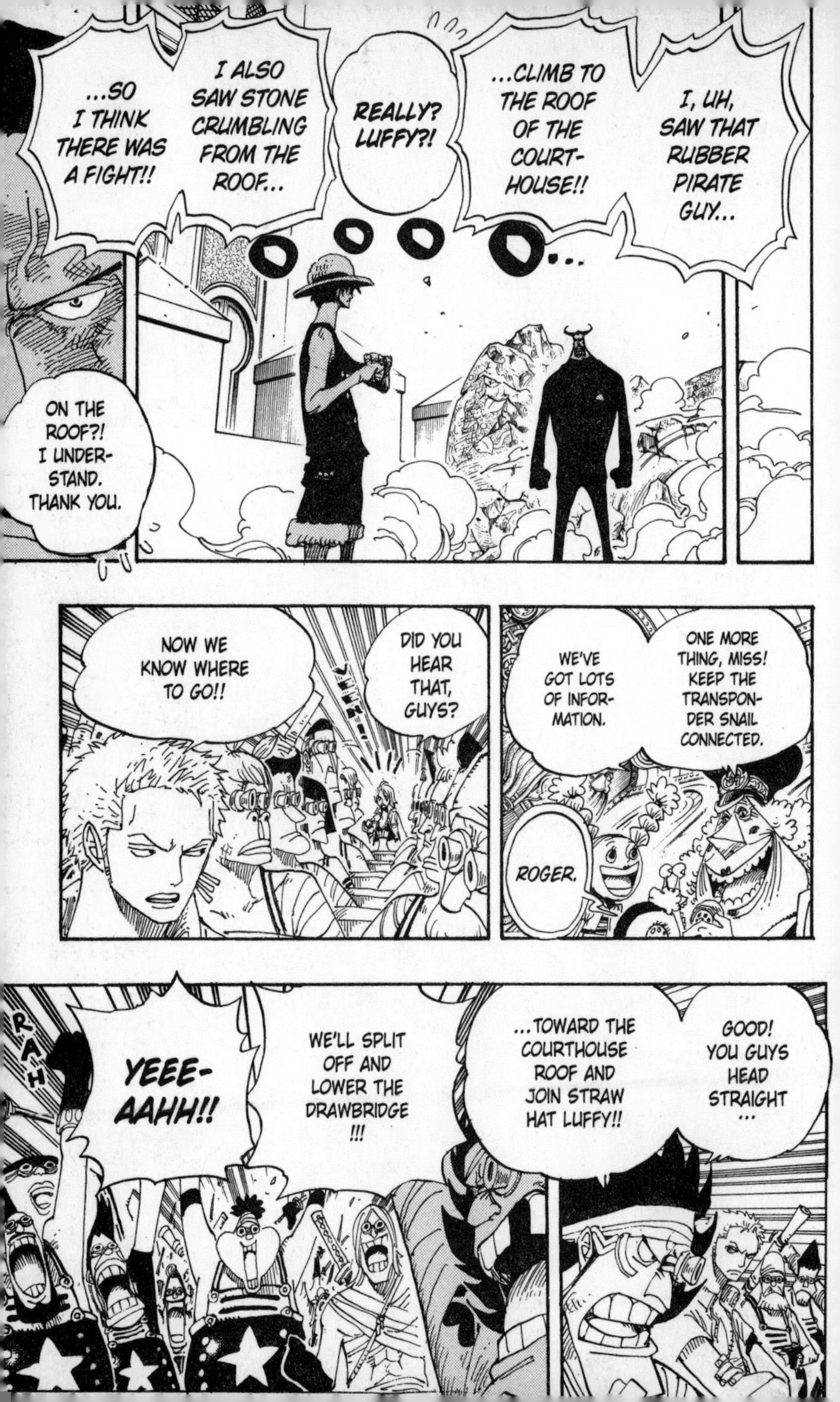
I, UH, SAW THAT RUBBER PIRATE GUY...
...CLIMB TO THE ROOF OF THE COURT-HOUSE!!
REALLY? LUFFY?!
I ALSO SAW STONE CRUMBLING FROM THE ROOF...
...SO I THINK THERE WAS A FIGHT!!
ON THE ROOF?! I UNDER-STAND. THANK YOU.
ONE MORE THING, MISS! KEEP THE TRANSPON-DER SNAIL CONNECTED.
WE'VE GOT LOTS OF INFOR-MATION.
ROGER.
DID YOU HEAR THAT, GUYS?
NOW WE KNOW WHERE TO GO!!
GOOD! YOU GUYS HEAD STRAIGHT...
...TOWARD THE COURTHOUSE ROOF AND JOIN STRAW HAT LUFFY!!
WE'LL SPLIT OFF AND LOWER THE DRAWBRIDGE!!!
YEEE-AAHH!!
RAH

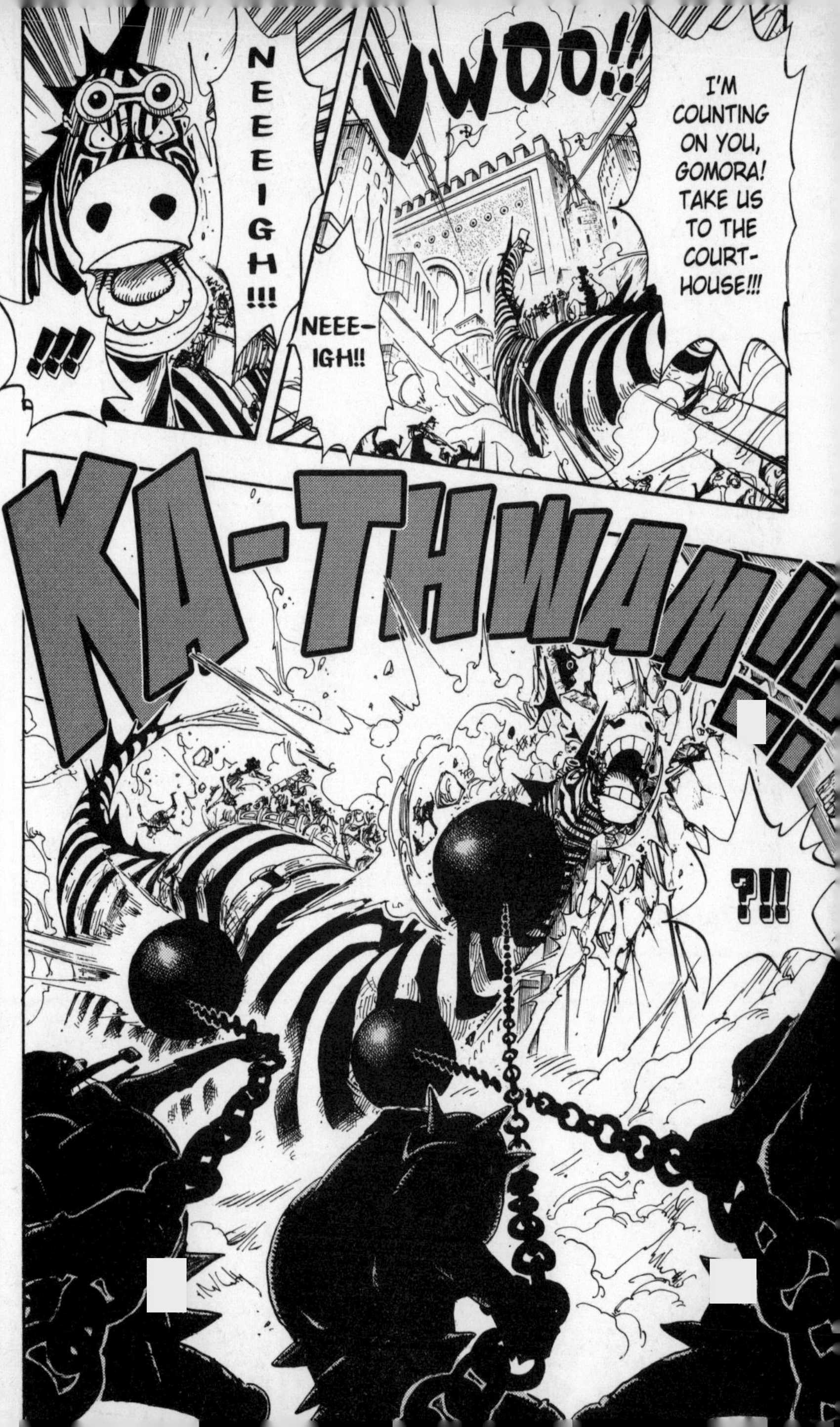

I'M COUNTING ON YOU, GOMORA! TAKE US TO THE COURT-HOUSE!!!
VWOO!!
NEEE-IGH!!
NEEEEIGH!!!
!!!
KA-THWAM!!!
?!!

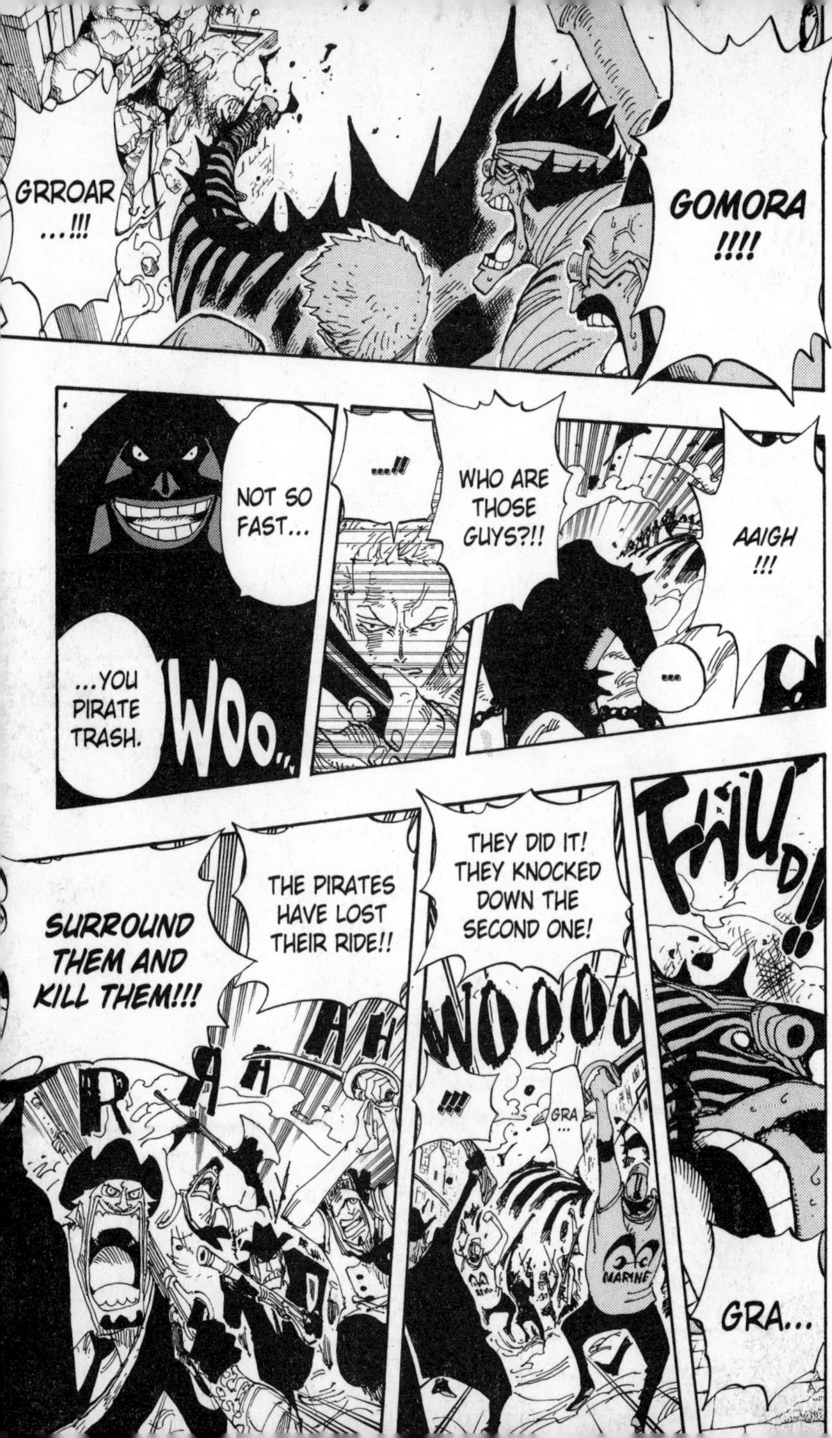
GOMORA !!!!
GRROAR ...!!!
AAIGH !!!
...
WHO ARE THOSE GUYS?!!
...!!
NOT SO FAST...
...YOU PIRATE TRASH.
WOO...
FWUD!!
GRA...
THEY DID IT! THEY KNOCKED DOWN THE SECOND ONE!
WOOOOO!!!
GRA...
THE PIRATES HAVE LOST THEIR RIDE!!
SURROUND THEM AND KILL THEM!!!
RAAAH

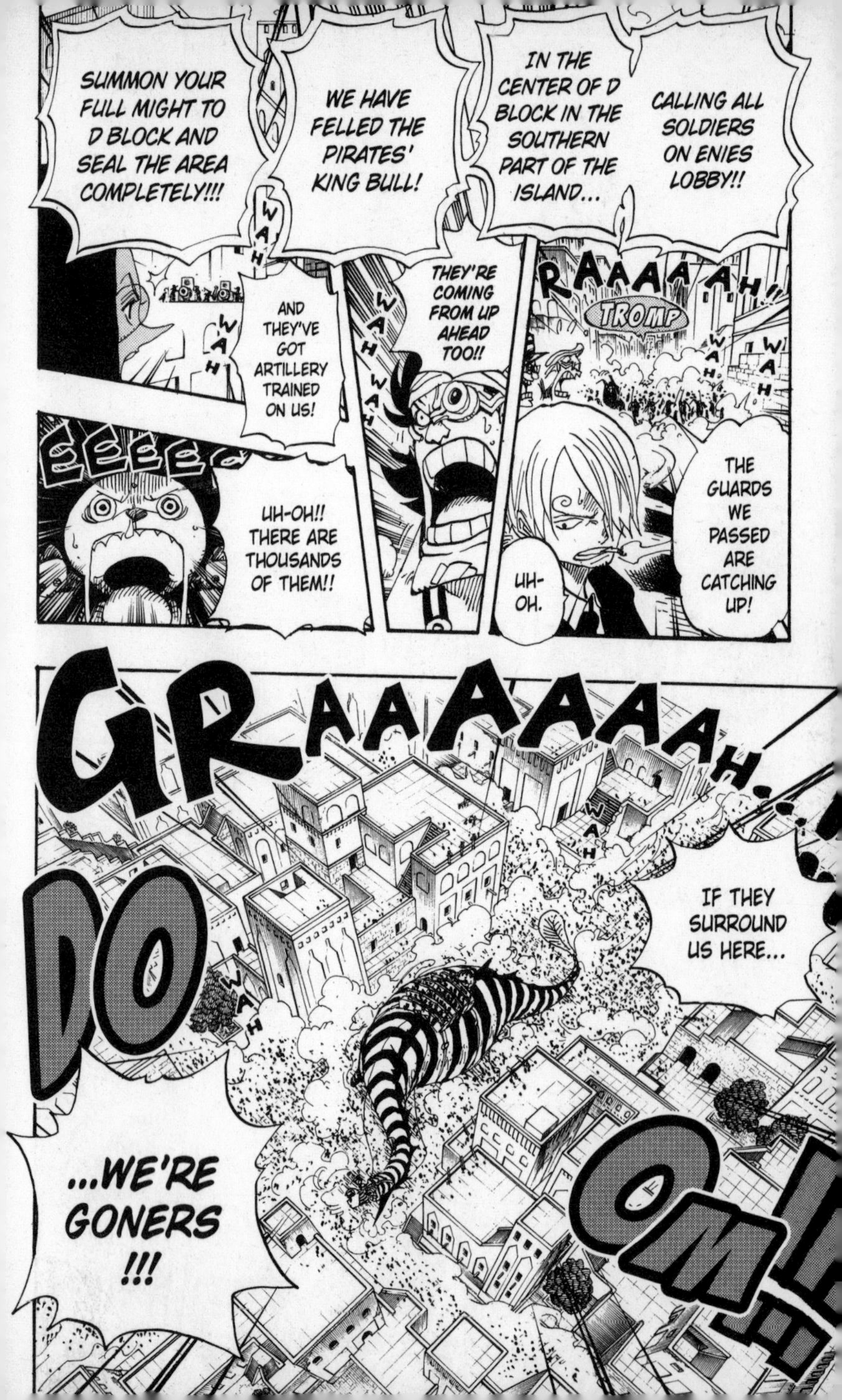
CALLING ALL SOLDIERS ON ENIES LOBBY!!
IN THE CENTER OF D BLOCK IN THE SOUTHERN PART OF THE ISLAND...
WE HAVE FELLED THE PIRATES' KING BULL!
SUMMON YOUR FULL MIGHT TO D BLOCK AND SEAL THE AREA COMPLETELY!!!
RAAAAAAH!!
TROMP
WAH
WAH
THE GUARDS WE PASSED ARE CATCHING UP!
UH-OH.
WAH
WAH
THEY'RE COMING FROM UP AHEAD TOO!!
WAH
WAH
AND THEY'VE GOT ARTILLERY TRAINED ON US!
EEEE
UH-OH!! THERE ARE THOUSANDS OF THEM!!
GRAAAAAAH..
WAH
IF THEY SURROUND US HERE...
WAH
DO
OM!!
...WE'RE GONERS!!!

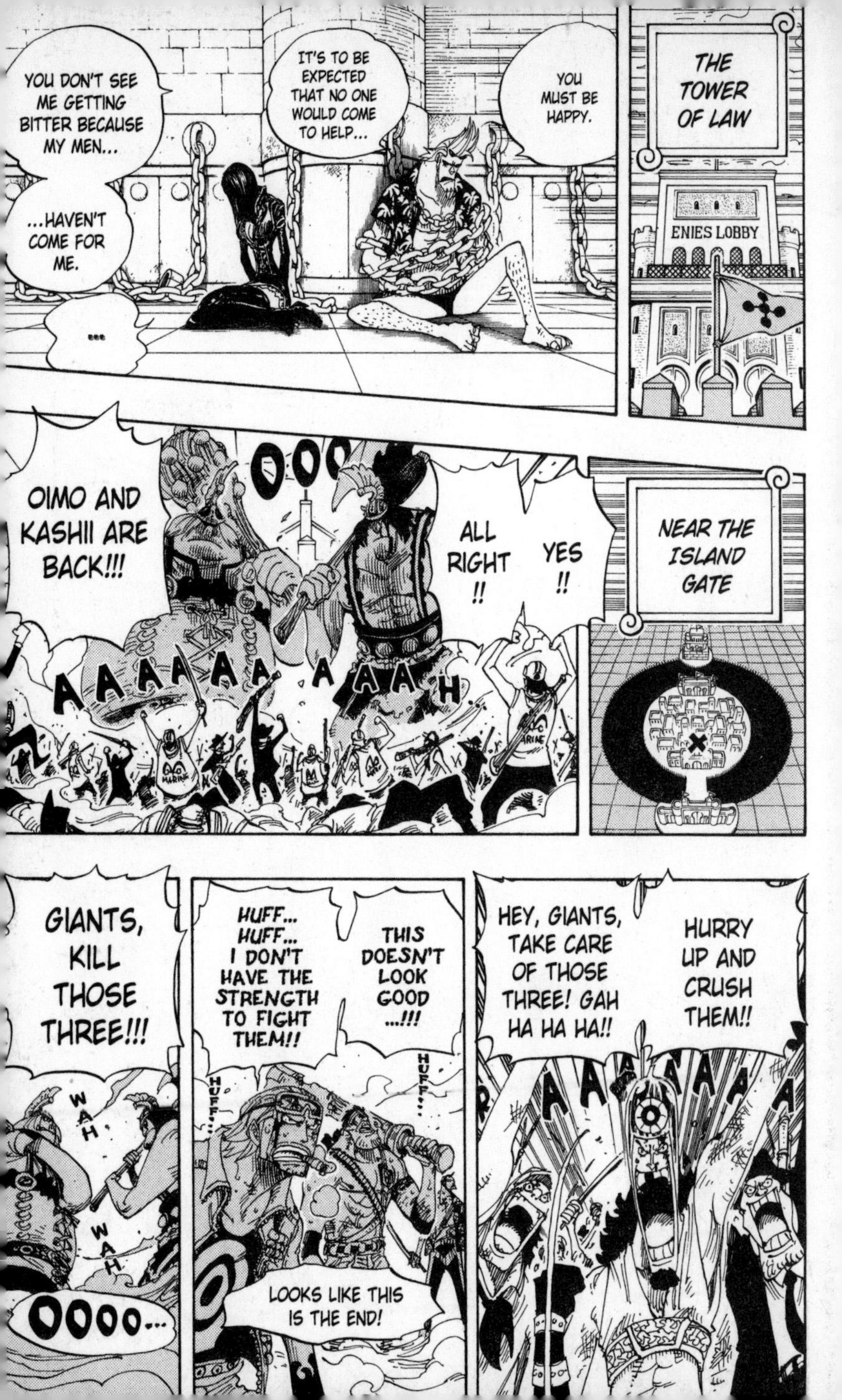
THE TOWER OF LAW
ENIES LOBBY
YOU MUST BE HAPPY.
IT'S TO BE EXPECTED THAT NO ONE WOULD COME TO HELP...
YOU DON'T SEE ME GETTING BITTER BECAUSE MY MEN...
...HAVEN'T COME FOR ME.
...
NEAR THE ISLAND GATE
YES!!
ALL RIGHT!!
OOO
OIMO AND KASHII ARE BACK!!!
AAAAAAAAAH.
HURRY UP AND CRUSH THEM!!
HEY, GIANTS, TAKE CARE OF THOSE THREE! GAH HA HA HA!!
AAAAAA
THIS DOESN'T LOOK GOOD...!!!
HUFF...
HUFF... HUFF... I DON'T HAVE THE STRENGTH TO FIGHT THEM!!
HUFF...
LOOKS LIKE THIS IS THE END!
GIANTS, KILL THOSE THREE!!!
WAH
WAH
OOOO...

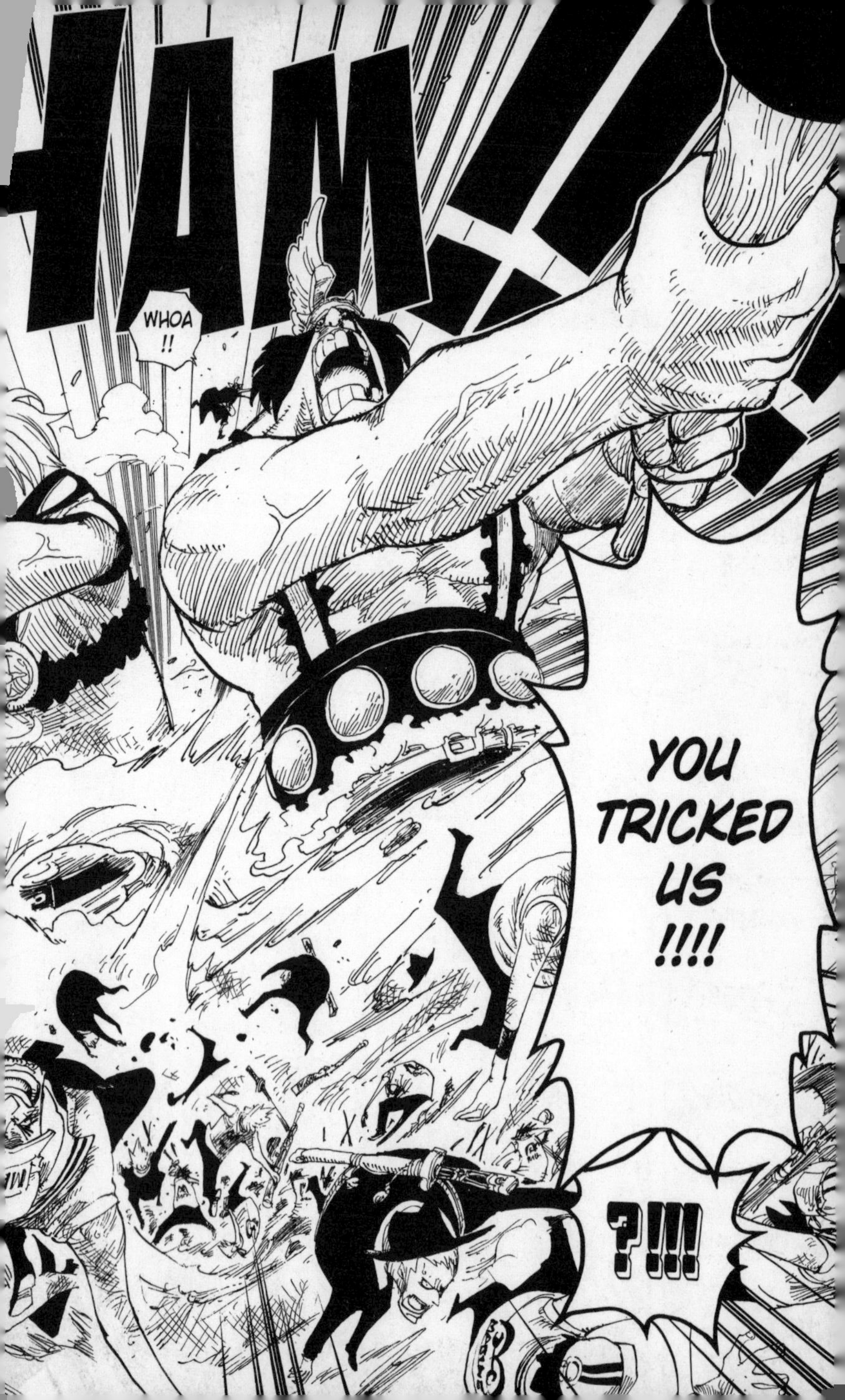
WHOA !!
YOU TRICKED US !!!!
?!!!

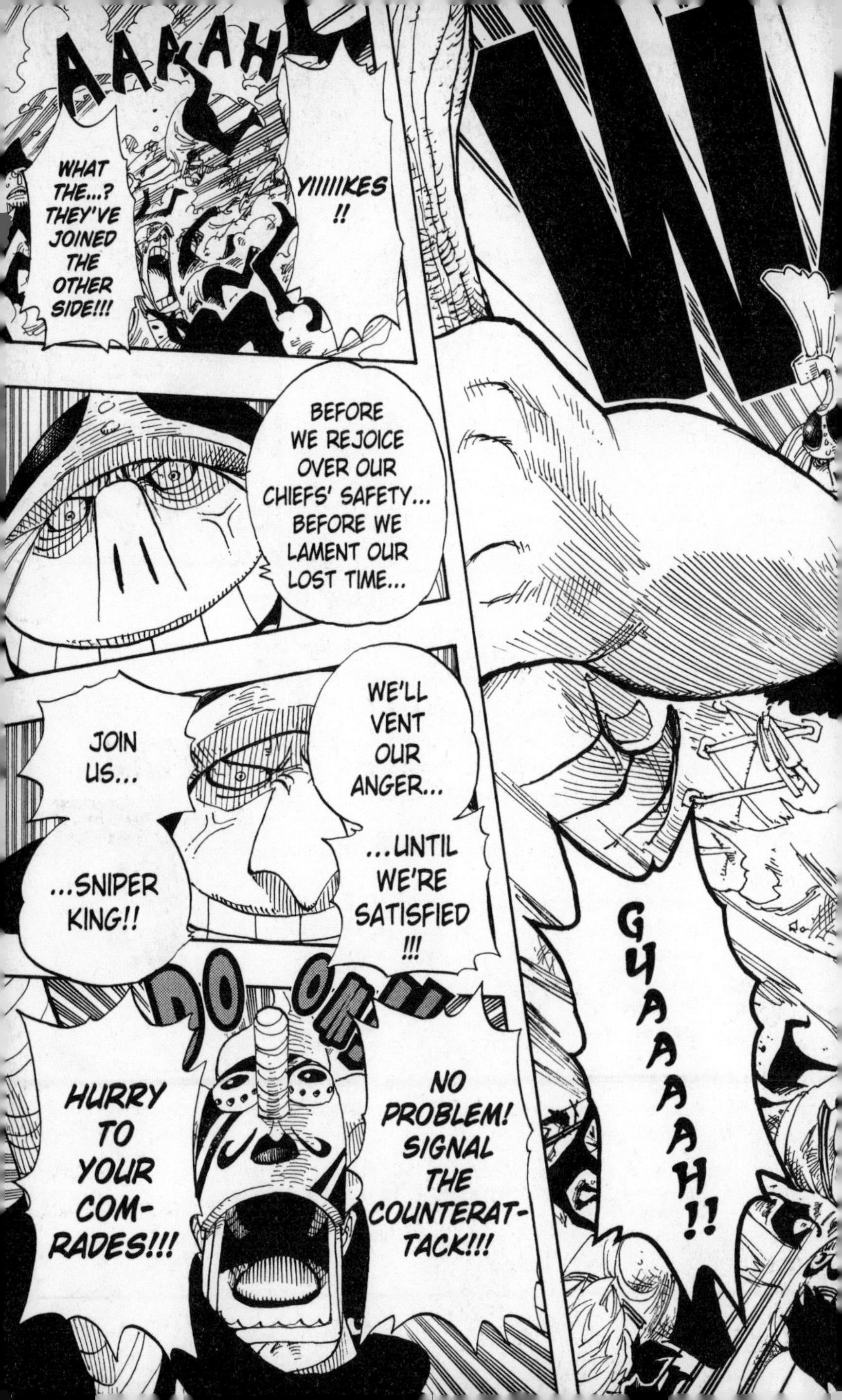
GUAAAAH!!
AAAAH
YIIIIIKES!!
WHAT THE...? THEY'VE JOINED THE OTHER SIDE!!!
BEFORE WE REJOICE OVER OUR CHIEFS' SAFETY... BEFORE WE LAMENT OUR LOST TIME...
WE'LL VENT OUR ANGER...
JOIN US...
...UNTIL WE'RE SATISFIED!!!
...SNIPER KING!!
DOOM
NO PROBLEM! SIGNAL THE COUNTERAT-TACK!!!
HURRY TO YOUR COM-RADES!!!

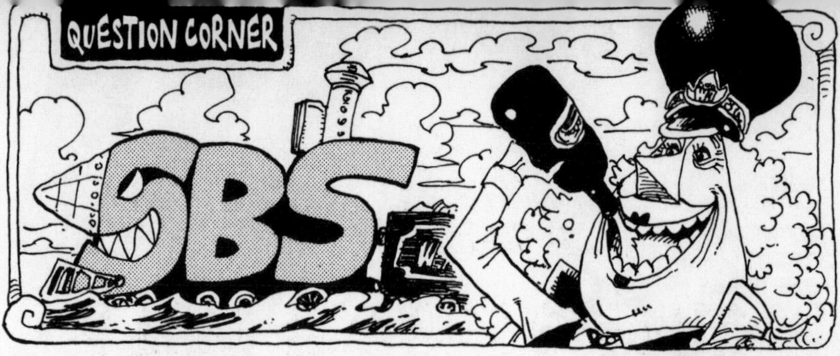
QUESTION CORNER
SBS

Q. Why is Franky fueled by cola?

--Shu

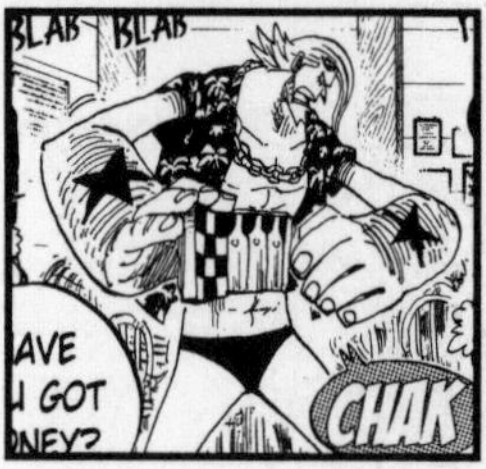
BLAB BLAB
CHAK

A: Because it tastes good.

Q: Master Oda, are you having fun drawing manga? You are? Good. I thought of a new technique for Luffy. It's called Gum-Gum Rain. He floats up with Gum-Gum Storm, and then rains down spit. What do you think? Hee hee hee.

--Ryuta

A: That's gross!! But it just might work!!

Q: Sensei… Hiya! I'd like to ask a favor… In the first panel of page 65 in volume 26, Chopper makes a fist, but his hand looks the same as usual!! (DA-DOOM) Would you please show me how Chopper does rock, paper and scissors?!

--Kachiwarigori

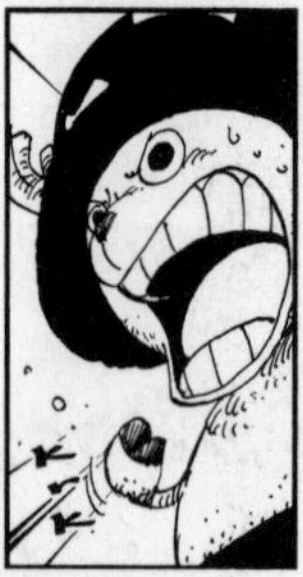

A: I see. The same as usual... He's making a fist, but it looks the same, huh? Hey, get out here, Chopper! Show us you can do rock, paper and scissors!

Chopper: *All right! I can do that!*

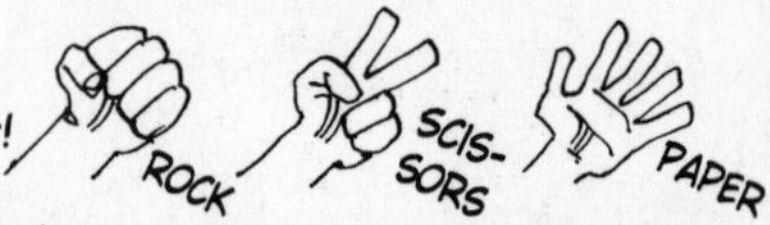
ROCK
SCIS-
SORS
PAPER

Oda: Good, good... You can make rock, scissors and paper very clearly... Hey, that's cheating! You did it in human form! No wonder it looked so good!

Chopper: Oh, I get it. I'm supposed to use my hoof?

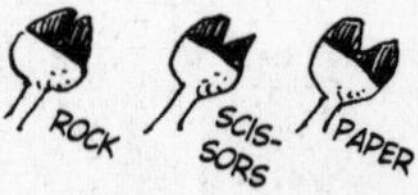
ROCK
SCIS-
SORS
PAPER

Oda: Okay, Chopper! Thanks!

Chapter 385:
THERE IS A WAY

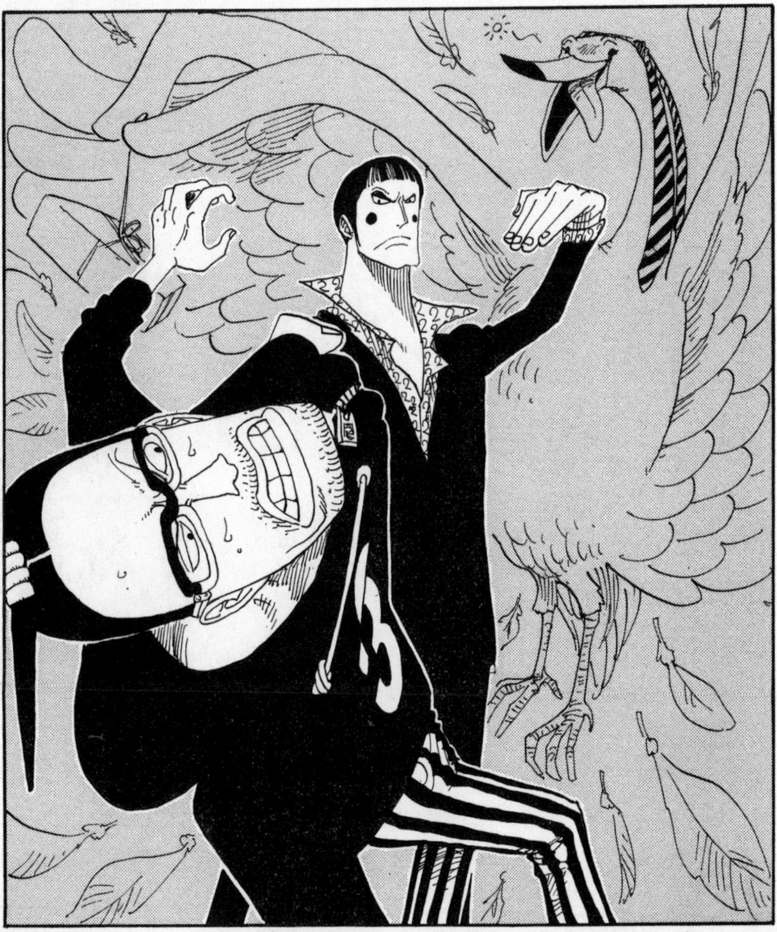

MS. GOLDEN WEEK'S BIG PLAN, A BAROQUE REUNION, VOL. 20:
"YOU MUST NOT FAIL IN LIFE"

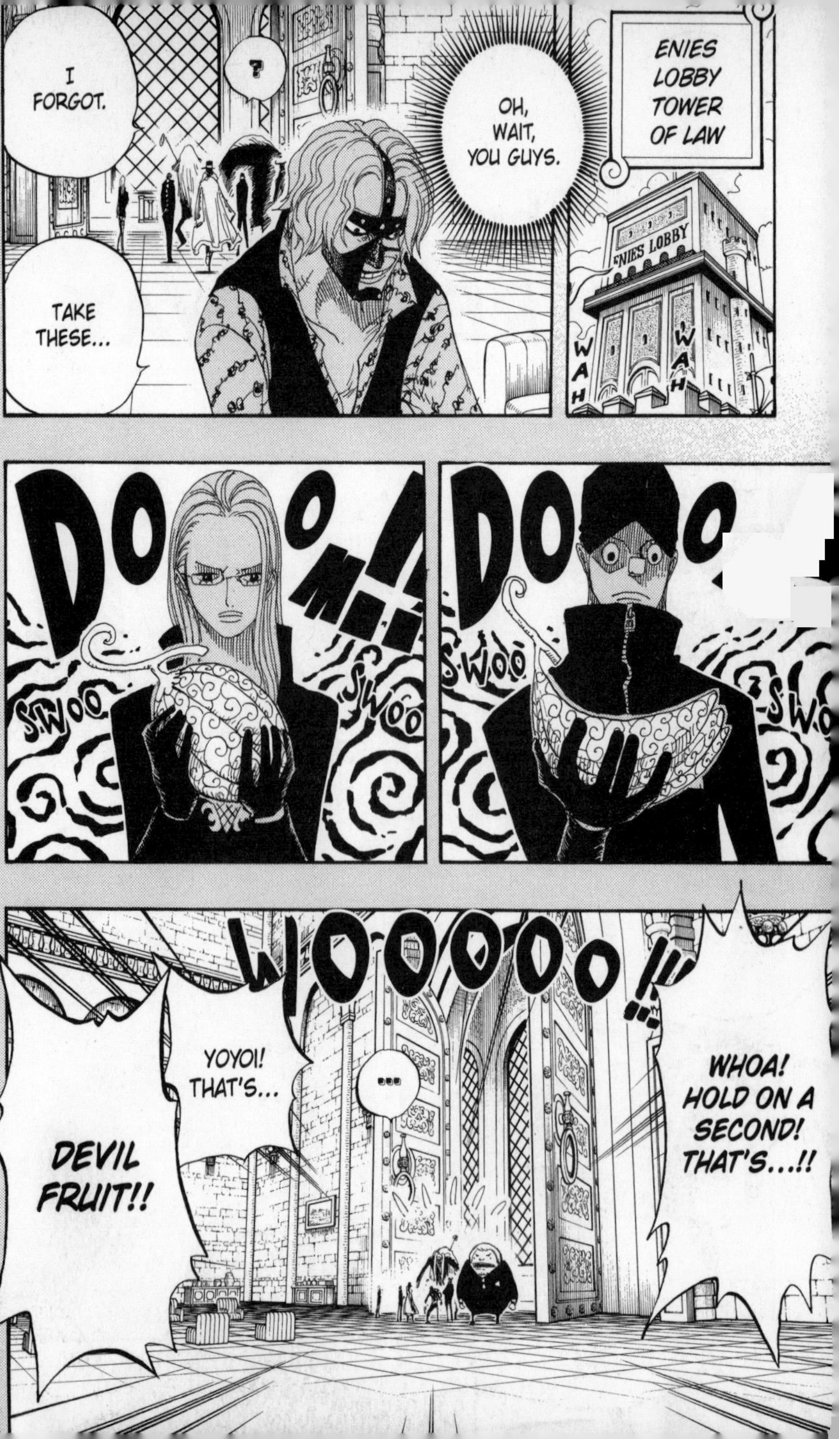
ENIES LOBBY TOWER OF LAW
ENIES LOBBY
WAH
WAH
OH, WAIT, YOU GUYS.
?
I FORGOT.
TAKE THESE...
DOO
SWOO
SWOO
DOOM!!
SWOO
SWOO
WOOOOOO!!
WHOA! HOLD ON A SECOND! THAT'S...!!
...
YOYOI! THAT'S...
DEVIL FRUIT!!

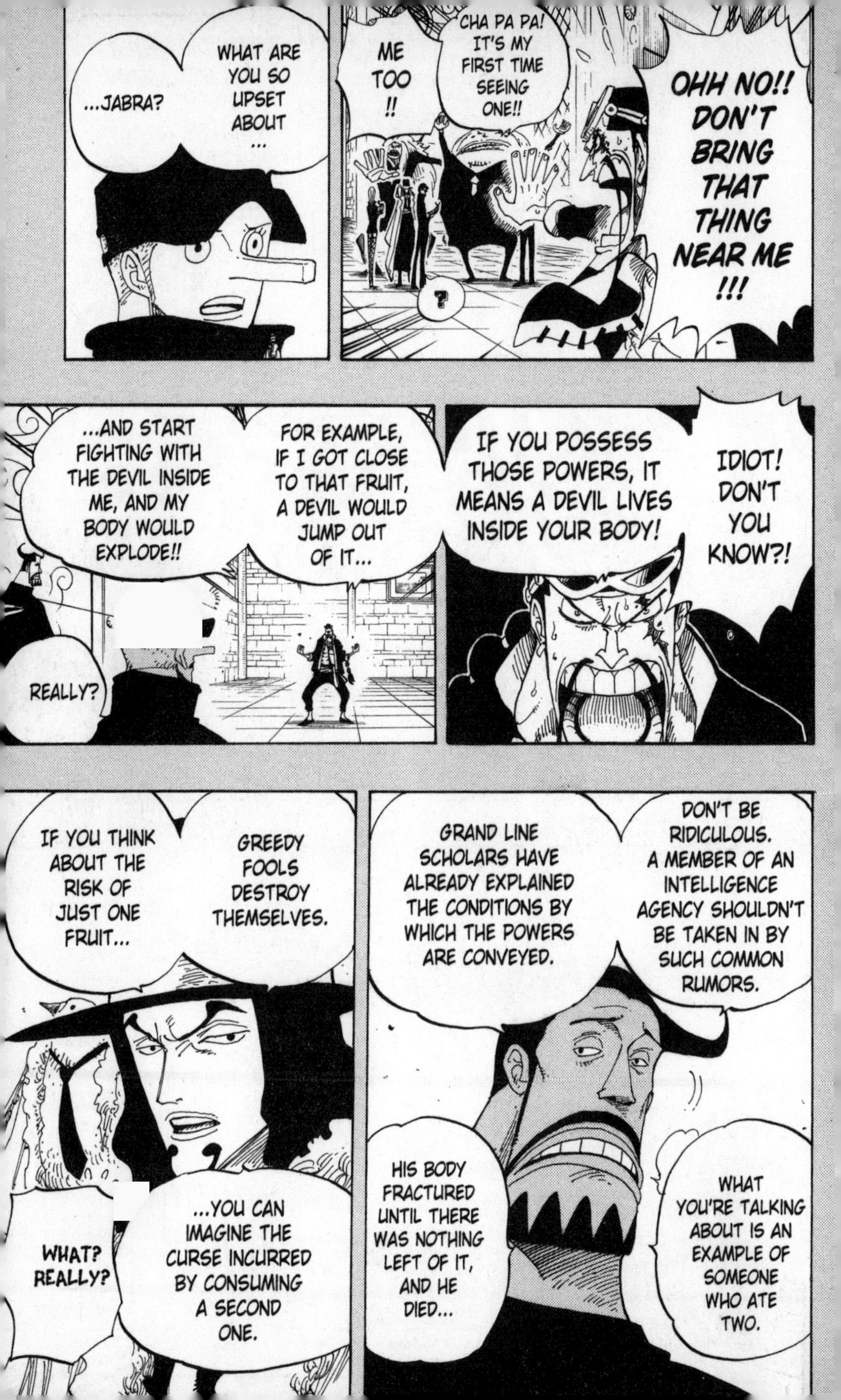
OHH NO!! DON'T BRING THAT THING NEAR ME!!!
CHA PA PA! IT'S MY FIRST TIME SEEING ONE!!
ME TOO!!
?
WHAT ARE YOU SO UPSET ABOUT...
...JABRA?
IDIOT! DON'T YOU KNOW?!
IF YOU POSSESS THOSE POWERS, IT MEANS A DEVIL LIVES INSIDE YOUR BODY!
FOR EXAMPLE, IF I GOT CLOSE TO THAT FRUIT, A DEVIL WOULD JUMP OUT OF IT...
...AND START FIGHTING WITH THE DEVIL INSIDE ME, AND MY BODY WOULD EXPLODE!!
REALLY?
DON'T BE RIDICULOUS. A MEMBER OF AN INTELLIGENCE AGENCY SHOULDN'T BE TAKEN IN BY SUCH COMMON RUMORS.
GRAND LINE SCHOLARS HAVE ALREADY EXPLAINED THE CONDITIONS BY WHICH THE POWERS ARE CONVEYED.
WHAT YOU'RE TALKING ABOUT IS AN EXAMPLE OF SOMEONE WHO ATE TWO.
HIS BODY FRACTURED UNTIL THERE WAS NOTHING LEFT OF IT, AND HE DIED...
GREEDY FOOLS DESTROY THEMSELVES.
IF YOU THINK ABOUT THE RISK OF JUST ONE FRUIT...
...YOU CAN IMAGINE THE CURSE INCURRED BY CONSUMING A SECOND ONE.
WHAT? REALLY?

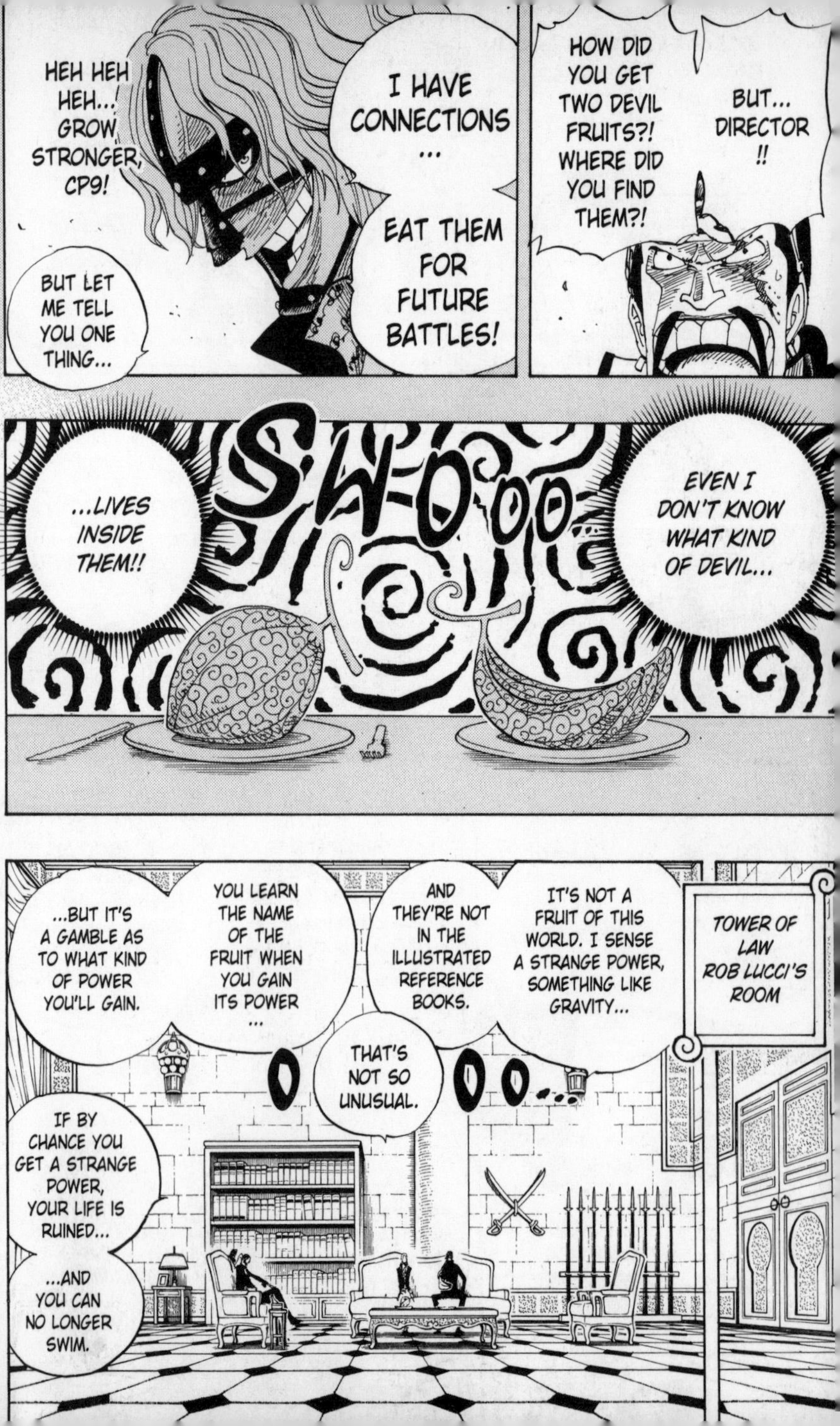
BUT... DIRECTOR !!
HOW DID YOU GET TWO DEVIL FRUITS?! WHERE DID YOU FIND THEM?!
I HAVE CONNECTIONS ...
EAT THEM FOR FUTURE BATTLES!
HEH HEH HEH...! GROW STRONGER, CP9!
BUT LET ME TELL YOU ONE THING...
EVEN I DON'T KNOW WHAT KIND OF DEVIL...
SWOOO
...LIVES INSIDE THEM!!
TOWER OF LAW ROB LUCCI'S ROOM
IT'S NOT A FRUIT OF THIS WORLD. I SENSE A STRANGE POWER, SOMETHING LIKE GRAVITY...
AND THEY'RE NOT IN THE ILLUSTRATED REFERENCE BOOKS.
THAT'S NOT SO UNUSUAL.
YOU LEARN THE NAME OF THE FRUIT WHEN YOU GAIN ITS POWER ...
...BUT IT'S A GAMBLE AS TO WHAT KIND OF POWER YOU'LL GAIN.
IF BY CHANCE YOU GET A STRANGE POWER, YOUR LIFE IS RUINED...
...AND YOU CAN NO LONGER SWIM.

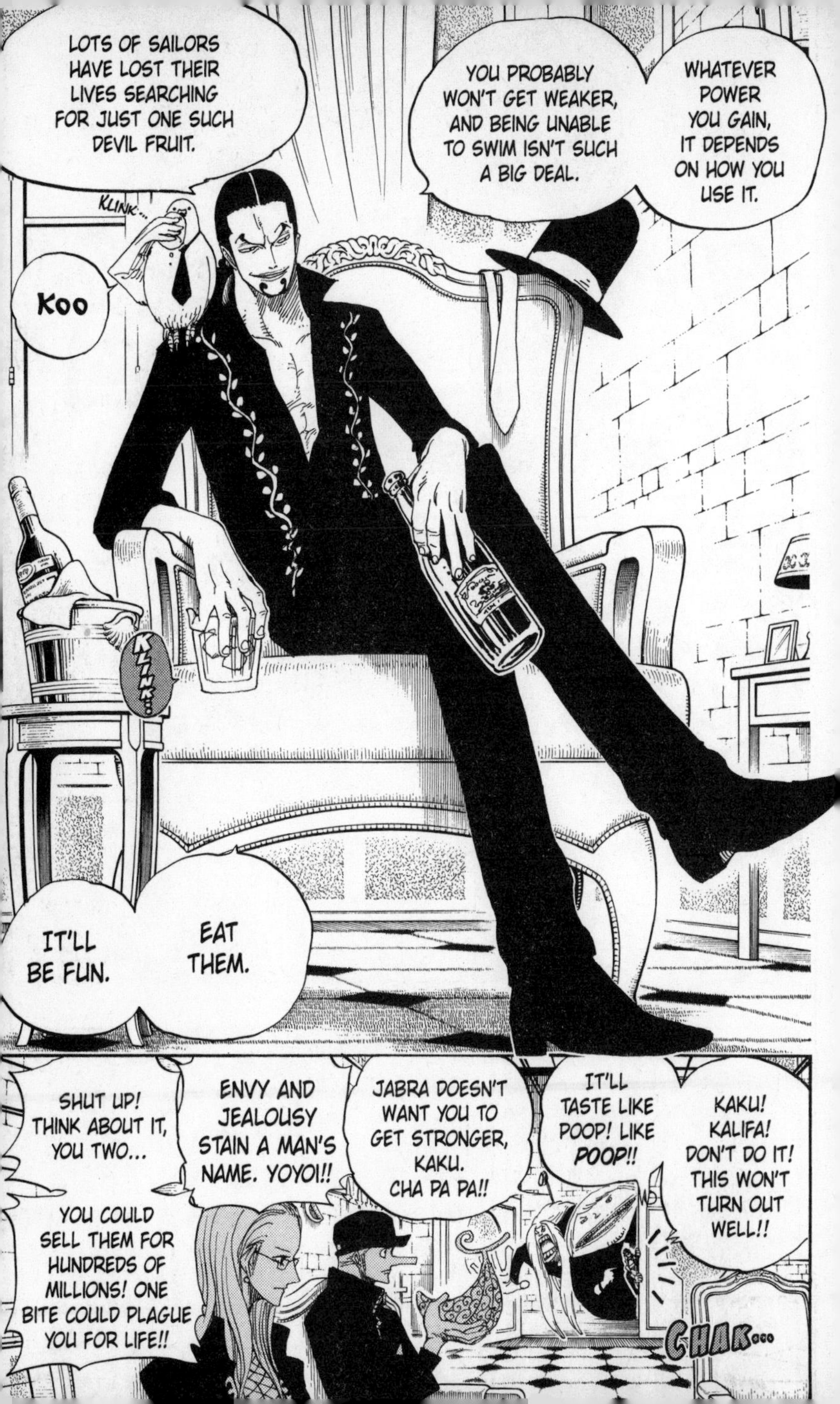
WHATEVER POWER YOU GAIN, IT DEPENDS ON HOW YOU USE IT.
YOU PROBABLY WON'T GET WEAKER, AND BEING UNABLE TO SWIM ISN'T SUCH A BIG DEAL.
LOTS OF SAILORS HAVE LOST THEIR LIVES SEARCHING FOR JUST ONE SUCH DEVIL FRUIT.
KLINK...
KOO
KLINK!!
EAT THEM.
IT'LL BE FUN.
KAKU! KALIFA! DON'T DO IT! THIS WON'T TURN OUT WELL!!
IT'LL TASTE LIKE POOP! LIKE POOP!!
JABRA DOESN'T WANT YOU TO GET STRONGER, KAKU. CHA PA PA!!
ENVY AND JEALOUSY STAIN A MAN'S NAME. YOYOI!!
SHUT UP! THINK ABOUT IT, YOU TWO...
YOU COULD SELL THEM FOR HUNDREDS OF MILLIONS! ONE BITE COULD PLAGUE YOU FOR LIFE!!
CHAK...

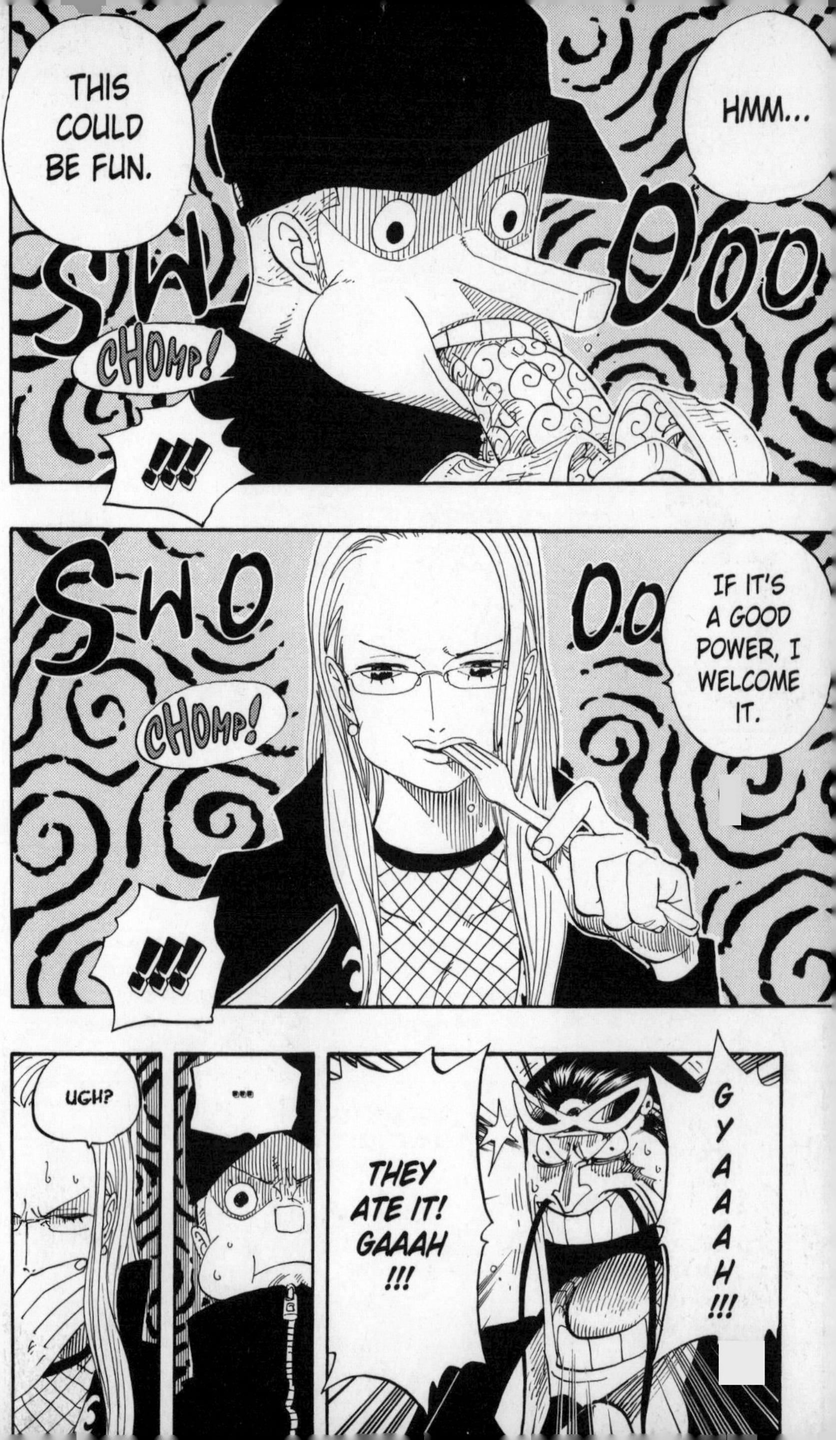
HMM...
THIS COULD BE FUN.
SWOOO
CHOMP!
!!!
IF IT'S A GOOD POWER, I WELCOME IT.
SWOOO
CHOMP!
!!!
GYAAAAH!!!
THEY ATE IT! GAAAH!!!
...
UGH?

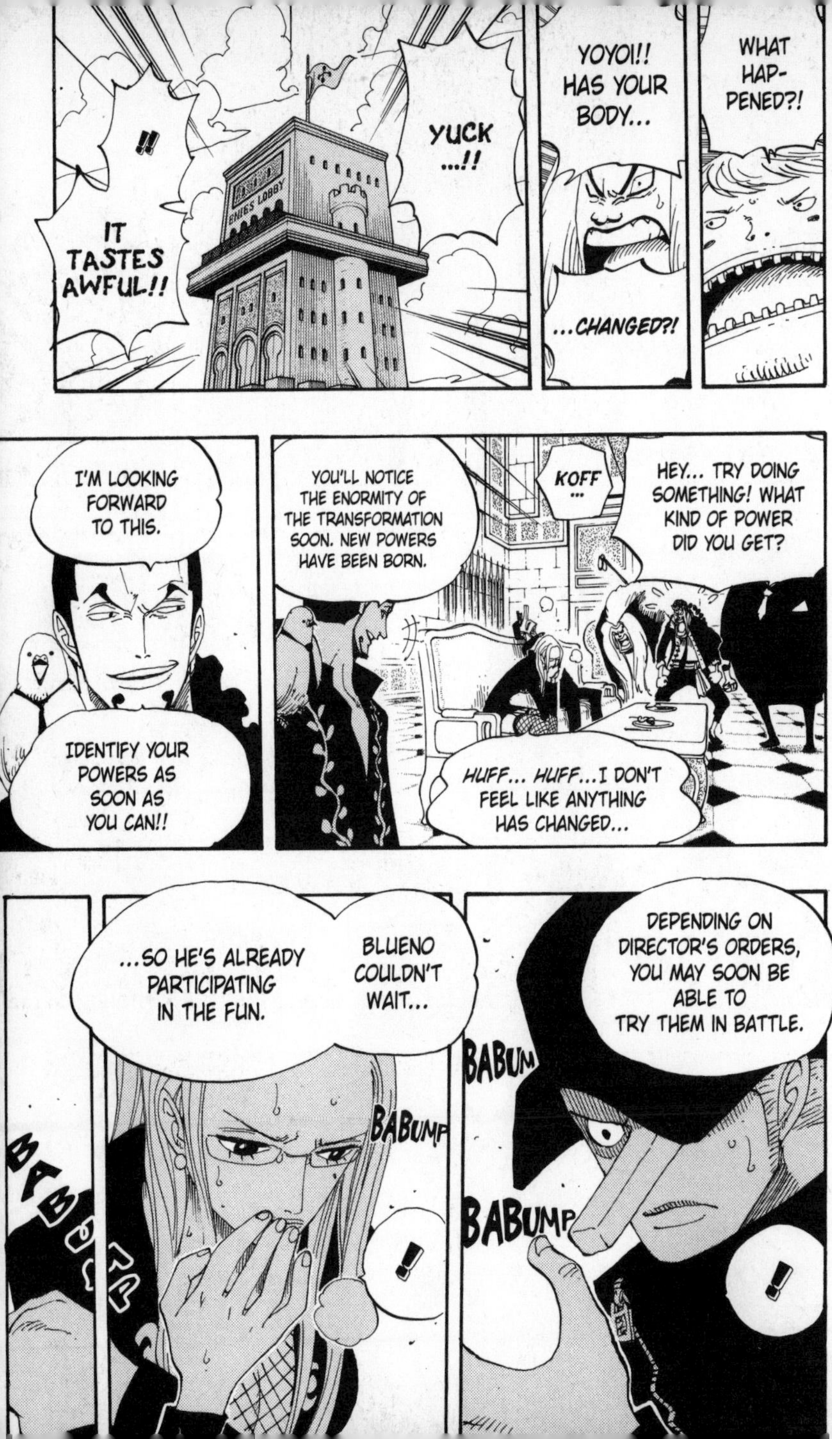
WHAT HAP-PENED?!
YOYOI!! HAS YOUR BODY...
...CHANGED?!
YUCK ...!!
!!
IT TASTES AWFUL!!
HEY... TRY DOING SOMETHING! WHAT KIND OF POWER DID YOU GET?
KOFF ...
YOU'LL NOTICE THE ENORMITY OF THE TRANSFORMATION SOON. NEW POWERS HAVE BEEN BORN.
HUFF... HUFF...I DON'T FEEL LIKE ANYTHING HAS CHANGED...
I'M LOOKING FORWARD TO THIS.
IDENTIFY YOUR POWERS AS SOON AS YOU CAN!!
DEPENDING ON DIRECTOR'S ORDERS, YOU MAY SOON BE ABLE TO TRY THEM IN BATTLE.
BABUM
BABUMP
!
BLUENO COULDN'T WAIT...
...SO HE'S ALREADY PARTICIPATING IN THE FUN.
BABUMP
!
BABUMP

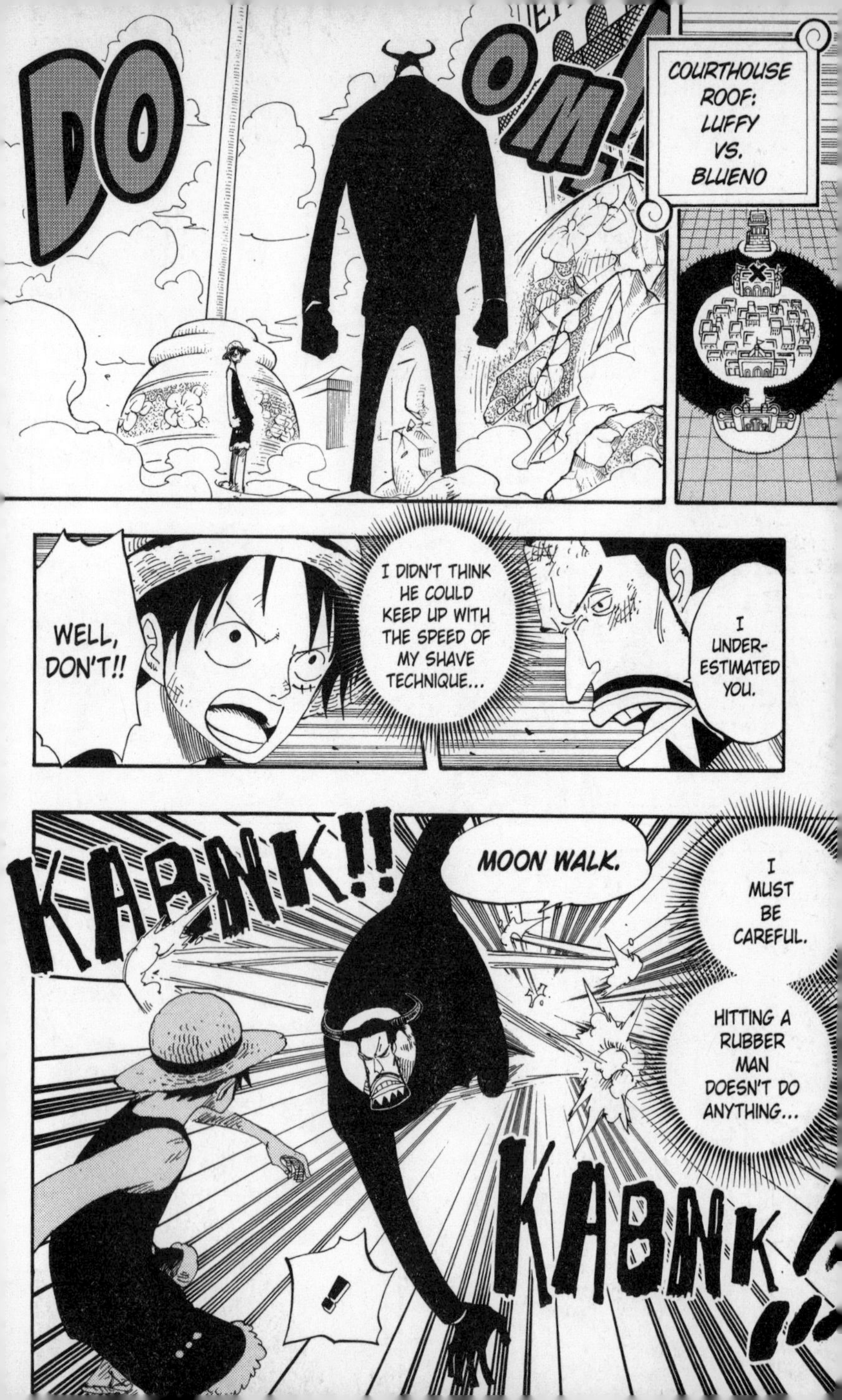
COURTHOUSE ROOF: LUFFY VS. BLUENO
DOOM
I UNDER-ESTIMATED YOU.
I DIDN'T THINK HE COULD KEEP UP WITH THE SPEED OF MY SHAVE TECHNIQUE...
WELL, DON'T!!
I MUST BE CAREFUL.
HITTING A RUBBER MAN DOESN'T DO ANYTHING...
MOON WALK.
KABNK!!
KABNK
!

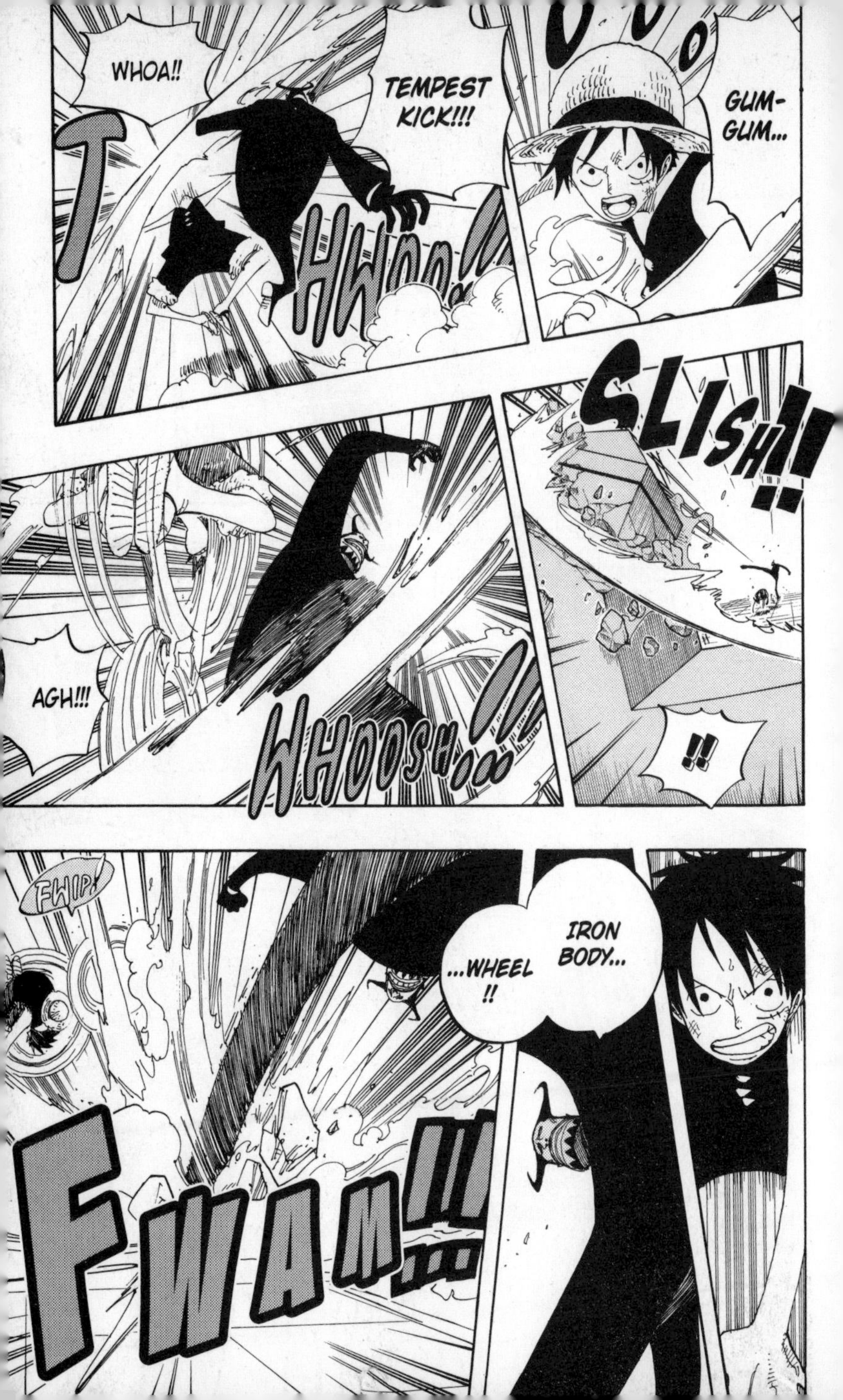

GUM-GUM...
TEMPEST KICK!!!
WHOA!!
SLISH!!
!!
WHOOSH...
AGH!!!
IRON BODY...
...WHEEL !!
FWIP!
FWAM!!

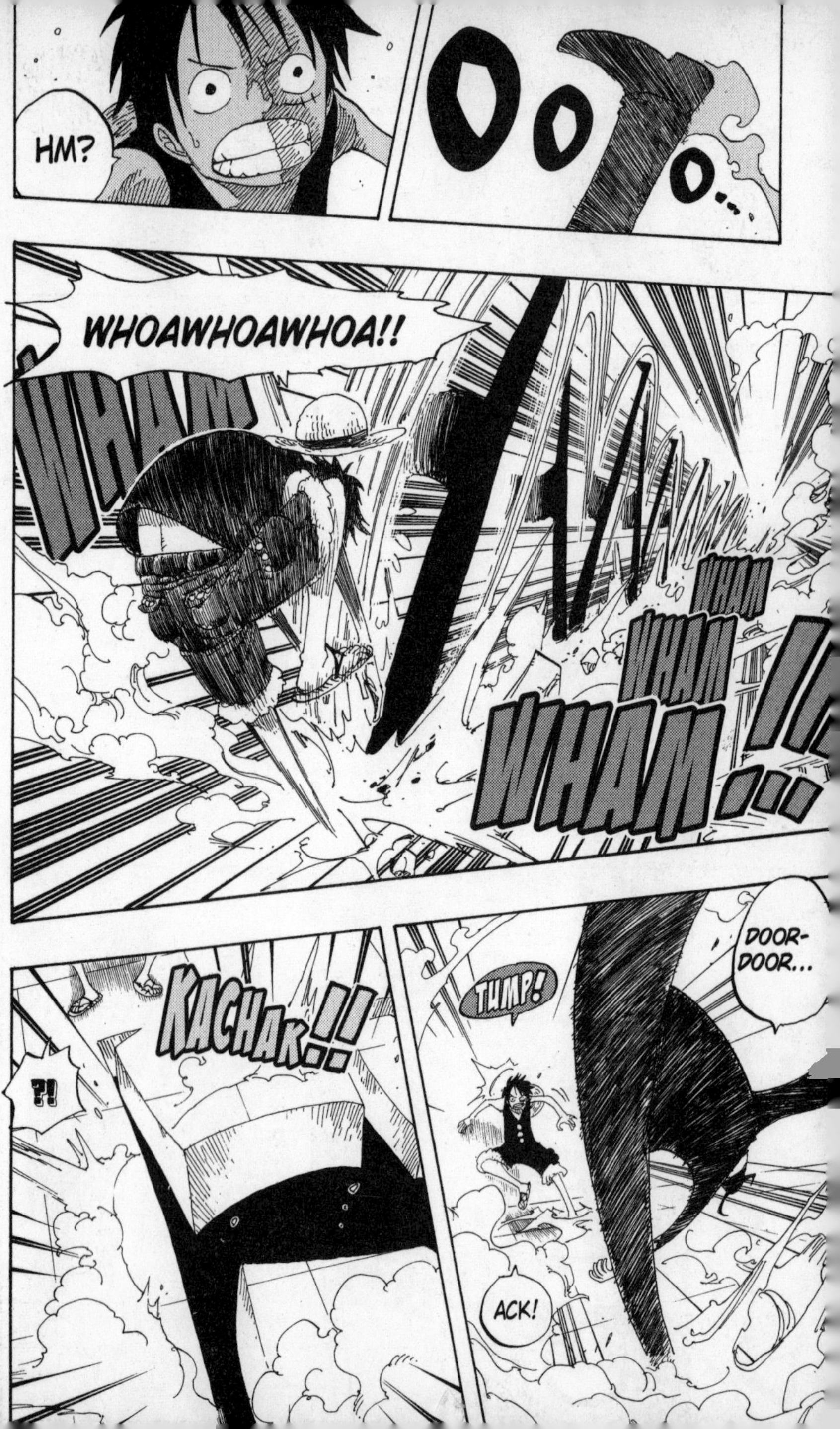
OOO...
HM?
WHOAWHOAWHOA!!
WHAM
WHAM
WHAM
WHAM...!!
DOOR-DOOR...
TUMP!
ACK!
KACHAK!!
?!

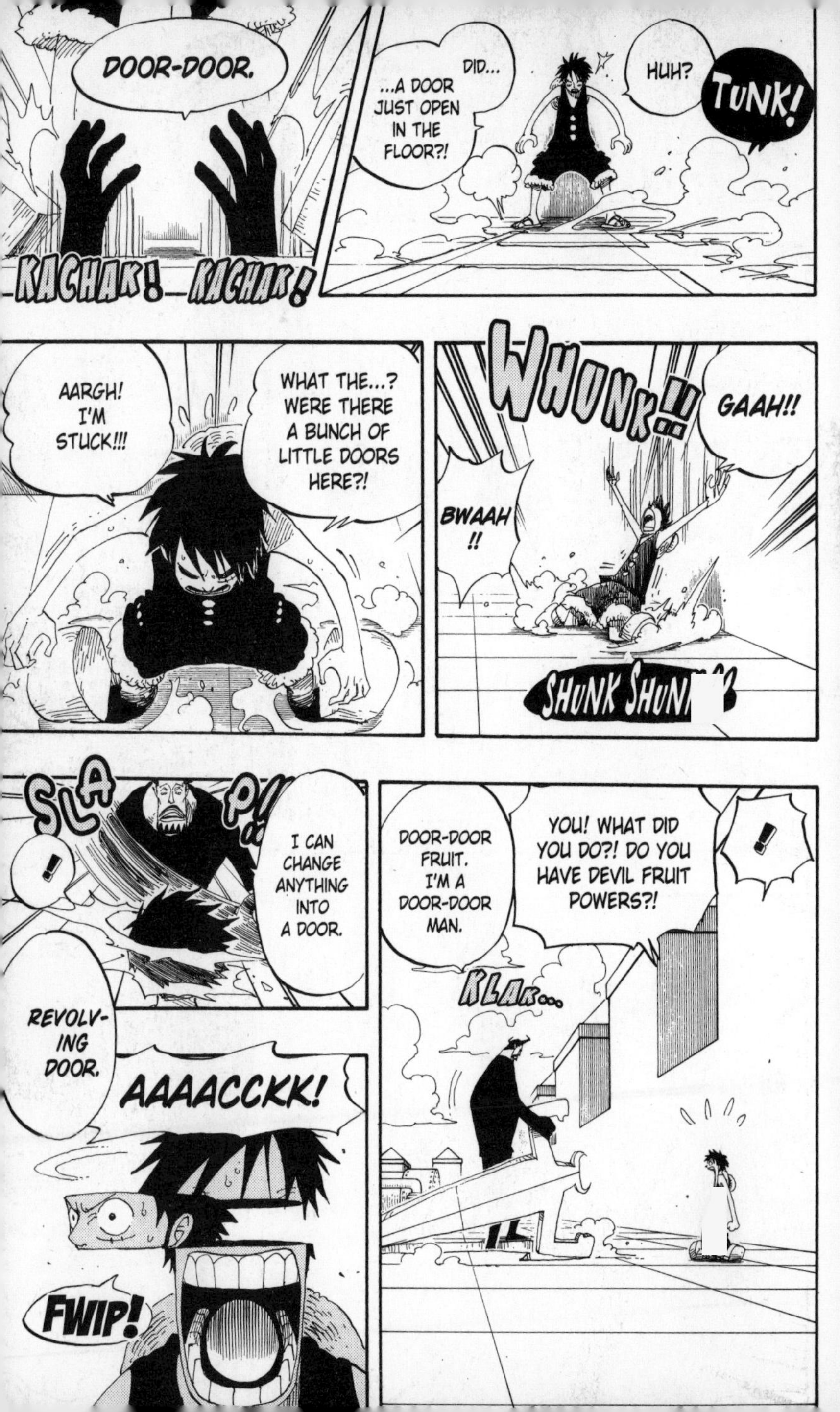
HUH?
TUNK!
DID...
...A DOOR JUST OPEN IN THE FLOOR?!
DOOR-DOOR.
KACHAK! KACHAK!
WHUNK!!
GAAH!!
BWAAH!!
SHUNK SHUN
WHAT THE...? WERE THERE A BUNCH OF LITTLE DOORS HERE?!
AARGH! I'M STUCK!!!
!
YOU! WHAT DID YOU DO?! DO YOU HAVE DEVIL FRUIT POWERS?!
DOOR-DOOR FRUIT. I'M A DOOR-DOOR MAN.
KLAK...
SLAP!
I CAN CHANGE ANYTHING INTO A DOOR.
!
REVOLVING DOOR.
AAAACCKK!
FWIP!

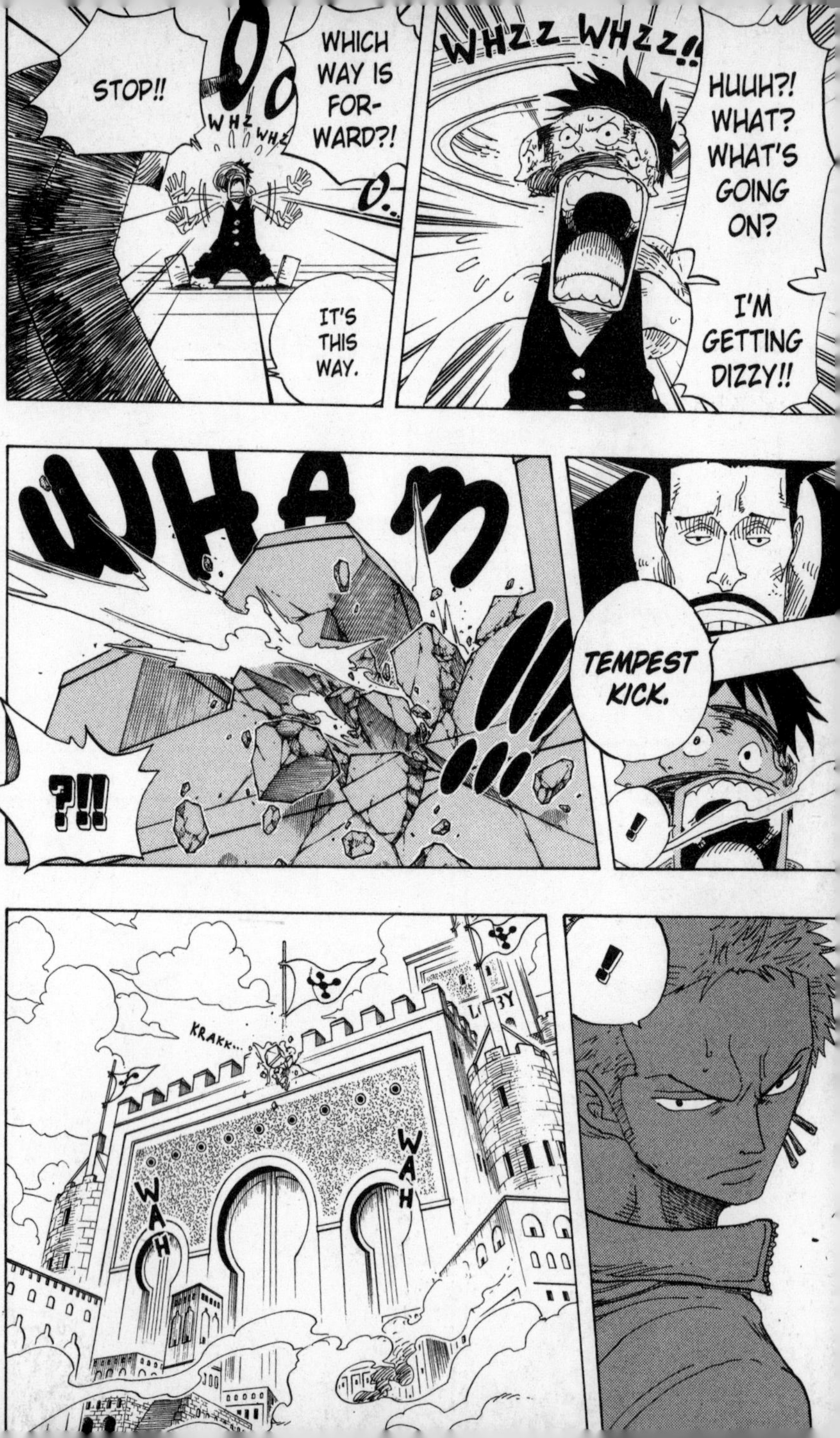
WHZZ WHZZ!!
HUUH?! WHAT? WHAT'S GOING ON?
I'M GETTING DIZZY!!
STOP!!
WHZ WHZ
WHICH WAY IS FOR-WARD?!
IT'S THIS WAY.
TEMPEST KICK.
!
WHAM
?!!
!
KRAKK...
WAH
WAH

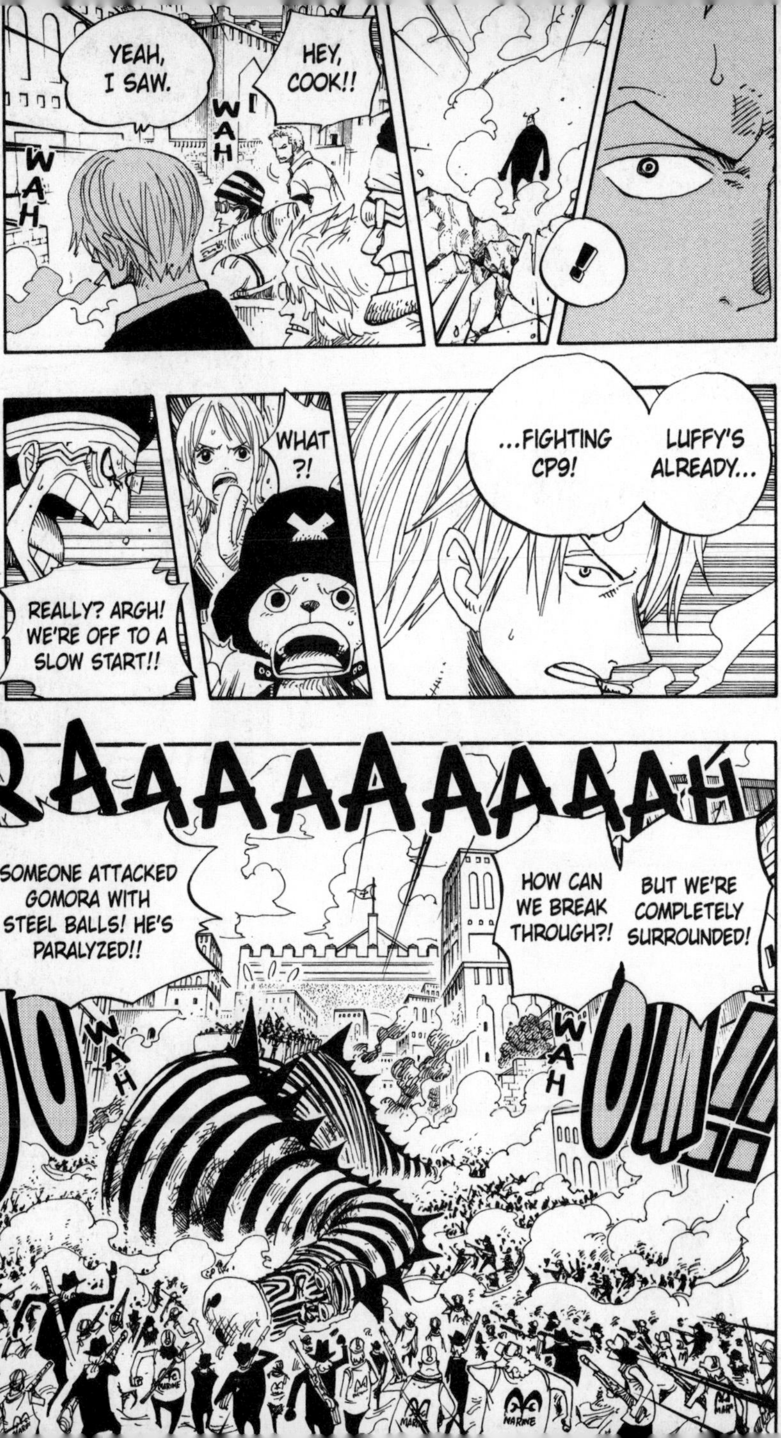
!
HEY, COOK!!
YEAH, I SAW.
WAH
WAH
LUFFY'S ALREADY...
...FIGHTING CP9!
WHAT?!
REALLY? ARGH! WE'RE OFF TO A SLOW START!!
RAAAAAAAAAAH
BUT WE'RE COMPLETELY SURROUNDED!
HOW CAN WE BREAK THROUGH?!
SOMEONE ATTACKED GOMORA WITH STEEL BALLS! HE'S PARALYZED!!
DOOM!!
WAH
WAH

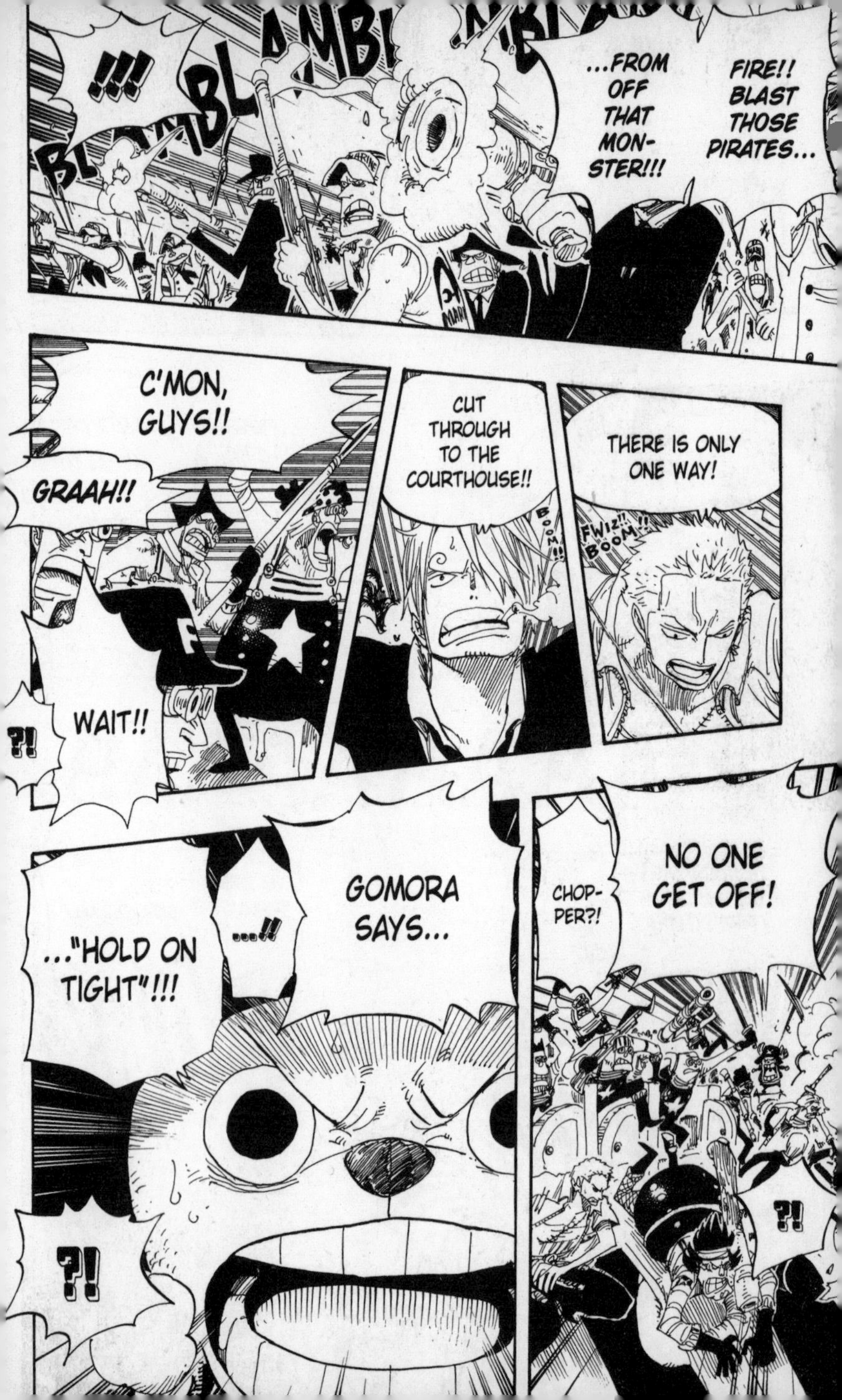

FIRE!! BLAST THOSE PIRATES...
...FROM OFF THAT MON-STER!!!
!!!
THERE IS ONLY ONE WAY!
FWIZ!! BOOM!!
CUT THROUGH TO THE COURTHOUSE!!
BOOM!!
C'MON, GUYS!!
GRAAH!!
WAIT!!
?!
NO ONE GET OFF!
CHOP-PER?!
?!
GOMORA SAYS...
...!!
..."HOLD ON TIGHT"!!!
?!

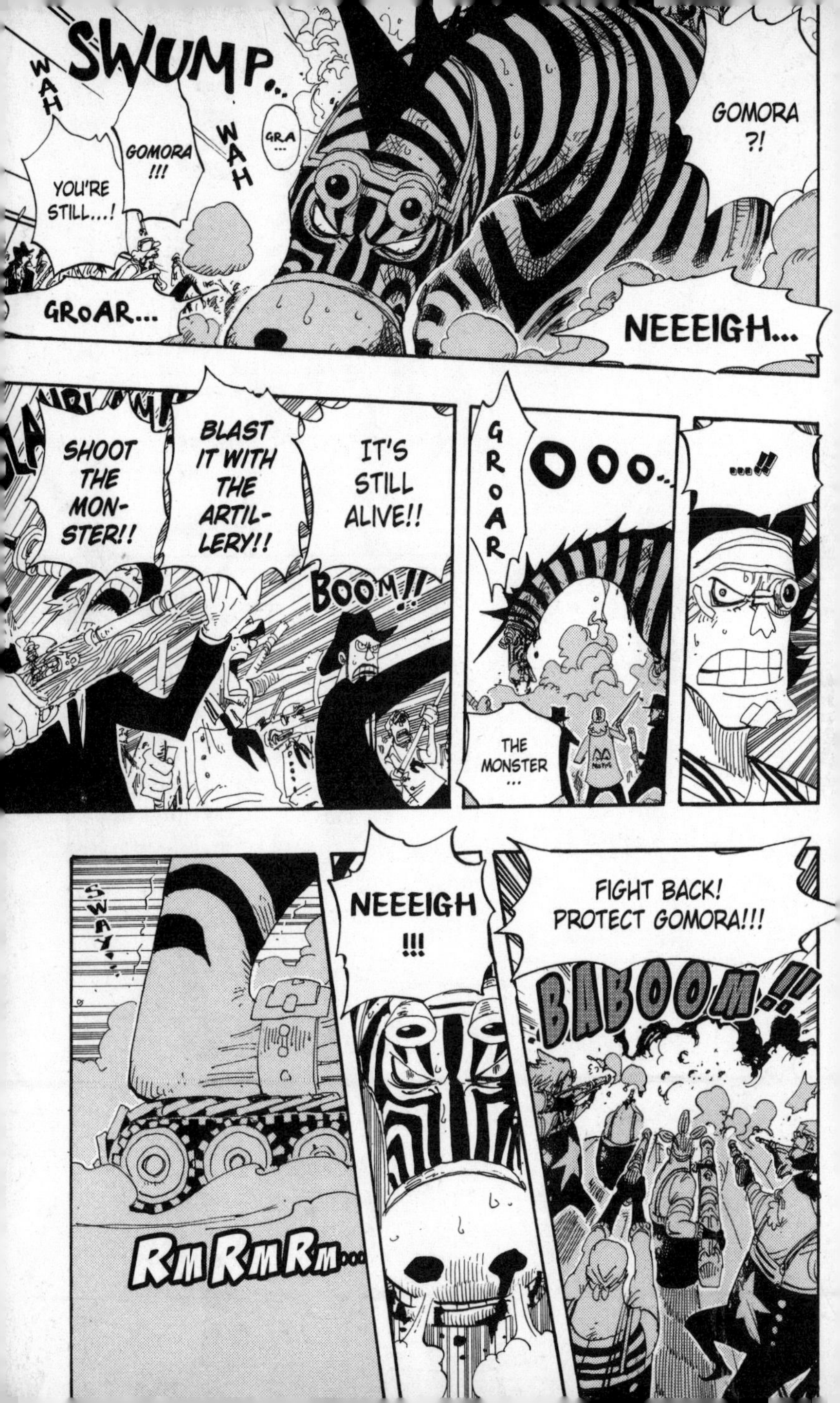
GOMORA ?!
NEEEIGH...
GRA ...
SWUMP...
WAH
WAH
GOMORA !!!
YOU'RE STILL...!
GROAR...
...!!
GROAR
OOO...
THE MONSTER ...
IT'S STILL ALIVE!!
BOOM!!
BLAST IT WITH THE ARTIL-LERY!!
SHOOT THE MON-STER!!
FIGHT BACK! PROTECT GOMORA!!!
BABOOM!!
NEEEIGH !!!
SWAY...
RMRMRM...

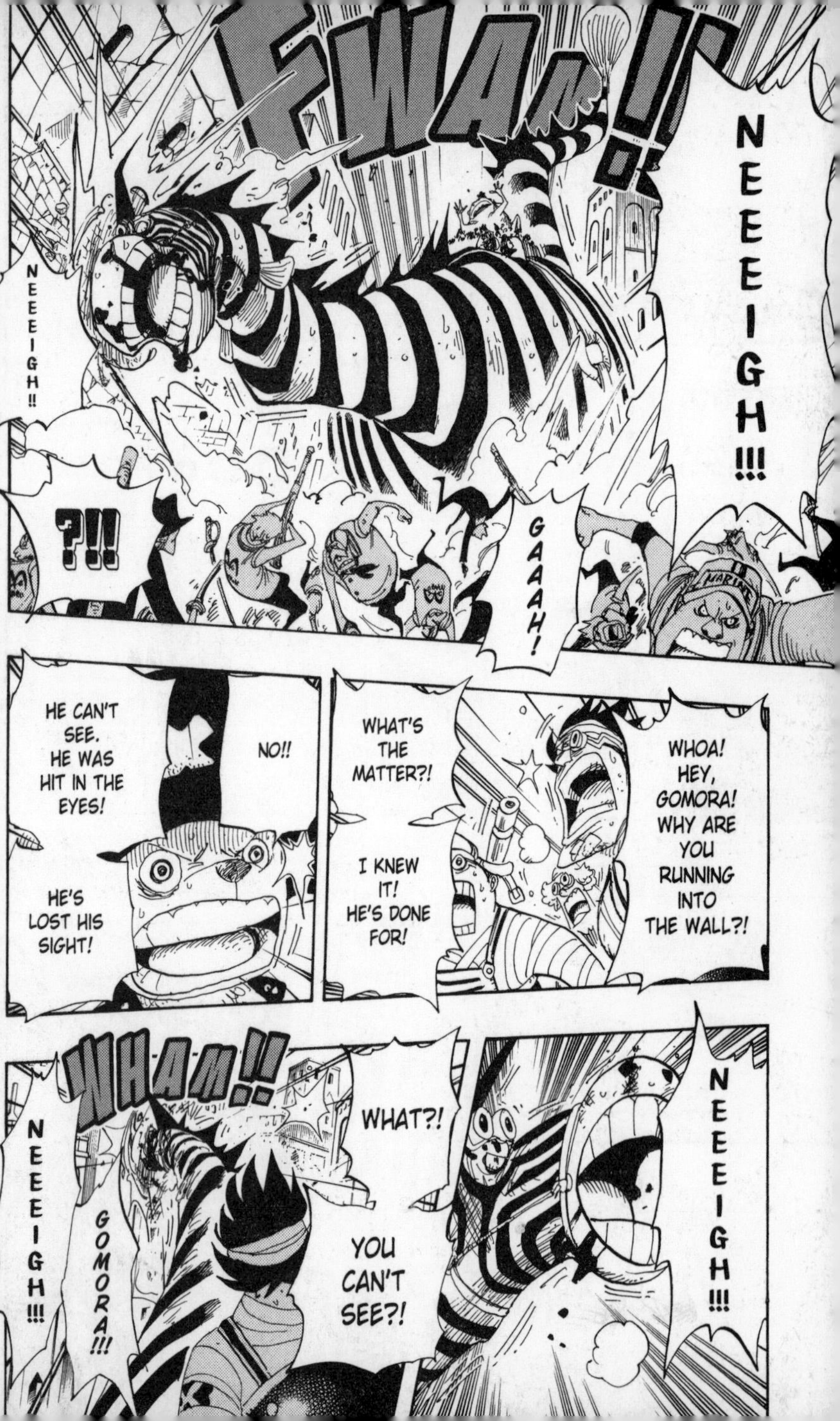
FWAM!!
NEEEIGH!!!
NEEEEIGH!!
GAAAH!
?!!
WHOA! HEY, GOMORA! WHY ARE YOU RUNNING INTO THE WALL?!
WHAT'S THE MATTER?!
I KNEW IT! HE'S DONE FOR!
NO!!
HE CAN'T SEE. HE WAS HIT IN THE EYES!
HE'S LOST HIS SIGHT!
NEEEEIGH!!!
WHAT?!
YOU CAN'T SEE?!
WHAM!!
GOMORA!!!
NEEEIGH!!!

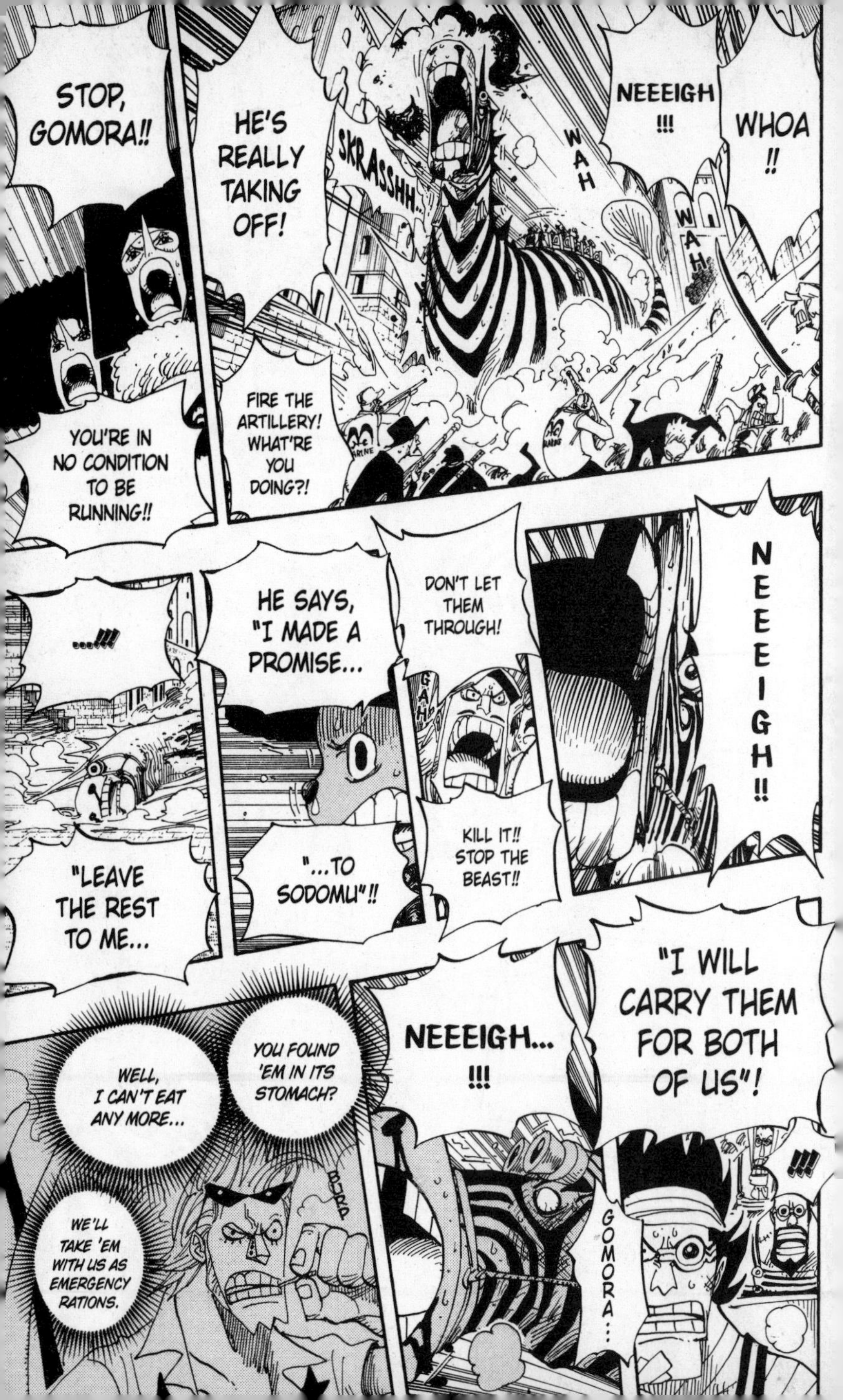
WHOA!!
NEEEIGH!!!
WAH
WAH
HE'S REALLY TAKING OFF!
SKRASSHH...
FIRE THE ARTILLERY! WHAT'RE YOU DOING?!
STOP, GOMORA!!
YOU'RE IN NO CONDITION TO BE RUNNING!!
NEEEIGH!!
DON'T LET THEM THROUGH!
GAH
KILL IT!! STOP THE BEAST!!
HE SAYS, "I MADE A PROMISE...
"...TO SODOMU"!!
...!!!
"LEAVE THE REST TO ME...
"I WILL CARRY THEM FOR BOTH OF US"!
NEEEIGH...!!!
!!!
GOMORA...
YOU FOUND 'EM IN ITS STOMACH?
WELL, I CAN'T EAT ANY MORE...
BURP
WE'LL TAKE 'EM WITH US AS EMERGENCY RATIONS.

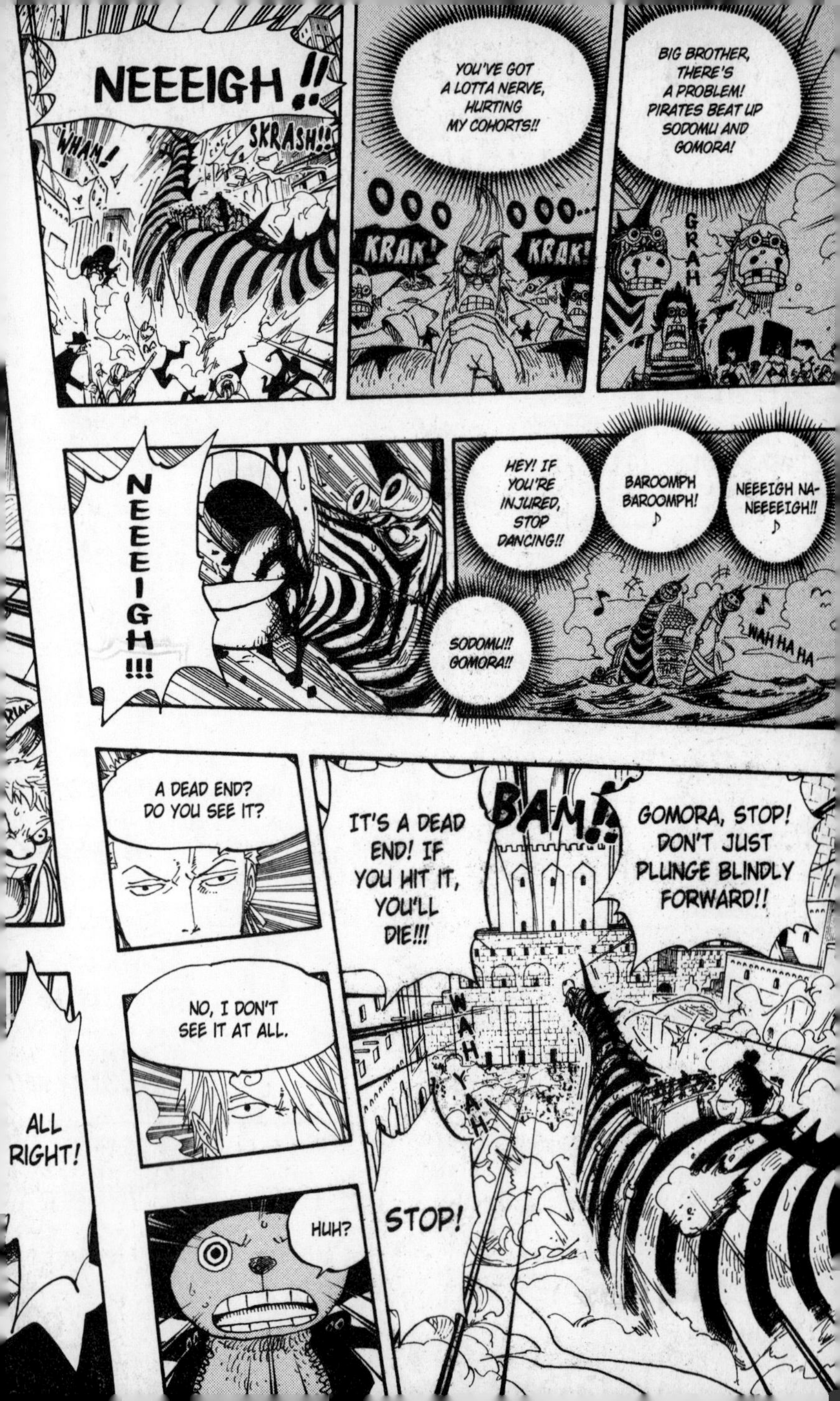
BIG BROTHER, THERE'S A PROBLEM! PIRATES BEAT UP SODOMU AND GOMORA!
GRAH
YOU'VE GOT A LOTTA NERVE, HURTING MY COHORTS!!
OOO
OOO...
KRAK!
KRAK!
NEEEIGH!!
SKRASH!!
WHAM!
NEEEIGH NA-NEEEEIGH!! ♪
BAROOMPH BAROOMPH! ♪
HEY! IF YOU'RE INJURED, STOP DANCING!!
SODOMU!! GOMORA!!
WAH HA HA
NEEEIGH!!!
GOMORA, STOP! DON'T JUST PLUNGE BLINDLY FORWARD!!
BAM!!
IT'S A DEAD END! IF YOU HIT IT, YOU'LL DIE!!!
WAHYAH
STOP!
A DEAD END? DO YOU SEE IT?
NO, I DON'T SEE IT AT ALL.
HUH?
ALL RIGHT!

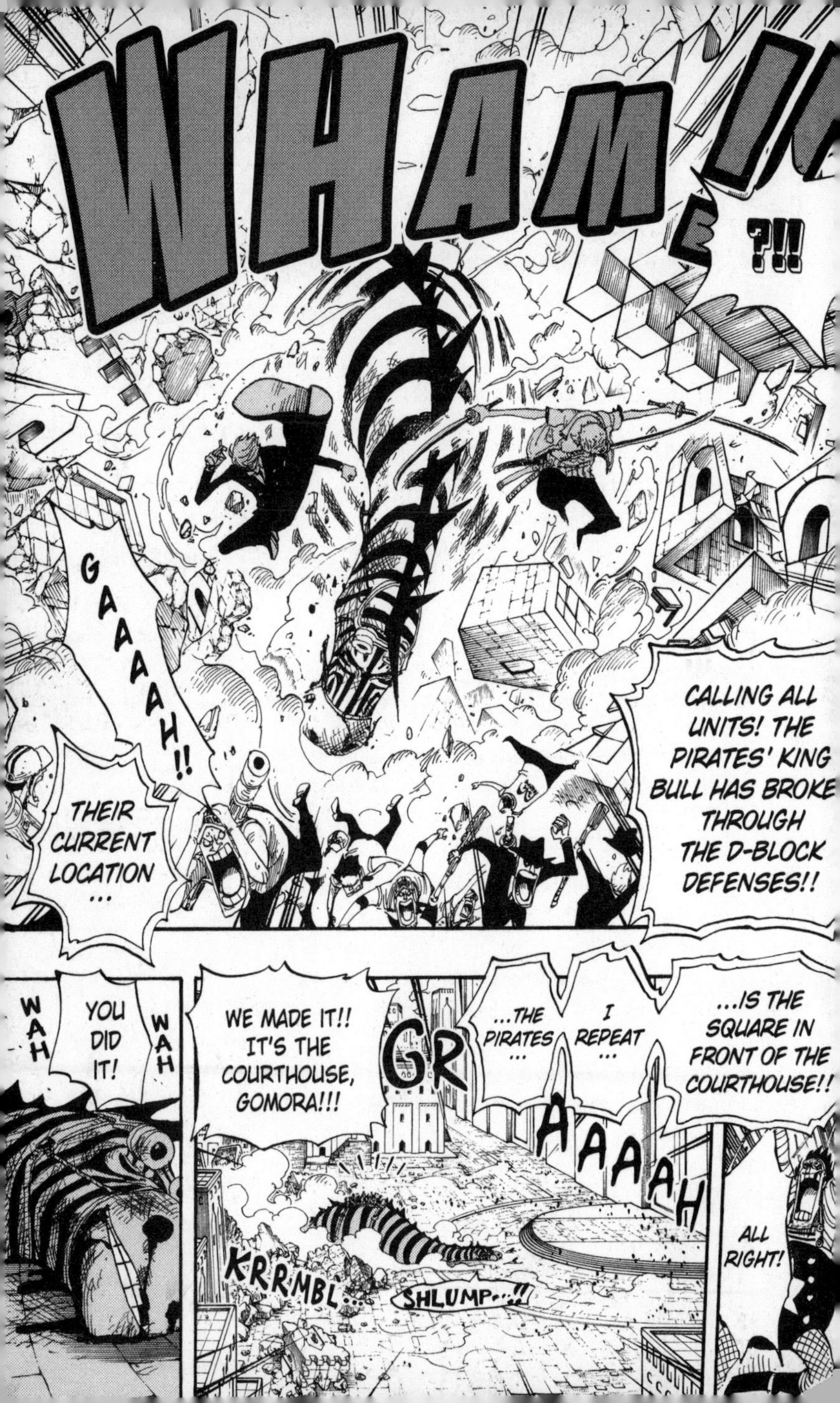
WHAM
?!!
CALLING ALL UNITS! THE PIRATES' KING BULL HAS BROKE THROUGH THE D-BLOCK DEFENSES!!
GAAAAAH!!
THEIR CURRENT LOCATION ...
...IS THE SQUARE IN FRONT OF THE COURTHOUSE!!
ALL RIGHT!
I REPEAT ...
...THE PIRATES ...
GRAAAAAH
WE MADE IT!! IT'S THE COURTHOUSE, GOMORA!!!
KRRMBL...
SHLUMP...!!
WAH
YOU DID IT!
WAH

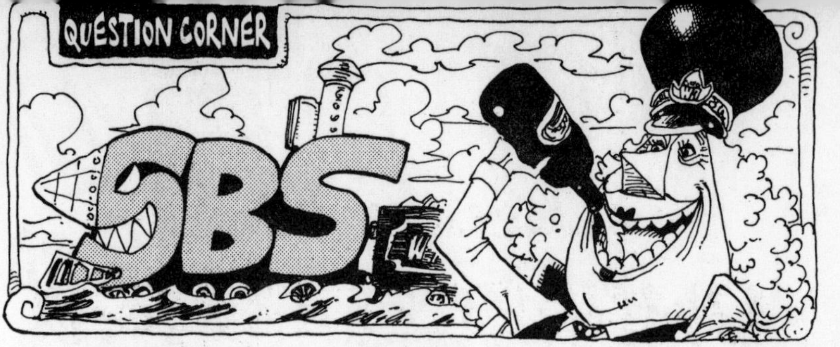
QUESTION CORNER
SBS

Q: Odachi, Wanze is awesome! Making noodles just by putting flour in your mouth! But...wouldn't you need water too?? Are you implying it's spit instead of water?! It's still cool though. And you can eat them as soon as they come out of his nose?! Raw?! You don't boil them? I love ramen, but I don't feel like eating that. How about you? For your dinner maybe?

--Umi

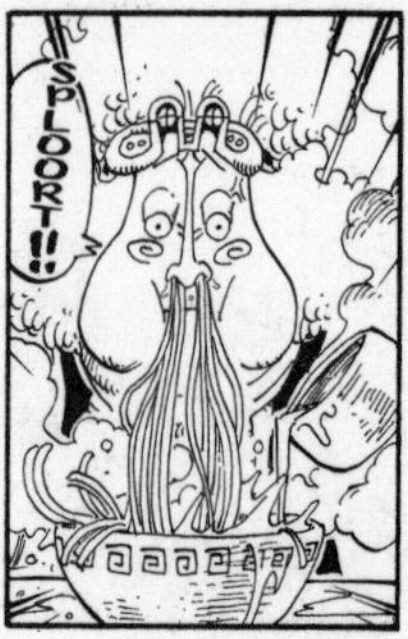
SPLOORT!!

A: Yeah, I always have delicious Wanze ramen for dinner! Yaay! Uh... no way!! If I ate that, I wouldn't feel like drawing anymore. Wanze really whipped up a storm! Green Gum☆Allergy in Osaka has a complaint too?!↓

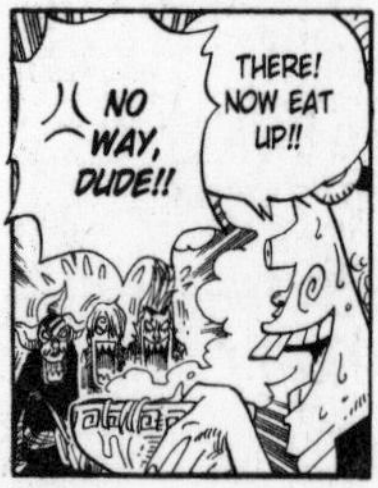
THERE! NOW EAT UP!!
NO WAY, DUDE!!

Q: I've got something to say to Wanze!! It's about the panel in which he offers ramen to Sanji and the others and says, "Eat up." ...Your thumb! Your thumb is in the soup, old man! No one can eat that! That's why the three of them got mad! Please tell Wanze that.

--Green Gum☆Allergy

A: That's not the only problem!! (BAM!!)

Q: Does everyone in *One Piece* cut their fingernails down to the quick?!

--Basil

A: Does it matter?!! (BABAM!!) The Question Corner is over!! (See you next volume.)

Chapter 386:
UNPRECEDENTED

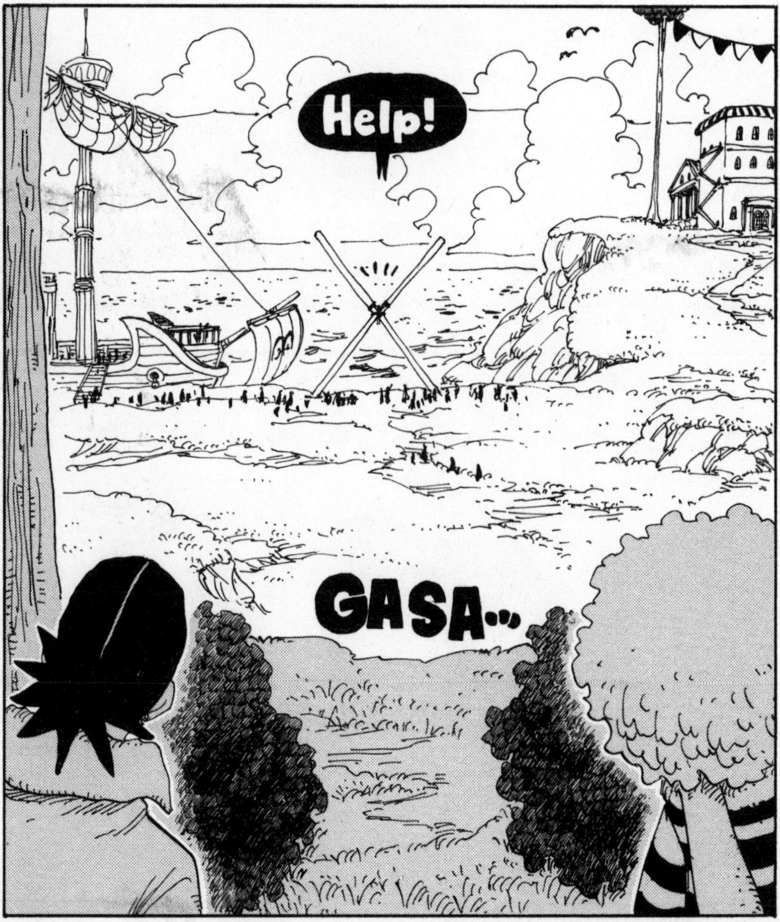
Help!
GASA...

MS. GOLDEN WEEK'S BIG PLAN, A BAROQUE REUNION, VOL. 21: "HELP!"

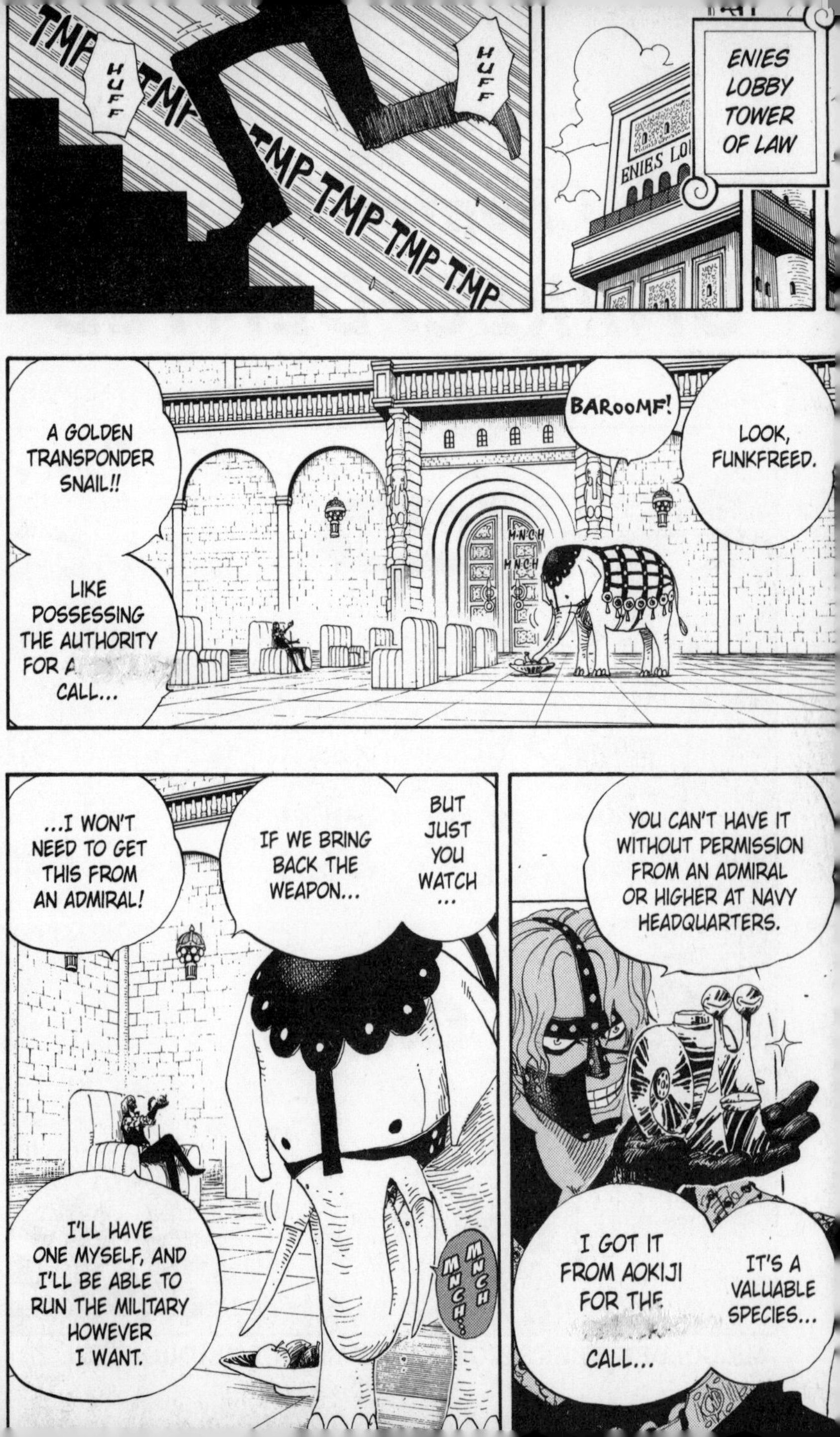
ENIES LOBBY TOWER OF LAW
ENIES LO
HUFF
HUFF
TMP TMP TMP TMP TMP TMP TMP
LOOK, FUNKFREED.
BAROOMF!
MNCH MNCH
A GOLDEN TRANSPONDER SNAIL!!
LIKE POSSESSING THE AUTHORITY FOR A
CALL...
YOU CAN'T HAVE IT WITHOUT PERMISSION FROM AN ADMIRAL OR HIGHER AT NAVY HEADQUARTERS.
IT'S A VALUABLE SPECIES...
I GOT IT FROM AOKIJI FOR THE
CALL...
BUT JUST YOU WATCH...
IF WE BRING BACK THE WEAPON...
...I WON'T NEED TO GET THIS FROM AN ADMIRAL!
I'LL HAVE ONE MYSELF, AND I'LL BE ABLE TO RUN THE MILITARY HOWEVER I WANT.
MNCH MNCH...

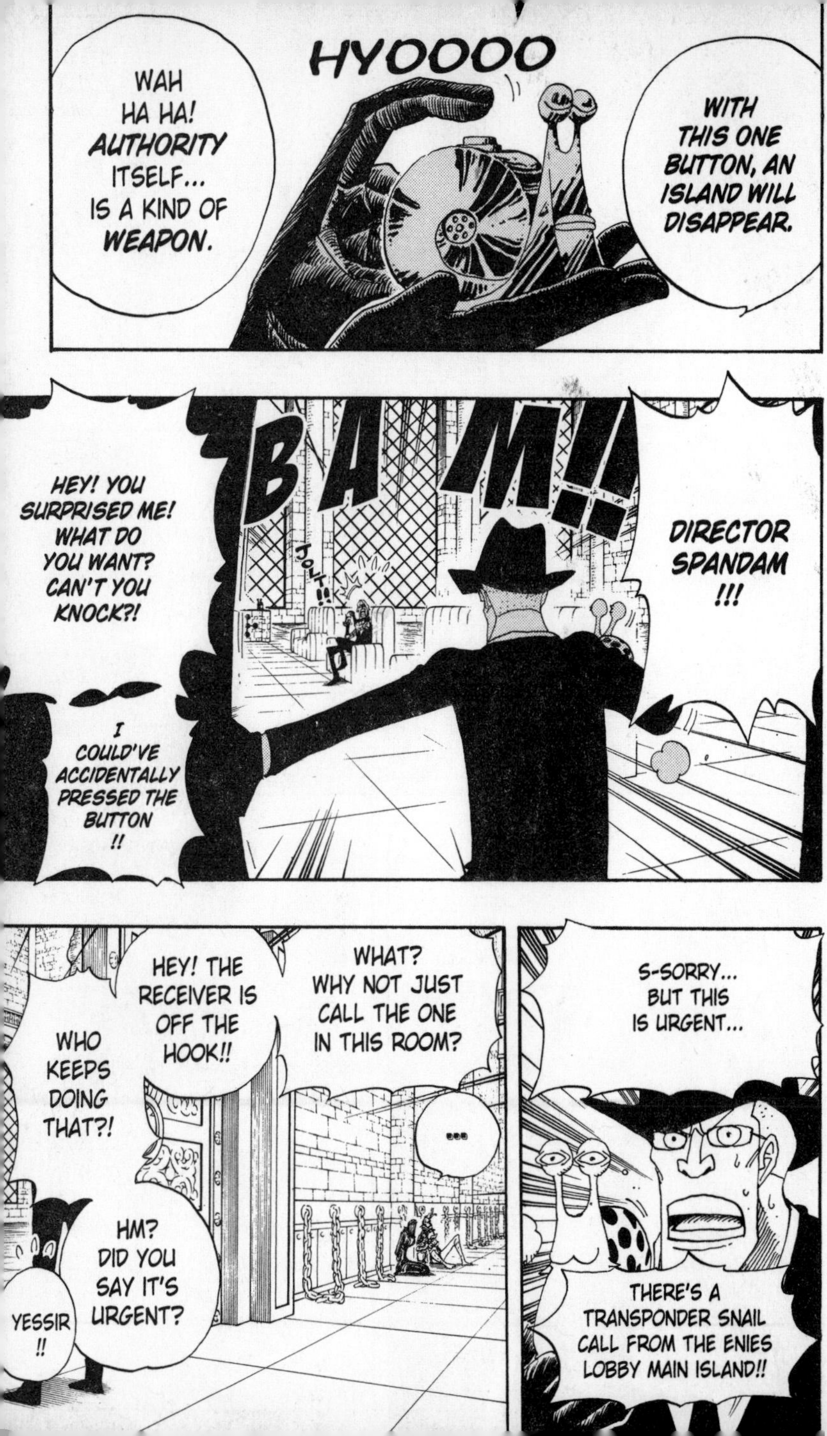
WITH THIS ONE BUTTON, AN ISLAND WILL DISAPPEAR.
HYOOOO
WAH HA HA! AUTHORITY ITSELF... IS A KIND OF WEAPON.
DIRECTOR SPANDAM!!!
BAM!!
JOLT!!
HEY! YOU SURPRISED ME! WHAT DO YOU WANT? CAN'T YOU KNOCK?!
I COULD'VE ACCIDENTALLY PRESSED THE BUTTON!!
S-SORRY... BUT THIS IS URGENT...
THERE'S A TRANSPONDER SNAIL CALL FROM THE ENIES LOBBY MAIN ISLAND!!
WHAT? WHY NOT JUST CALL THE ONE IN THIS ROOM?
HEY! THE RECEIVER IS OFF THE HOOK!!
WHO KEEPS DOING THAT?!
...
HM? DID YOU SAY IT'S URGENT?
YESSIR!!

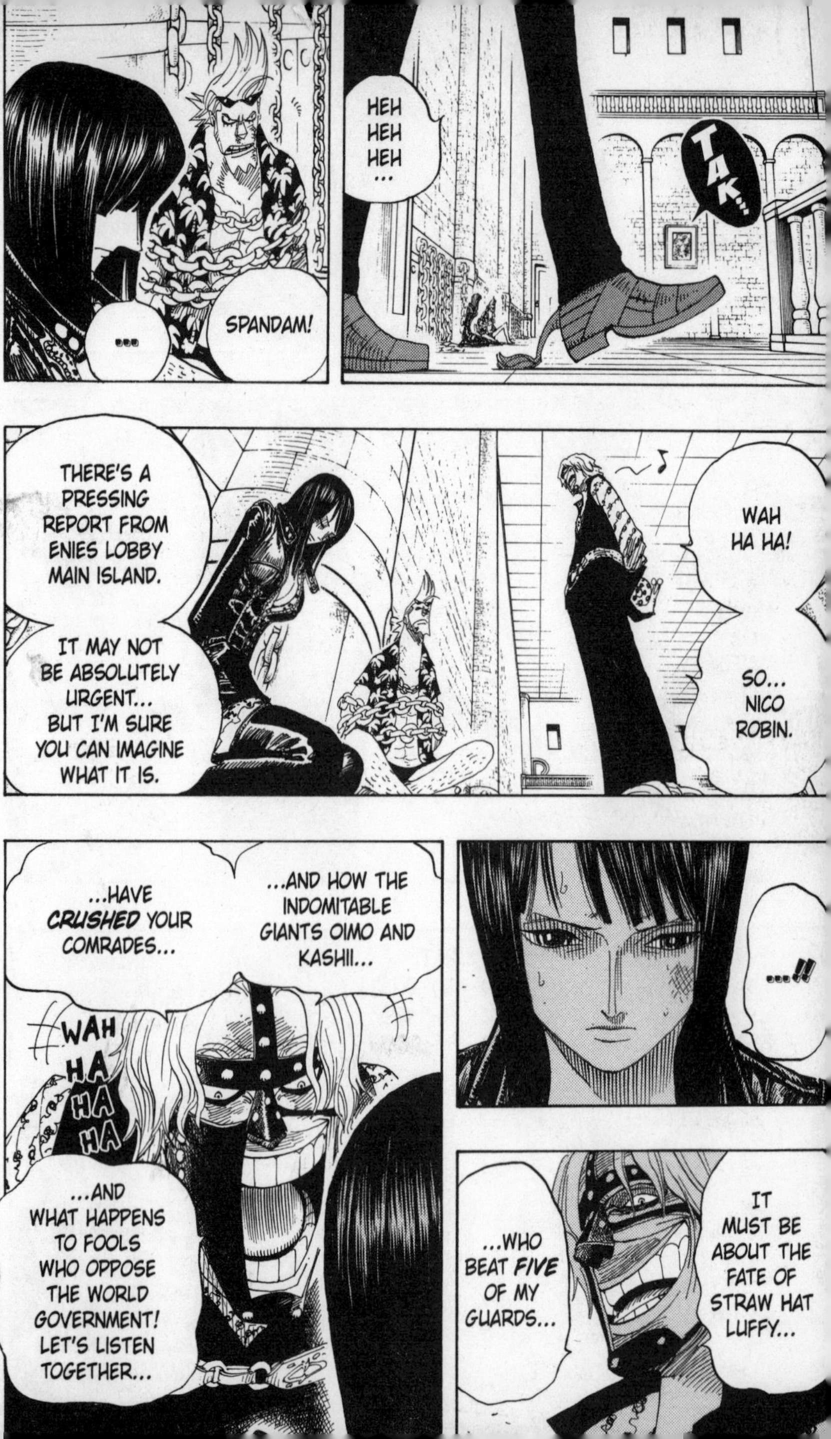
TAK...
HEH HEH HEH...
SPANDAM!
...
WAH HA HA!
SO... NICO ROBIN.
THERE'S A PRESSING REPORT FROM ENIES LOBBY MAIN ISLAND.
IT MAY NOT BE ABSOLUTELY URGENT... BUT I'M SURE YOU CAN IMAGINE WHAT IT IS.
...!!
IT MUST BE ABOUT THE FATE OF STRAW HAT LUFFY...
...WHO BEAT *FIVE* OF MY GUARDS...
...AND HOW THE INDOMITABLE GIANTS OIMO AND KASHII...
...HAVE *CRUSHED* YOUR COMRADES...
WAH HA HA HA HA
...AND WHAT HAPPENS TO FOOLS WHO OPPOSE THE WORLD GOVERNMENT! LET'S LISTEN TOGETHER...

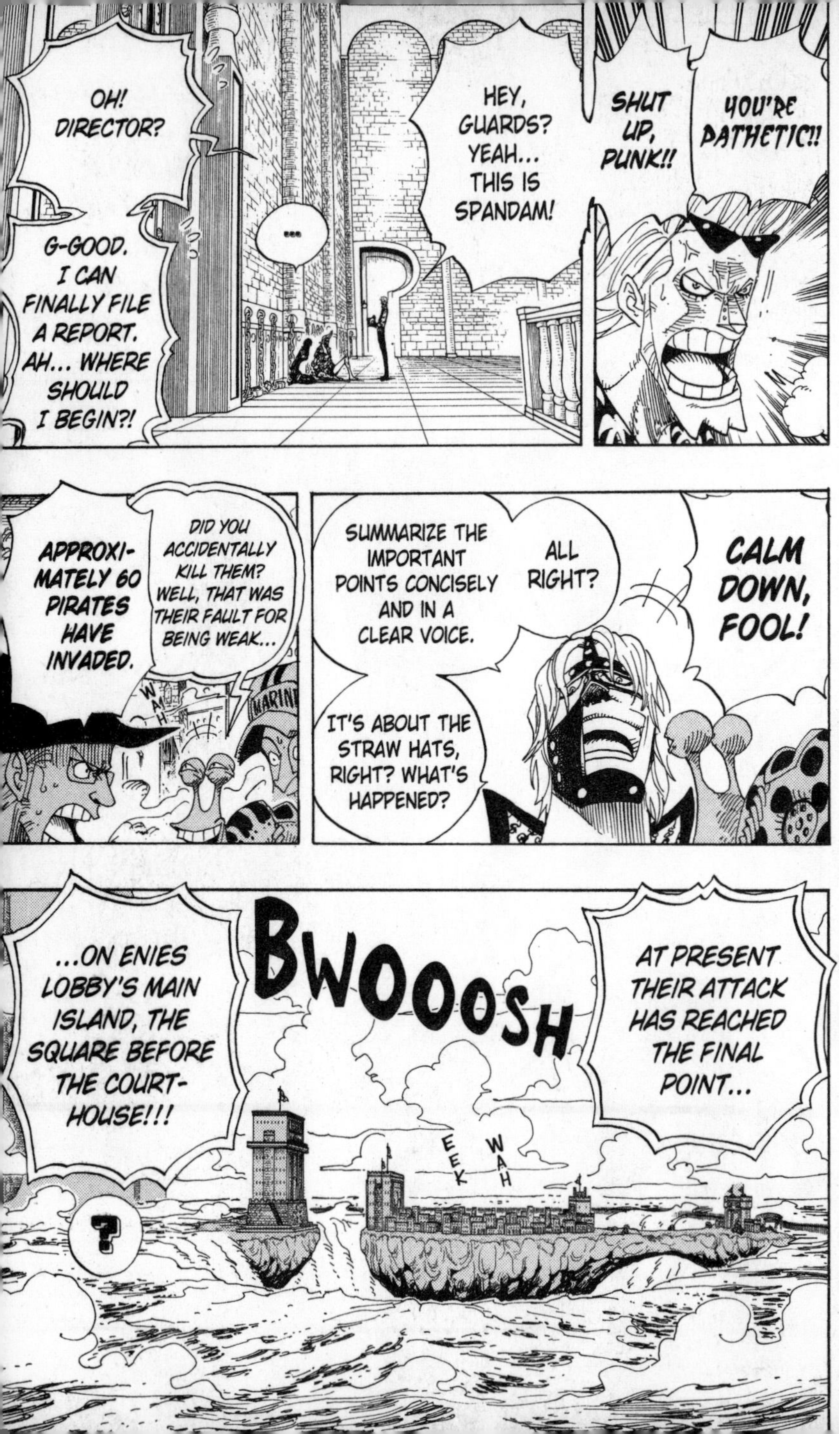
YOU'RE PATHETIC!!
SHUT UP, PUNK!!
HEY, GUARDS? YEAH... THIS IS SPANDAM!
...
OH! DIRECTOR?
G-GOOD. I CAN FINALLY FILE A REPORT. AH... WHERE SHOULD I BEGIN?!
CALM DOWN, FOOL!
ALL RIGHT?
SUMMARIZE THE IMPORTANT POINTS CONCISELY AND IN A CLEAR VOICE.
IT'S ABOUT THE STRAW HATS, RIGHT? WHAT'S HAPPENED?
DID YOU ACCIDENTALLY KILL THEM? WELL, THAT WAS THEIR FAULT FOR BEING WEAK...
APPROXI-MATELY 60 PIRATES HAVE INVADED.
WAH
AT PRESENT THEIR ATTACK HAS REACHED THE FINAL POINT...
BWOOOSH
WAH
EEK
...ON ENIES LOBBY'S MAIN ISLAND, THE SQUARE BEFORE THE COURT-HOUSE!!!
?

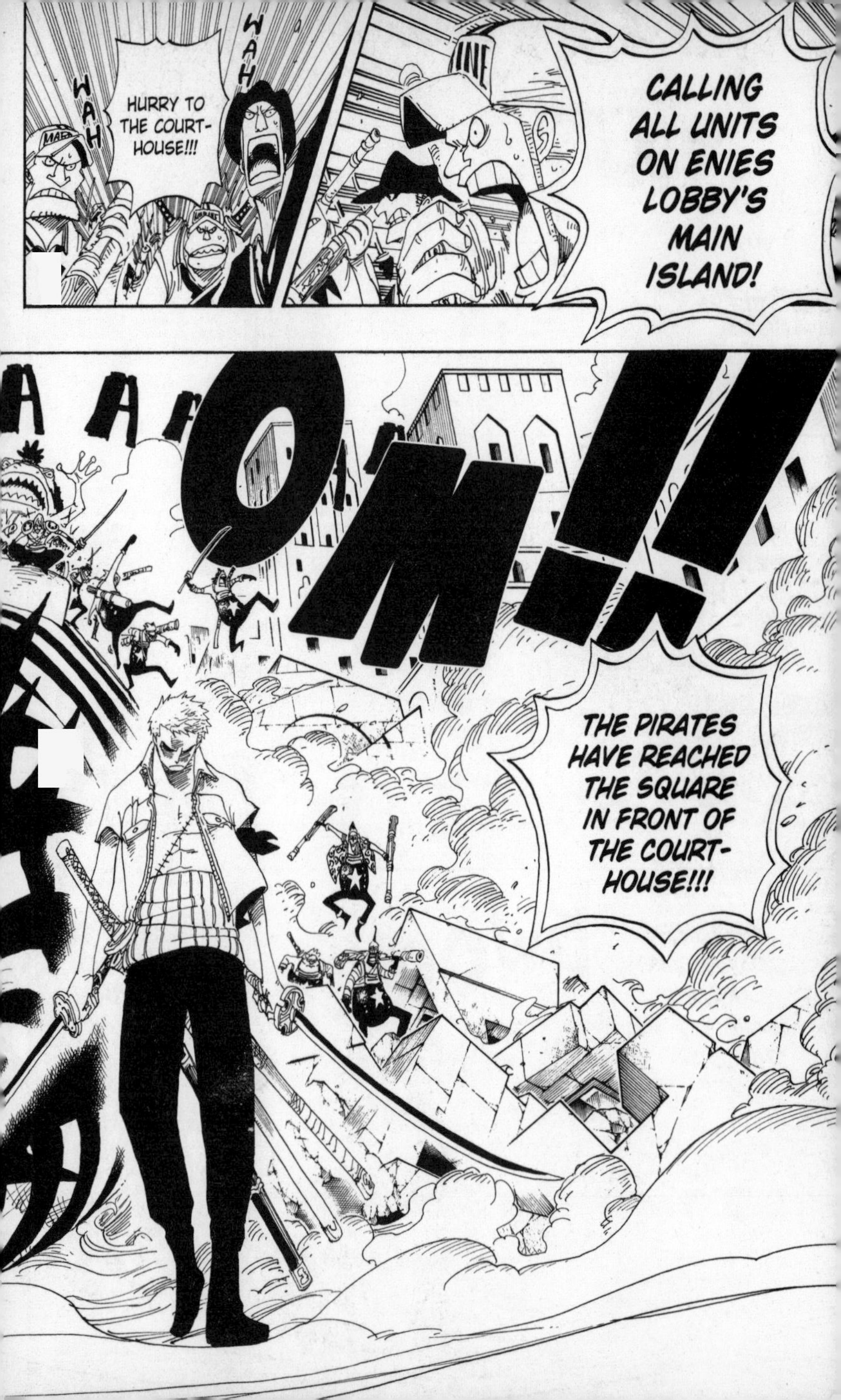
CALLING ALL UNITS ON ENIES LOBBY'S MAIN ISLAND!
WAH
HURRY TO THE COURT-HOUSE!!!
WAH
AAAOM!!
THE PIRATES HAVE REACHED THE SQUARE IN FRONT OF THE COURT-HOUSE!!!

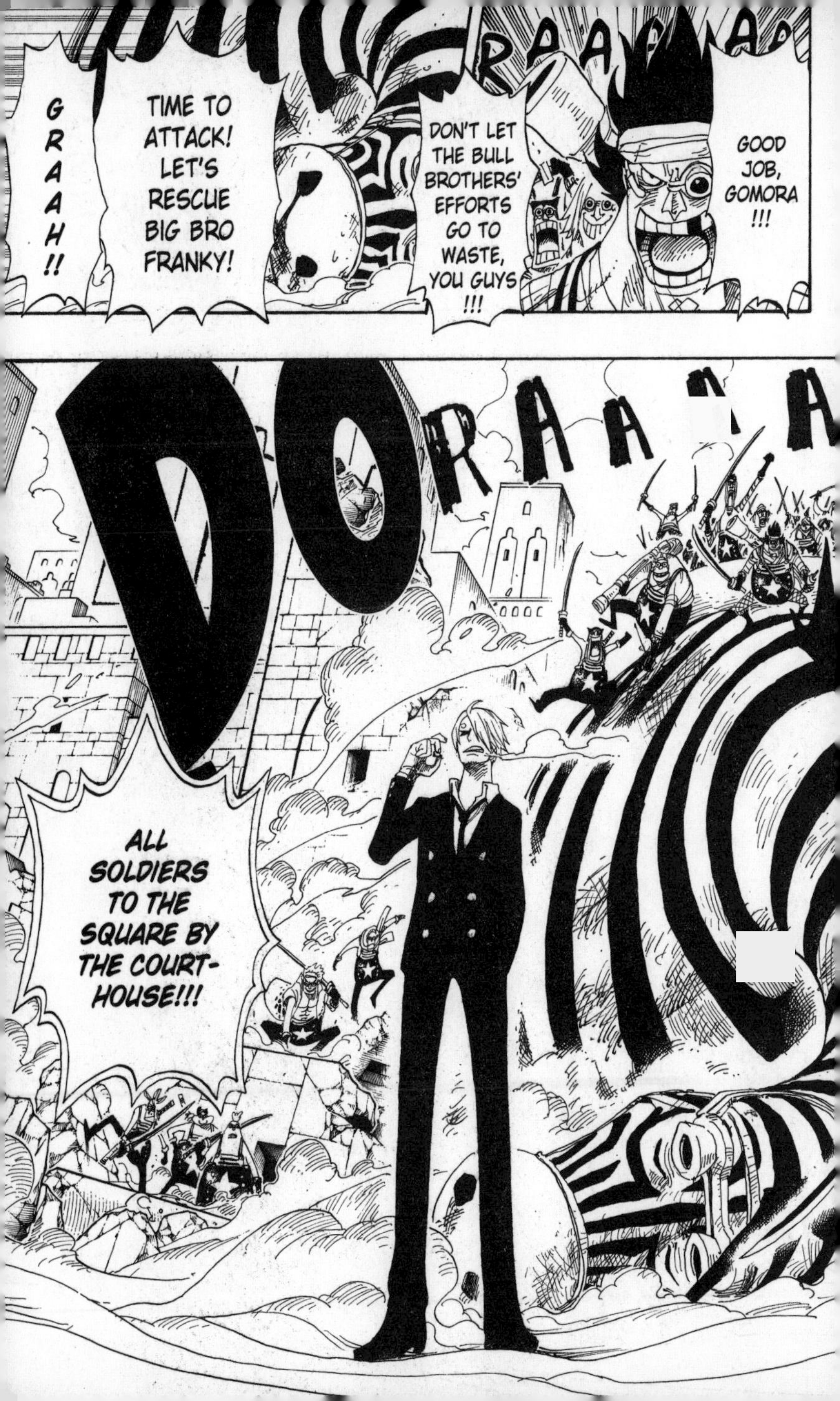
GOOD JOB, GOMORA!!!
DON'T LET THE BULL BROTHERS' EFFORTS GO TO WASTE, YOU GUYS!!!
TIME TO ATTACK! LET'S RESCUE BIG BRO FRANKY!
GRAAAH!!
ALL SOLDIERS TO THE SQUARE BY THE COURT-HOUSE!!!

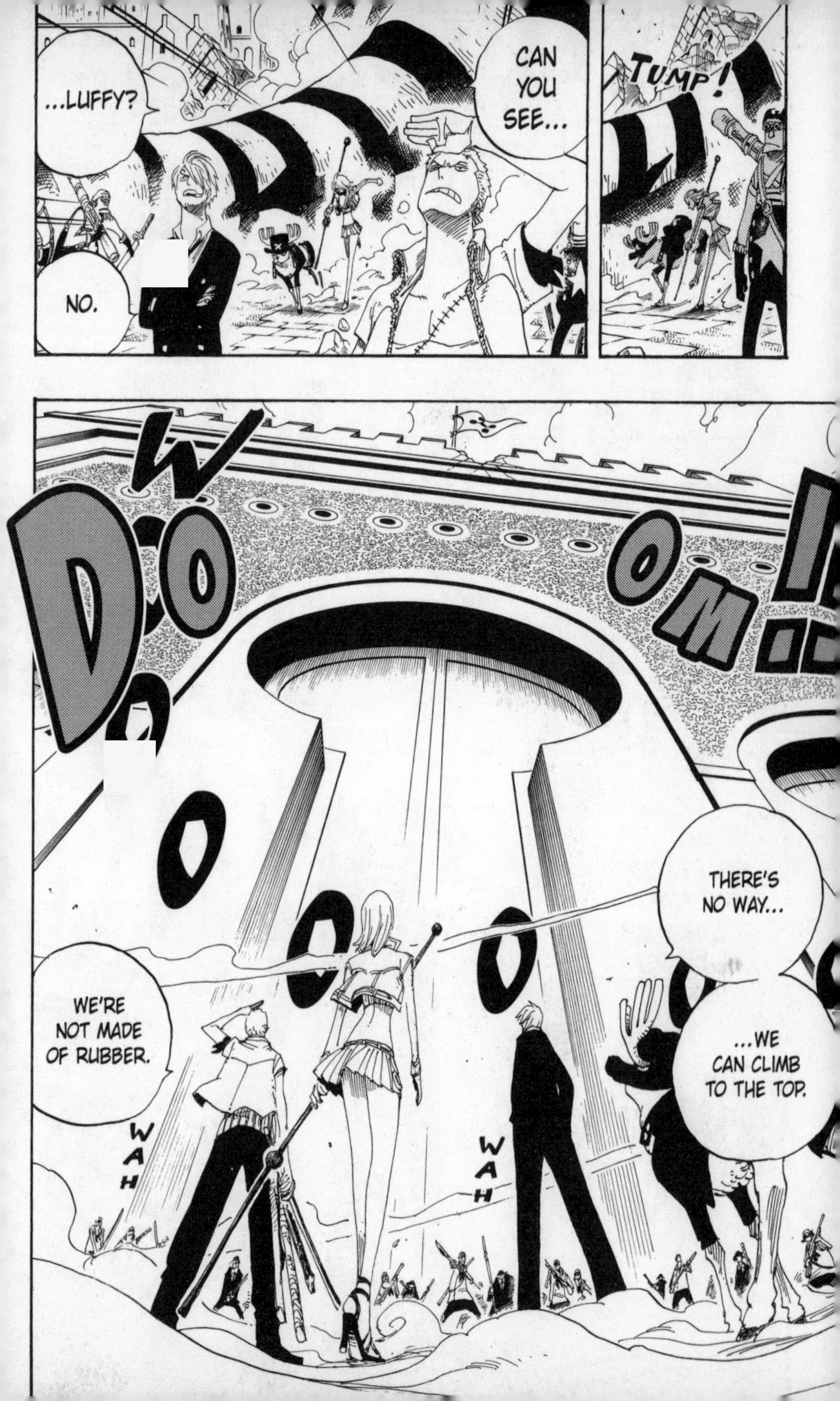
TUMP!
CAN YOU SEE...
...LUFFY?
NO.
DOOOOOOOM!!
THERE'S NO WAY...
...WE CAN CLIMB TO THE TOP.
WAH
WE'RE NOT MADE OF RUBBER.
WAH

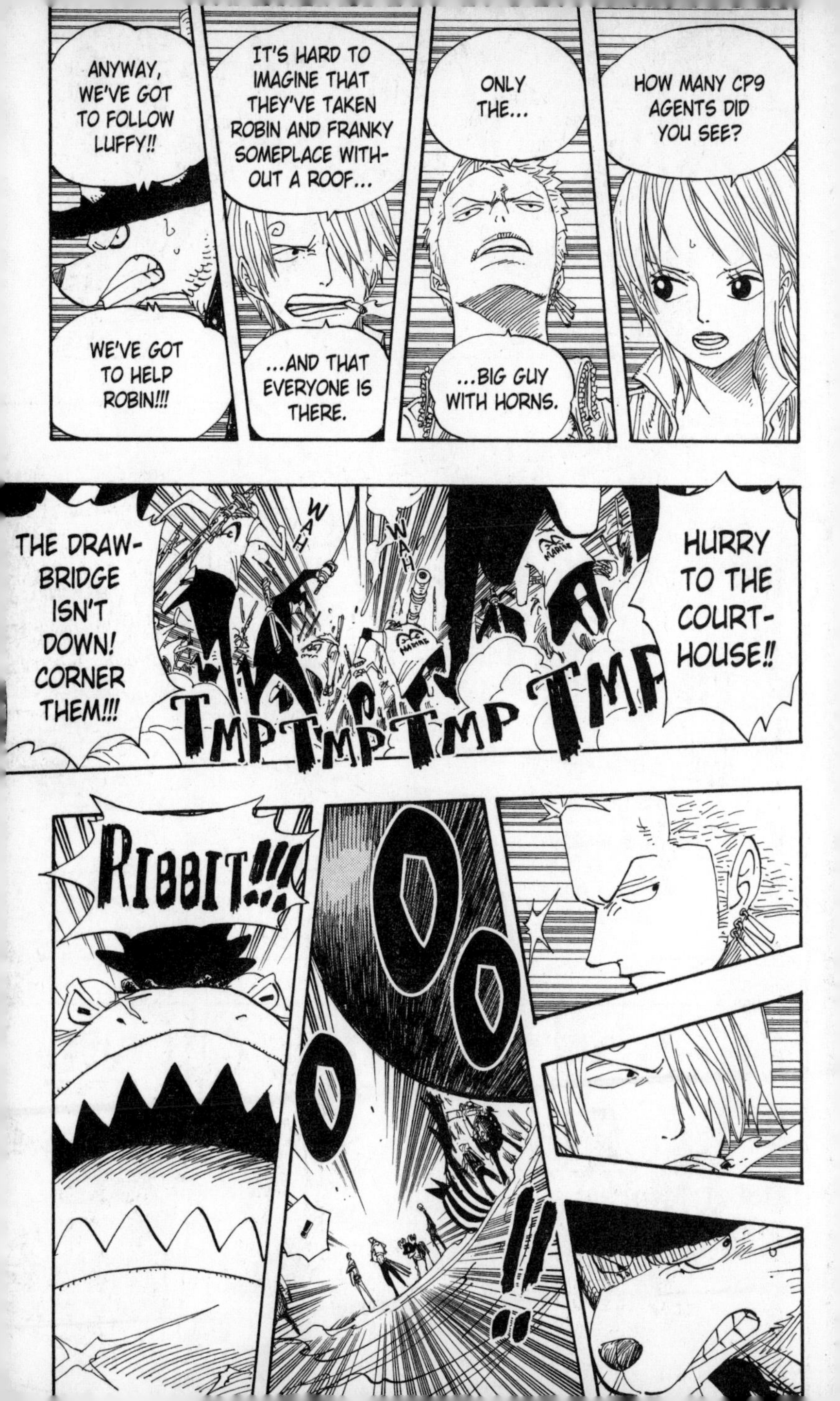
HOW MANY CP9 AGENTS DID YOU SEE?
ONLY THE...
...BIG GUY WITH HORNS.
IT'S HARD TO IMAGINE THAT THEY'VE TAKEN ROBIN AND FRANKY SOMEPLACE WITH-OUT A ROOF...
...AND THAT EVERYONE IS THERE.
ANYWAY, WE'VE GOT TO FOLLOW LUFFY!!
WE'VE GOT TO HELP ROBIN!!!
HURRY TO THE COURT-HOUSE!!
WAH
WAH
TMP TMP TMP TMP
THE DRAW-BRIDGE ISN'T DOWN! CORNER THEM!!!
!!
!
RIBBIT!!!

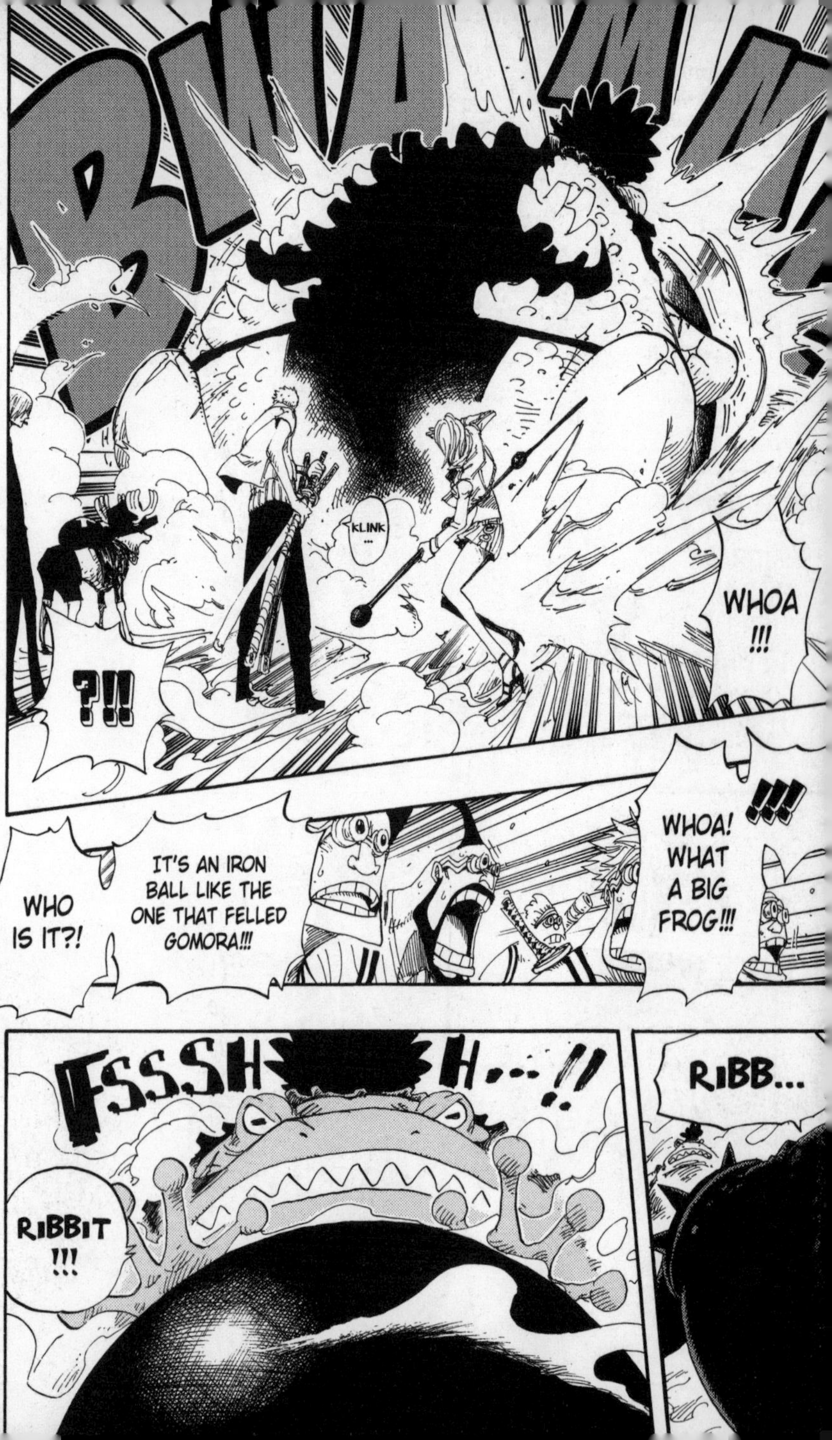
WHOA !!!
KLINK ...
?!!
!!!
WHOA! WHAT A BIG FROG!!!
IT'S AN IRON BALL LIKE THE ONE THAT FELLED GOMORA!!!
WHO IS IT?!
RIBB...
FSSSH...H...!!
RIBBIT !!!

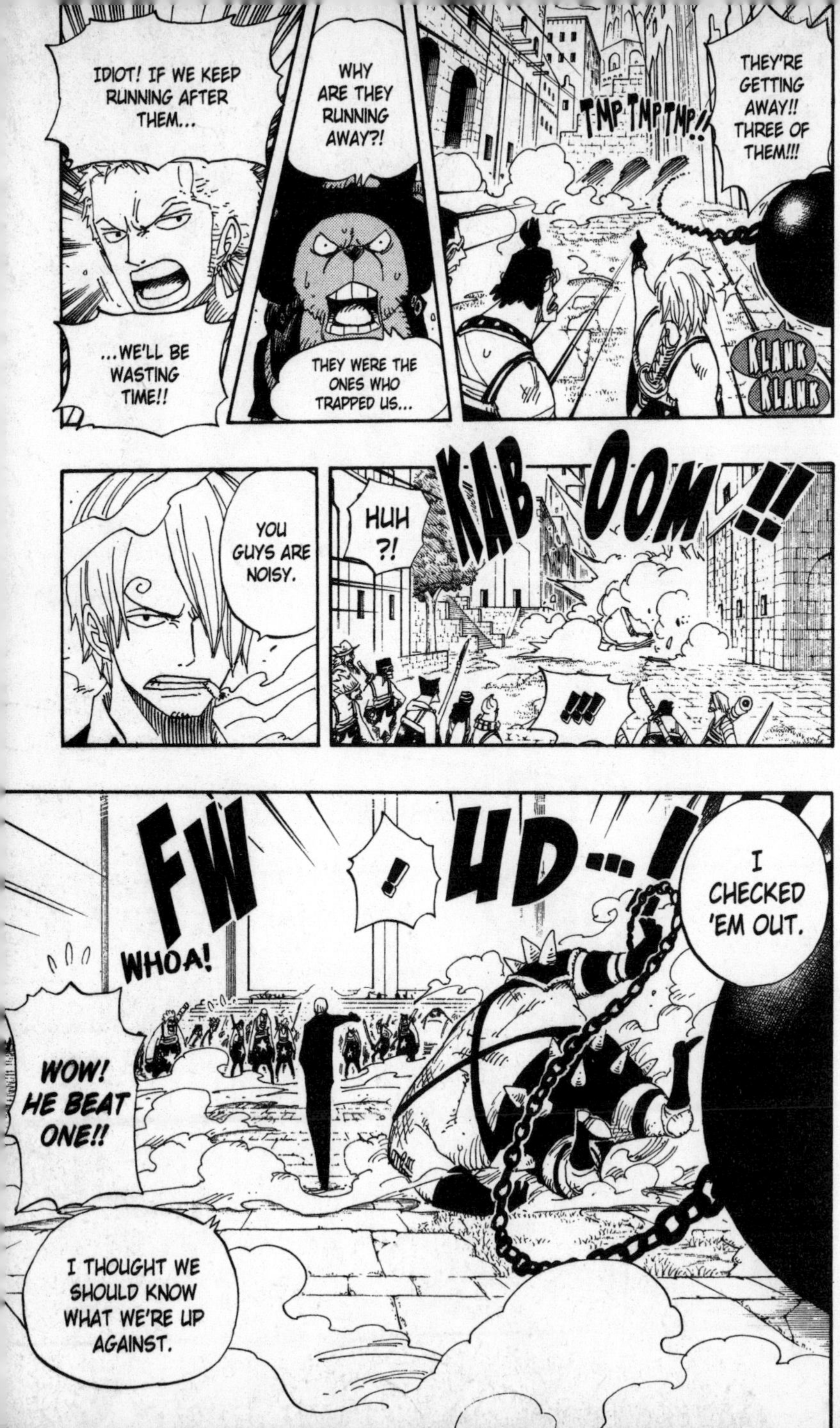
THEY'RE GETTING AWAY!! THREE OF THEM!!!
TMP TMP TMP!!
KLANK KLANK
WHY ARE THEY RUNNING AWAY?!
THEY WERE THE ONES WHO TRAPPED US...
IDIOT! IF WE KEEP RUNNING AFTER THEM...
...WE'LL BE WASTING TIME!!
KABOOM!!
HUH ?!
!!!
YOU GUYS ARE NOISY.
I CHECKED 'EM OUT.
FWUD...!
!
WHOA!
WOW! HE BEAT ONE!!
I THOUGHT WE SHOULD KNOW WHAT WE'RE UP AGAINST.

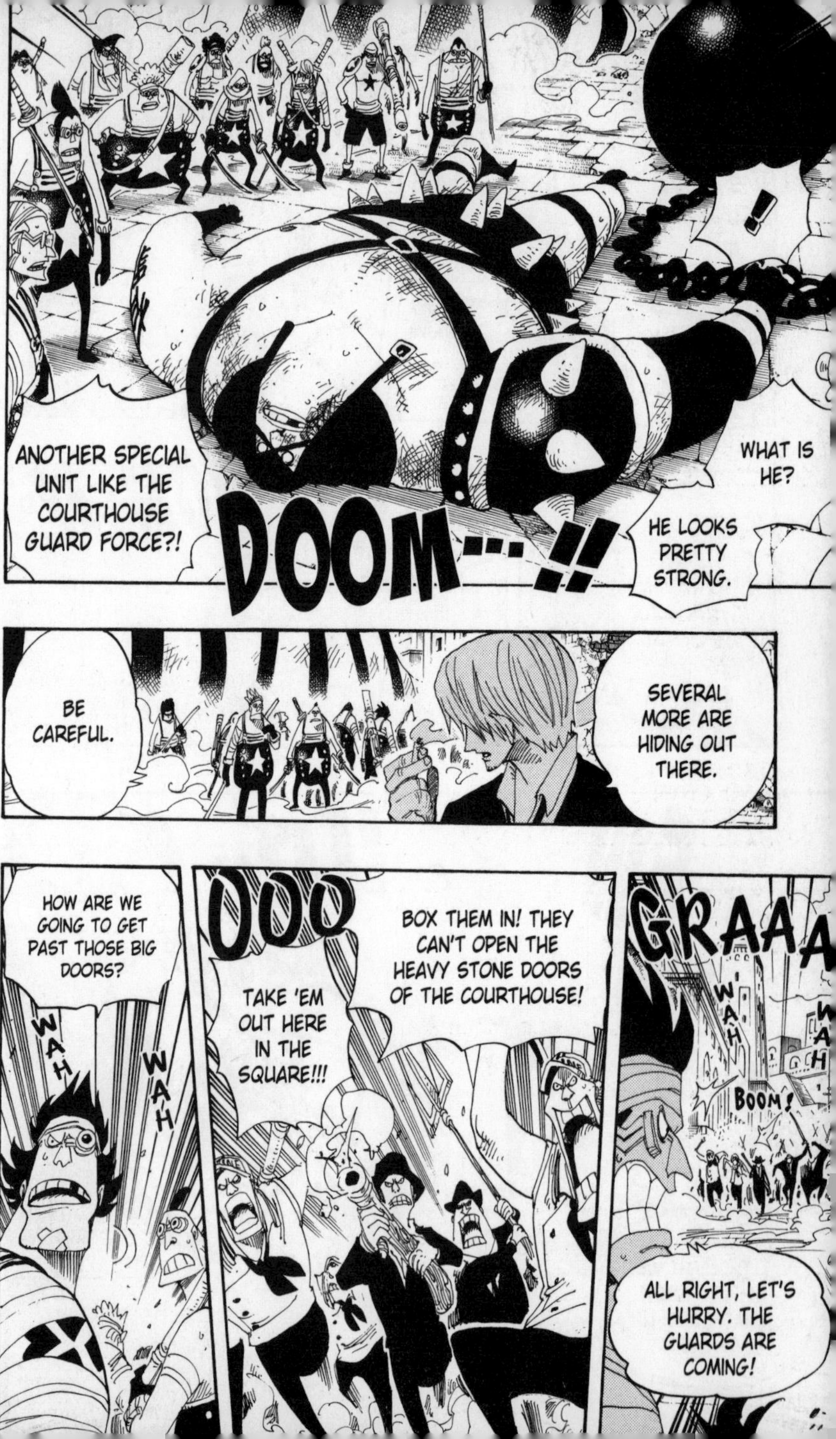
!
WHAT IS HE?
HE LOOKS PRETTY STRONG.
DOOM...!!
ANOTHER SPECIAL UNIT LIKE THE COURTHOUSE GUARD FORCE?!
SEVERAL MORE ARE HIDING OUT THERE.
BE CAREFUL.
GRAAA
WAH
WAH
BOOM!
ALL RIGHT, LET'S HURRY. THE GUARDS ARE COMING!
OOO
BOX THEM IN! THEY CAN'T OPEN THE HEAVY STONE DOORS OF THE COURTHOUSE!
TAKE 'EM OUT HERE IN THE SQUARE!!!
HOW ARE WE GOING TO GET PAST THOSE BIG DOORS?
WAH
WAH

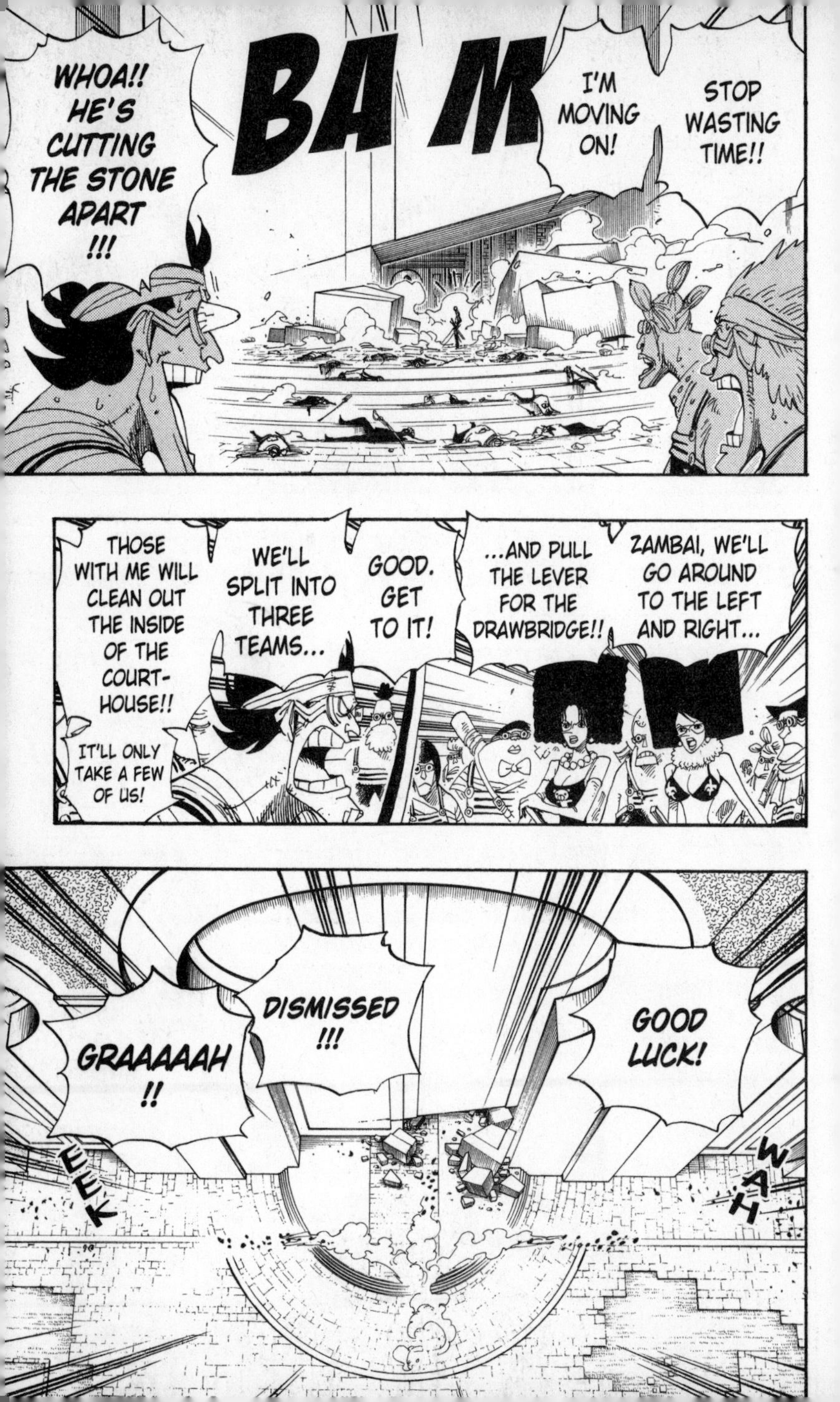
STOP WASTING TIME!!
I'M MOVING ON!
BAM
WHOA!! HE'S CUTTING THE STONE APART!!!
ZAMBAI, WE'LL GO AROUND TO THE LEFT AND RIGHT...
...AND PULL THE LEVER FOR THE DRAWBRIDGE!!
GOOD. GET TO IT!
WE'LL SPLIT INTO THREE TEAMS...
THOSE WITH ME WILL CLEAN OUT THE INSIDE OF THE COURTHOUSE!!
IT'LL ONLY TAKE A FEW OF US!
WAH
GOOD LUCK!
DISMISSED!!!
GRAAAAAH!!
EEEK

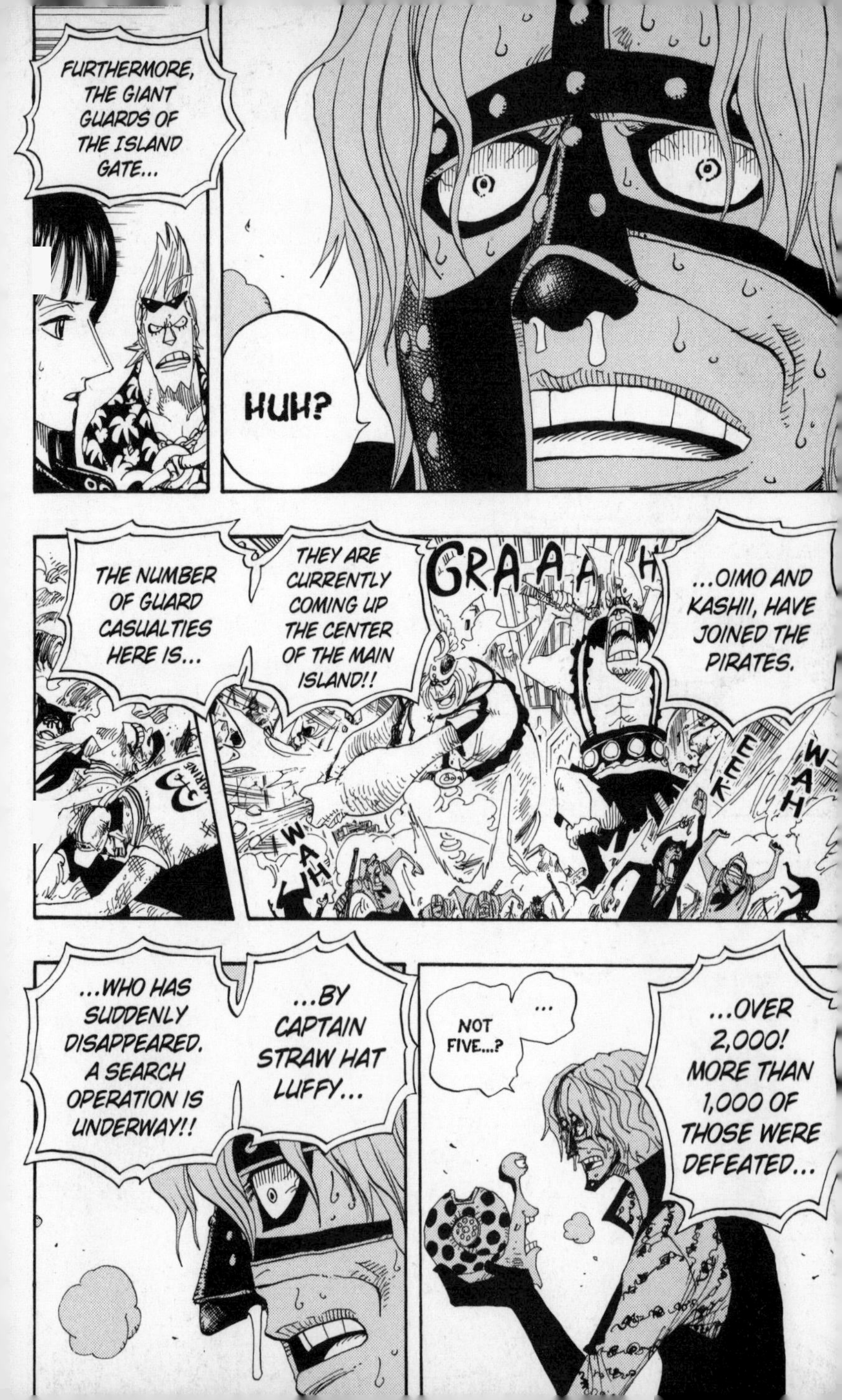
HUH?
FURTHERMORE, THE GIANT GUARDS OF THE ISLAND GATE...
...OIMO AND KASHII, HAVE JOINED THE PIRATES.
GRAAAH
THEY ARE CURRENTLY COMING UP THE CENTER OF THE MAIN ISLAND!!
THE NUMBER OF GUARD CASUALTIES HERE IS...
EEEK
WAH
WAH
...OVER 2,000! MORE THAN 1,000 OF THOSE WERE DEFEATED...
...
NOT FIVE...?
...BY CAPTAIN STRAW HAT LUFFY...
...WHO HAS SUDDENLY DISAPPEARED. A SEARCH OPERATION IS UNDERWAY!!

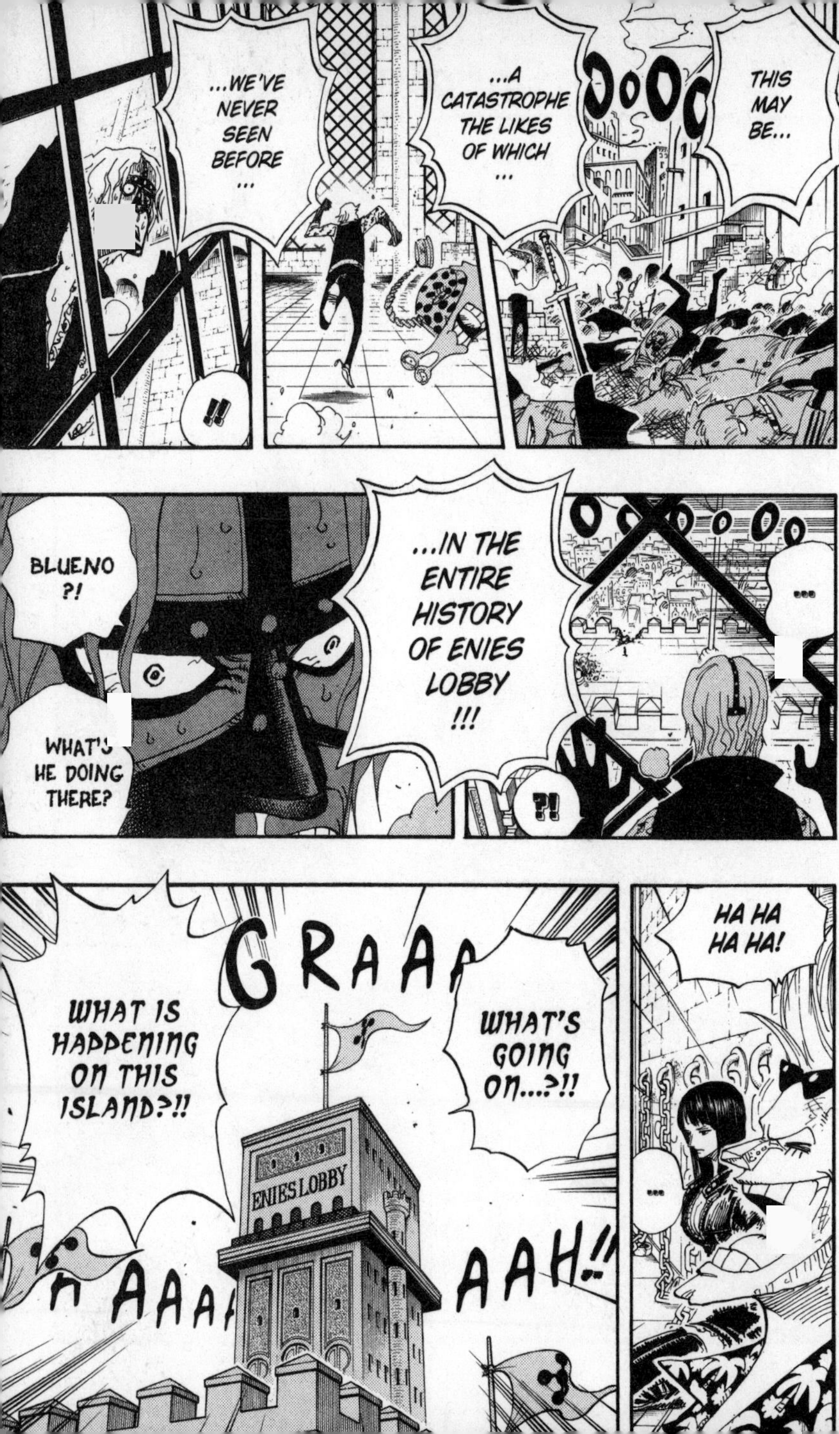

DOOO
THIS MAY BE...
...A CATASTROPHE THE LIKES OF WHICH ...
...WE'VE NEVER SEEN BEFORE ...
!!
...
?!
...IN THE ENTIRE HISTORY OF ENIES LOBBY !!!
BLUENO ?!
WHAT'S HE DOING THERE?
HA HA HA HA!
...
WHAT'S GOING ON...?!!
GRAA
WHAT IS HAPPENING ON THIS ISLAND?!!
ENIES LOBBY
AAA
AAH!!

Chapter 387: GEAR

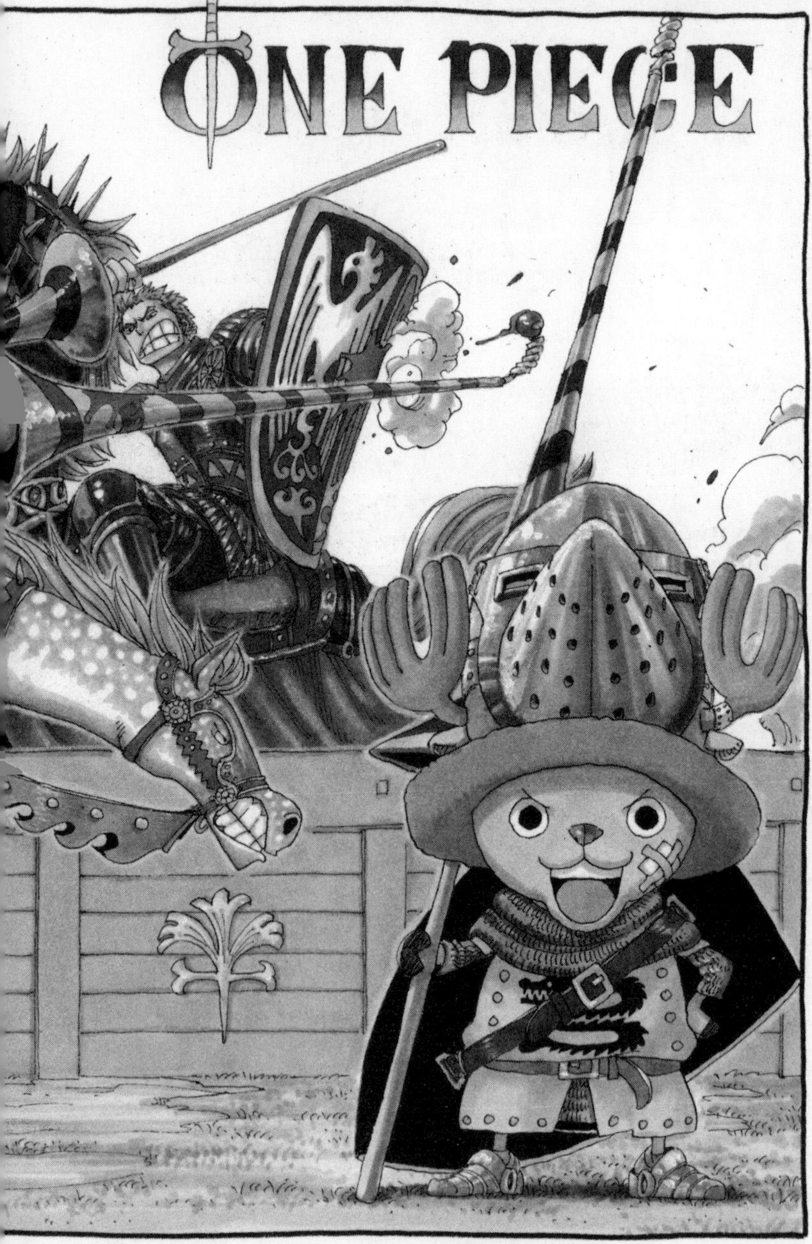
ONE PIECE

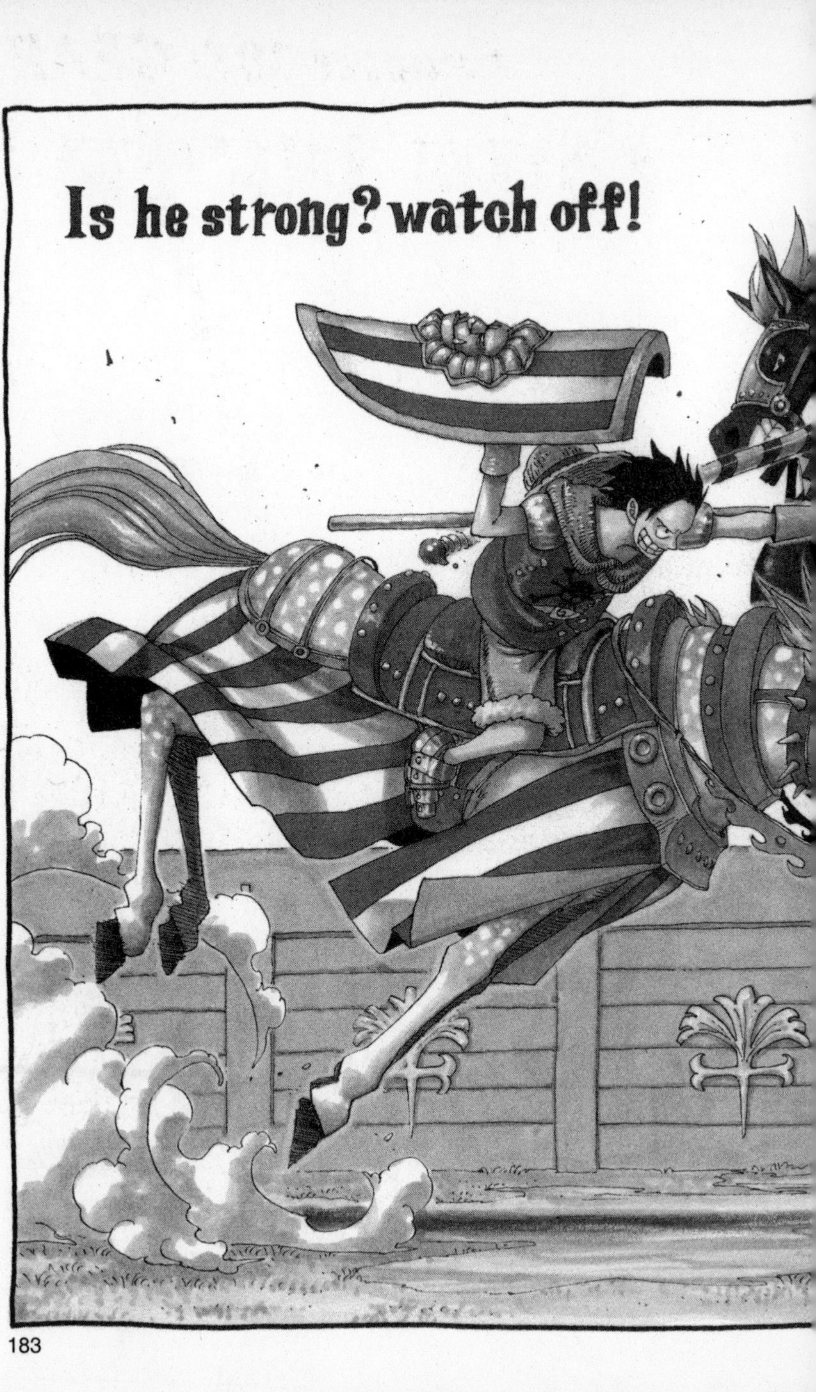
Is he strong? watch off!

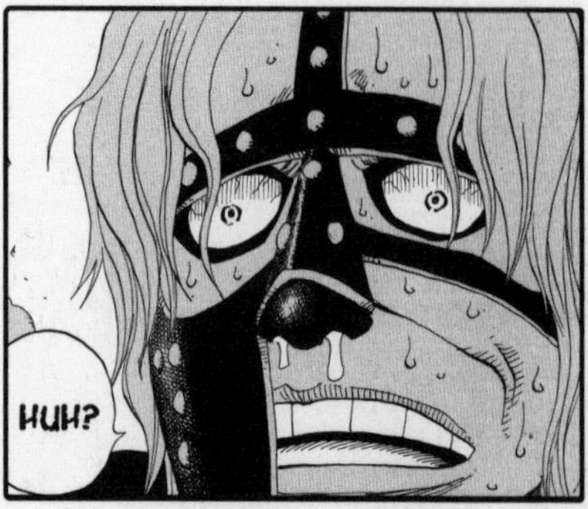
HUH?

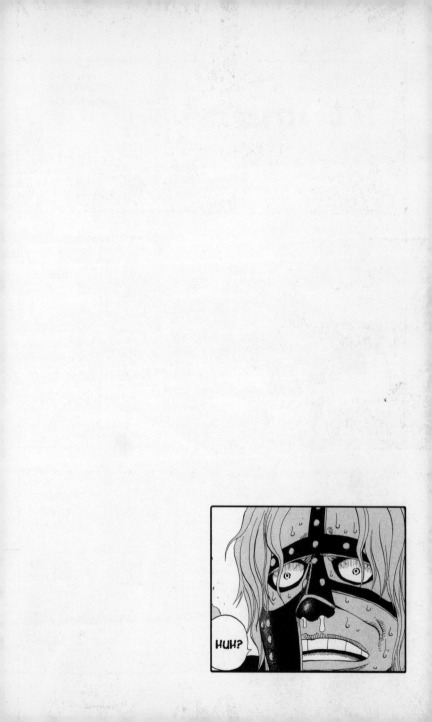

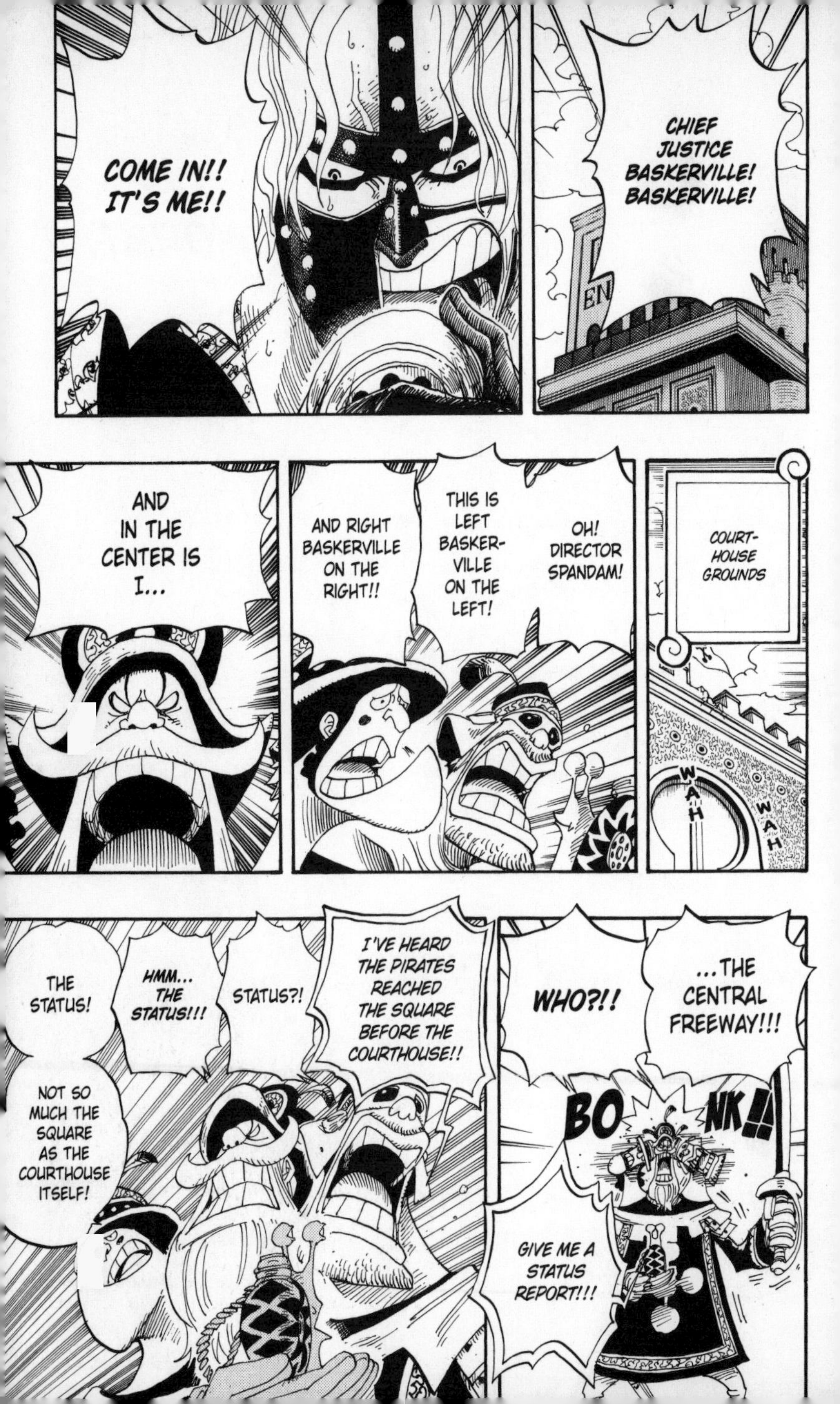
CHIEF JUSTICE BASKERVILLE! BASKERVILLE!
COME IN!! IT'S ME!!
COURT-HOUSE GROUNDS
WAH
WAH
OH! DIRECTOR SPANDAM!
THIS IS LEFT BASKER-VILLE ON THE LEFT!
AND RIGHT BASKERVILLE ON THE RIGHT!!
AND IN THE CENTER IS I...
...THE CENTRAL FREEWAY!!!
WHO?!!
BONK!!
GIVE ME A STATUS REPORT!!!
I'VE HEARD THE PIRATES REACHED THE SQUARE BEFORE THE COURTHOUSE!!
STATUS?!
HMM... THE STATUS!!!
THE STATUS!
NOT SO MUCH THE SQUARE AS THE COURTHOUSE ITSELF!

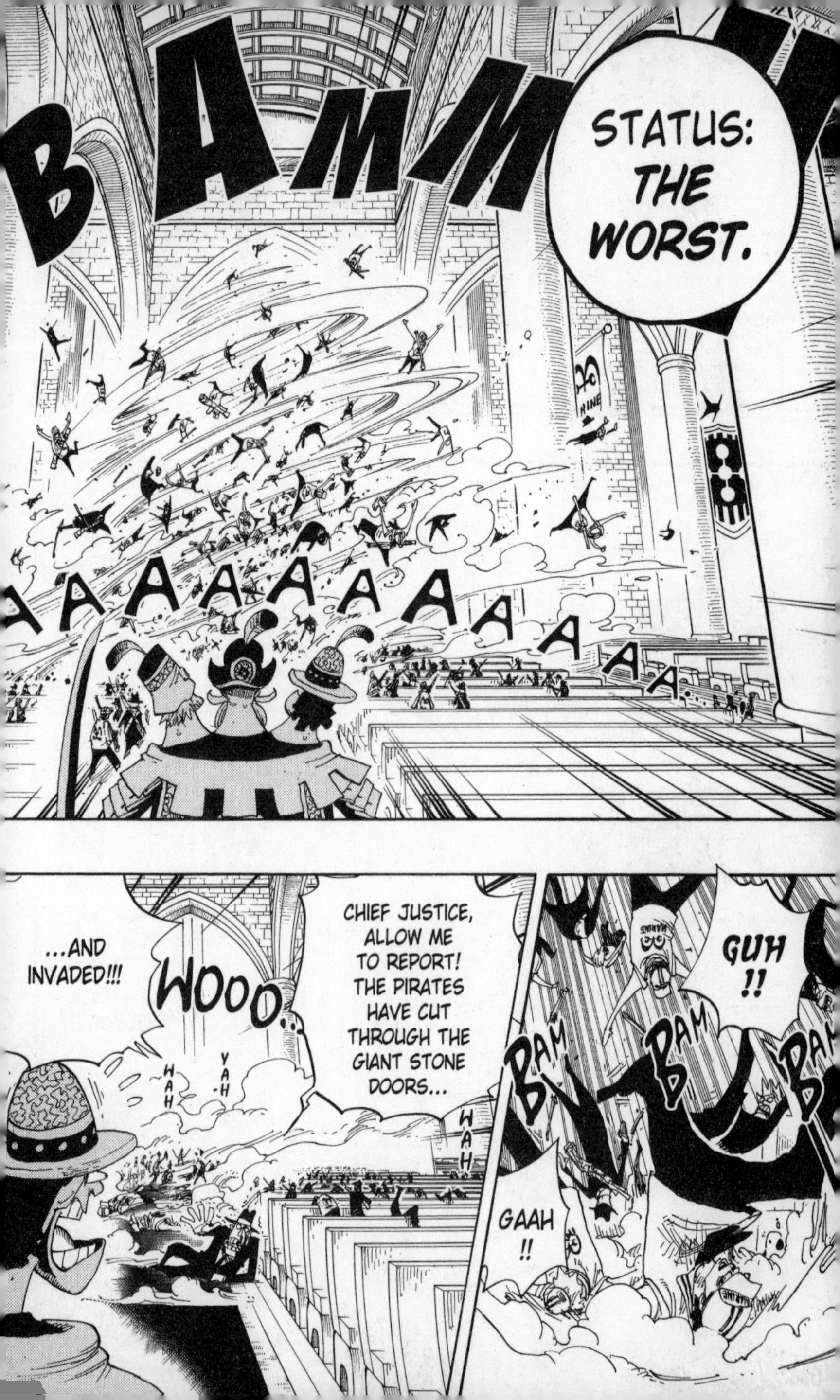
BAMM
STATUS: THE WORST.
AAAAAAAAAAA
GUH!!
BAM BAM BAM
GAAH!!
CHIEF JUSTICE, ALLOW ME TO REPORT! THE PIRATES HAVE CUT THROUGH THE GIANT STONE DOORS...
...AND INVADED!!!
WOOO
YAH
WAH
WAH

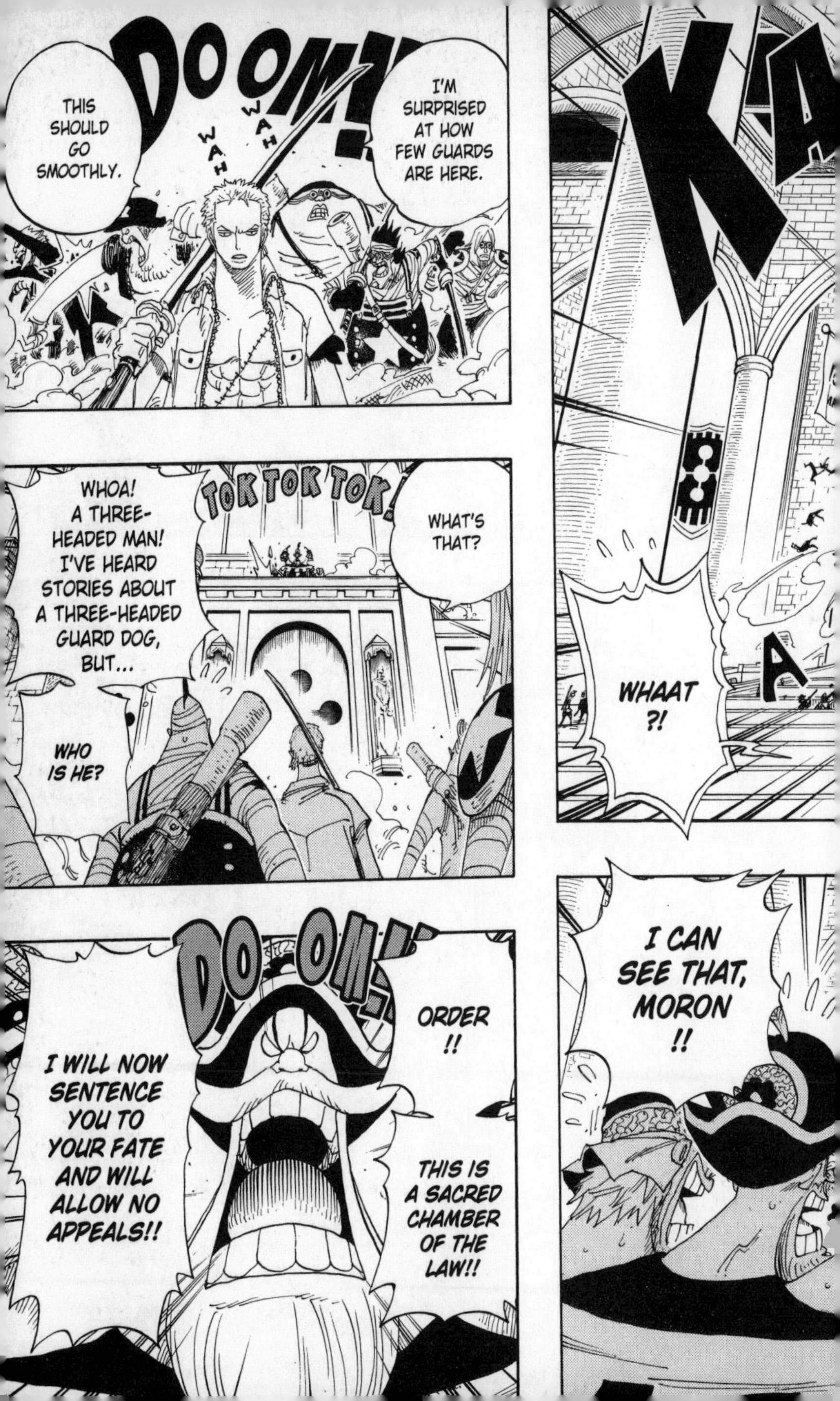
KA
A
WHAAT ?!
I'M SURPRISED AT HOW FEW GUARDS ARE HERE.
DOOM!
WAH WAH
THIS SHOULD GO SMOOTHLY.
WHAT'S THAT?
TOK TOK TOK!
WHOA! A THREE-HEADED MAN! I'VE HEARD STORIES ABOUT A THREE-HEADED GUARD DOG, BUT...
WHO IS HE?
I CAN SEE THAT, MORON !!
ORDER !!
DOOM!
THIS IS A SACRED CHAMBER OF THE LAW!!
I WILL NOW SENTENCE YOU TO YOUR FATE AND WILL ALLOW NO APPEALS!!

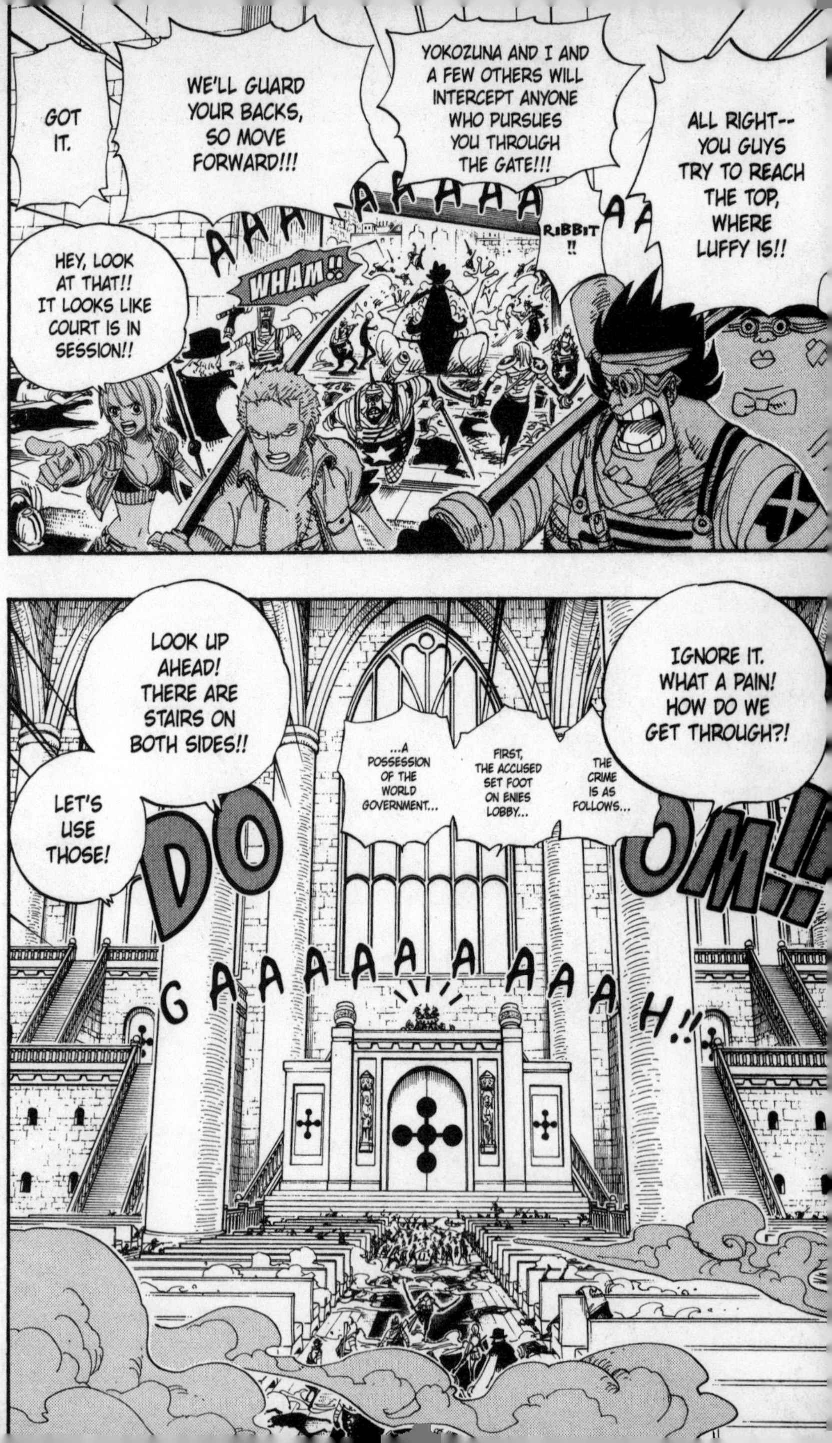
ALL RIGHT-- YOU GUYS TRY TO REACH THE TOP, WHERE LUFFY IS!!
YOKOZUNA AND I AND A FEW OTHERS WILL INTERCEPT ANYONE WHO PURSUES YOU THROUGH THE GATE!!!
WE'LL GUARD YOUR BACKS, SO MOVE FORWARD!!!
GOT IT.
RIBBIT!!
WHAM!!
HEY, LOOK AT THAT!! IT LOOKS LIKE COURT IS IN SESSION!!
IGNORE IT. WHAT A PAIN! HOW DO WE GET THROUGH?!
THE CRIME IS AS FOLLOWS...
FIRST, THE ACCUSED SET FOOT ON ENIES LOBBY...
...A POSSESSION OF THE WORLD GOVERNMENT...
LOOK UP AHEAD! THERE ARE STAIRS ON BOTH SIDES!!
LET'S USE THOSE!
DO
OM!!
GAAAAAAAAH!!

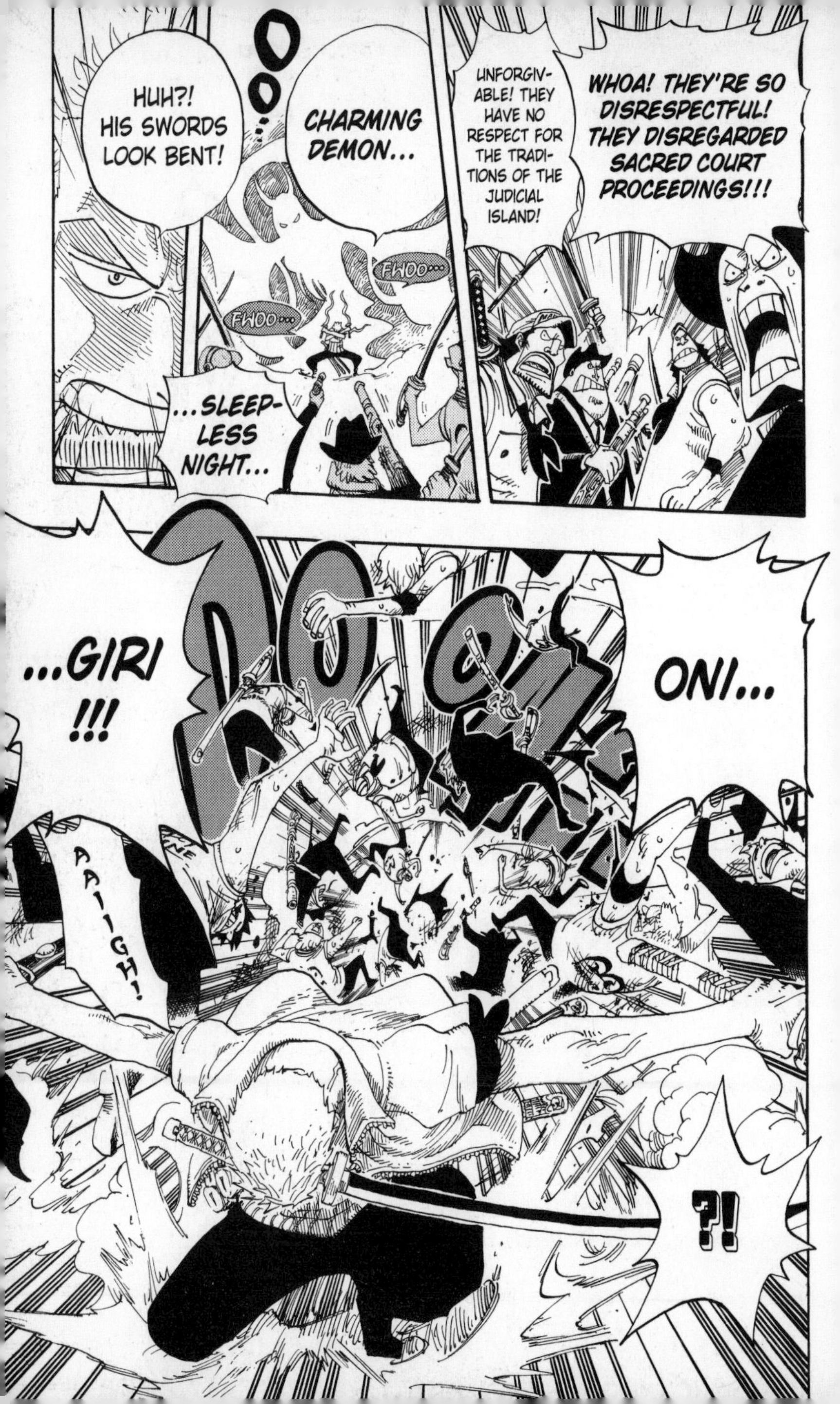
WHOA! THEY'RE SO DISRESPECTFUL! THEY DISREGARDED SACRED COURT PROCEEDINGS!!!
UNFORGIV-ABLE! THEY HAVE NO RESPECT FOR THE TRADI-TIONS OF THE JUDICIAL ISLAND!
CHARMING DEMON...
FWOO...
FWOO...
...SLEEP-LESS NIGHT...
HUH?! HIS SWORDS LOOK BENT!
ONI...
...GIRI !!!
AAIIGH!
?!

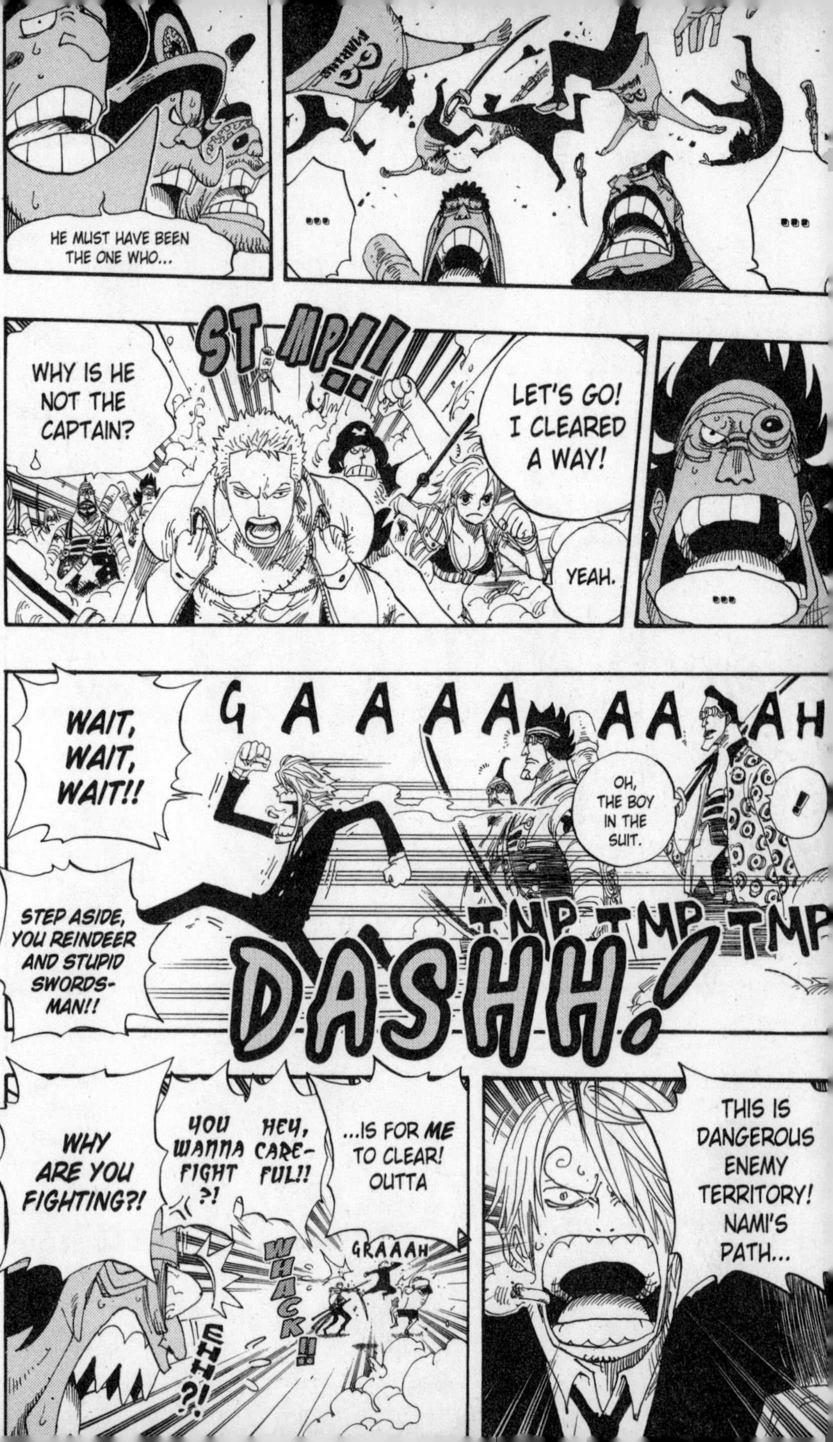
...
...
HE MUST HAVE BEEN THE ONE WHO...
...
ST MP!!
LET'S GO! I CLEARED A WAY!
YEAH.
WHY IS HE NOT THE CAPTAIN?
G A A A A A A A H
OH, THE BOY IN THE SUIT.
!
WAIT, WAIT, WAIT!!
STEP ASIDE, YOU REINDEER AND STUPID SWORDS-MAN!!
TMP TMP TMP
DASHH!
THIS IS DANGEROUS ENEMY TERRITORY! NAMI'S PATH...
...IS FOR ME TO CLEAR! OUTTA
HEY, CARE-FUL!!
YOU WANNA FIGHT?!
WHY ARE YOU FIGHTING?!
GRAAAH
WHACK!!
EHH?!

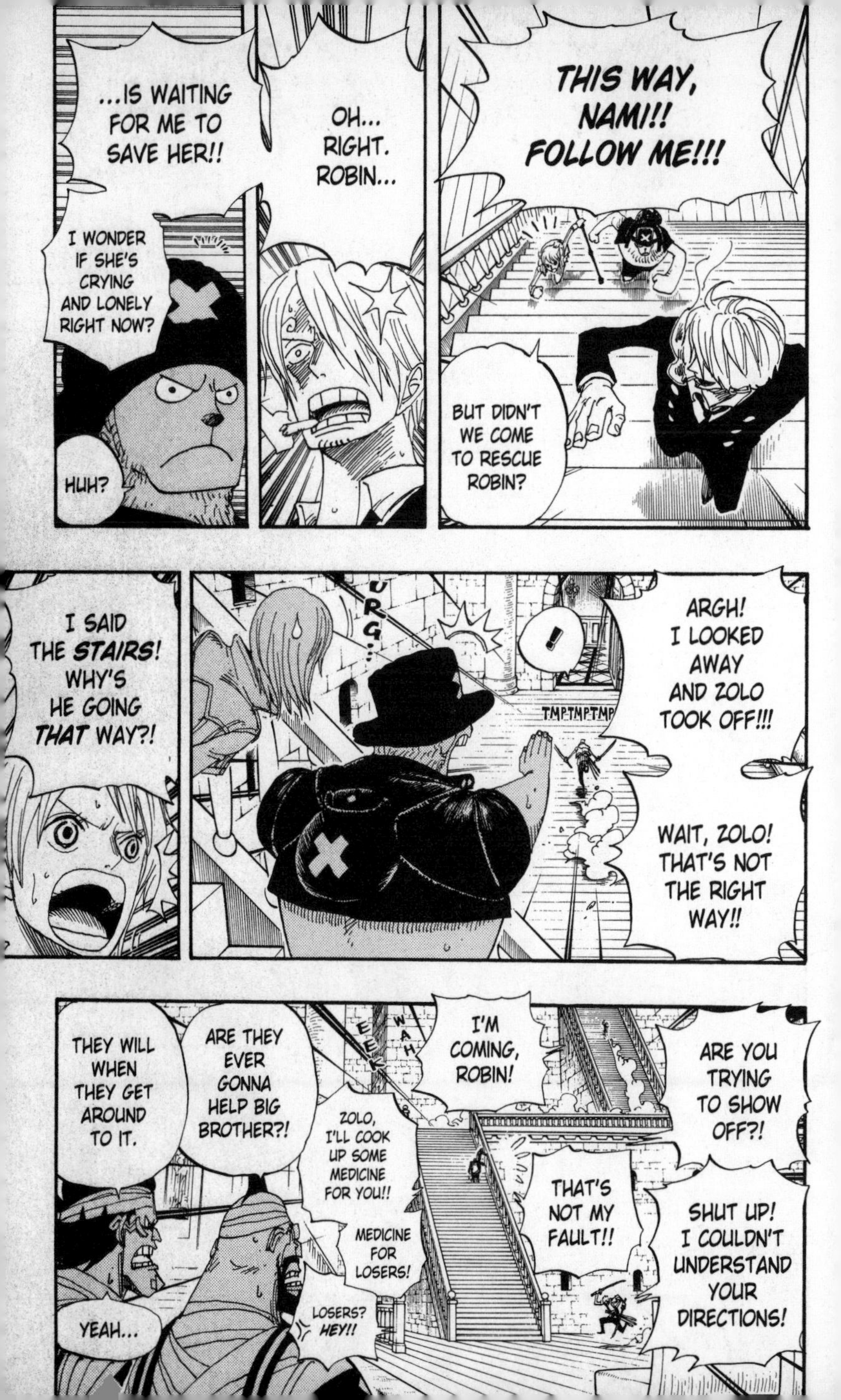
THIS WAY, NAMI!! FOLLOW ME!!!
BUT DIDN'T WE COME TO RESCUE ROBIN?
OH... RIGHT. ROBIN...
...IS WAITING FOR ME TO SAVE HER!!
I WONDER IF SHE'S CRYING AND LONELY RIGHT NOW?
HUH?
ARGH! I LOOKED AWAY AND ZOLO TOOK OFF!!!
!
URG...
TMPTMPTMP
WAIT, ZOLO! THAT'S NOT THE RIGHT WAY!!
I SAID THE *STAIRS*! WHY'S HE GOING *THAT* WAY?!
ARE YOU TRYING TO SHOW OFF?!
I'M COMING, ROBIN!
WAH
EEEK
SHUT UP! I COULDN'T UNDERSTAND YOUR DIRECTIONS!
THAT'S NOT MY FAULT!!
ZOLO, I'LL COOK UP SOME MEDICINE FOR YOU!!
MEDICINE FOR LOSERS!
LOSERS? *HEY!!*
ARE THEY EVER GONNA HELP BIG BROTHER?!
THEY WILL WHEN THEY GET AROUND TO IT.
YEAH...

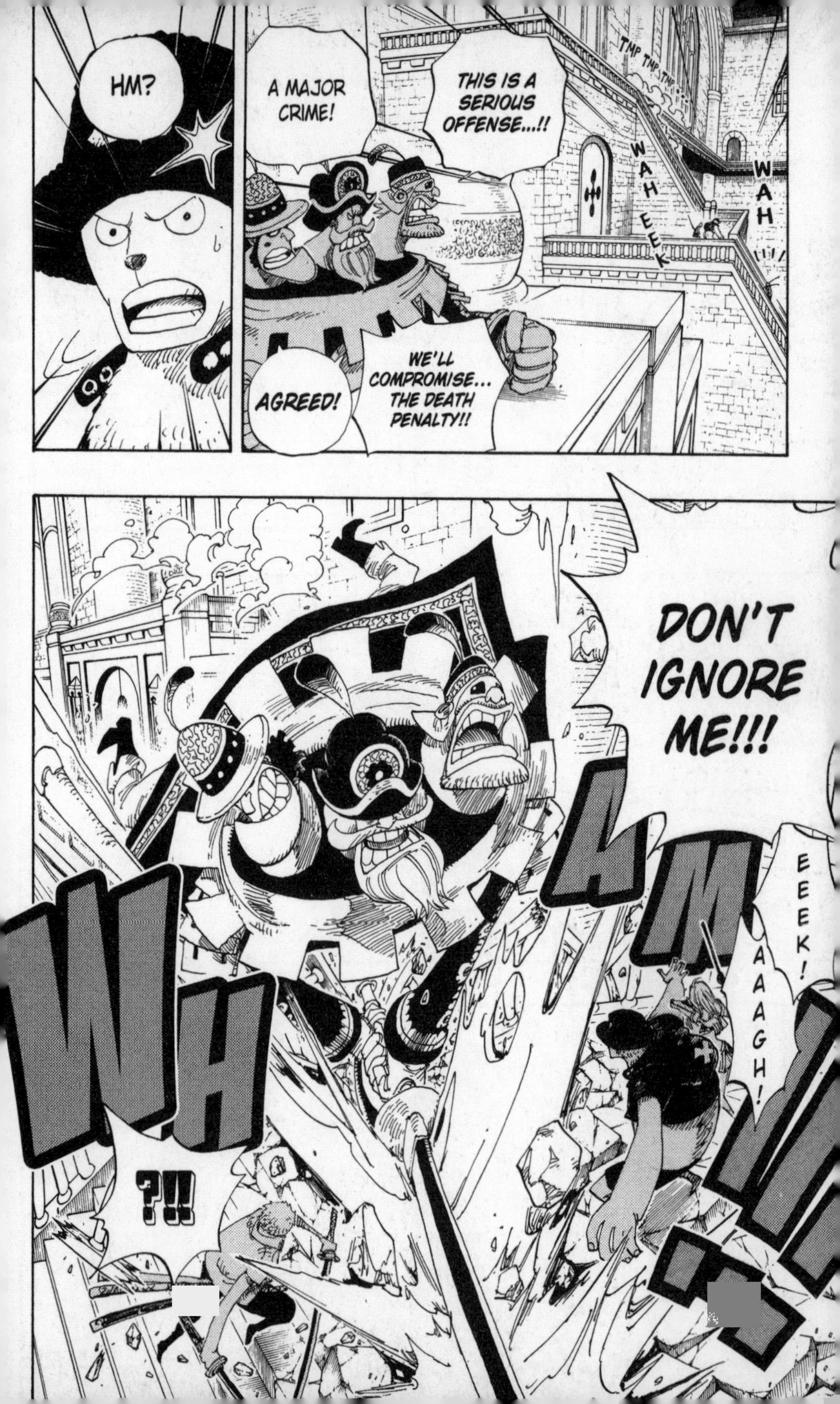
TMP TMP TMP
WAH
WAH EEK
THIS IS A SERIOUS OFFENSE...!!
A MAJOR CRIME!
WE'LL COMPROMISE... THE DEATH PENALTY!!
AGREED!
HM?
DON'T IGNORE ME!!!
EEEK!
AAAAGH!
WHAM!!
?!!

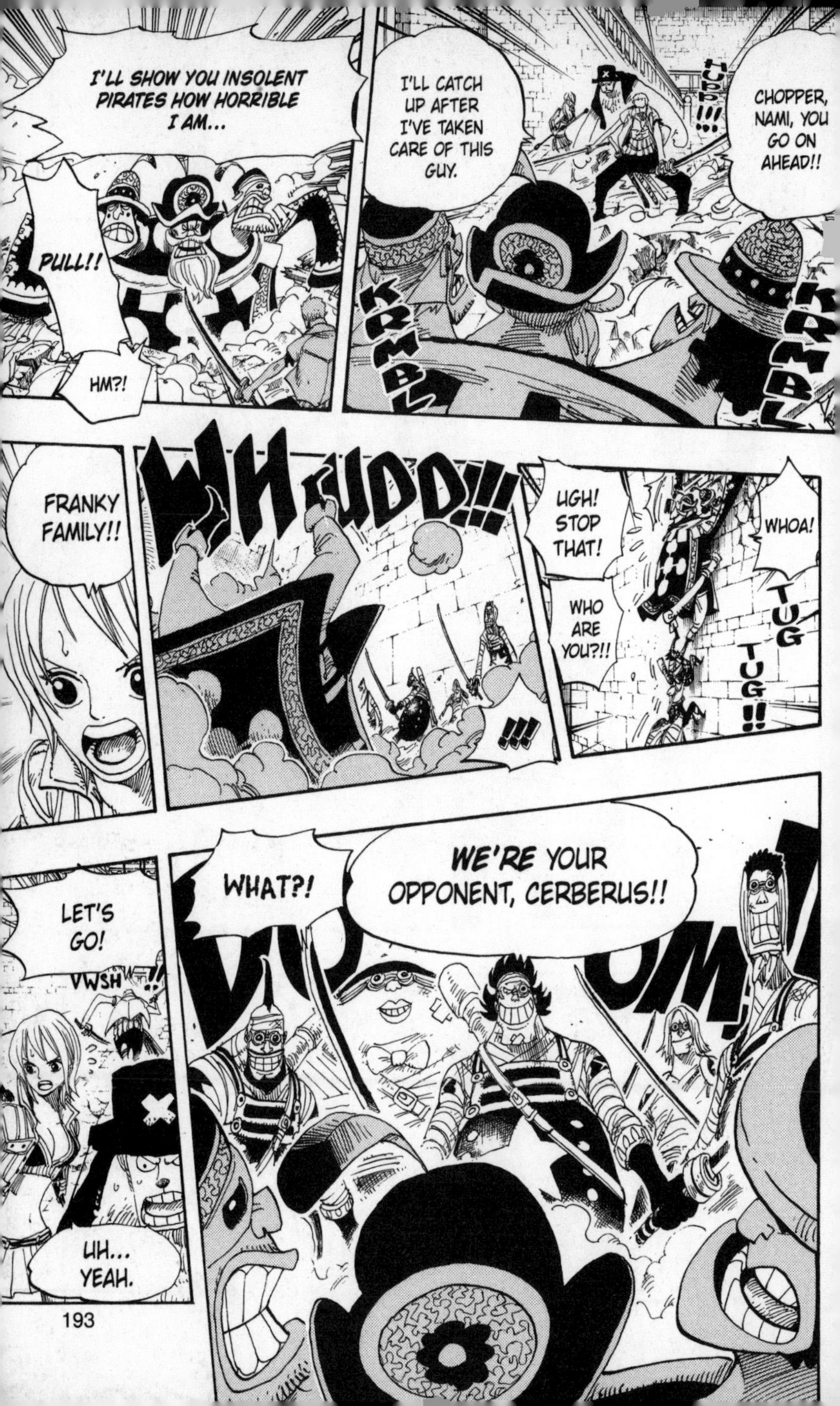
CHOPPER, NAMI, YOU GO ON AHEAD!!
HUPP!!!
I'LL CATCH UP AFTER I'VE TAKEN CARE OF THIS GUY.
KRMBL
KRMBL
I'LL SHOW YOU INSOLENT PIRATES HOW HORRIBLE I AM...
PULL!!
HM?!
WHOA!
UGH! STOP THAT!
WHO ARE YOU?!!
TUG
TUG!!
WHUDD!!!
!!!
FRANKY FAMILY!!
WE'RE YOUR OPPONENT, CERBERUS!!
WHAT?!
LET'S GO!
VWSH
UH... YEAH.

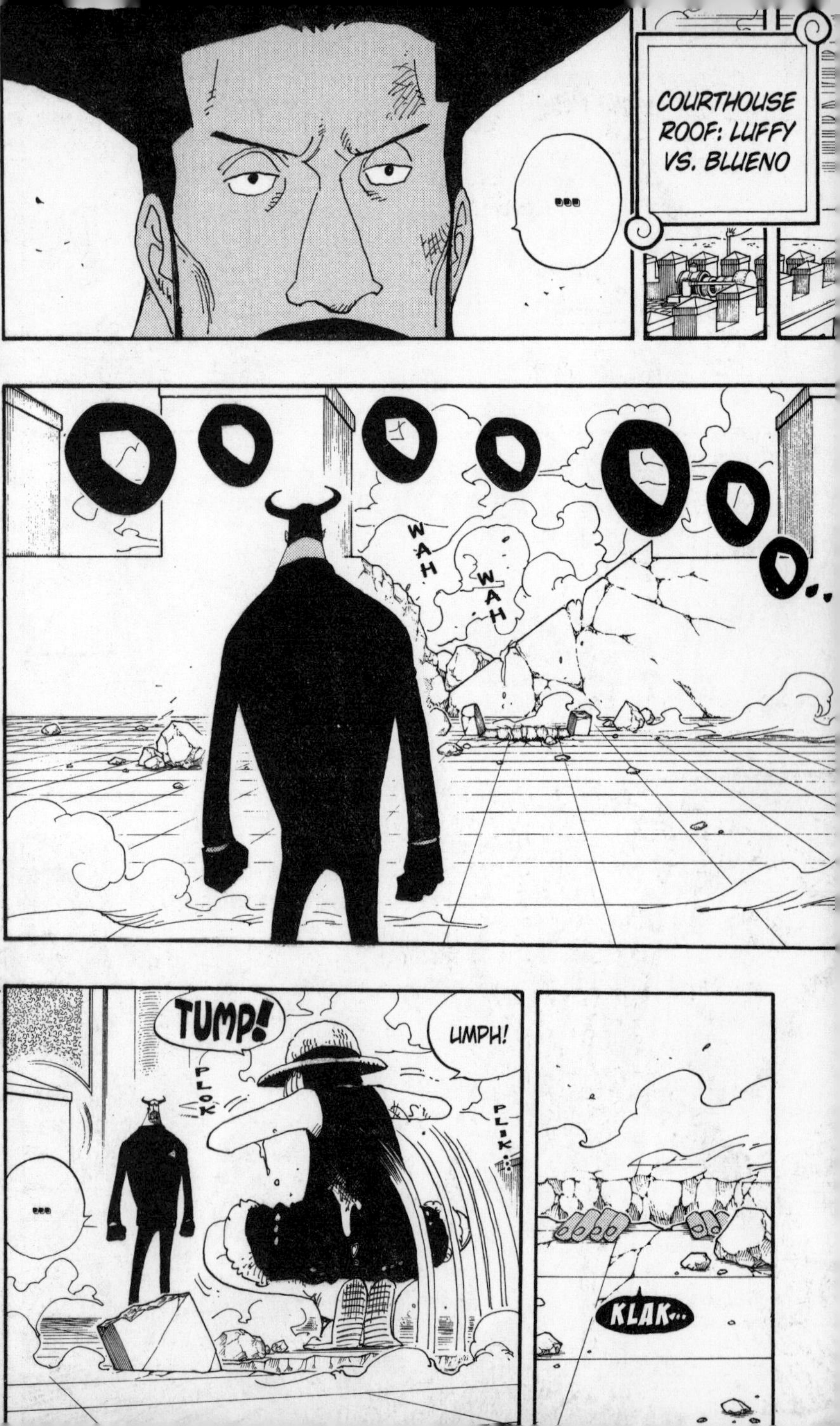
COURTHOUSE ROOF: LUFFY VS. BLUENO
...
OOOOOOO...
WAH
WAH
UMPH!
PLIK...
TUMP!
PLOK
...
KLAK...

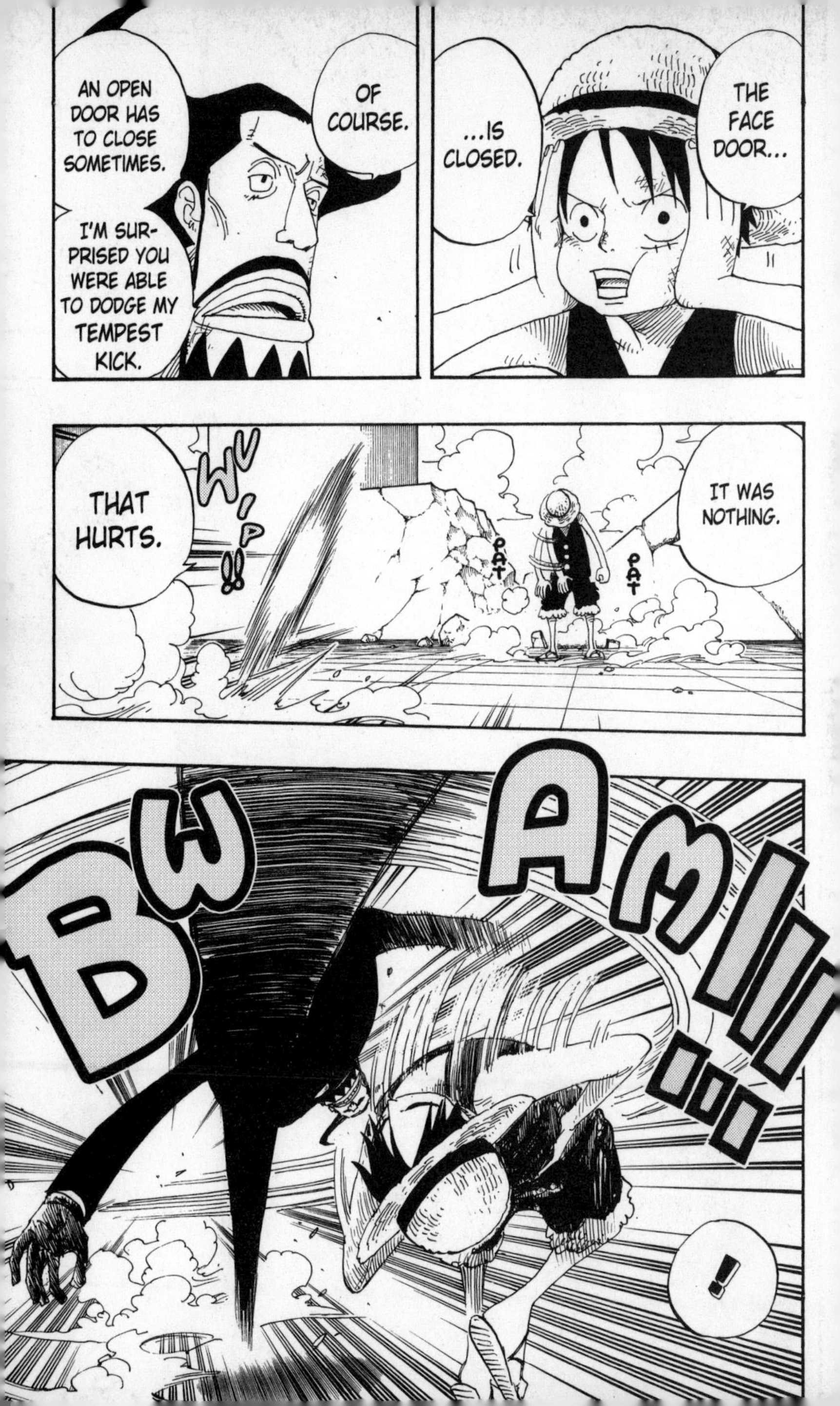
THE FACE DOOR...
...IS CLOSED.
OF COURSE.
AN OPEN DOOR HAS TO CLOSE SOMETIMES.
I'M SUR-PRISED YOU WERE ABLE TO DODGE MY TEMPEST KICK.
IT WAS NOTHING.
PAT
PAT
WHIP!!
THAT HURTS.
BWAM!!!
!

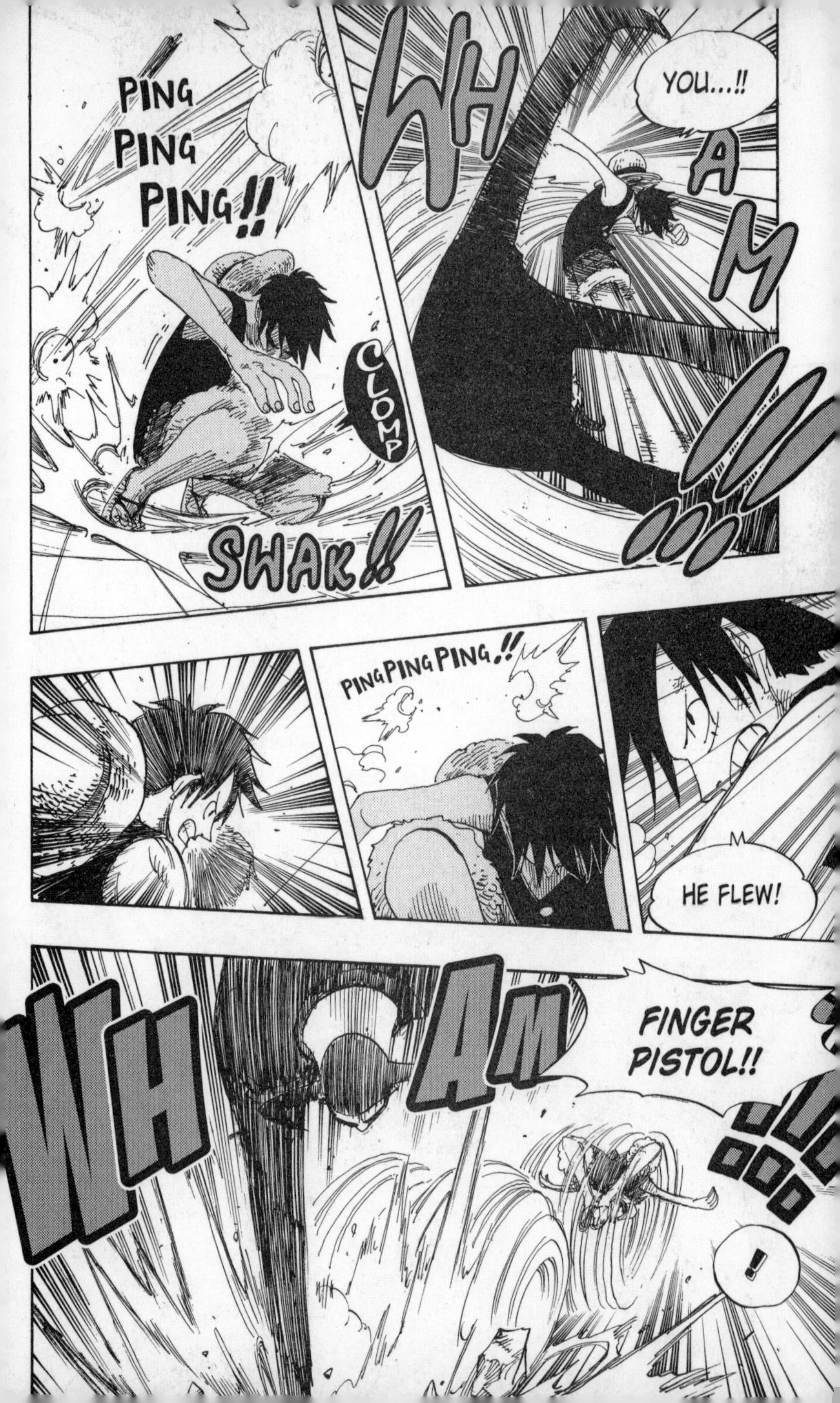

YOU...!!
WHAM!!
PING PING PING!!
CLOMP
SHAK!!
HE FLEW!
PING PING PING!!
FINGER PISTOL!!
!
WHAM!!

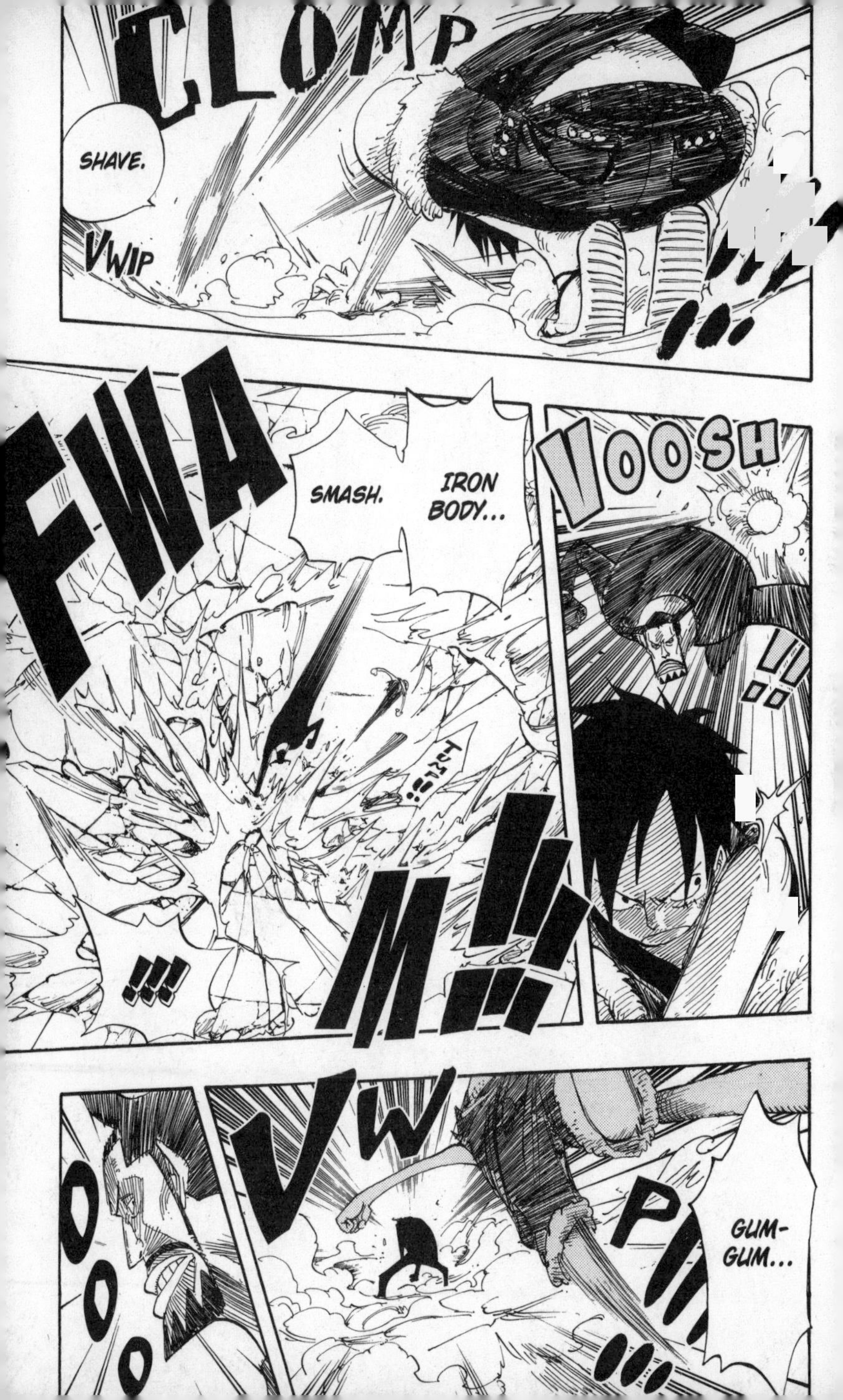
CLOMP
SHAVE.
VWIP
VOOSH
IRON BODY...
SMASH.
FWA
TUMP!!
M!!!
GUM-GUM...
P!!
VW
OOO

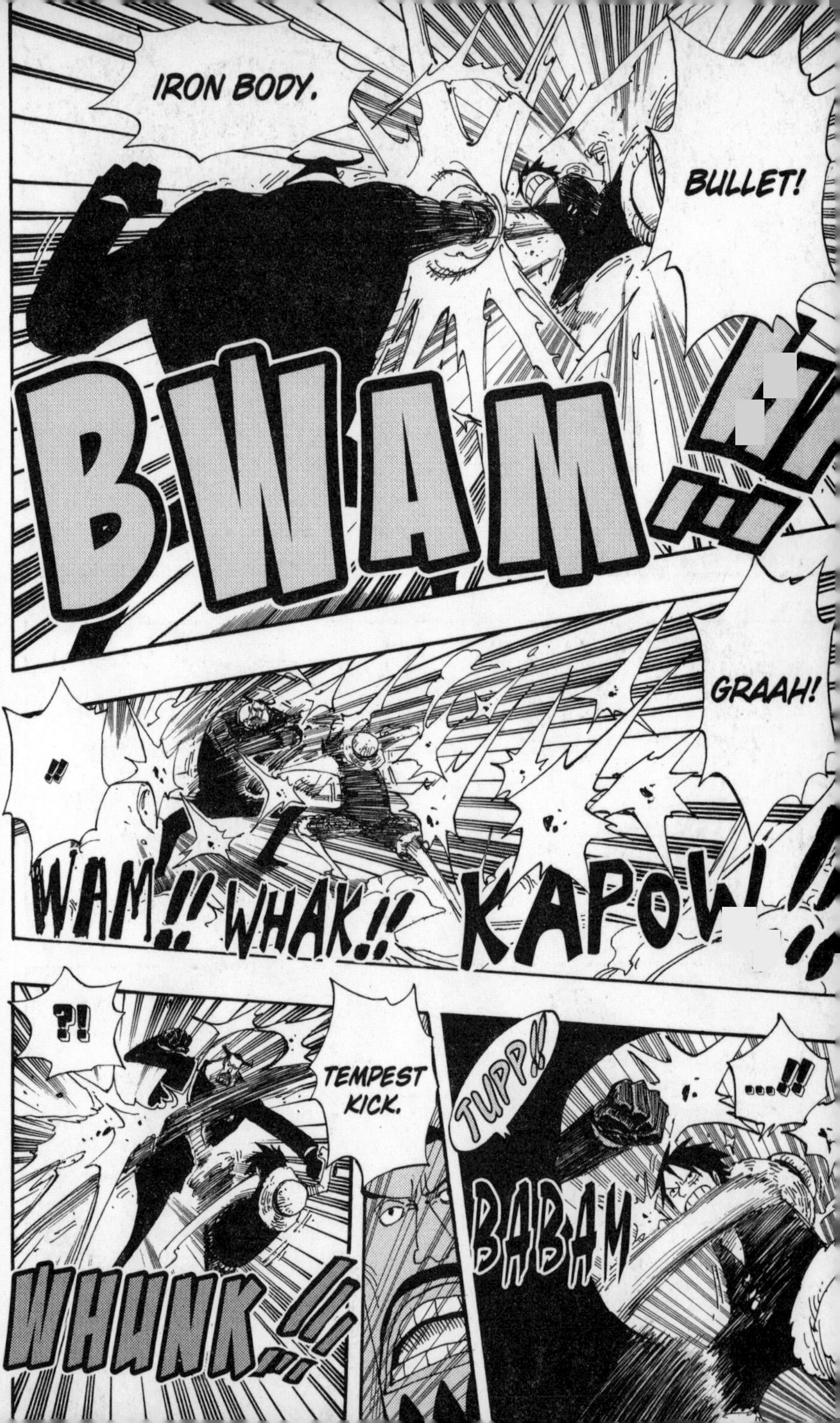
BULLET!
IRON BODY.
BWAM!!
GRAAH!
!!
KAPOW!!
WHAK!!
WAM!!
...!!
TUPP!!
BABAM
TEMPEST KICK.
?!
WHUNK!!

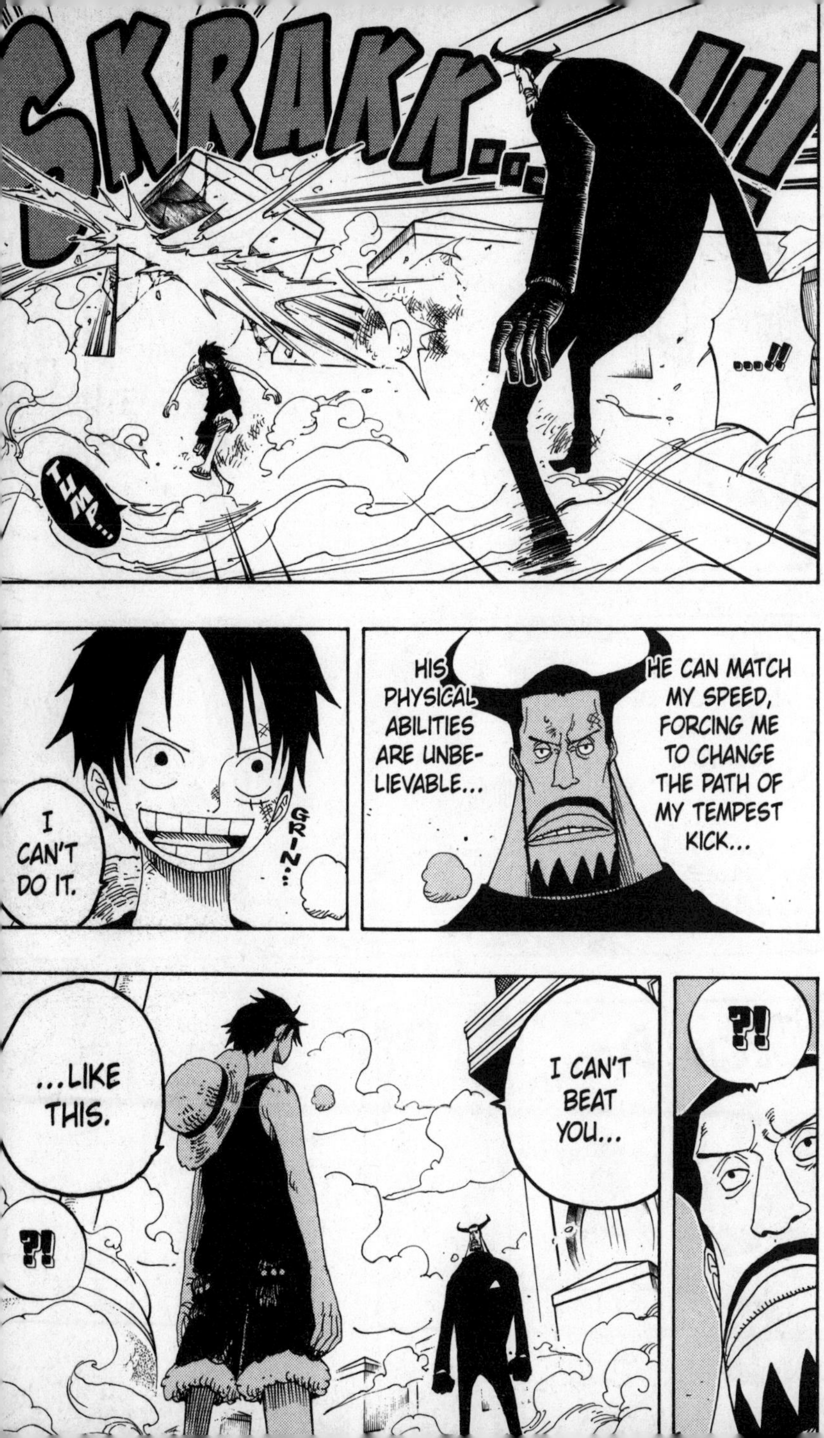
SKRAKK...!!!
...!!
TUMP...
HE CAN MATCH MY SPEED, FORCING ME TO CHANGE THE PATH OF MY TEMPEST KICK...
HIS PHYSICAL ABILITIES ARE UNBE-LIEVABLE...
GRIN...
I CAN'T DO IT.
?!
I CAN'T BEAT YOU...
...LIKE THIS.
?!

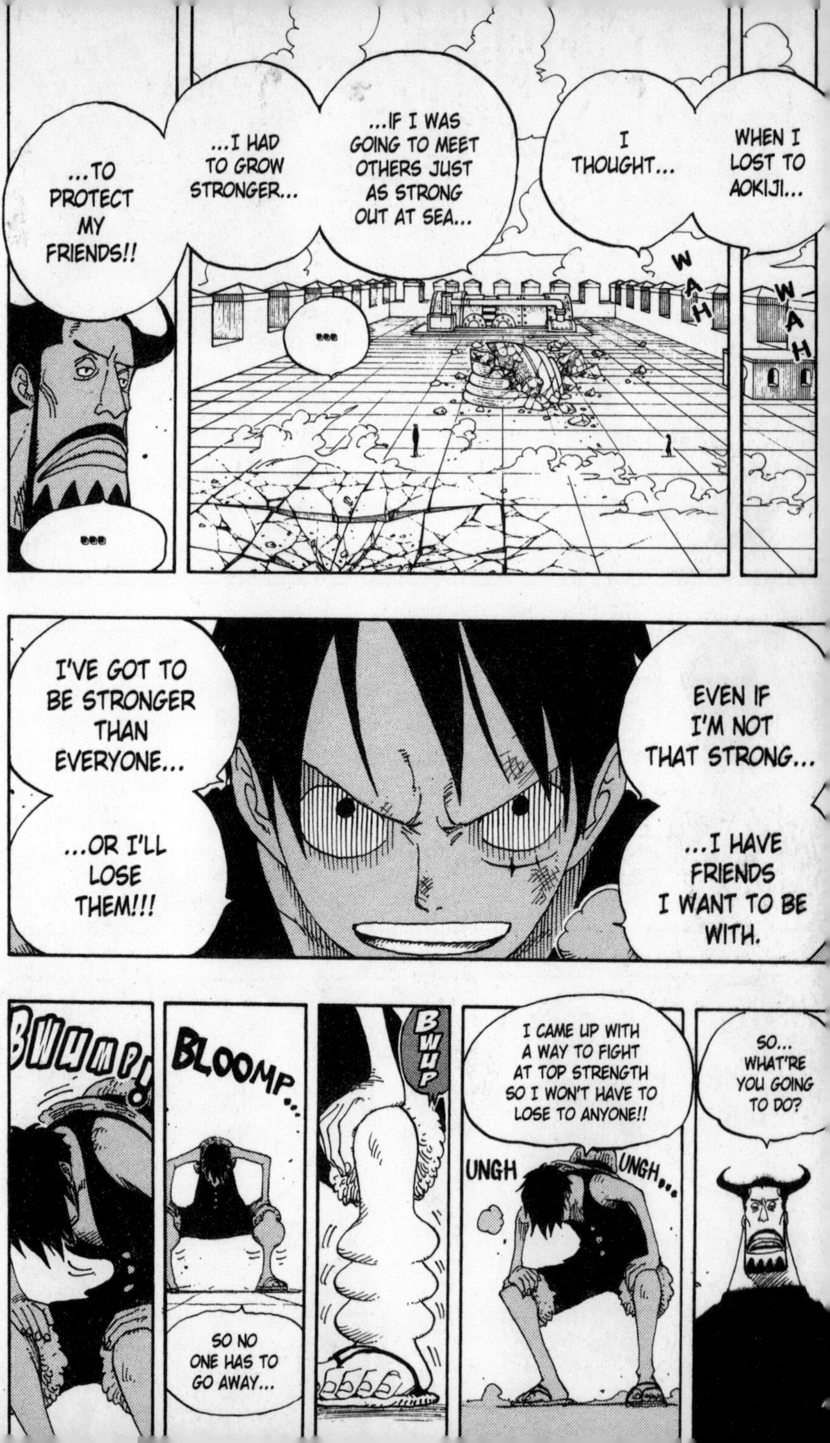
WHEN I LOST TO AOKIJI...
WAH
WAH
I THOUGHT...
...IF I WAS GOING TO MEET OTHERS JUST AS STRONG OUT AT SEA...
...I HAD TO GROW STRONGER...
...
...TO PROTECT MY FRIENDS!!
...
EVEN IF I'M NOT THAT STRONG...
...I HAVE FRIENDS I WANT TO BE WITH.
I'VE GOT TO BE STRONGER THAN EVERYONE...
...OR I'LL LOSE THEM!!!
SO... WHAT'RE YOU GOING TO DO?
I CAME UP WITH A WAY TO FIGHT AT TOP STRENGTH SO I WON'T HAVE TO LOSE TO ANYONE!!
UNGH...
UNGH
BWUP
BLOOMP...
SO NO ONE HAS TO GO AWAY...
BWUMP!!

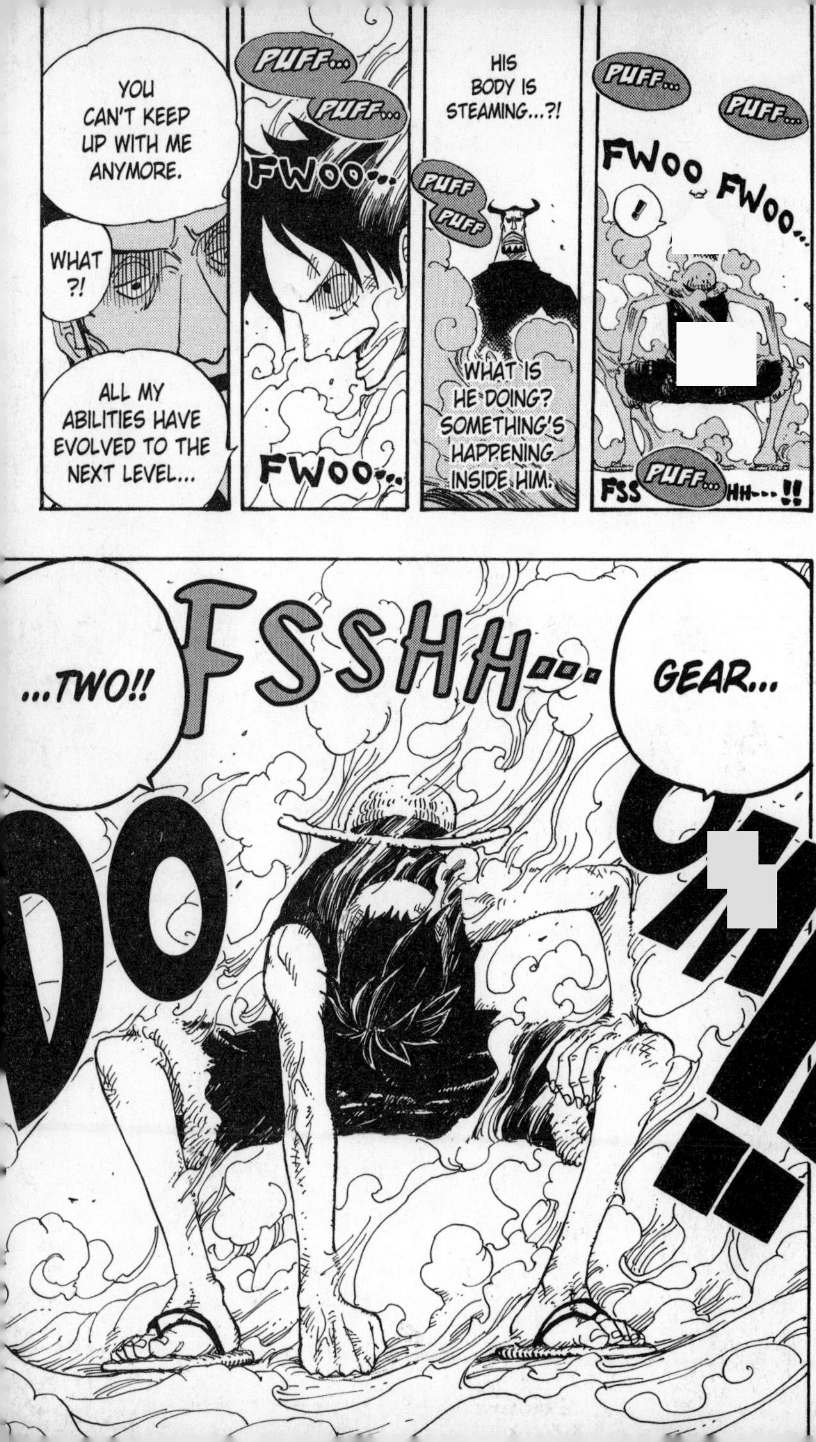
PUFF...
PUFF...
FWOO FWOO...
!
FSS
PUFF...
HH...!!
HIS BODY IS STEAMING...?!
PUFF
PUFF
WHAT IS HE DOING? SOMETHING'S HAPPENING INSIDE HIM.
PUFF...
PUFF...
FWOO...
FWOO...
YOU CAN'T KEEP UP WITH ME ANYMORE.
WHAT ?!
ALL MY ABILITIES HAVE EVOLVED TO THE NEXT LEVEL...
GEAR...
FSSHH...
...TWO!!
DO

CONTINUED FROM VOL. 39

The first *One Piece*

"FAN FAVORITE MOVES" CONTEST RESULTS!

TENTH PLACE (410 VOTES)

SINGLE-SWORD STYLE DRAW AND RESHEATH TECHNIQUE: LION SONG

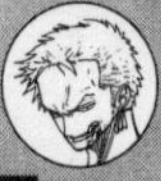

RORONOA ZOLO

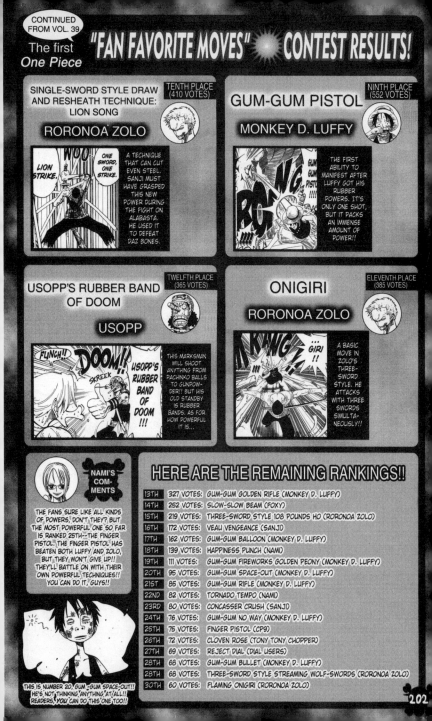

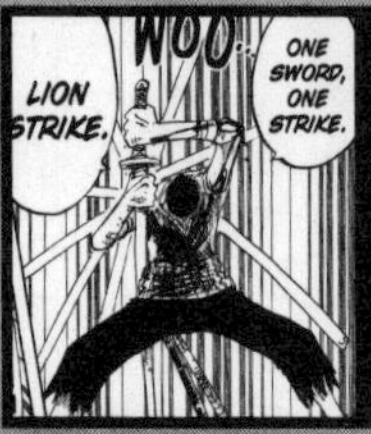
ONE SWORD, ONE STRIKE.
WOO...
LION STRIKE.

A TECHNIQUE THAT CAN CUT EVEN STEEL. SANJI MUST HAVE GRASPED THIS NEW POWER DURING THE FIGHT ON ALABASTA. HE USED IT TO DEFEAT DAZ BONES.

NINTH PLACE (552 VOTES)

GUM-GUM PISTOL

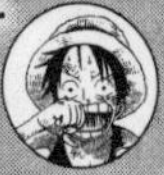

MONKEY D. LUFFY

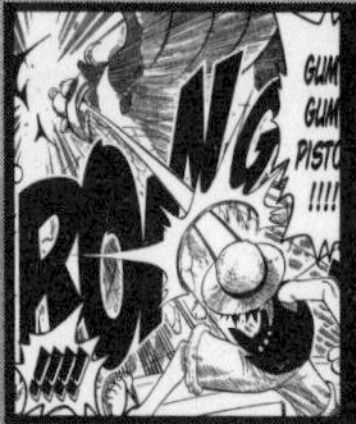
GUM GUM PISTO !!!!
!!!!

THE FIRST ABILITY TO MANIFEST AFTER LUFFY GOT HIS RUBBER POWERS. IT'S ONLY ONE SHOT, BUT IT PACKS AN IMMENSE AMOUNT OF POWER!!

TWELFTH PLACE (365 VOTES)

USOPP'S RUBBER BAND OF DOOM

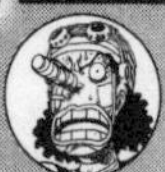

USOPP

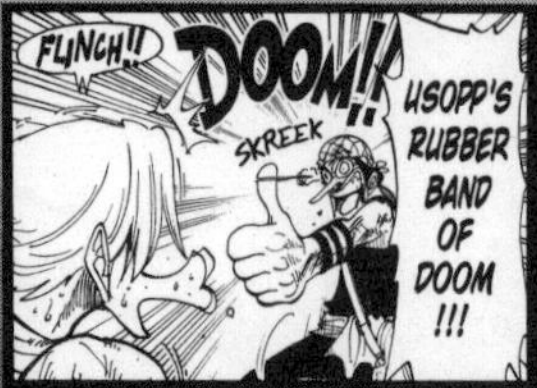
USOPP'S RUBBER BAND OF DOOM !!!
DOOM!!
FLINCH!!
SKREEK

THIS MARKSMAN WILL SHOOT ANYTHING FROM PACHINKO BALLS TO GUNPOWDER!! BUT HIS OLD STANDBY IS RUBBER BANDS. AS FOR HOW POWERFUL IT IS...

ELEVENTH PLACE (385 VOTES)

ONIGIRI

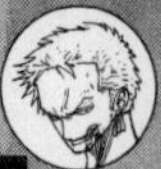

RORONOA ZOLO

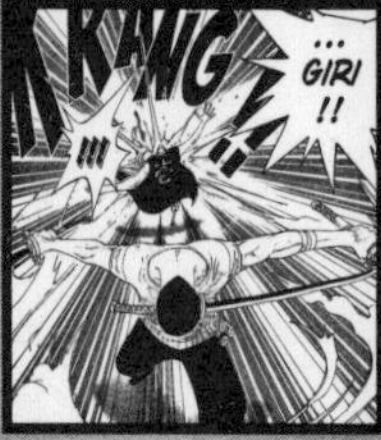
...GIRI !!
!!!

A BASIC MOVE IN ZOLO'S THREE-SWORD STYLE. HE ATTACKS WITH THREE SWORDS SIMULTANEOUSLY!!

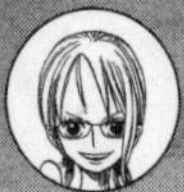

NAMI'S COMMENTS

THE FANS SURE LIKE ALL KINDS OF POWERS, DON'T THEY? BUT THE MOST POWERFUL ONE SO FAR IS RANKED 25TH--THE FINGER PISTOL. THE FINGER PISTOL HAS BEATEN BOTH LUFFY AND ZOLO, BUT THEY WON'T GIVE UP!! THEY'LL BATTLE ON WITH THEIR OWN POWERFUL TECHNIQUES!! YOU CAN DO IT, GUYS!!

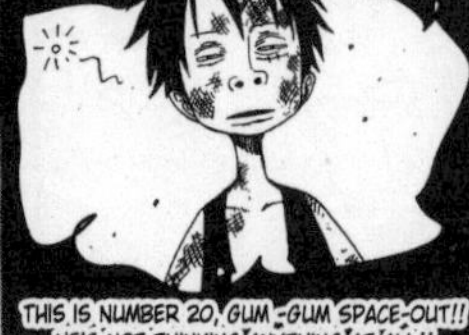

THIS IS NUMBER 20, GUM-GUM SPACE-OUT!! HE'S NOT THINKING ANYTHING AT ALL!! READERS, ***YOU*** CAN DO THIS ONE TOO!!

HERE ARE THE REMAINING RANKINGS!!

13TH	327 VOTES:	GUM-GUM GOLDEN RIFLE (MONKEY D. LUFFY)
14TH	252 VOTES:	SLOW-SLOW BEAM (FOXY)
15TH	219 VOTES:	THREE-SWORD STYLE 108 POUNDS HO (RORONOA ZOLO)
16TH	172 VOTES:	VEAU VENGEANCE (SANJI)
17TH	162 VOTES:	GUM-GUM BALLOON (MONKEY D. LUFFY)
18TH	139 VOTES:	HAPPINESS PUNCH (NAMI)
19TH	111 VOTES:	GUM-GUM FIREWORKS GOLDEN PEONY (MONKEY D. LUFFY)
20TH	95 VOTES:	GUM-GUM SPACE-OUT (MONKEY D. LUFFY)
21ST	85 VOTES:	GUM-GUM RIFLE (MONKEY D. LUFFY)
22ND	82 VOTES:	TORNADO TEMPO (NAMI)
23RD	80 VOTES:	CONCASSER CRUSH (SANJI)
24TH	76 VOTES:	GUM-GUM NO WAY (MONKEY D. LUFFY)
25TH	75 VOTES:	FINGER PISTOL (CP9)
26TH	72 VOTES:	CLOVEN ROSE (TONY TONY CHOPPER)
27TH	69 VOTES:	REJECT DIAL (DIAL USERS)
28TH	68 VOTES:	GUM-GUM BULLET (MONKEY D. LUFFY)
28TH	68 VOTES:	THREE-SWORD STYLE STREAMING WOLF-SWORDS (RORONOA ZOLO)
30TH	60 VOTES:	FLAMING ONIGIRI (RORONOA ZOLO)

Chapter 388:
GEAR TWO

*"SURRENDER"

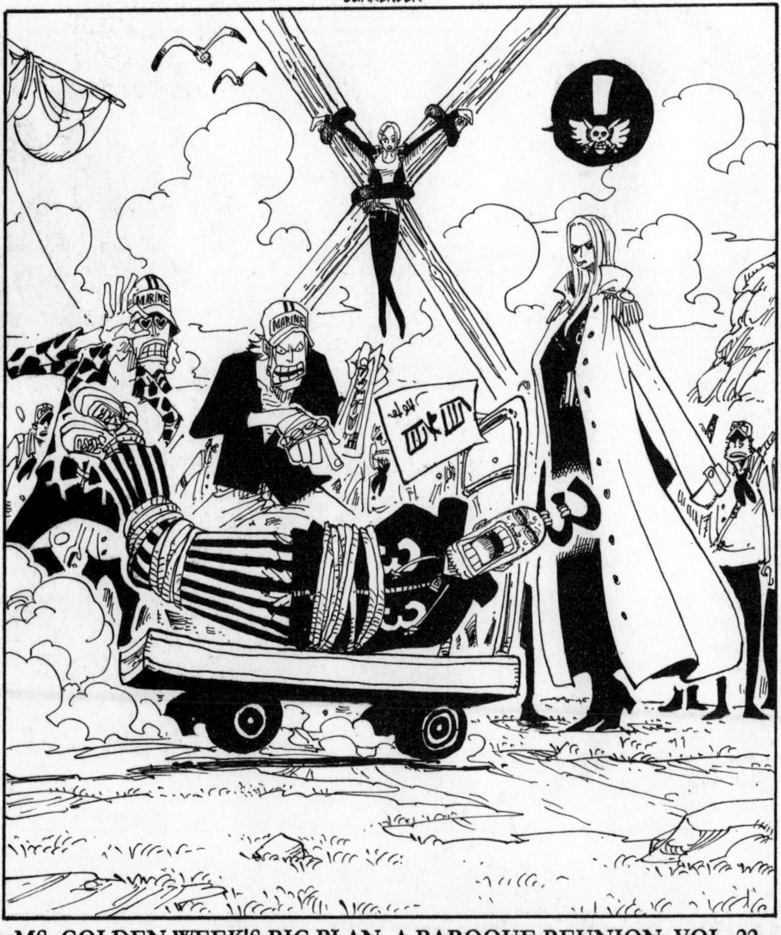
!

MS. GOLDEN WEEK'S BIG PLAN, A BAROQUE REUNION, VOL. 22:
"MR. 3 SURRENDERS?!"

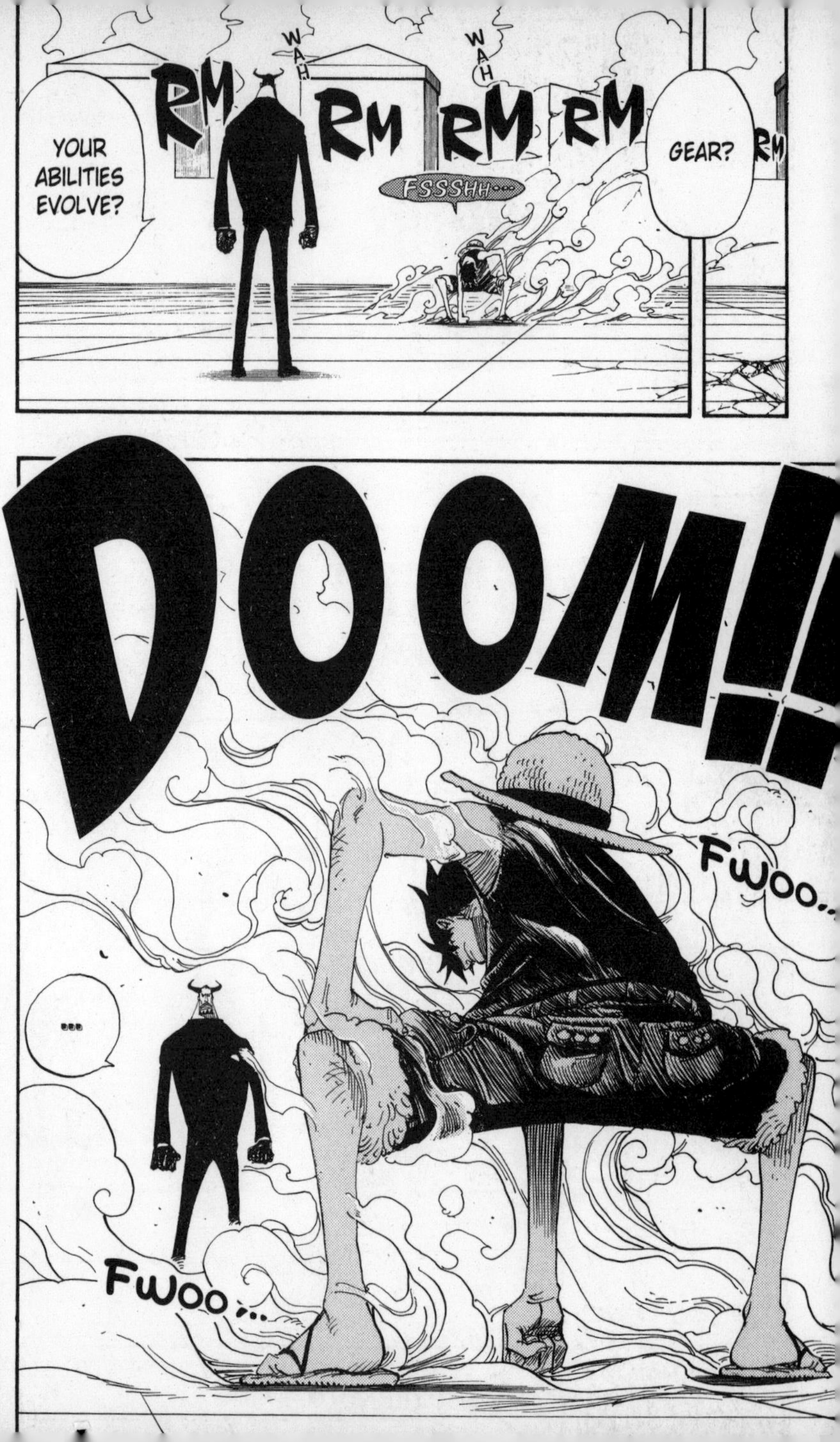
GEAR?
RM
WAH
WAH
RM RM RM RM
FSSSHH...
YOUR ABILITIES EVOLVE?
DOOM!!
Fwoo...
...
Fwoo...

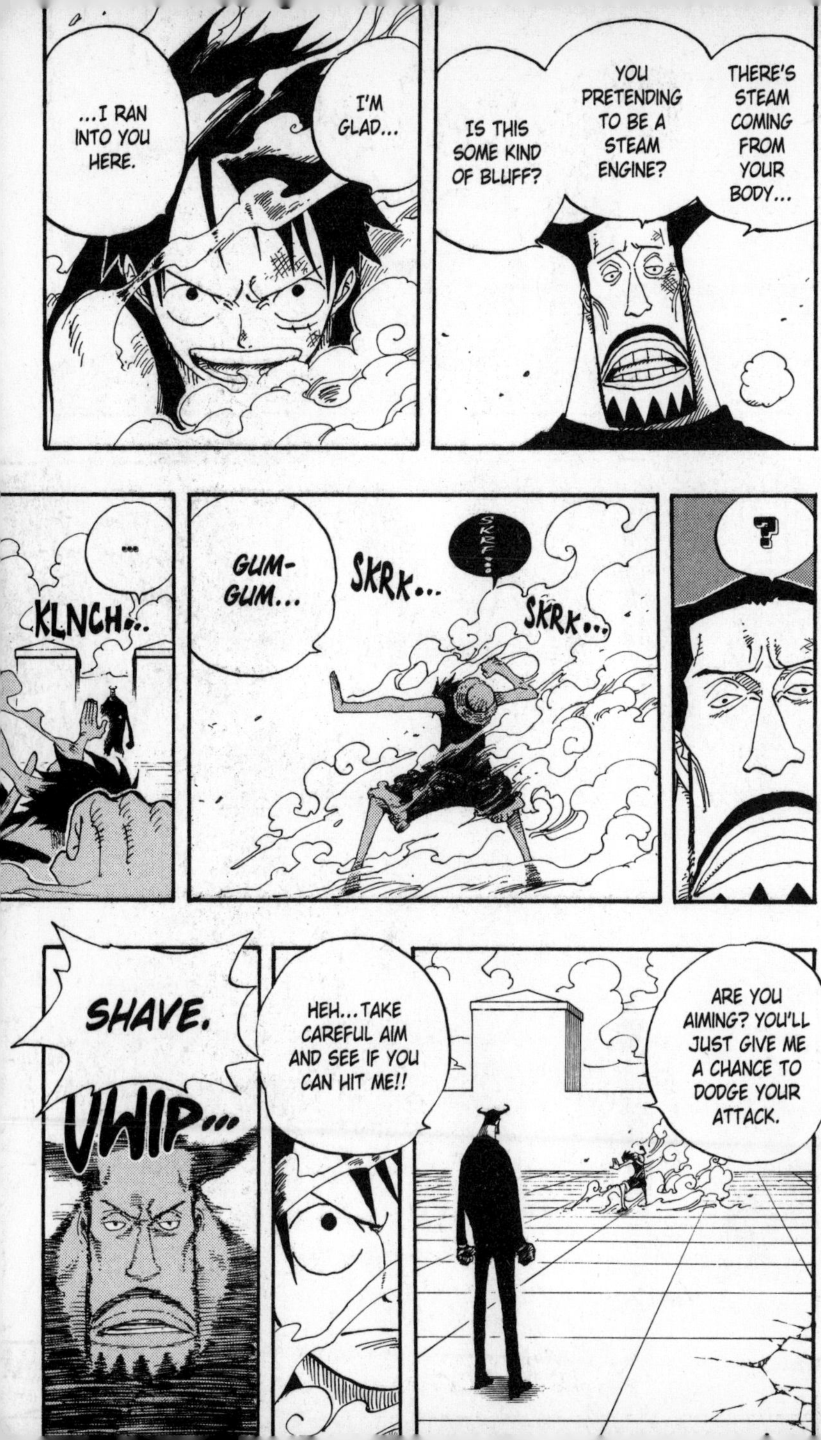
THERE'S STEAM COMING FROM YOUR BODY...
YOU PRETENDING TO BE A STEAM ENGINE?
IS THIS SOME KIND OF BLUFF?
I'M GLAD...
...I RAN INTO YOU HERE.
?
SKRF...
SKRK...
SKRK...
GUM-GUM...
...
KLNCH...
ARE YOU AIMING? YOU'LL JUST GIVE ME A CHANCE TO DODGE YOUR ATTACK.
HEH...TAKE CAREFUL AIM AND SEE IF YOU CAN HIT ME!!
SHAVE.
VWIP...

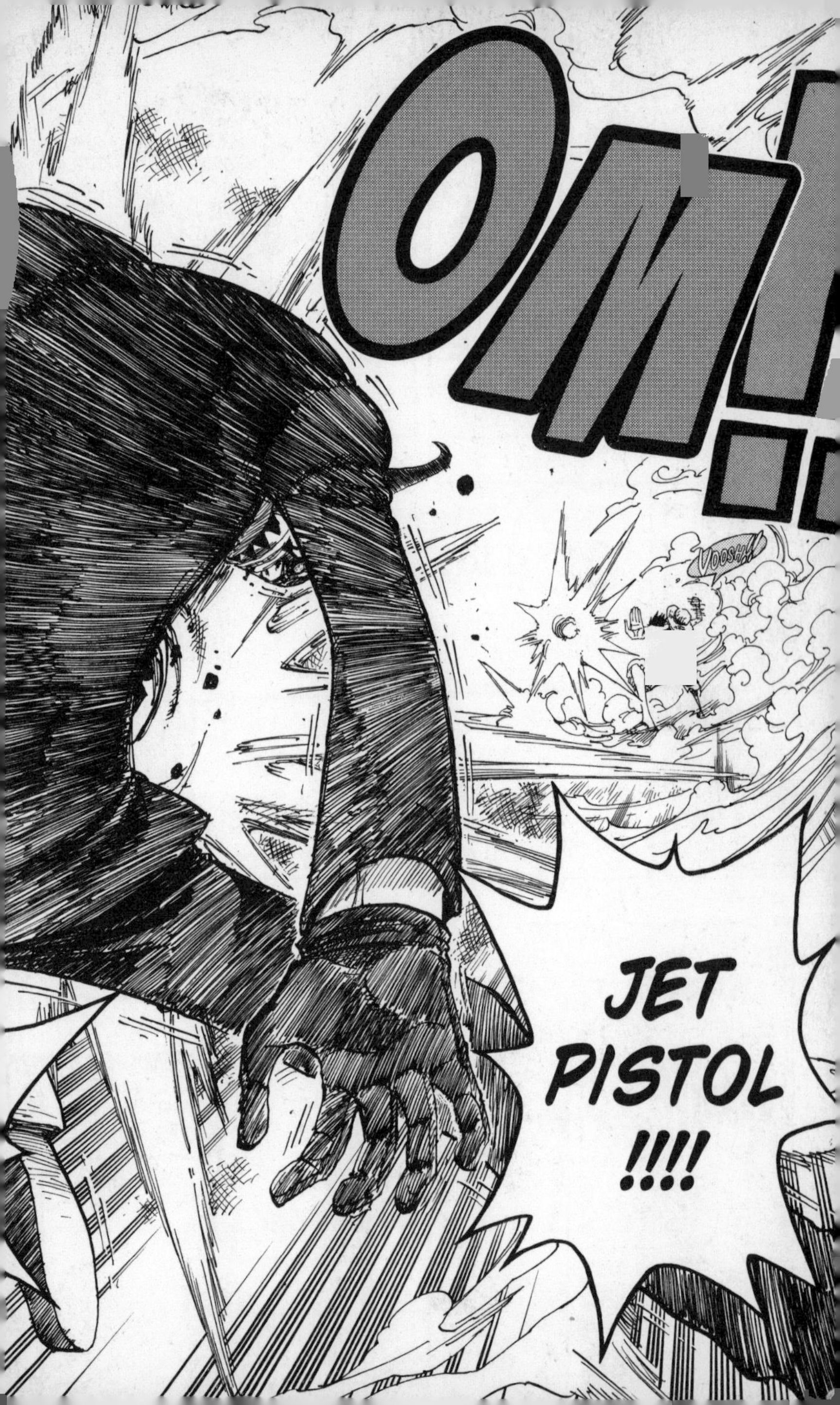
ON!!
VOOSH!!
JET PISTOL !!!!

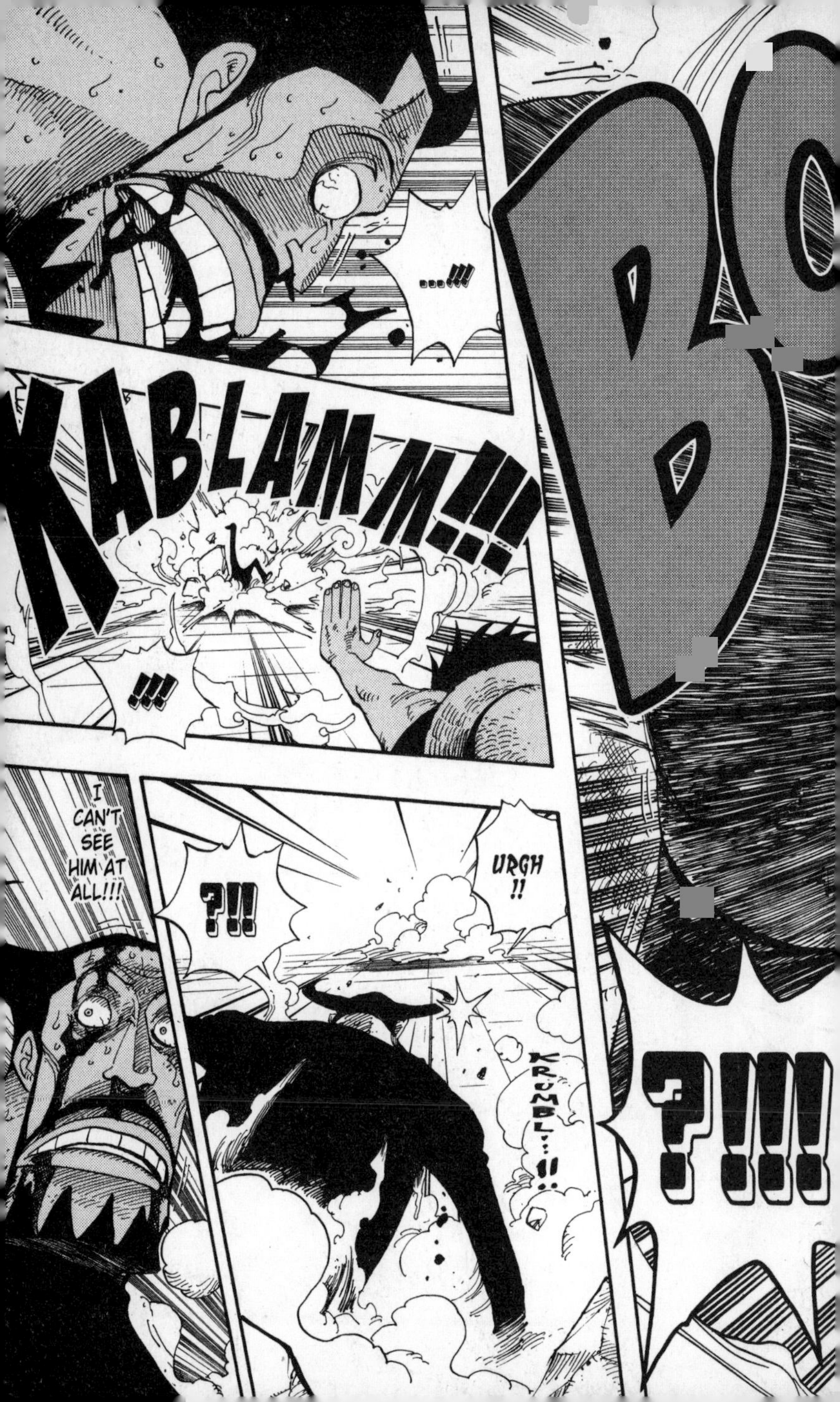
?!!!
...!!!
KABLAMM!!!
!!!
URGH !!
?!!
KRUMBL...!!
I CAN'T SEE HIM AT ALL!!!

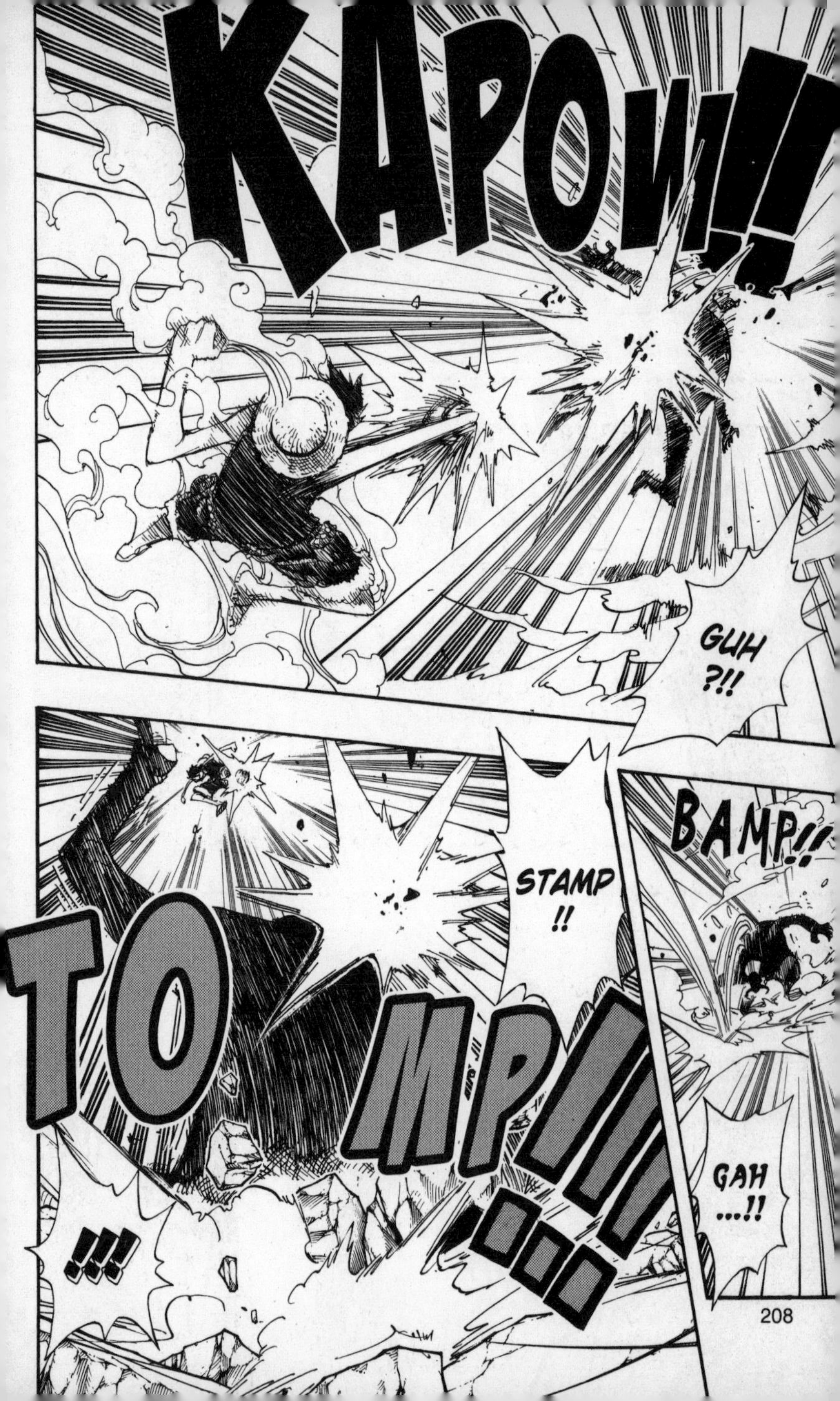

KAPOW!!
GUH ?!!
BAMP!!
GAH ...!!
STAMP !!
TOMP!!...!!!

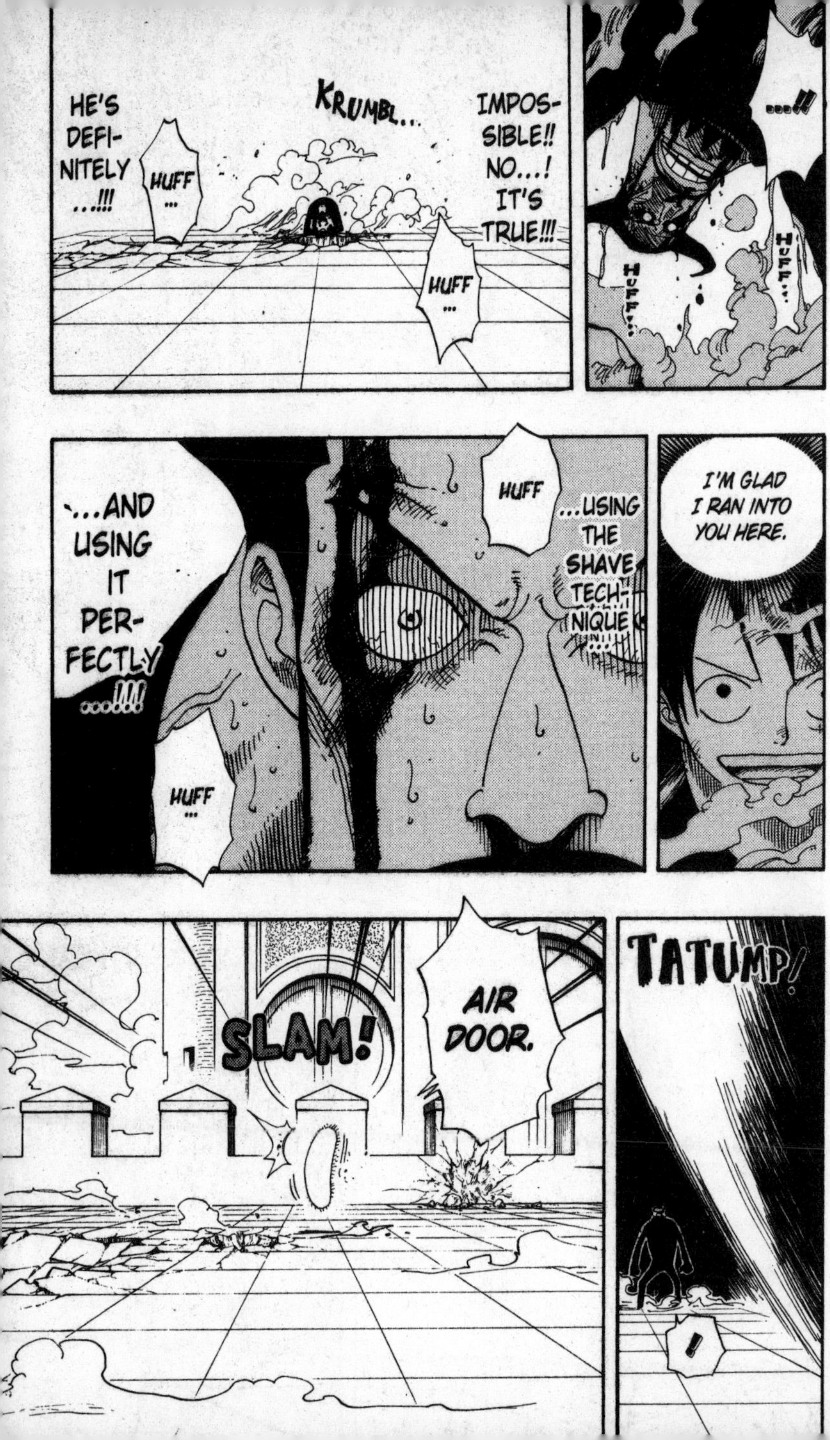
...!!
HUFF...
HUFF...
IMPOSSIBLE!! NO...! IT'S TRUE!!!
KRUMBL...
HUFF...
HE'S DEFINITELY...!!!
HUFF...
I'M GLAD I RAN INTO YOU HERE.
HUFF
...USING THE SHAVE TECHNIQUE...!!!
...AND USING IT PERFECTLY...!!!
HUFF...
TATUMP!
!
AIR DOOR.
SLAM!

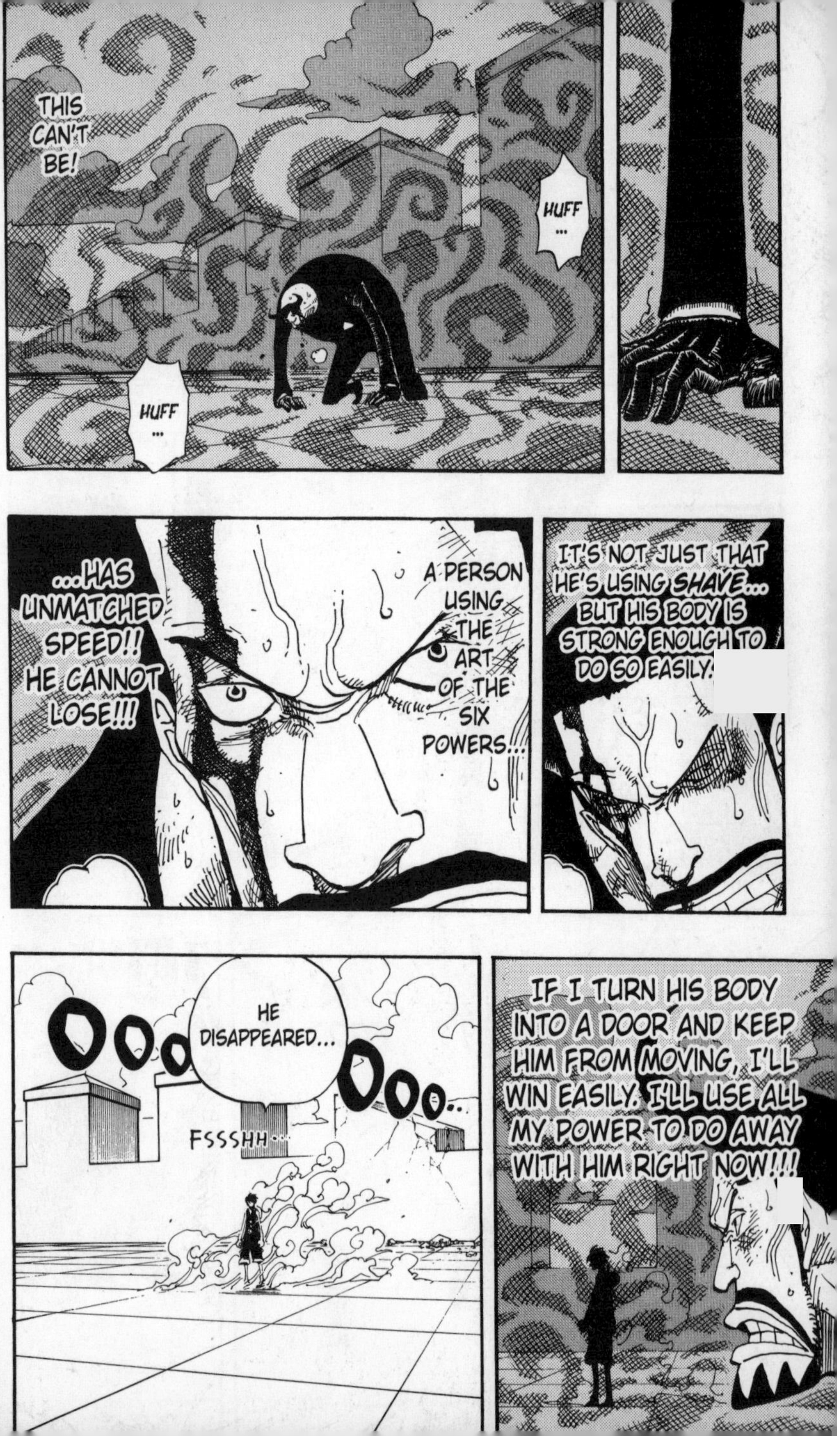
HUFF ...
THIS CAN'T BE!
HUFF ...
IT'S NOT JUST THAT HE'S USING *SHAVE*... BUT HIS BODY IS STRONG ENOUGH TO DO SO EASILY.
A PERSON USING THE ART OF THE SIX POWERS...
...HAS UNMATCHED SPEED!! HE CANNOT LOSE!!!
IF I TURN HIS BODY INTO A DOOR AND KEEP HIM FROM MOVING, I'LL WIN EASILY. I'LL USE ALL MY POWER TO DO AWAY WITH HIM RIGHT NOW!!!
OOO
HE DISAPPEARED...
OOO...
FSSSHH...

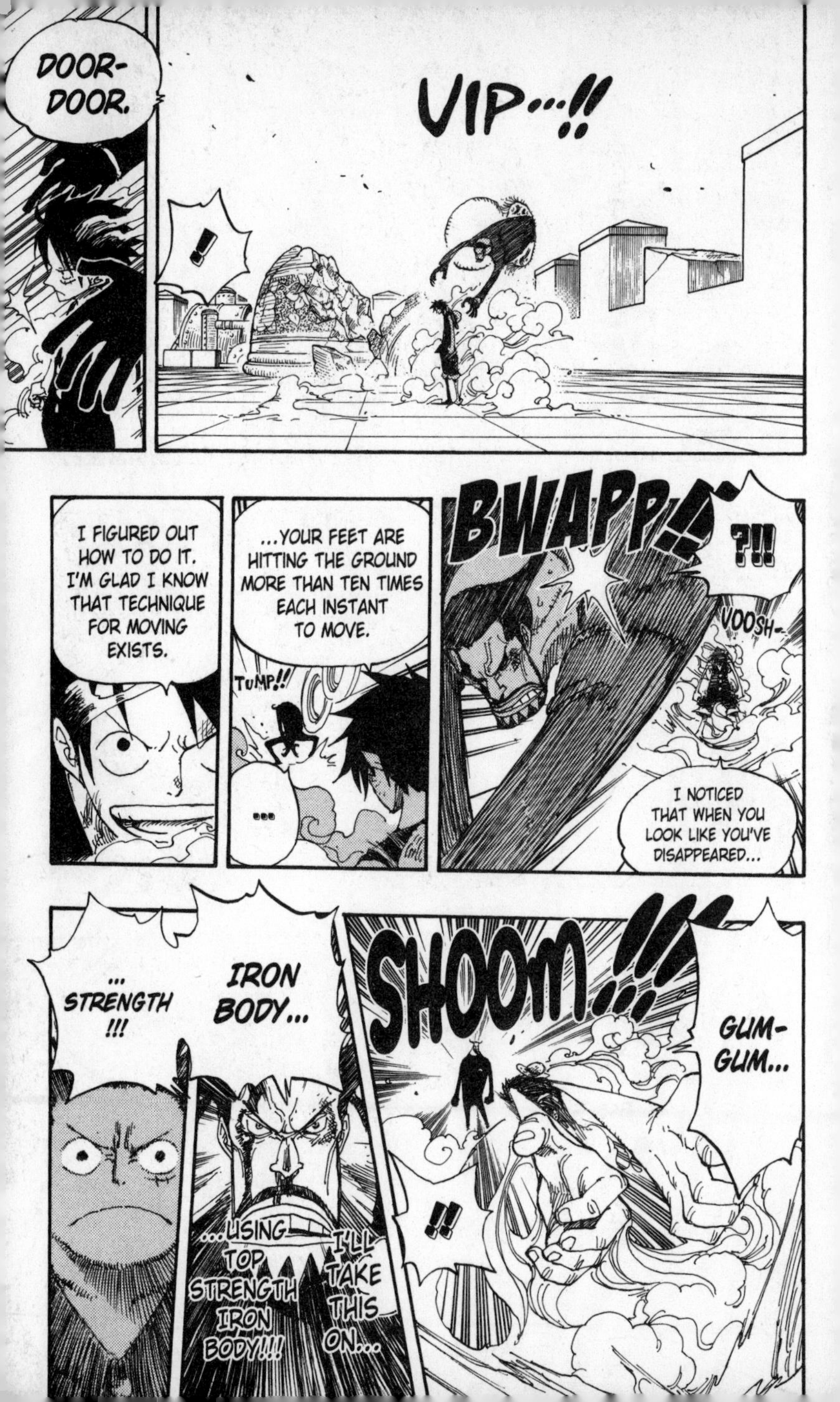
VIP...!!
!
DOOR-DOOR.
BWAPP!!
?!!
VOOSH-
I NOTICED THAT WHEN YOU LOOK LIKE YOU'VE DISAPPEARED...
...YOUR FEET ARE HITTING THE GROUND MORE THAN TEN TIMES EACH INSTANT TO MOVE.
TUMP!!
...
I FIGURED OUT HOW TO DO IT. I'M GLAD I KNOW THAT TECHNIQUE FOR MOVING EXISTS.
SHOOM...!!
GUM-GUM...
!!
IRON BODY...
I'LL TAKE THIS ON...
...USING TOP STRENGTH IRON BODY!!!
... STRENGTH !!!

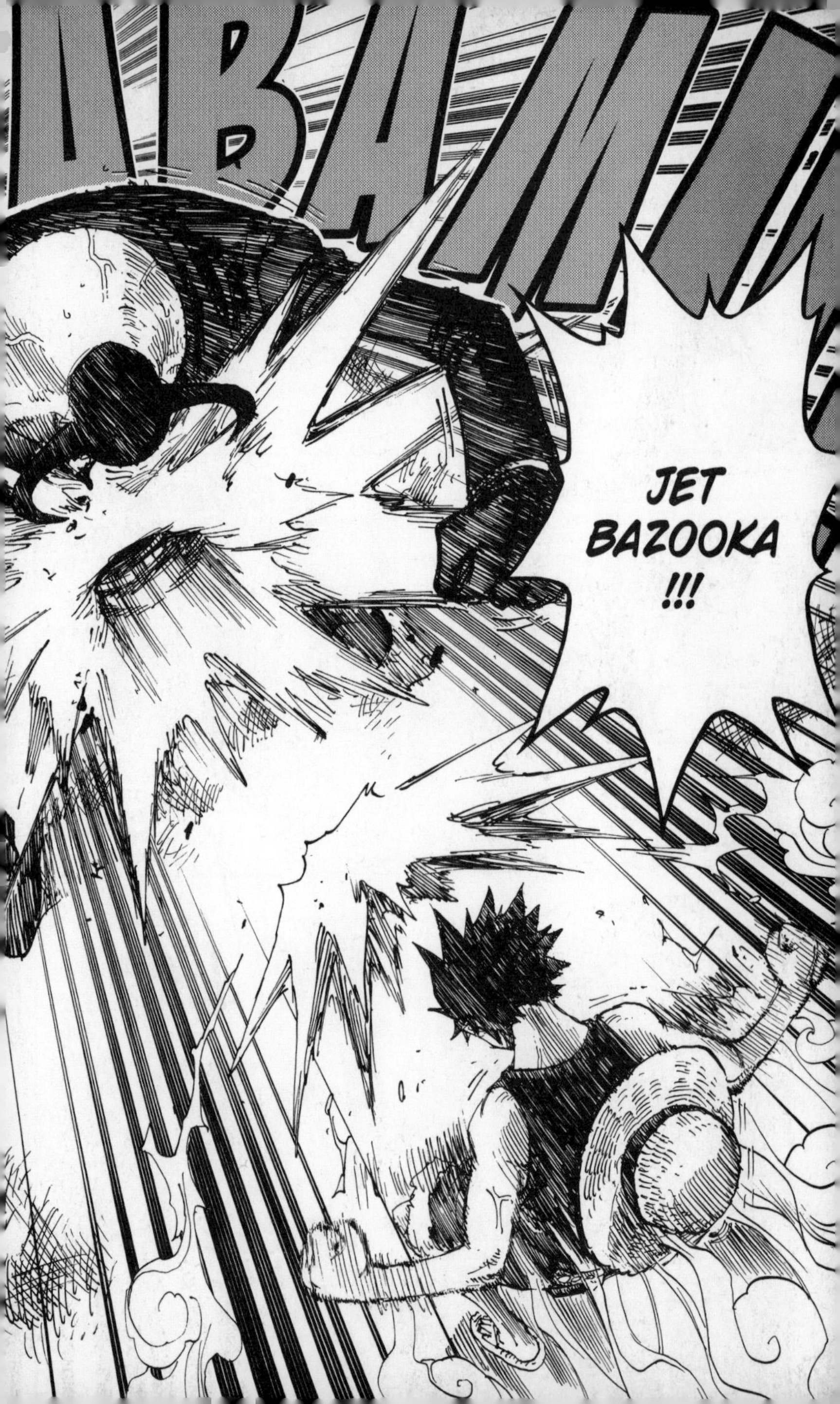
JET BAZOOKA !!!

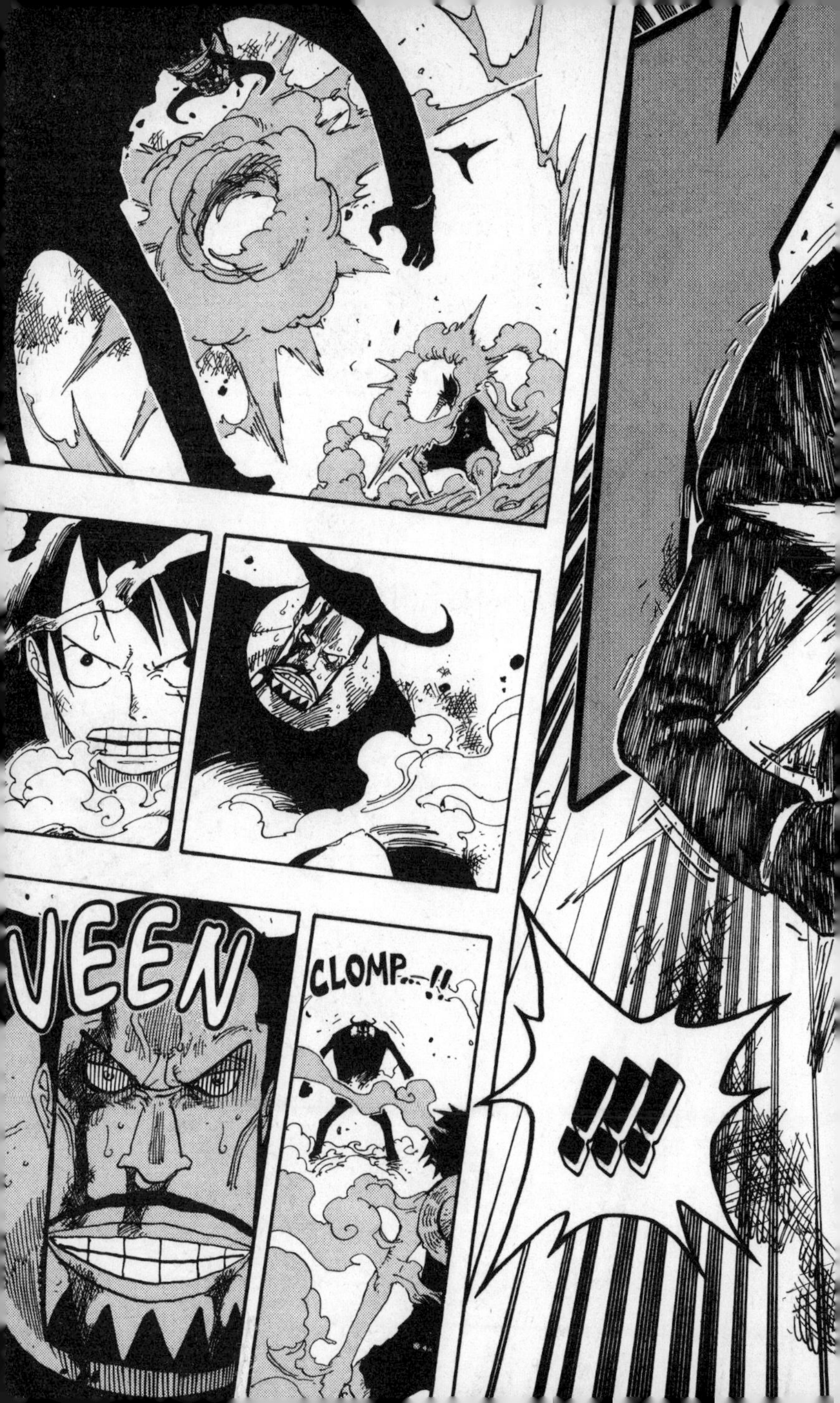

!!!
CLOMP...!!
VEEN

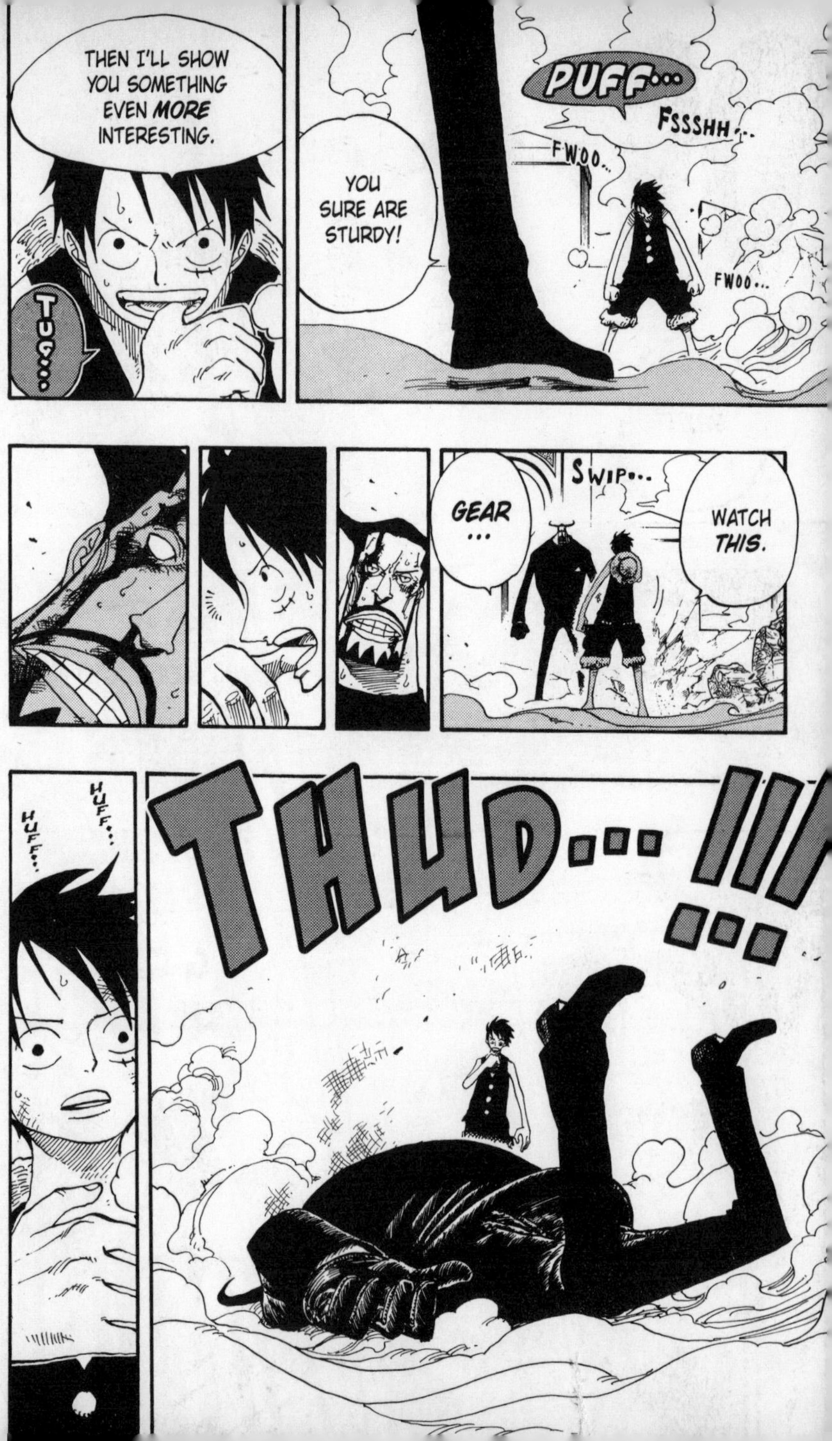
PUFF...
FSSSHH...
FWOO...
FWOO...
YOU SURE ARE STURDY!
THEN I'LL SHOW YOU SOMETHING EVEN MORE INTERESTING.
TUG...
WATCH THIS.
SWIP...
GEAR ...
THUD... !!!
...
HUFF...
HUFF...

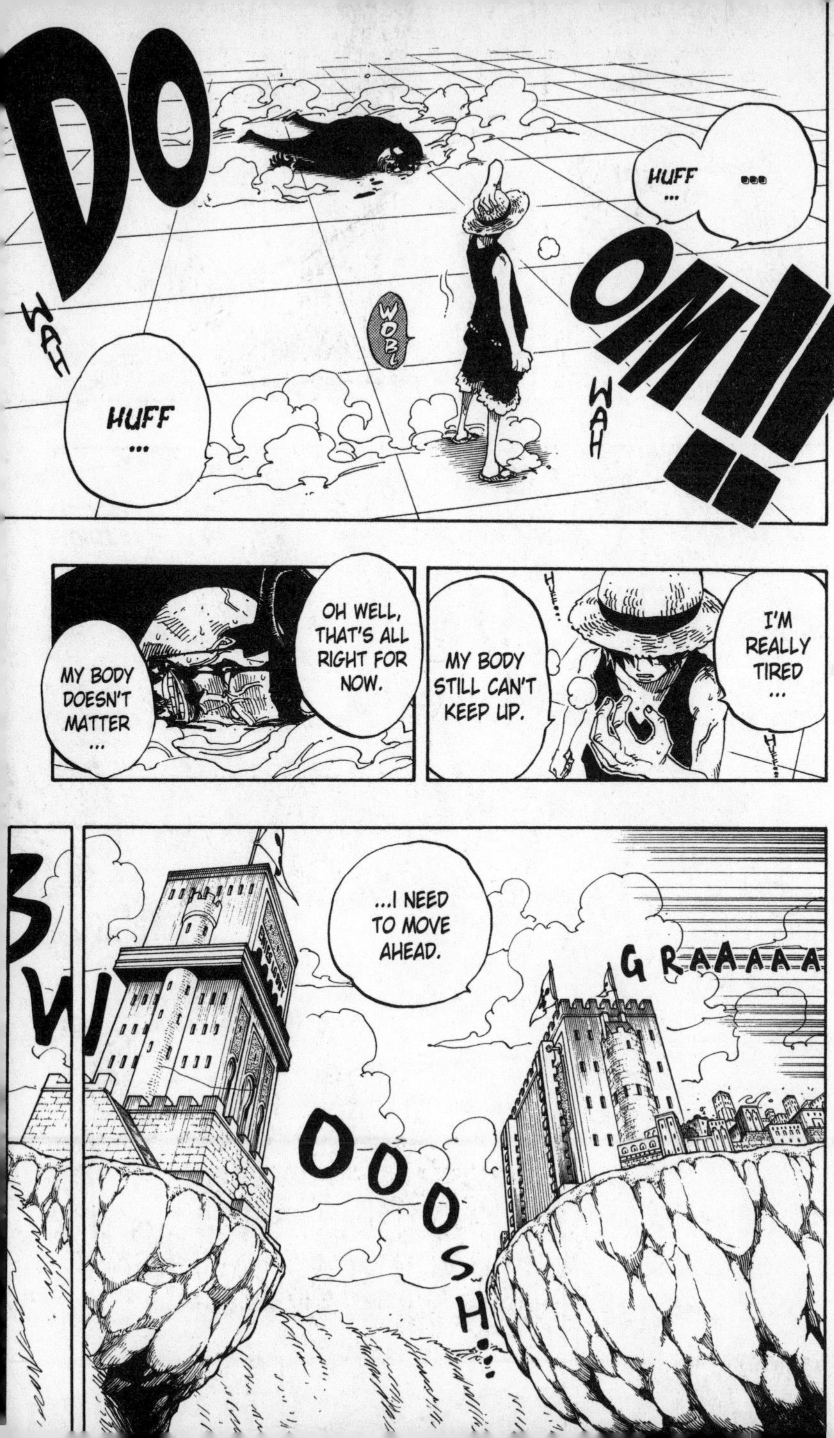
HUFF ... ...
DOOM!!
WAH
WAH
WOBL
HUFF ...
I'M REALLY TIRED ...
HUF...
HUF...
MY BODY STILL CAN'T KEEP UP.
OH WELL, THAT'S ALL RIGHT FOR NOW.
MY BODY DOESN'T MATTER ...
GRAAAAA
...I NEED TO MOVE AHEAD.
BWOOOSH!!

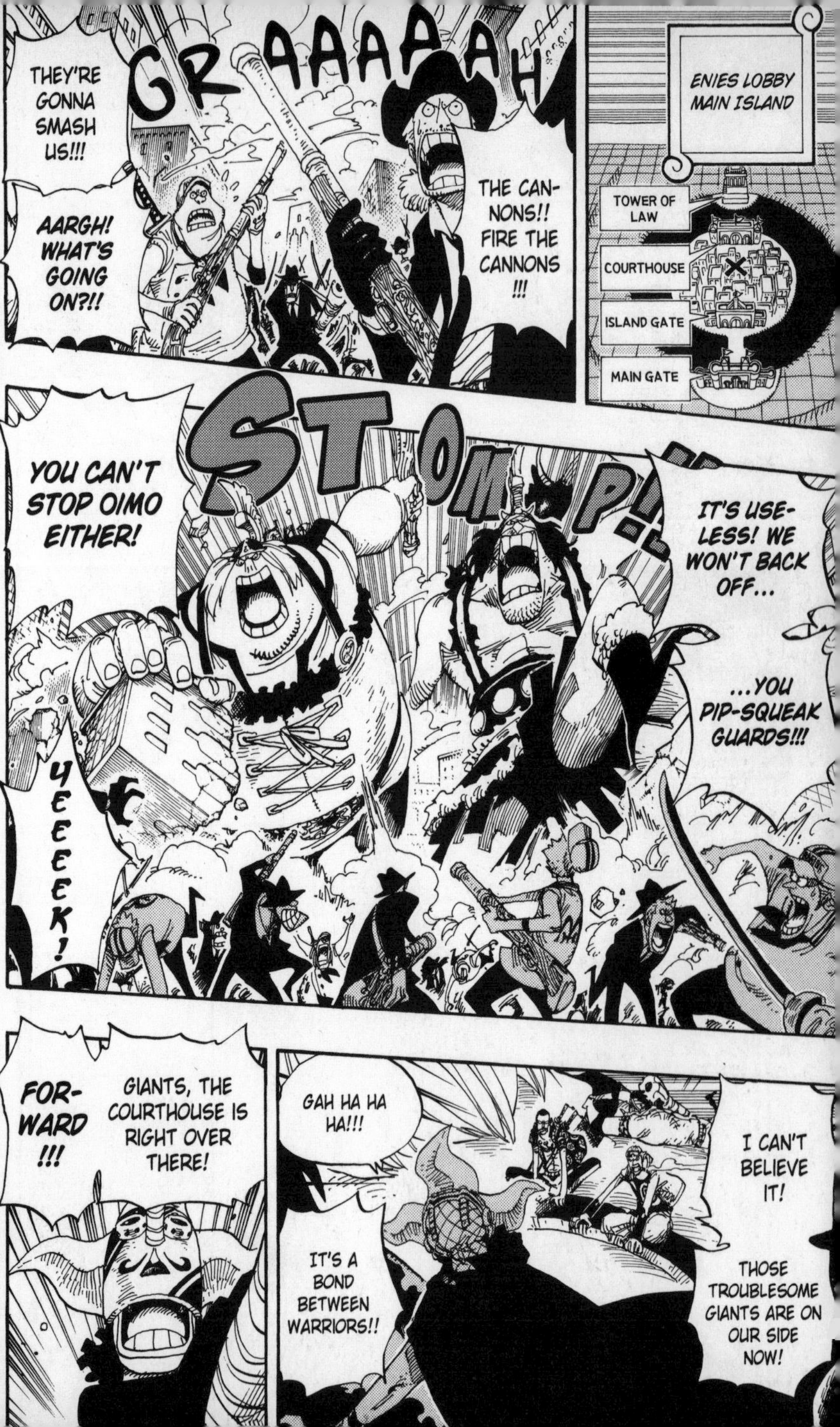
ENIES LOBBY MAIN ISLAND
TOWER OF LAW
COURTHOUSE
ISLAND GATE
MAIN GATE
GRAAAPAH
THE CAN-NONS!! FIRE THE CANNONS!!!
THEY'RE GONNA SMASH US!!!
AARGH! WHAT'S GOING ON?!!
IT'S USE-LESS! WE WON'T BACK OFF...
...YOU PIP-SQUEAK GUARDS!!!
STOMP!!
YOU CAN'T STOP OIMO EITHER!
YEEEEEK!
I CAN'T BELIEVE IT!
GAH HA HA HA!!!
THOSE TROUBLESOME GIANTS ARE ON OUR SIDE NOW!
IT'S A BOND BETWEEN WARRIORS!!
GIANTS, THE COURTHOUSE IS RIGHT OVER THERE!
FOR-WARD!!!

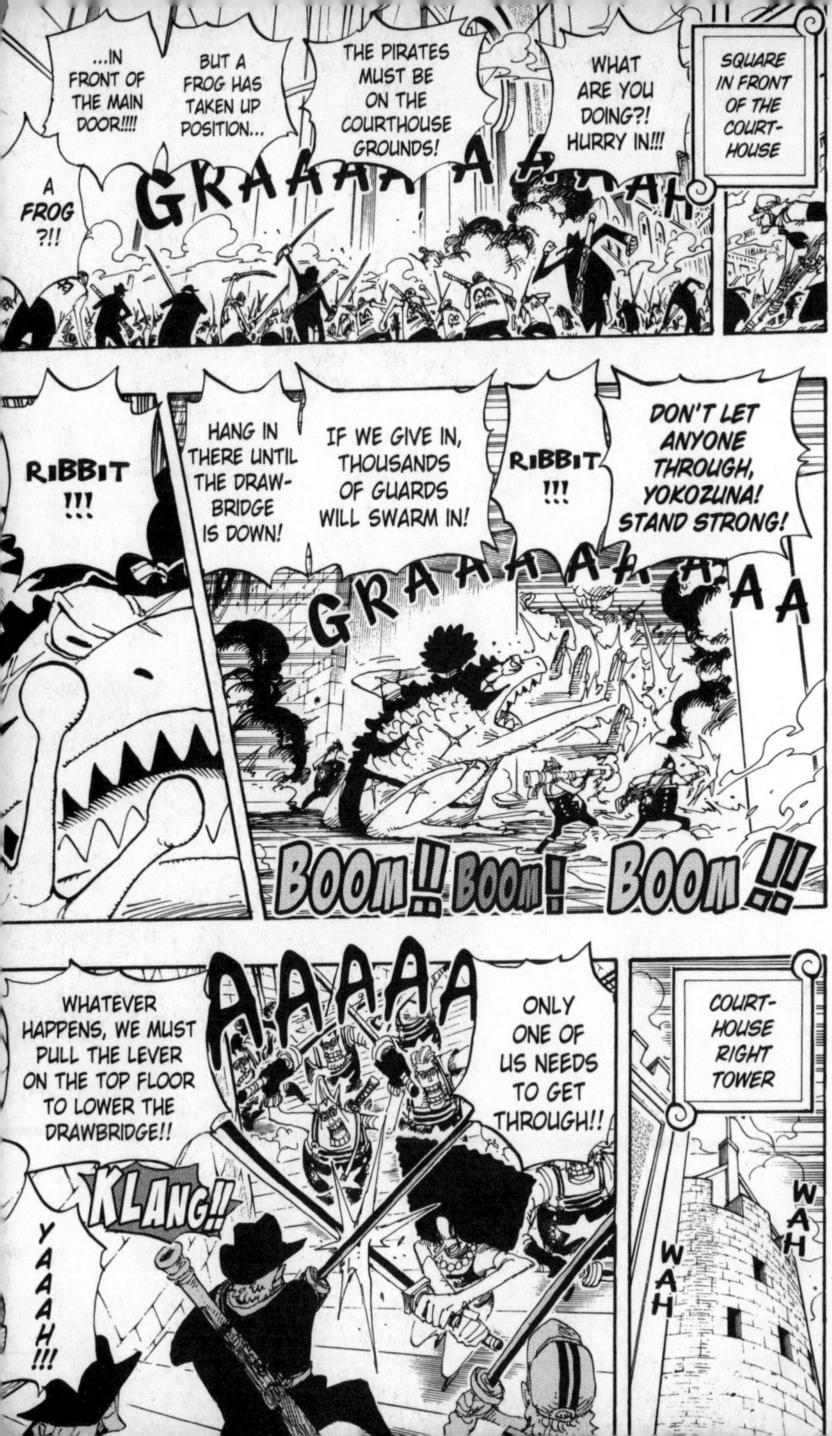
SQUARE IN FRONT OF THE COURT-HOUSE
WHAT ARE YOU DOING?! HURRY IN!!!
THE PIRATES MUST BE ON THE COURTHOUSE GROUNDS!
BUT A FROG HAS TAKEN UP POSITION...
...IN FRONT OF THE MAIN DOOR!!!!
A FROG ?!!
GRAAAAAAAH
DON'T LET ANYONE THROUGH, YOKOZUNA! STAND STRONG!
RIBBIT !!!
IF WE GIVE IN, THOUSANDS OF GUARDS WILL SWARM IN!
HANG IN THERE UNTIL THE DRAW-BRIDGE IS DOWN!
GRAAAAAAAA
BOOM!! BOOM! BOOM!!
RIBBIT !!!
COURT-HOUSE RIGHT TOWER
WAH
WAH
ONLY ONE OF US NEEDS TO GET THROUGH!!
AAAAA
WHATEVER HAPPENS, WE MUST PULL THE LEVER ON THE TOP FLOOR TO LOWER THE DRAWBRIDGE!!
KLANG!!
YAAAAH!!!

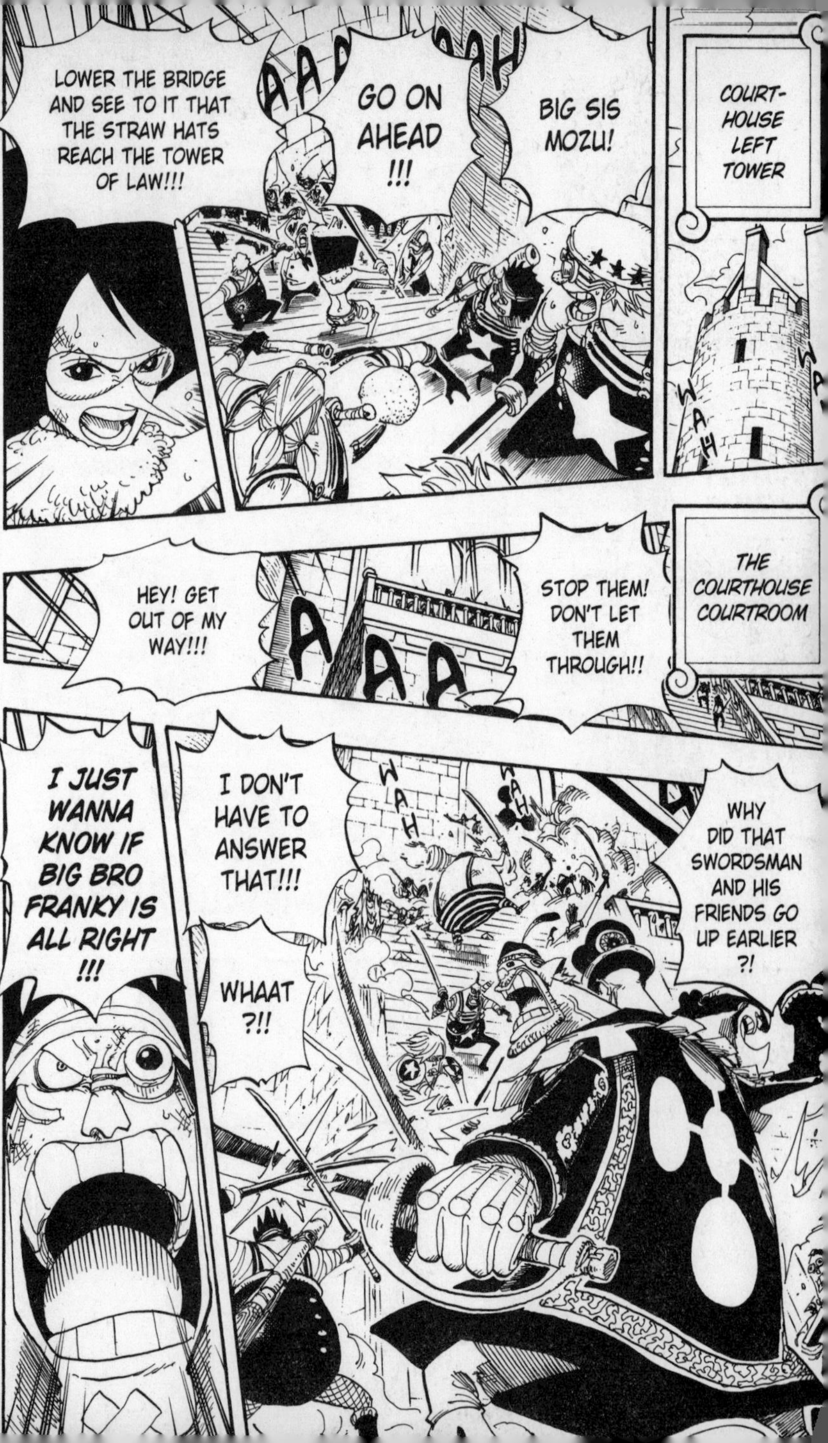
COURT-HOUSE LEFT TOWER
WAH
WAH
BIG SIS MOZU!
GO ON AHEAD !!!
LOWER THE BRIDGE AND SEE TO IT THAT THE STRAW HATS REACH THE TOWER OF LAW!!!
THE COURTHOUSE COURTROOM
STOP THEM! DON'T LET THEM THROUGH!!
AAA
HEY! GET OUT OF MY WAY!!!
WHY DID THAT SWORDSMAN AND HIS FRIENDS GO UP EARLIER ?!
WAH
WAH
I DON'T HAVE TO ANSWER THAT!!!
WHAAT ?!!
I JUST WANNA KNOW IF BIG BRO FRANKY IS ALL RIGHT !!!

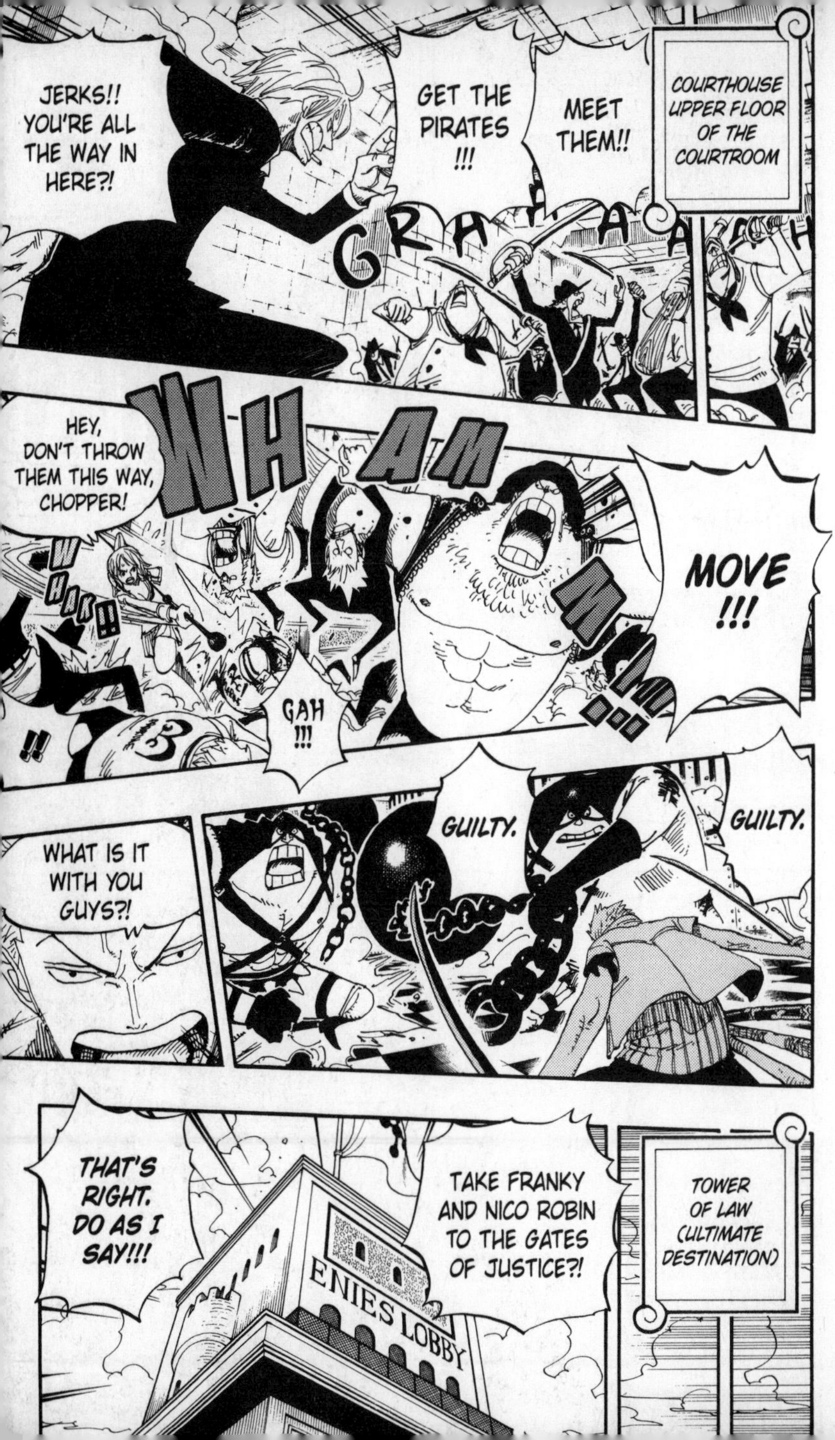

COURTHOUSE UPPER FLOOR OF THE COURTROOM
MEET THEM!!
GET THE PIRATES !!!
JERKS!! YOU'RE ALL THE WAY IN HERE?!
MOVE !!!
WHAM
HEY, DON'T THROW THEM THIS WAY, CHOPPER!
GAH !!!
WHAK!!
GUILTY.
GUILTY.
WHAT IS IT WITH YOU GUYS?!
TOWER OF LAW (ULTIMATE DESTINATION)
TAKE FRANKY AND NICO ROBIN TO THE GATES OF JUSTICE?!
THAT'S RIGHT. DO AS I SAY!!!
ENIES LOBBY

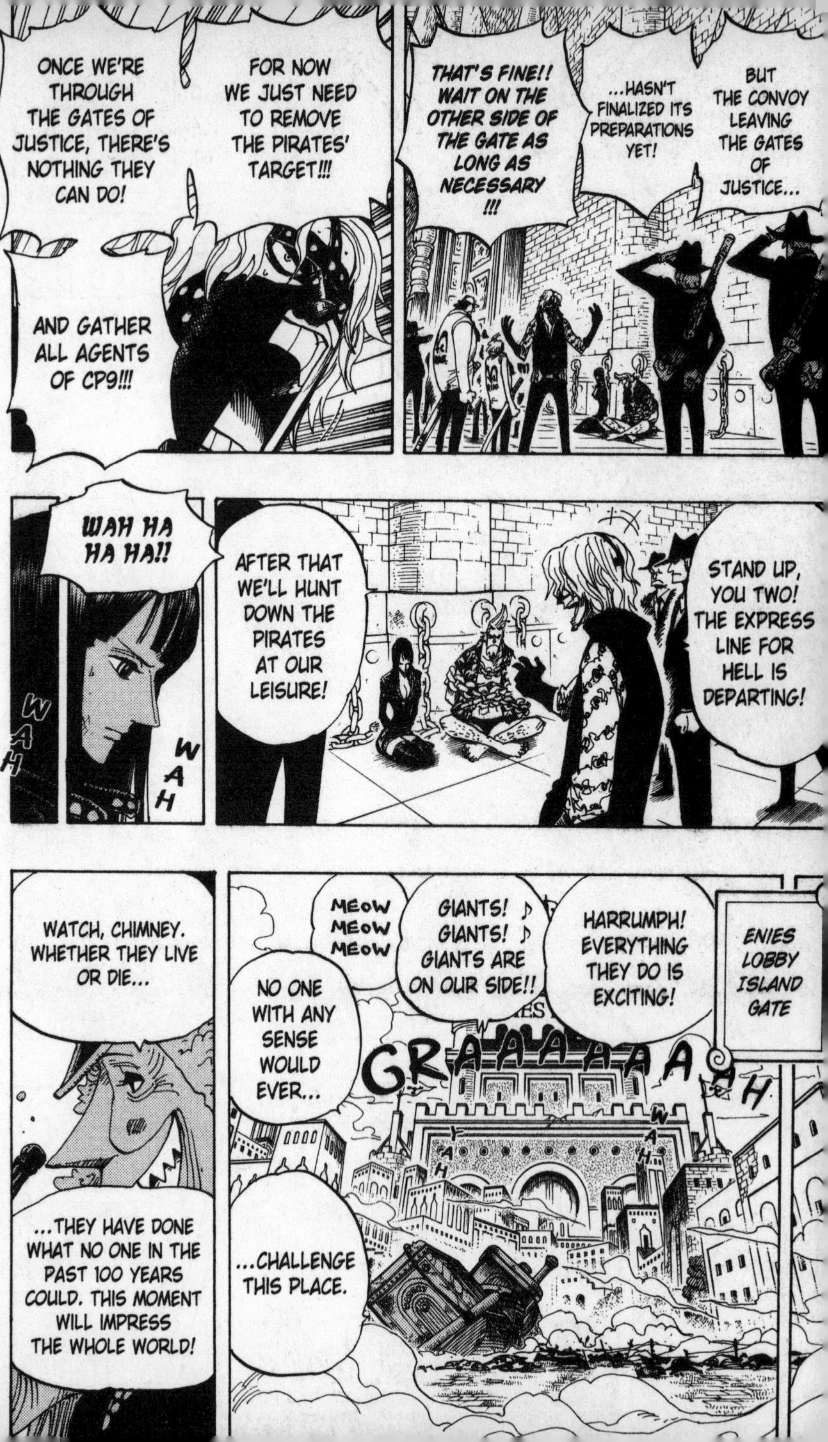
BUT THE CONVOY LEAVING THE GATES OF JUSTICE...
...HASN'T FINALIZED ITS PREPARATIONS YET!
THAT'S FINE!! WAIT ON THE OTHER SIDE OF THE GATE AS LONG AS NECESSARY!!!
FOR NOW WE JUST NEED TO REMOVE THE PIRATES' TARGET!!!
ONCE WE'RE THROUGH THE GATES OF JUSTICE, THERE'S NOTHING THEY CAN DO!
AND GATHER ALL AGENTS OF CP9!!!
STAND UP, YOU TWO! THE EXPRESS LINE FOR HELL IS DEPARTING!
AFTER THAT WE'LL HUNT DOWN THE PIRATES AT OUR LEISURE!
WAH HA HA HA!!
WAH
WAH
ENIES LOBBY ISLAND GATE
HARRUMPH! EVERYTHING THEY DO IS EXCITING!
GIANTS! ♪ GIANTS! ♪ GIANTS ARE ON OUR SIDE!!
MEOW MEOW MEOW
NO ONE WITH ANY SENSE WOULD EVER...
GRAAAAAAAH
...CHALLENGE THIS PLACE.
WATCH, CHIMNEY. WHETHER THEY LIVE OR DIE...
...THEY HAVE DONE WHAT NO ONE IN THE PAST 100 YEARS COULD. THIS MOMENT WILL IMPRESS THE WHOLE WORLD!

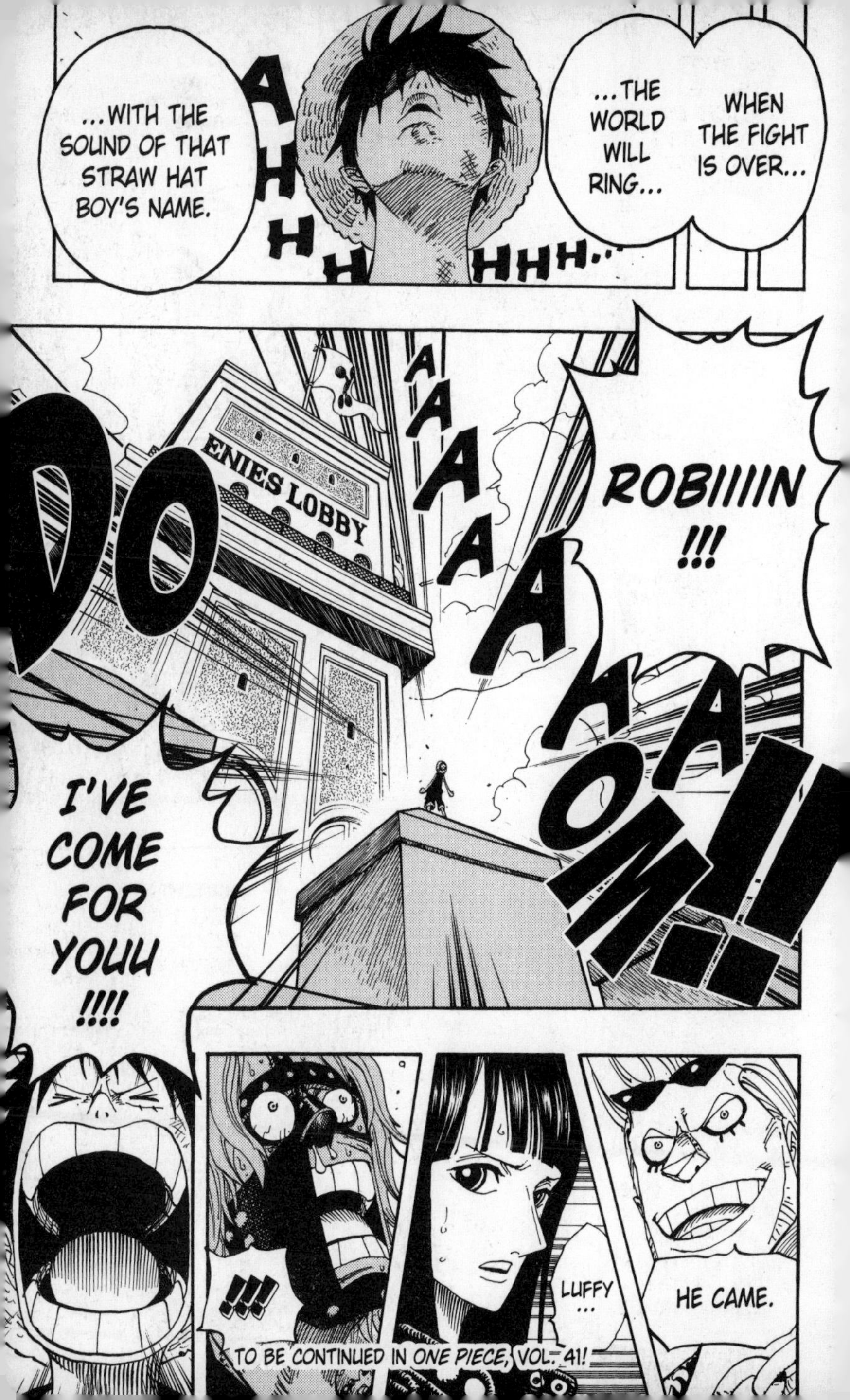
WHEN THE FIGHT IS OVER...
...THE WORLD WILL RING...
...WITH THE SOUND OF THAT STRAW HAT BOY'S NAME.
ROBIIIIN !!!
I'VE COME FOR YOUU !!!!
HE CAME.
LUFFY ...
!!!
TO BE CONTINUED IN ONE PIECE, VOL. 41!

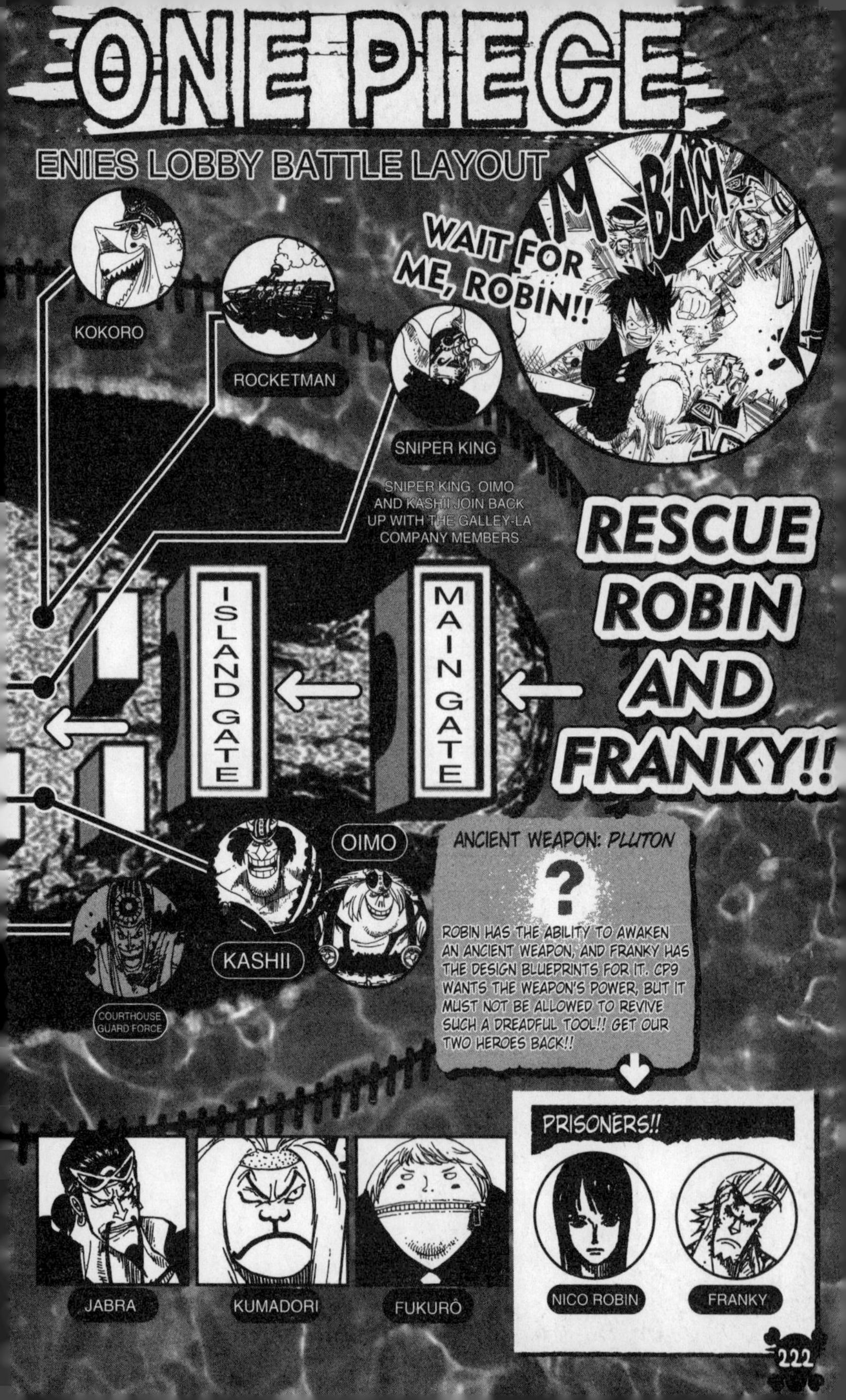
ONE PIECE
ENIES LOBBY BATTLE LAYOUT
BAM
WAIT FOR ME, ROBIN!!
KOKORO
ROCKETMAN
SNIPER KING
SNIPER KING, OIMO AND KASHII JOIN BACK UP WITH THE GALLEY-LA COMPANY MEMBERS
RESCUE ROBIN AND FRANKY!!
MAIN GATE
ISLAND GATE
OIMO
KASHII
COURTHOUSE GUARD FORCE
ANCIENT WEAPON: PLUTON
?
ROBIN HAS THE ABILITY TO AWAKEN AN ANCIENT WEAPON, AND FRANKY HAS THE DESIGN BLUEPRINTS FOR IT. CP9 WANTS THE WEAPON'S POWER, BUT IT MUST NOT BE ALLOWED TO REVIVE SUCH A DREADFUL TOOL!! GET OUR TWO HEROES BACK!!
PRISONERS!!
NICO ROBIN
FRANKY
JABRA
KUMADORI
FUKURO

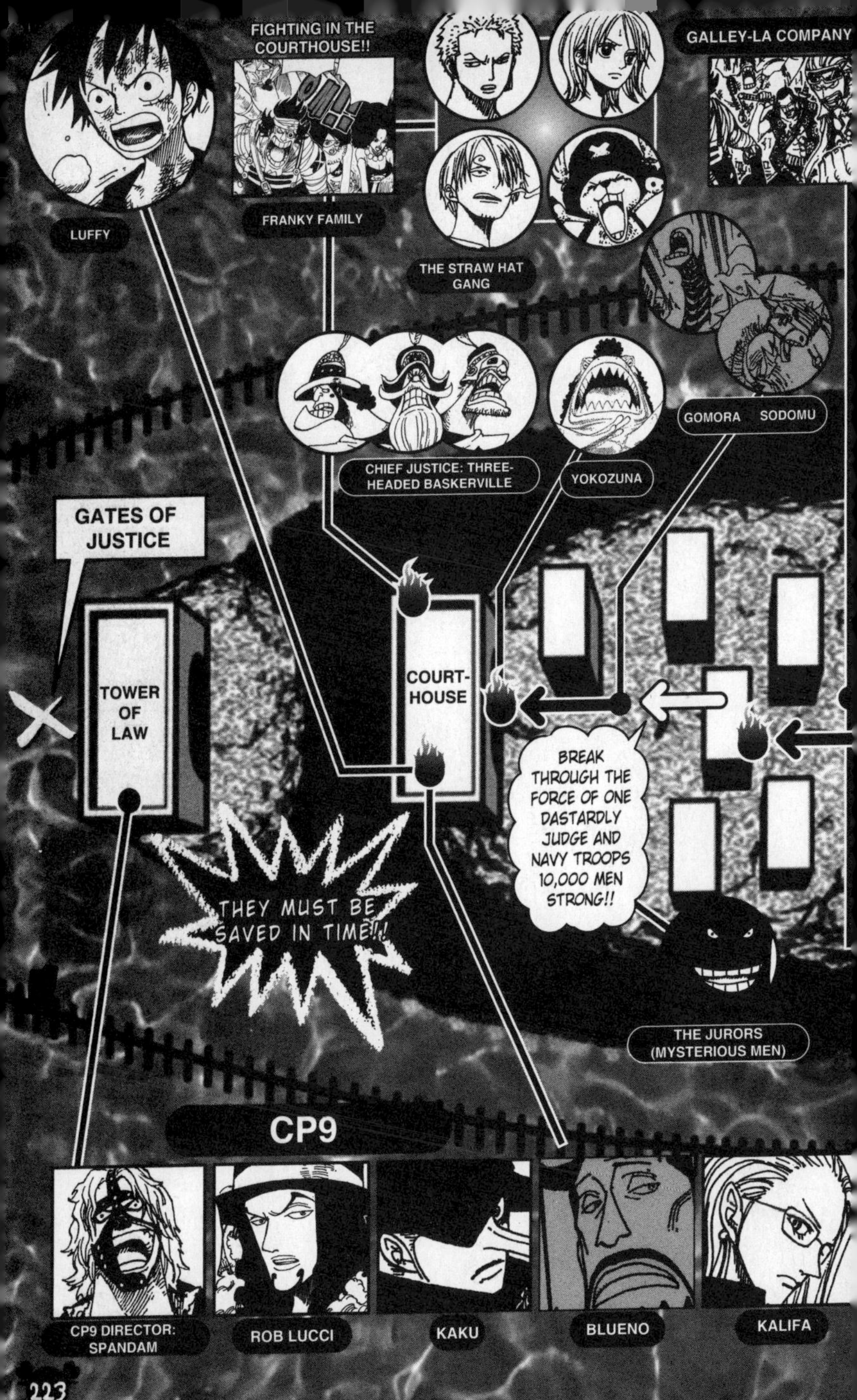
GALLEY-LA COMPANY
THE STRAW HAT GANG
FIGHTING IN THE COURTHOUSE!!
FRANKY FAMILY
LUFFY
GOMORA
SODOMU
YOKOZUNA
CHIEF JUSTICE: THREE-HEADED BASKERVILLE
GATES OF JUSTICE
TOWER OF LAW
COURT-HOUSE
BREAK THROUGH THE FORCE OF ONE DASTARDLY JUDGE AND NAVY TROOPS 10,000 MEN STRONG!!
THEY MUST BE SAVED IN TIME!!
THE JURORS (MYSTERIOUS MEN)
CP9
KALIFA
BLUENO
KAKU
ROB LUCCI
CP9 DIRECTOR: SPANDAM

COMING NEXT VOLUME:

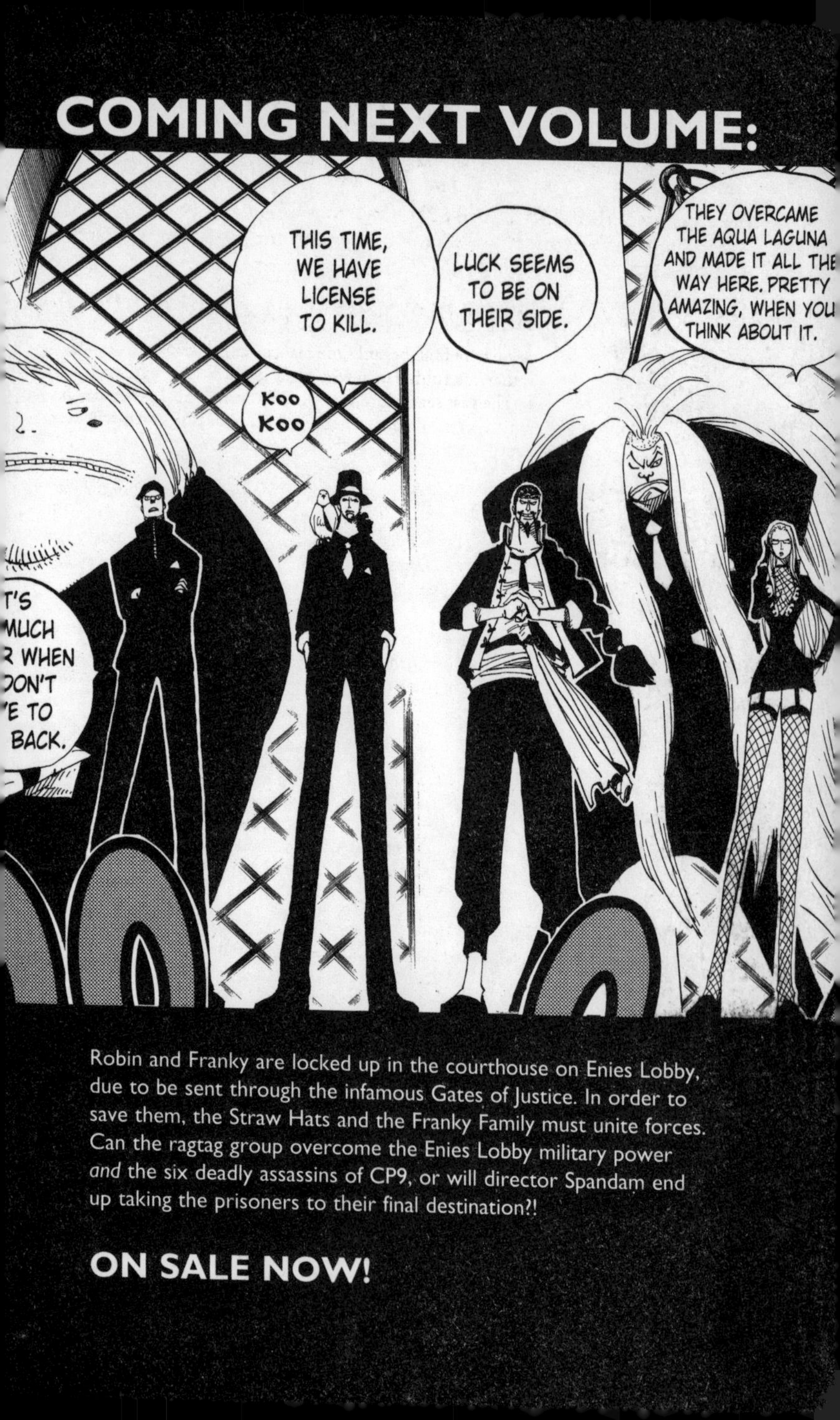
THEY OVERCAME THE AQUA LAGUNA AND MADE IT ALL THE WAY HERE. PRETTY AMAZING, WHEN YOU THINK ABOUT IT.
LUCK SEEMS TO BE ON THEIR SIDE.
THIS TIME, WE HAVE LICENSE TO KILL.
KOO KOO
T'S MUCH R WHEN DON'T 'E TO BACK.

Robin and Franky are locked up in the courthouse on Enies Lobby, due to be sent through the infamous Gates of Justice. In order to save them, the Straw Hats and the Franky Family must unite forces. Can the ragtag group overcome the Enies Lobby military power *and* the six deadly assassins of CP9, or will director Spandam end up taking the prisoners to their final destination?!

ON SALE NOW!

Set Sail with

Read all about **MONKEY D. LUFFY**'s adventures as he sails around the world assembling a motley crew to join him on his search for the legendary treasure "**ONE PIECE.**" For more information, check out **onepiece.viz.com**.

EAST BLUE
(Vols. 1-12)
Available now!

See where it all began! One man, a dinghy and a dream. Or rather… a rubber man who can't swim, setting out in a tiny boat on the vast seas without any navigational skills. What are the odds that his dream of becoming King of the Pirates will ever come true?

BAROQUE WORKS
(Vols. 12-24)
Available now!

Friend or foe? Ms. Wednesday is part of a group of bounty hunters—or isn't she? The Straw Hats get caught up in a civil war when they find a princess in their midst. But can they help her stop the revolution in her home country before the evil Crocodile gets his way?!

SKYPIEA
(Vols. 24-32)
Available now!

Luffy's quest to become King of the Pirates and find the elusive treasure known as "One Piece" continues…in the sky! The Straw Hats sail to Skypiea, an airborne island in the midst of a territorial war and ruled by a short-fused megalomaniac!

WATER SEVEN
(Vols. 32-46)
Available from February 2010!

The *Merry Go* has been a stalwart for the Straw Hats since the beginning, but countless battles have taken their toll on the ship. Luckily, their next stop is Water Seven, where a rough-and-tumble crew of shipwrights awaits their arrival!

THRILLER BARK
(Vols. 46-50)
Available from May 2010!

Luffy and crew get more than they bargained for when their ship is drawn toward haunted Thriller Bark. When Gecko Moria, one of the Warlords of the Sea, steals the crew's shadows, they'll have to get them back before the sun rises or else they'll all turn into zombies!

SABAODY
(Vols. 50-54)
Available from June 2010!

On the way to Fish-Man Island, the Straw Hats disembark on the Sabaody archipelago to get soaped up for their undersea adventure! But it's not too long before they get caught up in trouble! Luffy's made an enemy of an exalted World Noble when he saves Camie the mermaid from being sold on the slave market, and now he's got the Navy after him too!

IMPEL DOWN
(from Vol. 54)
Available from July 2010!

Luffy's brother Ace is about to be executed! Held in the Navy's maximum security prison Impel Down, Luffy needs to find a way to break in to help Ace escape. But with murderous fiends for guards inside, the notorious prisoners start to seem not so bad. Some are even friendly enough to give Luffy a helping hand!

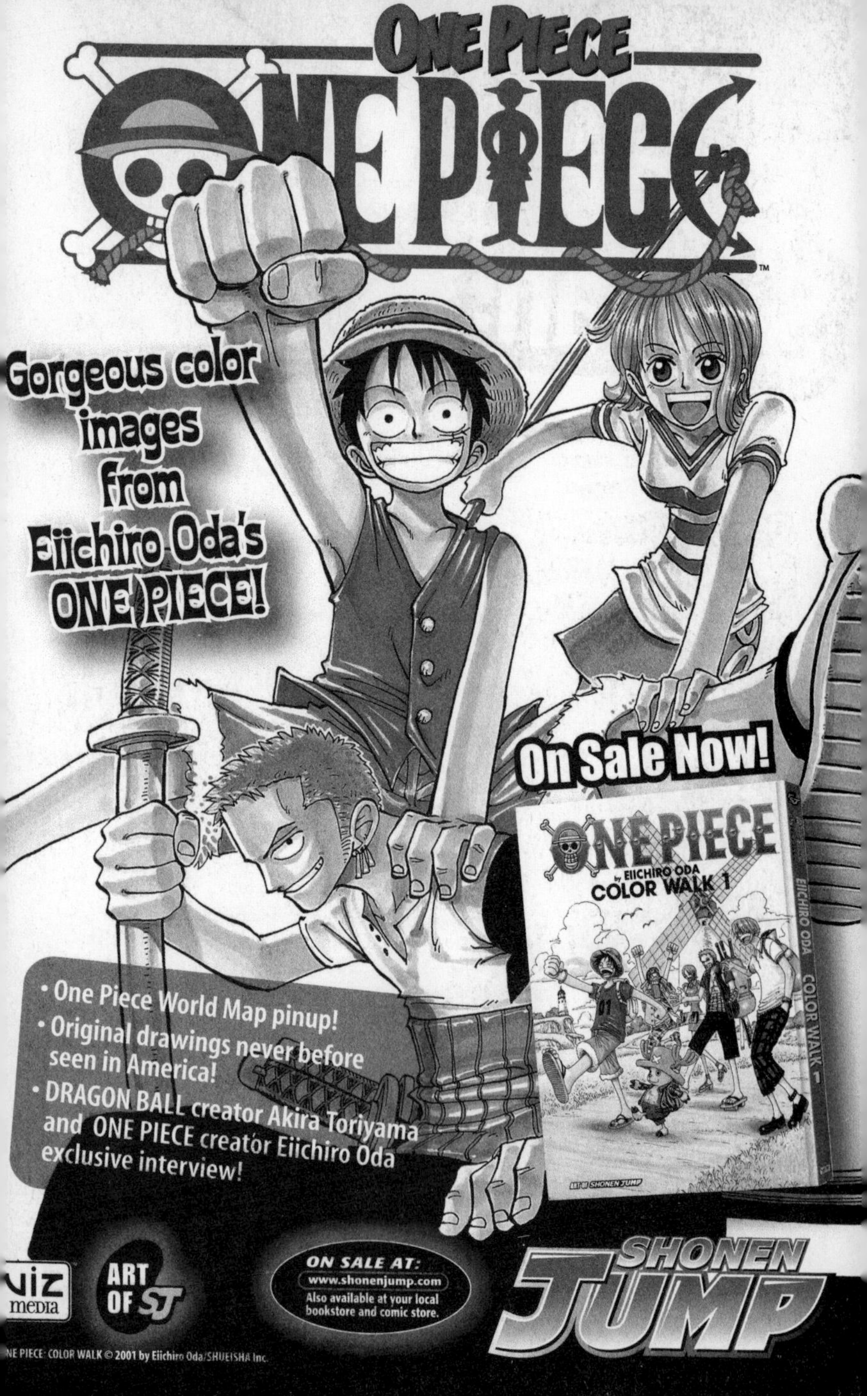
ONE PIECE
ONE PIECE
Gorgeous color images from Eiichiro Oda's ONE PIECE!
On Sale Now!
ONE PIECE
by EIICHIRO ODA
COLOR WALK 1
EIICHIRO ODA COLOR WALK 1
ART OF SHONEN JUMP
• One Piece World Map pinup!
• Original drawings never before seen in America!
• DRAGON BALL creator Akira Toriyama and ONE PIECE creator Eiichiro Oda exclusive interview!
viz media
ART OF SJ
ON SALE AT:
www.shonenjump.com
Also available at your local bookstore and comic store.
SHONEN JUMP
NE PIECE: COLOR WALK © 2001 by Eiichiro Oda/SHUEISHA Inc.

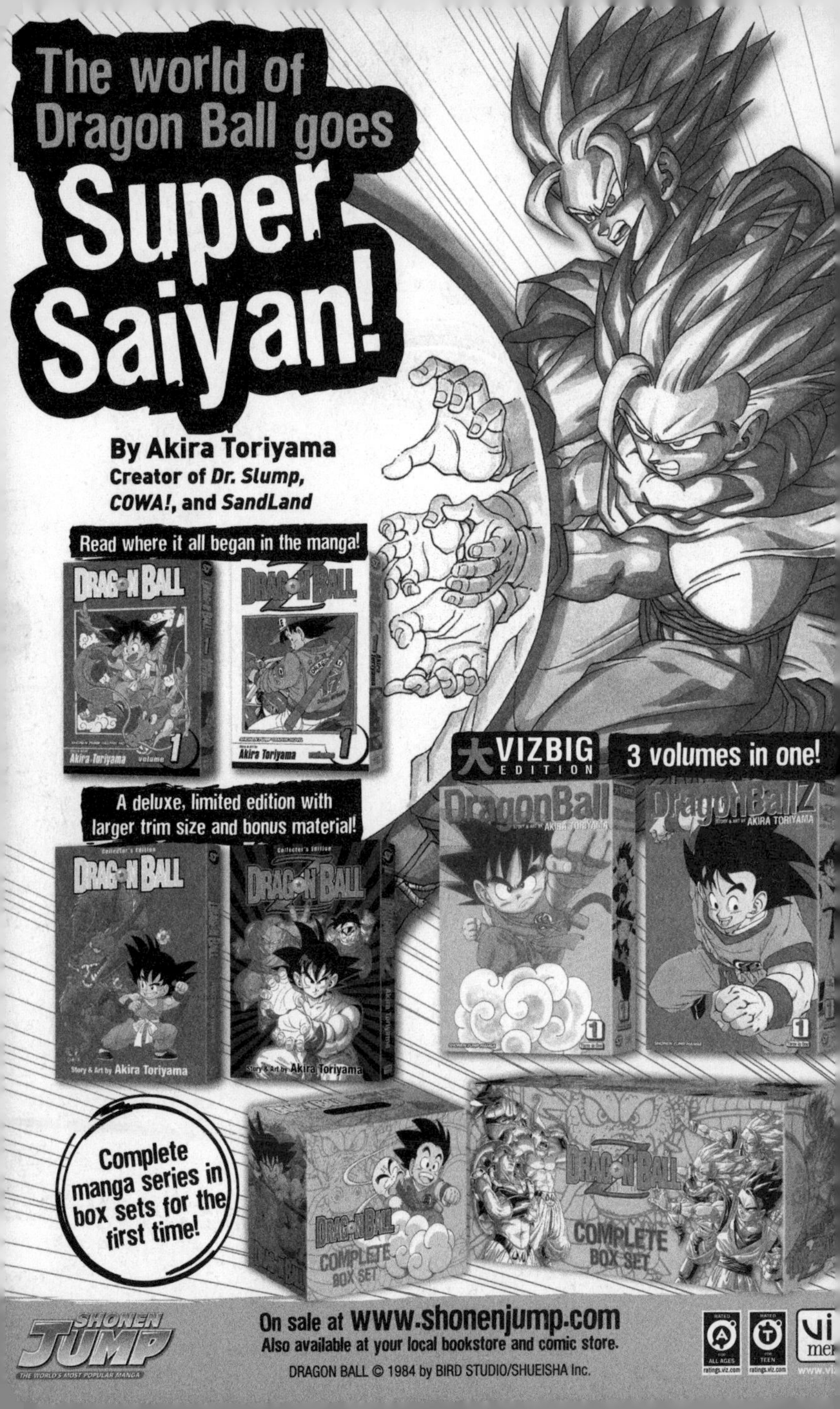
The world of Dragon Ball goes
Super Saiyan!
By Akira Toriyama
Creator of Dr. Slump, COWA!, and SandLand
Read where it all began in the manga!
DRAGON BALL
Akira Toriyama volume 1
DRAGON BALL Z
Akira Toriyama volume 1
A deluxe, limited edition with larger trim size and bonus material!
Collector's Edition
DRAGON BALL
Story & Art by Akira Toriyama
Collector's Edition
DRAGON BALL Z
Story & Art by Akira Toriyama
大 VIZBIG EDITION
3 volumes in one!
DragonBall
STORY & ART BY AKIRA TORIYAMA
DragonBallZ
STORY & ART BY AKIRA TORIYAMA
Complete manga series in box sets for the first time!
DRAGON BALL COMPLETE BOX SET
DRAGON BALL Z COMPLETE BOX SET
SHONEN JUMP
THE WORLD'S MOST POPULAR MANGA
On sale at www.shonenjump.com
Also available at your local bookstore and comic store.
DRAGON BALL © 1984 by BIRD STUDIO/SHUEISHA Inc.
RATED A FOR ALL AGES ratings.viz.com
RATED T FOR TEEN ratings.viz.com

SAVE 50% OFF
THE COVER PRICE!

IT'S LIKE GETTING 6 ISSUES
FREE!

OVER 350+ PAGES PER ISSUE

SHONEN JUMP

THE WORLD'S MOST POPULAR MANGA

This monthly magazine contains 7 of the coolest manga available in the U.S., PLUS anime news, and info about video & card games, toys AND more!

❏ **I want 12 HUGE issues of SHONEN JUMP for only $29.95*!**

NAME

ADDRESS

CITY/STATE/ZIP

EMAIL ADDRESS   **DATE OF BIRTH**

❏ YES, send me via email information, advertising, offers, and promotions related to VIZ Media, SHONEN JUMP, and/or their business partners.

❏ **CHECK ENCLOSED** (payable to SHONEN JUMP)   ❏ **BILL ME LATER**

CREDIT CARD: ❏ **Visa** ❏ **Mastercard**

ACCOUNT NUMBER   **EXP. DATE**

SIGNATURE

CLIP&MAIL TO:
SHONEN JUMP Subscriptions Service Dept.
P.O. Box 515
Mount Morris, IL 61054-0515

P9GNC1

* Canada price: $41.95 USD, including GST, HST, and QST. US/CAN orders only. Allow 6-8 weeks for delivery.
ONE PIECE © 1997 by Eiichiro Oda/SHUEISHA Inc. BLEACH © 2001 by Tite Kubo/SHUEISHA Inc.
NARUTO © 1999 by Masashi Kishimoto/SHUEISHA Inc.

RATED TEEN
ratings.viz.com

VIZ MEDIA
www.viz.com